Joseph Fong • Brian Siu (Eds.)

Multimedia, Knowledge-Based and Object-Oriented Databases

Springer

Joseph Fong
Department of Computer Science
City University of Hong Kong
Tat Chee Avenue
Kowloon
Hong Kong

Brian Siu
Division of Technology
City University of Hong Kong
Tat Chee Avenue
Kowloon
Hong Kong

Library of Congress Cataloging-in-Publication Data
Multimedia, knowledge-based, and object-oriented databases/Joseph Fong,
Brian Siu, eds.
p. cm.
Includes index.
ISBN 981-3083-00-X
1. Multimedia systems. 2. Expert systems (Computer science). 3. Object-oriented databases. I. Fong, Joseph. II. Siu, Brian
QA76.575.M8335 1996 96-17841
005.74–dc20 CIP

CR Subject Classification (1991): H.5.1, H.2.4, D.1.5

ISBN 981-3083-00-X

Printed in Hong Kong

Typesetting: Camera-ready by authors
5 4 3 2 1 0

Foreword

This workshop, the seventh in a series of annual events, aims at providing a forum for database researchers and practitioners to share their recent experience and results in various areas of database research and development.

This year the program focuses on the themes of multimedia, knowledge-based and object-oriented databases. These are timely topics, as they are of keen interest to both database developers as well as researchers. The program contains reports on both commercial activities in these areas, in the Industrial Stream, and research contributions in the Academic Program.

The Hong Kong Computer Society and the workshop program committee met in January to select 20 papers to be presented in the Academic Program. Those papers include authors from Hong Kong and beyond: Asia, Australia, Europe and North America are all represented in the workshop.

The papers have been assigned to three tracks, although they do not correspond exactly to the multimedia, knowledge-based and object-oriented areas, as the number of accepted paper was not equal in each area. However, we hope the categorization will help attendees in selecting which presentations to attend.

This series of workshops has been organized by the Hong Kong Computer Society in cooperation with ACM Hong Kong. We thank the referees and the members of the program committee for their efforts to make the workshop a success, and express our gratitude to the sponsoring companies and institutions.

David Maier
Program Committee Co-chairman
March 1996

Preface

The first International Hong Kong Computer Society Database Workshop was held in Hong Kong in 1989. This book covers the seventh annual database workshop in the series.

The main theme of this workshop concerns with advance database technologies in the area of multimedia database, knowledge-based database and object-oriented databases. It's goal is to search for the third generation of post-relational database models which will require larger data sets, enhanced capability in data type, multimedia support, complex object, rule processing and archival storage. The objective of this workshop is to bring together database practitioners, researchers and vendors to share and explore their methodologies and experience of advance database systems.

This workshop includes 27 papers from 10 countries. On behalf of the Hong Kong Computer Society Database Special Interest Group Workshop Program Committee and Workshop Organizing Committee, I would like to take this opportunity to express my thanks to those who contributed to this function, and trust you will find this a useful and practical database technology reference book.

Joseph Fong
Program Committee Co-chairman
March 1996

Advisory Committee

N.V. Balasubramanian	City University of Hong Kong, Hong Kong
F.Y.L. Chin	Hong Kong University, Hong Kong
T.Y. Cheung	City University of Hong Kong, Hong Kong
Stephen Harrold	City University of Hong Kong, Hong Kong
S.L. Hung	City University of Hong Kong, Hong Kong
George Leung	Hong Kong Computer Society, Hong Kong
F.H. Lochosvky	Hong Kong University of Science & Technology, Hong Kong
David Maier	Oregon Graduate Institute of Science and Technology, USA
Daniel Yeung	Hong Kong Polytechnic University, Hong Kong

Program Committee

Program Committee Chair

Joseph Fong	City University of Hong Kong, Hong Kong
David Maier	Oregon Graduate Institute of Science & Technology, USA

Program Committee

Jiannong Cao	City University of Hong Kong, Hong Kong
Daniel Cheung	Borland (Hong Kong) Ltd, Hong Kong
To-yat Cheung	City University of Hong Kong, Hong Kong
Francis Chin	University of Hong Kong, Hong Kong
Pamela Drew	Hong Kong University of Science & Technology, Hong Kong
Joseph Fong	City University of Hong Kong, Hong Kong
S.L. Hung	City University of Hong Kong, Hong Kong
Laurie Kan	Microsoft Hong Kong Limited, Hong Kong
Kamalakar Karlapalem	Hong Kong University of Science & Technology, Hong Kong
Ken Law	City University of Hong Kong, Hong Kong
John Lee	Hong Kong Polytechnic University, Hong Kong
K.S. Leung	Chinese University of Hong Kong, Hong Kong
Qing Li	Hong Kong University of Science & Technology, Hong Kong
Fred Lochovsky	Hong Kong University of Science & Technology, Hong Kong
Vincent Lum	Chinese University of Hong Kong, Hong Kong
David Maier	Oregon Graduate Institute of Science & Technology, USA

Organizing Committee

Organizing Chair

Irene Kwan — Hong Kong Polytechnic University, Hong Kong
Brian Siu — City University of Hong Kong, Hong Kong

Secretary

Bonnie Lau — Chinese University of Hong Kong, Hong Kong

Treasurer

Penny Pang — Hong Kong Baptist University, Hong Kong

Publication

S.L. Hung — City University of Hong Kong, Hong Kong

Registration

Theresa Leung — Hong Kong Computer Society
Jacky Yu — Hong Kong Computer Society

Publicity

Karen Wan — Hewlett-Packard Hong Kong Limited
Danny Ha — Databank Training & Consulting Services Limited

Tutorial

Kevin Ho — Cafe de Coral Group Limited

Photograph

Paul Kwan — Mexx Far East Hong Kong Limited
Tommy Ho — Hong Kong Computer Society
Michael Tsui — Sybase Hong Kong Limited

Local Arrangement

Vivian Wong — Oracle Hong Kong Limited, Hong Kong

Sponsors

Borland (HK) Ltd

Computer Associates International Ltd
Hong Kong Computer Society

Department of Computer Science,
City University of Hong Kong

Divison of Technology,
City University of Hong Kong

Daprtment of Computing,
Hong Kong Polytechnic University

Informix Software (HK) Ltd

Microsoft Hong Kong Ltd

Oracle System Hong Kong Ltd

Progress Software Corporation Ltd

Sybase Hong Kong Ltd

WinClient Technologies (HK) Ltd

Table of Contents

Keynote Paper

Invited Papers

Multimedia Databases

Knowledge-based Databases

Object-Oriented Databases

Industrial Stream Papers

Poster Session Papers

Bringing Knowledge to Bear: Challenges for Decision Support Databases

David Maier
Oregon Graduate Institute, USA

Mary Edie Meredith
Sequent Computer Systems, USA

Leonard Shapiro
Portland State University, USA

Abstract. A flurry of buzzwords awaits anyone investigating database technology for decision support: data warehouse, multidimensional database, on-line analytical processing, star schema, slicing, dicing, drill-down and roll-up. We introduce the area via an example based on a long-ago project to design a repository on energy information for the US Department of Energy. Once we have introduced some terminology, we explore research issues associated with decision support databases, including representation, software architecture, query processing, modeling and metadata management.

1 Introduction

Back in 1979, one of us (Maier) was doing his first serious database design for the US Department of Energy (DOE). In response to the Arab oil embargo of 1973, and the resulting energy shortage, the DOE had started gathering data on energy import, export, production, transport, storage and use in the US, down to the level of individual oil wells and pipelines, in some cases. States and energy companies were required to report monthly on production, energy in storage, conversion, and so forth. The purpose of this data gathering effort was that in times of future energy shortage or dislocation (such as a flood blocking a rail line and halting coal deliveries), federal decision makers would be able to assess the severity of a problem, predict its extent (both temporally and geographically) and suggest actions to ameliorate it (generate more electricity at gas-fired power plants and have coal-fired plants back off, for example).

In practice, the data were nearly useless for supporting decision makers with an urgent problem to solve. The difficulty was that the data, though timely and comprehensive, had been assembled in somewhere between 51 and 53 separate databases. (We never got a definitive count.) These databases did not interoperate. (Remember, it was the mid-1970's.) When an energy emergency arose, the response was to dump the contents of various databases to paper, and stick piles of printouts into a room with a bunch of people, who would try to compare and collate it manually. About two weeks later, the people would emerge from the room with some kind of assessment of the problem, by which time the problem had either resolved itself or become a crisis.

Thus, although the DOE had the information they needed to analyze energy emergencies, they could not bring it effectively to bear in support of decision makers analyzing those emergencies. Having the data partitioned into 50 or so independent databases was probably necessary, in order to divide and conquer the problem of data modeling and collection for such a broad area.

Enter the Energy Emergency Management Information System (EEMIS) [CRO79a, CRO79b, CRO79c, DAC79]. The goal of EEMIS was to pull data out of the 50-odd individual databases into a single database, where cross-sector analyses could be answered without consuming several boxes of paper. EEMIS was to be what today we would call a *data warehouse*—a central repository that combines and summarizes data from multiple sources on an enterprise-wide basis. In the case of EEMIS, the enterprise was all the energy in the United States.

The job of producing the conceptual model for EEMIS was contracted to the Technology Assessment Group of the Department of Energy and Environment at Brookhaven National Laboratory in New York state. The staff there had one look at it and promptly subcontracted the job to a group of professors and graduate students at the State University of New York at Stony Brook. They struggled with the design problem for a semester, and came up with a design that was a cross between a relational and hierarchical schema, with about 145 field types and 190 segments.

From a high level, the domain didn't seem that complex. There were types of energy whose amounts were measured at certain time periods, for energy facilities and transportation links. For example,

> There were 635,000 barrels of Saudi Arabian Light crude oil in the Exxon storage facility at Bergen, New Jersey at the end of April, 1978, or
>
> 2.43 million cubic feet of natural gas moved between the Getty Bastion Bay gas processing plant and the Lake Charles LNG terminal in June, 1975.

It seems simple enough. Why the need for hundreds of fields and record types? The problem was all the summary data that was needed. As a simple example, while oil well production figures were reported monthly, in addition, quarterly and yearly totals were of interest. Life gets a bit more complex when considering forms of energy. There are individual *energy types*, such as Aviation Gasoline, Propane and Labuan Light Crude Oil. Energy types belong to *energy groups*, such as Gasoline, Light Products and Foreign Crude. Groups form *categories*, for instance, Wet Gas and Crude Oil. From categories there are *sectors*, such as coal, petroleum and natural gas. At the top of the hierarchy is the "Universal" form of energy. (See Fig. 1.)

Facilities were more complicated still, as there were two ways to classify them, by function and by geographic location. *Function* classified a facility as to what role it played in the energy chain of import or extraction, conversion, storage, and export or consumption. Examples of facility functions are crude storage, refinery, underground natural gas storage and military consumer. Functions are further combined into *sectors*, such as petroleum, natural gas or large consumer. (See Fig. 2.)

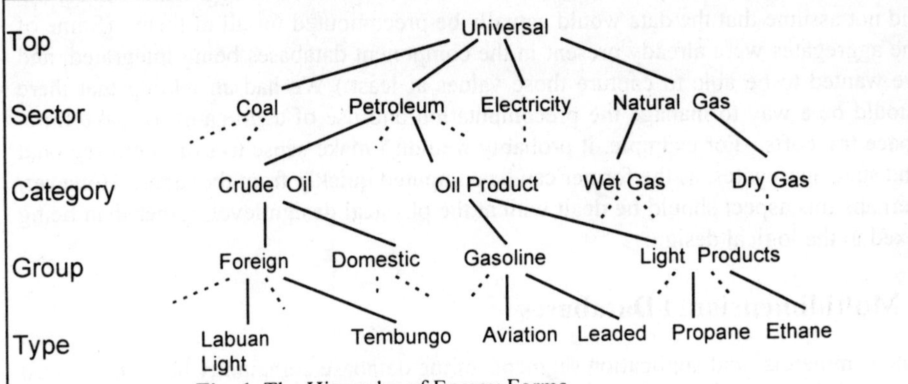

Fig. 1. The Hierarchy of Energy Forms

Geographically, the primary grouping was by political boundary: county, state, region (Pacific Northwest, Mid-Atlantic), nation. However, there were also non-political areas, such as oil fields, that cut across state or even regional boundaries.

Transportation links were handled similarly to facilities. A link was categorized by its *mode* (pipeline, rail, barge, truck, oxcart, etc.), the functions of the source and destination facilities it connected, and its geographic location. The last was problematic, as a pipeline, say, could cross many areas.

Finally, there was a grand classification over both facilities and links called "RES Function" (for Reference Energy System, a particular model). It was a broad classification that spanned energy sectors and had classifications such as "extraction", "transmission" and "refining and conversion."

One of the big debates during the database design was whether or not to store aggregated values. On the one hand, computing, say, a national total of all petroleum

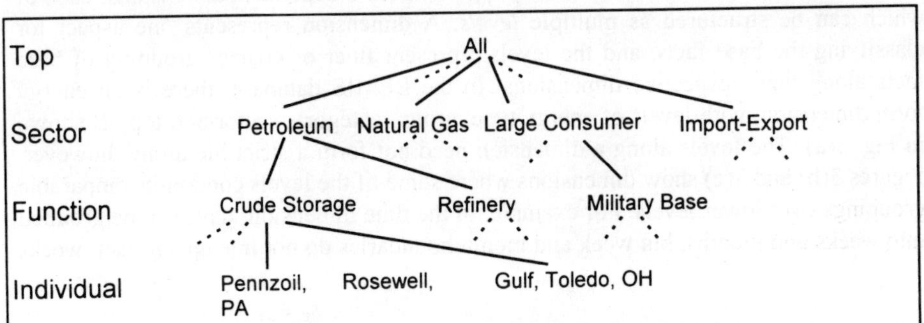

Fig. 2. The Hierarchy of Facility Functions

production over a five-year period from monthly information on individual refineries would take an unacceptable amount of time. However, precomputing and storing all possible aggregations of interest would be prohibitive in space usage. Furthermore, it was not clear that we could predefine all the aggregates needed, since arbitrary interest. In the end, we provided for the schema to store many aggregate values, but did not assume that the data would actually be precomputed for all of them. (Some of the aggregates were already present in the component databases being integrated, and we wanted to be able to capture those values at least.) We had an inkling that there should be a way to manage the precomputation and use of aggregates to make time-space tradeoffs. For example, it probably wouldn't make sense to store both regional and state aggregates, as the former can be computed quickly from the latter. However, perhaps this aspect should be dealt with at the physical design level, rather than being fixed in the logical design.

2 Multidimensional Databases

The commercial and application segments of the database community have recognized for a while a frequent pattern of base facts and aggregate dimensions occurring in decision-support databases [DEM94, FIN95, FRA94, KIM95, SQU95]. The research community in only beginning to devote its attention to this area [GRA96, HAR96, SAL95]. (However, there has been a history of work in processing aggregation queries [CHA95].) There are dozens of front-end and back-end products currently on the market to support datasets of this form. Let us be a bit more precise in our characterization.

We will define a *multidimensional database*[1] (MDDB) as one that stores one or more kinds of *base facts*, and connects them to *dimensional information*. The base facts typically contain numeric fields, which are aggregated via summary, taking optima (max and min), computing averages and so forth, via the classifications defined in the dimensional information. The dimensional information can also be used to select subsets of the base facts. The EEMIS database had base facts on amounts and costs of energy, and dimensional information on time, energy form, and link and facility function and geography.

The dimensional information consists of one or more independent *dimensions*, each of which can be structured as multiple *levels*. A dimension represents one aspect for classifying the base facts, and the levels represent finer or coarser grouping of base facts along their respective dimensions. In the EEMIS database, there is an energy form dimension, with levels of energy type, group, category, sector and top, as shown in Fig. 3(a). The levels along a dimension need not form a strict hierarchy, however. Figures 3(b) and 3(c) show dimensions where some of the levels contain incomparable groupings over lower levels. For example, in the time dimension, days can be grouped into weeks and months, but week and month boundaries do not line up. (In fact, weeks

---

[1] There is another kind of dataset that could be called multidimensional, as found in many scientific and engineering applications. There the dimensions of the dataset represent continuous independent variables, such as time, latitude, longitude and altitude, and values at the interstices are measurements of dependent variables, such as temperature or pressure. While such datasets offer interesting challenges of their own, we do not include them in what we mean by MDDBs.

and years don't line up exactly, but some commercial calendars have conventions for making them line up.)

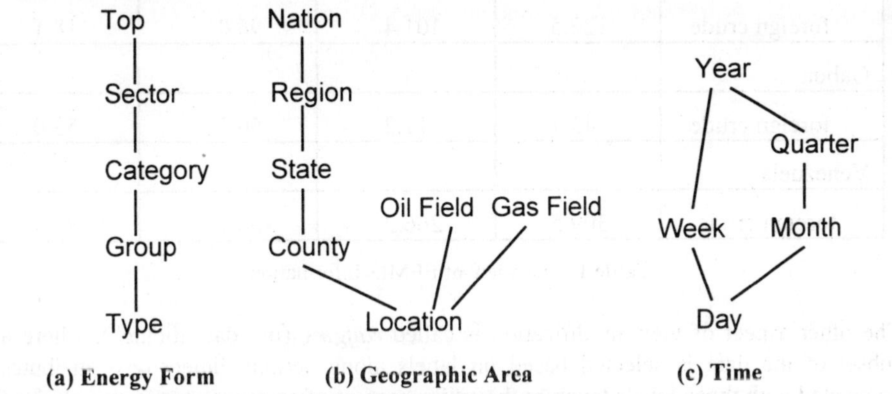

Fig. 3. Levels Within Different Dimensions

Most MDDB tools have a component to let a database designer declare and populate the dimensions when setting up a database, but end users might still want to define new groupings dynamically, such as combining months into two-month periods. We will refer to the alternative values within one level of a dimension as *labels*, though we do not mean to imply they are always strings. For instance, "Coal" is a label at the sector level of the energy form dimension.

The common access patterns characterize an MDDB as much as the structural features. MDDBs may be used to generate standard reports, or support a particular canned application, but more interesting is their use in On-Line Analytical Processing (OLAP) [COD94, THE95]. OLAP is ad hoc, exploratory data analysis, where a decision make is seeking patterns, trends, anomalies, correlations and so forth in order to better understand the history, current status or future of some aspect of the enterprise. OLAP usage of data is best characterized by the sequences of operations that users perform, rather than just the style of single queries. (The terminology we use is borrowed mainly from Kenan Technologies [KEE94].)

A session will often start with *browsing*, or "surfing", the database, looking at different parts of it until some item of interest appears. For example, in the EEMIS database, a user might start by looking through oil imports quarter by quarter or country by country. Once an area of interest is found, the user may tune his or her view of it. One way to modify the view is via *rotation* (also called "data slicing"). End-user OLAP tools generally let users view data in a spreadsheet-style display (see Table 1), with labels from one or more dimensions on the rows and columns, and base values or aggregates of those values in the cells. Rotation allows the user to change which dimensions occur along each side. For example, a view of the EEMIS data might want to show energy groups on one side, and states on the other (energy form versus facility-location dimensions) or country and energy group portrayed against calendar quarters (facility-location and energy form versus time dimensions.)

Imports	Q1 76	Q2 76	Q3 76	Q4 76
Algeria				
foreign crude	122.5	101.4	96.0	118.1
Gabon				
foreign crude	43.7	11.2	50.3	53.0
Venezuela				
foreign crude	309.5	266.2	300.1	288.3

Table 1. One View of EEMIS Information

The other aspect of view modification is called *ranging* (or "data dicing"), where a subset of the data is selected based on labels along certain dimensions, attributes connected with those labels (such as the sulfur content of an energy type), or values of the cell data. In Table 1, the view has been limited to three countries, the foreign crude group and calendar quarters from 1976.

Imports	Q1 76	Q2 76	Q3 76	Q4 76	1976
Algeria					
foreign crude	122.5	101.4	96.0	118.1	438.0
Gabon					
foreign crude	43.7	11.2	50.3	53.0	158.2
Anguille	8.1	7.1	9.5	8.0	32.7
Gamba	30.6	0.0	35.5	38.3	104.4
Mandji	5.0	4.1	5.3	6.7	21.1
Venezuela					
foreign crude	309.5	266.2	300.1	288.3	1164.1

Table 2. Drilling Down and Rolling Up

The other main kind of OLAP manipulation is to shift the level of aggregation along the dimensions. Going to a lower level of aggregation is called *drilling down*, while going to a more aggregated view is called *rolling up*. For example, in Table 1, the user may wonder about the dip in imports from Gabon in the second quarter, and could decide to drill down to the energy type level under Gabon, and perhaps roll up the quarters in the time dimension to yearly totals, as shown in Table 2. (Note that it is possible to have more than one level of aggregation showing for a dimension at one time.) The modified view shows that exports of one type of crude dropped to zero, perhaps because of a break in a pipeline or problems at a shipping port. Many other forms of aggregation are used, besides simple sums: rankings, percentiles, running totals, and so forth. Other forms of derived data, such as differences and ratios, are also of interest.

We have touched on the fundamentals of MDDBs, and will now consider some of the research issues they engender.

3 Research Issues

3.1 Representation

Given the kinds of information and operations common for an MDDB, what are the possible representations for MDDB data?

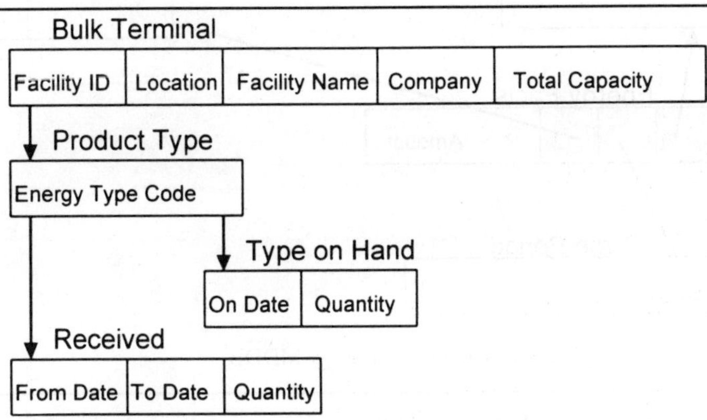

Fig. 4. Schema for Oil Product Bulk Terminal

The Original Schema

In retrospect, the recommended design for the EEMIS data warehouse was not well matched to OLAP-style queries. The structure of the data tended to overly reflect the organization of the component data sources, which were biased to the reporting structure of the data. That structure tended to overdecompose data relative to the way that users wanted to access it. The EEMIS schema was also biased towards certain dimensions, based on where new labels are likely to be added to a level. For example, new facilities are not added frequently, nor are new energy types, but new time periods are added every month. Thus, EEMIS ended up with hierarchical schemas with facility information at the top, then energy form information, and time periods at the bottom. For example, Fig. 4 shows a simplified version of the schema for an oil product bulk terminal (a kind of storage facility).

Facilities with different functions ended up being represented in different hierarchies, because they had different attributes. This organization supports roll-ups along the temporal dimension adequately, and roll-ups across energy type are not too bad to compute. Roll-ups over facility location or sector are difficult because records from different hierarchies are involved.

Stars and Snowflakes

MDDBs implemented in relational DBMSs usually have a schema that does not emphasize one dimension over another. Instead, there is a logical schema build around a fact table that is linked to one or more dimension tables. The simplest form is often called a *star* schema—the base table is portrayed in the center, and the dimension tables arrayed around it, as shown in Fig. 5. The ENERGY FACT records contain foreign keys for the three dimension tables.

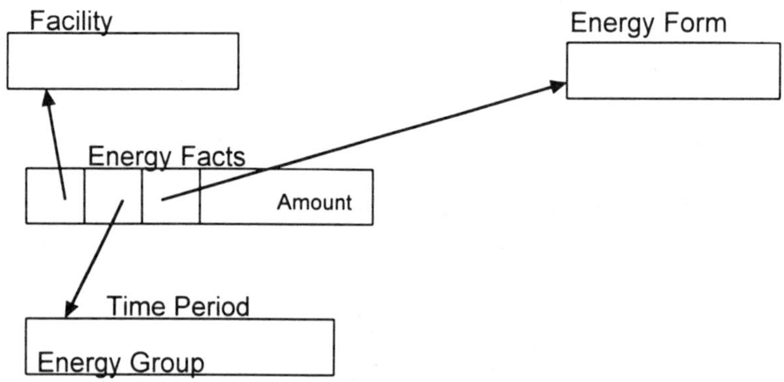

Fig. 5. Star Schema for Energy MDDB

Usually, a relational schema needs to be more complicated than this, because of the richness of information in some dimensions. It may be that a dimension has independent subdimensions, such as the location and function aspects of the facility dimension, or that storing labels for all hierarchy levels in a single table creates redundant information. For instance, rows in ENERGY FORM will repeat the relationship between an energy group and its category many times. The redundancy can be worse if there are attributes functionally determined by associated labels, such as the name of the energy commission for a state. Thus, the dimension tables can be broken out further, becoming a *snowflake* schema, as in Fig. 6. There are other variations on the theme. For example, the schema for the TPC-D benchmarks is essentially a snowflake schema, but with two fact tables.

Many OLAP-style queries can be answered using SQL queries against star and snowflake schemas, via joins of the fact table with one or more dimension tables, grouping on label fields and aggregating on fact fields. However, such queries can be expensive to compute, and SQL cannot express all varieties of aggregates.

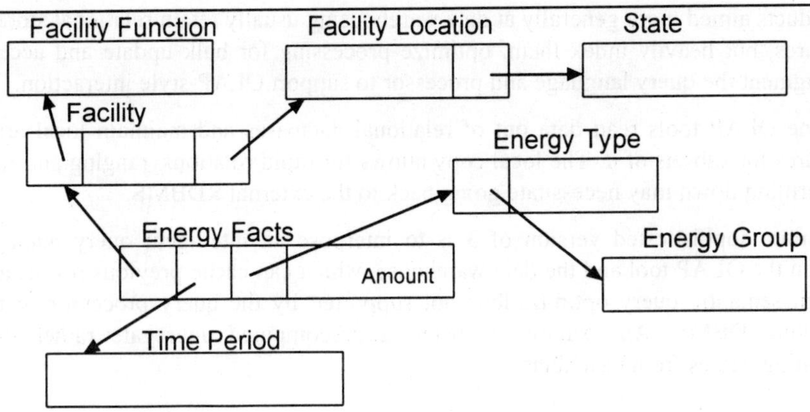

Fig. 6. Snowflake Schema for Energy MDDB

Array Representation

A third approach is adopted by some MDDB products that have their own storage managers. That approach is to store the base values in a n_1 by n_2 by ... by n_k array, where n_i is the number of labels at the lowest level in the ith dimension, there being k dimensions in all. The representation has the advantage that label information is stored once, external to the array, and the array stores only base values. Ranging can be done by indexing into the array. The exact set of cells for a particular roll-up can be calculated easily as well. A downside is that base facts might not be dense in all dimensions. For example, crude oil energy types are generally associated with single countries. Gabon exports Gamba crude oil, but no other country does, so the intersection of Gamba and any other country will always have a zero value. Thus, sparse array structuring techniques are need for space efficiency.

Research Issues

Are there any other natural representations for MDDBs? Would there be any advantage to hybrid schemes that combined snowflake and array representations?

3.2 Architectures

There have been a several software architectures proposed for MDDBs [KEE94, RED95]. We list some of them below.

1. Products aimed at supporting MDDBs might provide special storage structures, such as to hold the array representation of the last section. Those structures can be augmented with indexes on labels and precomputed aggregates along some dimensions. There are questions of scaleability with this approach.

2. Products aimed more generally at data warehousing usually retain relational storage structures, but heavily index them, optimize processing for bulk update and access, and augment the query language and processor to support OLAP-style interaction.

3. Some OLAP tools read data out of relational databases and maintain local array structures for subsets of it. The local copy allows for rapid rotations, ranging and roll-ups. Drilling down may necessitate going back to the external RDBMS.

4. A more sophisticated version of 3 is to interpose an intelligent query manager between the OLAP tool and the data warehouse, which can cache previous results and perform semantic query optimizations not supported by the query processor of the underlying DBMS. An example is using a precomputed aggregate rather than calculating values from base facts.

Research Issues

What are the trade-offs between such architectures? Does it make sense to have specialized MDDB or warehouse DBMS, or should conventional systems be augmented to handle such applications?

3.3 Queries and Access Methods

MDDBs present a rich domain for research on query processing and access methods, as well as query language design. One important aspect is that OLAP sessions consist of sequences of related queries, with high likelihood of overlap. The problem is not quite the same as multiple query optimization, as the queries are known all at once. Thus, strategies must speculatively store previous query results or subexpressions. Proposals on how to organize such information are starting to appear [SAL95, HAR96].

OLAP queries often want data aggregated at multiple levels in the same answer. The Data Cube [GRA96] is an approach to extend SQL to express such patterns and provide a specialized operator to compute them.

There is also opportunity for work on semantic query optimization. Materialized views, especially on aggregates, are often added for performance reasons. Another performance technique is to split a fact table into a union of smaller ones, say based on year. However, just defining views or decompositions is not enough. The query optimizer needs to recognize equivalences among expressions and know when to modify a query to go to the materialized view, or simplify it to use one part of a decomposition. Right now, these techniques generally require intervention from outside the database to revise queries.

There is also much work to do on beefing up conventional relational query processing techniques to perform better on decision-support queries, such as are typified by the TPC-D benchmark. Some of our own work has shown the efficiency of query transforms aimed at aggregates, the addition of a bit-join operator, and specialized search heuristics. Certain parts of these queries contribute very little to the overall evaluation time, but consume large amounts of optimization time. Quickly finding a "good enough" plan is better than taking forever to get the optimal plan for such subexpressions.

Research Issues

What other techniques can be applied to sequences of OLAP queries? Are there new auxiliary access structures that would aid in evaluating these kinds of queries? How should query optimizers be modified to take advantage of such auxiliary information?

3.4 Modeling Issues

While the multidimensional view of data captures much of the modeling complexity of the EEMIS database, there are still some issues not addressed.

Alternative Viewpoints

The examples in this paper have dealt largely with aggregating amounts of energy along time, energy form and facility dimensions. That view is appropriate for supporting decision makers who are concerned with status and trends in energy production and storage. However, there is another viewpoint that might be used to organize the data that is more suited to decision makers concerned with disruptions in the transport of energy and local shortages. They want a unifying view of the energy system as a network flow, with sources, sinks, intermediate nodes and connecting edges. The concern is not so much actual production and storage, as it is excess capacity and potential routings. Rather than applying statistical reductions to the data, such decision makers want to use operations research algorithms. This viewpoint probably entails a least some change in the classification dimensions for the data, as well as what kinds of values are going to be aggregated. For example, the latency of a mode of transport now becomes important, in addition to its capacity, or the amount of empty space in an oil tank is as interesting as how much oil is already in it. (The EEMIS schema ended up adding some auxiliary structures to support the network-flow viewpoint, but all-in-all that viewpoint was undersupported.)

Research Issue: Can a single data warehouse adequately handle two diverse organizational schemes over the same base data?

Non-Uniform Hierarchy

The dimension hierarchies we presented showed uniform depth in classification. In fact, that was an oversimplification. For example, in the geographic hierarchy, there was no breakdown for regions, states and counties for foreign countries. Hence, one could drill down on the United States, but not on, say, Saudi Arabia. In the energy form hierarchy, there was no differentiation at the category, group or type levels for electricity—kilowatts are kilowatts. Also, while the EEMIS hierarchies had uniform levels across them, that arrangement may have been artificial. In the geographic dimension, not every facility had an associated oil or gas field. There is no *a priori* reason to expect that the natural levels of classification for production facilities would be the same as for energy consumers. In fact, the consumption sector in EEMIS could have used an additional level of classification based on size.

Research Issue: How can MDDB models and tools accommodate non-uniform dimension hierarchies?

Instances, Intervals and Time Shifts

The time dimension has some of the most complex semantics. While the finest granularity in that dimension was monthly reports, "April 1976" did not mean the same thing in all contexts. In some cases, it means a value associated with the entire month of April (or a one-month period ending in April), such as for production from a gas well. In other cases, it means a measurement at a particular time in the month, such as quantity on hand at a storage facility. In the EEMIS data sources, the dates of measurement were not uniform within a month. Thus, it was possible that storage facility A reported figures for 10 April, and facility B reported for 25 April. Figures for A and B might count the same oil twice, if it moved between A and B between the 10th and the 25th. It may be that such problems are more a manifestation of poor design of reporting protocols rather than inherent modeling problems, or that different aspects of time are handled adequately by current temporal data models. However, different data sources that are feeding into a data warehouse may well have different time conventions, and features for interpolation and adjustment would be useful.

Research Issue: Are current approaches to time in databases adequate for MDDBs, or are new capabilities needed?

Regularizing Data

The data being combined in an MDDB may not have uniform domains for the values being aggregated. For example, a company tracking sales might count individual items at retail outlets, but use case lots in recording institutional sales. Obviously, the units have to be reconciled before aggregating across retail and institutional segments. In the EEMIS domain, different energy sectors had different ways of measuring energy: barrels of petroleum, cubic feet of natural gas, tons of coals, kilowatt-hours of electricity. Combinations across sectors demanded conversion to a common measure, such as BTUs. (The conversion is non-trivial in some cases—the BTUs in a barrel of crude oil depend on the specific gravity of its energy type.) Converting everything to common units as it enters the MDDB is probably not acceptable, as a user wants to see the normal units when looking at a single sector.

Not all regularization problems are simple unit conversions. There may be different conventions for descriptive labels in different parts of a business. Converting to a common system upon entry into the MDDB would again deprive users of looking at data in its most natural form, and might also lose information if disparate attributes have to be mapped into a "least common denominator" domain.

Research Issue: What is a good means to allow heterogeneity of data at lower levels of detail, while automatically regularizing it on roll up to higher levels of aggregation?

Specialization

The hierarchies found in MDDBs are not the same as the specialization hierarchies supported in object-oriented databases (OODBs). Dimensional hierarchies ultimately are used to relate states of data items—which instances at a finer level combine to form an aggregate instance at a coarser level. OODB hierarchies concern operations and express relationships between types, not instances. They are good for capturing semantics of data items that aren't wholly identical in structure.

There were places in the EEMIS design where an OO-style hierarchy would have been useful. There are many similarities between an oil refinery and a natural gas processing plant. It would have been helpful to capture that transportation links are in fact a kind of storage facility for "in-transit" energy. The amount of coal on a rail line or oil in a pipeline can be non-trivial. Current approaches to MDDBs demand uniformity in the dimensional entities, which may mean omitting information in order to fit a common pattern.

Research Issue: Can the MDDB view of data be combined with object-oriented models to allow some heterogeneity in dimensional information, while capturing commonalities for broad aggregates?

3.5 Metadata

The underlying data sources that are used to create an MDDB are never as uniform as the MDDB schema would indicate. First off, there are issues of completeness. The various states and companies reporting data to the DOE varied greatly in how promptly they supplied information. Thus, a particular reporting period might have base data missing for multiple months. Decision makers need to use the partial data nonetheless. The problems are how to compute functions such as averages when values are missing, and how to indicate to a user that a particular aggregate was computed from incomplete data.

Another problem is that some data sources do not record data at the lowest level of granularity in all dimensions. Some of the EEMIS data sources bottomed out at the group level along the energy form dimension, and at the state level in the facility-location subdimension. Thus, it would not be possible to drill down to arbitrary levels in the EEMIS data everywhere in the database.

A third problem is that certain label values might not be present explicitly in a data source. A database on crude oil imports might not contain "crude oil" as an explicit value in any field.

Research Issues

What kinds of metadata are needed to capture the variability in data completeness and granularity that is sure to arise in an MDDB? How can end-user tools exploit that metadata to properly annotate results and indicate legality of operations?

4 Summary

While multidimensional database applications have been around for decades, there has been a recent increase of interest fueled by the growth of data warehouse approaches. We have set forth research issues in the areas of representation, architecture, query, modeling and metadata, and there are surely dozens more problems of which we are not yet aware.

Acknowledgments

The authors would like to thank Lois Delcambre, Kaye Van Valkenburg and the DISC Decision-Support study group for ideas and help that went into this paper.

5 References

[CHA95] S. Chaudhuri and K. Shim. An overview of cost-based optimization of queries with aggregates. *Data Engineering* 18(3), September 1995.

[COD94] E. F. Codd and S. B. Codd. OLAP (on-line analytical processing). White paper, E. F. Codd & Associates, 1994.

[CRO79a] K. Croteau, J. Heller, T. Krawiec, D. Maier and B. Russell. The conceptual model for EEMIS. Dept. of Computer Science, SUNY Stony Brook, April 1979.

[CRO79b] K. Croteau, J. Heller, T. Krawiec, D. Maier, B. Russell and P. Wolk. Final report: The conceptual model for EEMIS. Dept. of Computer Science, SUNY Stony Brook, June 1979.

[CRO79c] K.Croteau, A. S. Kydes and D. Maier. EEMIS data sector correspondence with conceptual database design. Brookhaven National Laboratory Report BNL 51091, July 1979.

[DAC79] J. D'Acierno, A. Hermelee, C. P. Frederickson and K. Van Valkenburg. Methodology for coding the Energy Emergency Management Information System. Brookhaven National Laboratory Report BNL 51086, November 1979.

[DEM94] M. Demarest. Building the data mart. *DBMS*, June 1994.

[FIN95] R. Finkelstein. MDD: Database reaches the next dimension. *Database Programming & Design* 8(4), April 1995.

[FRA94] M. Frank. A drill-down analysis of multidimensional databases. *DBMS*, June 1994.

[GRA96] J. Gray, A. Bosworth, A. Layman and H. Pirahesh. Data Cube: A relational aggregation operator generalizing group-by, cross-tab and sub-totals. *Proc. Twelfth Intl. Conf. on Data Engineering*, IEEE, New Orleans, February-March 1996.

[HAR96] V. Harinarayan, A. Rajaraman and J. D. Ullman. Implementing data cubes efficiently. To be presented at the ACM SIGMOD Intl. Conf. on Management of Data, June 1996.

[KEE94] Kenan Technologies. An introduction to multidimensional database technology. Kenan Systems Corporation, One Main Street, Cambridge, MA 02142, 1994 (?).

[KIM95] R. Kimball and K. Strehlo. Why decision support fails and how to fix it. *ACM SIGMOD Record* 24(3), September 1995.

[RED95] Red Brick Systems. The data warehouse: The competitive advantage for the 1990's. White paper, 485 Alberto Way, Los Gatos, CA 95032, March 1995.

[SAL95] B. Salzberg and A. Reuter. Indexing for aggregation. Unpublished memorandum, College of Computer Science, Northwestern University, 1995.

[SQU95] C. Squire. Data extraction and transformation for the data warehouse. *Proc. ACM SIGMOD Intl. Conf. on Management of Data*, San Jose, May 1995.

[THE95] L. Thé. OLAP answers tough business questions. *Datamation*, May 1, 1995.

OODB Support for Software Process Management[1]

Chunnian Liu
Department of Computer ScienceBeijing
Polytechnic University
Beijing 100022, P.R.C
Email: bpvliu@public.bta.net.cn

Abstract. Software Process Technology (SPT) is a new research area in Software Engineering (SE). SPT systems require DB support. This paper investigates the trend of the OODB application to SPT. We present and analyze the requirements to DB support for SPT systems, examining typical SPT systems to see how they design their repositories with these requirements in mind, and why almost all SPT systems use OODB (at least logically) as the repository. Finally we point out the most important extensions needed to fully support software process modeling and management.

1 Introduction

Software Process Technology (SPT) is a new research area in Software Engineering (SE). A *software development process (software process* or *process*, in short) is the sum of software engineering activities required to develop and maintain a target software product. SPT studies the methods, formalism and tools supporting software processes. The main topics in SPT are:

-- Understanding software processes;
-- Describing formally software processes (i.e. *process modeling*);
-- Process automation based on process models (planning, scheduling, enacting, controlling, etc.);
-- Supporting process evolution and process model evolution;
-- Supporting long-term, nested, cooperative processes;
-- Improving software processes.

In [LIU91], we have identified 5 major paradigms in SPT research:

-- Active DB paradigm (e.g. Adele-TEMPO);
-- Rule based paradigm (e.g. Marvel, ALF);
-- Petri-net based paradigm (e.g. MELMAC, SPADE);
-- Process programming paradigm (e.g. APPL/A);
-- Hybrid paradigm (e.g. EPOS).

All SPT systems, whatever paradigms they are taking, relay on a centered software engineering database. This is not surprising, because process information (artifacts, activities, tools, resource, policies, and history) must be stored and maintained in some centered repository. What more interesting is that, almost all

[1] This work is partly supported by the National Science Foundation of China (NSFC).

SPT systems use Object-Oriented (OO) DBMS. The retionale is that, nowadays only OO data models and OODBs can satisfy the following requirements which are demanded by SPT systems:

-- Data representing software product and process have very complex structure.
-- Data have various semantic constraints.
-- Schema (a set of type definitions) evolves dynamically.
-- DB is operated on with various SE tools, while the tools are represented in DB as data.
-- DB applications to SPT are usually long-term, nested, cooperating transactions.
-- SPT systems and users are distributed over computer networks.

This paper investigates the trend of the OODB application to software process technology(SPT). We analyze the above requirements in more detail, examining typical SPT systems, [BAN94], [BEL94], [CAN94], [CON95], [DEI90], [KAI88], [SUT90], to see how they design their repositories with these requirements in mind, and why they use OODB (at least logically) as the repository. Finally we point out the most important extensions to fully support software process modeling and management.

2 Data Model

In this paper, *data model* means a set of type constructors (with syntax and semantics) and a set of operations applied to the data; A *schema* is a collection of type definitions. A particular database is built with a schema. In terms of SPT, a schema is a *process model* -- a formal description of the software development process, consisting mainly of type definitions for the software artifacts and software development activities (or *tasks*).
Almost all SPT systems use OO (Object-Oriented) data model, or ERA (Entity-Relation-Attribute) data model with OO extensions. The common features are described in the following subsections.

2.1 Entities and Relations

Both entities and relations are objects, having types and instances. A type is a *class* of instances, in terms of OO.

In SPT, entities represent software artifacts and software development tasks. An entity type definition contains its name, a list of supertypes, and a list of attribute definitions. An entity instance has unique identity.

Relations express connections between entities. In SPT, software product structure, task decomposition, object derivation, and even the type hierarchy, all can be described with relations (between artifacts, between tasks, between tasks and artifacts, and between type definitions, respectively). Most SPT systems only allow binary relations. A relation type definition contains its name, a pair of entity types connected by the relation, cardinality, a list of supertypes, and a list of attribute definitions. A relation instance (relationship) has no identity -- a relationship *r* is identified by the pair of source and destination entity instances (*src, des*) connected by *r*.

2.2 Complex Objects

In SPT systems, objects represent components of software product and process in various granularity, having nested structure. Each *complex (composite) object* is composed of several subobjects. Complex objects can be represented by *aggregation:* either by aggregate type constructors (set, list, etc.), or by implicit/explicit *composition* relationships. A composition relationship connects the superobject to the subobject. The cardinality could be N:N in general, but for efficiency reason it should be 1:N. Any entity instance that occurs as the superobject in a composition relationship is a complex object.

2.3 Attributes

An attribute definition contains its name, domain, and a tag indicating whether it is single-or-multi valued. Besides ordinary domains such as integer, boolean, etc., user-defined attribute domains should be offered by the data model used in SPT systems. For example, *long fields* domains are needed for text, source files, binary object code, bitmap images, etc.

2.4 Type Hierarchy

In SPT systems there are many types. Type definitions are organized in a hierarchical structure. A type can be specified as a subtype of its supertype. Subtypes inherit attributes and properties of their supertypes, while being able to add new ones and/or refine existing ones. This *subtyping* facility and the related *inheritance* rules allow more generic operations working at the appropriate abstraction levels and avoid redundancy. In the example of section 3 we will see part of the type hierarchy for task types.

2.5 Methods and Triggers

In SPT systems, users are allowed to specify new or type-specific operations performed on the database. In order to maintain consistency, operations should be encapsulated with data (i.e. operations is defined in types). This is the main characteristic of OODB, called *methods*.

Many SPT systems also have *triggers*. Triggers are ECA (Event-Condition-Action) rules specified in types. When the Event occurs in the DB, the Condition is tested, and if it holds, the Action is executed. In many SPT systems, the data model allows methods and triggers specified in (both entity and relation) type definitions.

For example, Adele-TEMPO [2] provides a quite complicate trigger mechanism. An event is defined by a method name and a condition, a trigger is defined as

PRE/POST/AFTER/ERROR ON event DO program. Whenever the method is executed, the event occurs. There are 4 kinds of triggers: *PRE* triggers effecting (i.e. checking condition and executing program) before method execution; *POST* triggers effecting after method execution; *AFTER* triggers effecting after the transaction is committed; *ERROR* triggers effecting when the transaction is aborted. Triggers can be specified in entity or relation types, and for relation triggers, events should be specified as occurring upon the source entity *src* or the destination entity *des*.

Methods and triggers can be used to specify resource-sharing problems which occur frequently in the SPT area (such as change propagation, etc.).

3 Schema Evolution

During the long lifetime of a software development project, many changes in the process and/or in the schema could arise. For example:

-- Redesign activity could systematically change the product structure of the target software.

-- The product structure could be changed dynamically, e.g. by #include statements in a C file.

-- The product types could be changed statically or dynamically (e.g., new types are added).

-- The task types could be changed statically(in customization)or dynamically (during execution).

Examples of the last kind of changes are: new tasks are introduced during process customization to a particular project or user; new tools are integrated into the environment in the mid of the project, etc.

SPT systems put great demands on the database wrt. schema evolution. To deal with this problem, the following two mechanisms become necessary:

First, the data model must be *reflective*. That is, the process model (the schema) can be manipulated (by meta-process) as ordinary data. In some SPT systems, attributes and methods are specified in two levels: type-level and instance-level. Instance-level attributes and methods are the ordinary ones relevant to instances. Type-level attributes are used for process planning and execution, type-level methods are used for process and schema evolution. For example, in EPOS [8], we have the following definitions of TaskEntity type for all tasks, and its subtype Build for executable code derivation tasks. In these definitions, some type-level methods (e.g. t_create, t_change, t_delete) operate on types, exactly for the purpose of schema modification.

```
ENTITY_TYPE TaskEntity IS Entity;        %% TaskEntity is a subtype of Entity
  INSTANCE_LEVEL:
    ATTRIBUTE                            %% each instance has a value for an attri. specified here
      TaskState : STRING := "created";   %% format:  name: domain  := initial_value
    METHOD                               %% operations on instances
      i_convert:                         %% to convert instances to sub/super types
```

```
  TYPE_LEVEL:
    ATTRIBUTE                          %% type_level attributes, used for process planning
                                       %% and execution,
      ......                               %% see the following subtype "Build" for details
    METHOD                               %% operations on type, executed by meta-process,
                                           %% can be used for schema modification
      t_create                           %%  to create a new subtype
      t_change                           %%  to change type definition
      t_delete                           %%  to delete existing type
      i_create                           %%  to create a new instance of the type
END TaskEntity;
-----------------------------------------------------------------------------------------------
ENTITY_TYPE Interactor IS TaskEntity;    %% Interactor is a subtype of TaskEntity
  ......
ENTITY_TYPE Deriver IS Interactor;       %% Deriver is a subtype of Interactor
  ......
-----------------------------------------------------------------------------------------------
ENTITY_TYPE Build IS Deriver;          %% Build is a subtype of Deriver
  TYPE_LEVEL
    ATTRIBUTE                            %% information used for process  planning and
                                       %% execution
      pre_static: "input is coded";     %% pre-condition, used for process planning
      pre_dynamic:                              %% timing conditions, used for process scheduling
and
                                        %% execution
      code: nil                                     %% procedural description of the task (tool
activation,
                                       %% etc.); but for high-level tasks like Build, code is
                                       %% "nil" because the task will be broke-down to
                                       %% subtasks, see attribute "decomposition" below
      post_static: "output is created";  %% post-condition, used for process planning
      post_dynamic:                        %% used for exception handling
      formal_parameters:                  %% specifying the types of input/output objects
        prog_family --> exe_code;
      decomposition: {compile, link}     %% "Build" task will be achieved by subtasks "compile"
                                       %% and "link" used for process planning, or task
                                         %% break-down
END Build;
```

Secondly, there must be some ways to support dynamic schema evolution, that is, to change schema without halting the whole project. For example, In EPOS [CON95], we have the incremental replanning mechanism to adjust the existing process plans according to the new schema; in MELMAC[DEI90], a mechanism based on *modification points* is used to cope with local changes in the schema dynamically. However, while process model evolution is recognized as a very important research issue in SPT, it is also a very difficult problem. The progress has been limited so far, much more has to be done in this direction.

4 Database vs. Workspace

Storing and representing data in a centered repository is not sufficient for a SPT system. The user of the SPT system must employ usual software engineering tools to do real work. This is performed in *Workspace*. A workspace, among other things, must contain ordinary files and directories since they are the only entities known by usual tools such as editors and compilers. The difference between database and workspace is two-fold: first, any kind of information with any complex structure and in any abstraction level can be stored in the database, while the workspace has relatively simple data model; secondly, the database contains all objects and their versions, while only the relevant part of the database is present in a given workspace, and in a single version since standard tools do not recognize version concepts.

Clearly, the centered database (DB) and multiple workspaces (WSs) must work in symbiosis. That is, activities in DB and WSs must be controlled and synchronized, to maintain the correspondence and consistency between DB and WSs. A nice solution to this problem is to regard a WS as a *sub-database* (see, for example, Adele-TEMPO [BEL94]). A sub-database is a subset of the centered repository (described formally by a product structure), so all DBMS services (local version, queries, short transactions, data protections, etc.) are available in each WS. On the other hand, a sub-database has also a partial File System representation, which is a WS. This mechanism offers users and tools working in a standard Unix environment while enjoying all DB service. The relationship sub-DB <--> WS is maintained by the Configuration Management (CM) system which is included in any substantial SPT systems.

5 Long , Nested, Cooperating Transactions

In SPT, tasks may be arbitrary long-lived. At extreme, a task could encompass an entire project, being active until maintenance of the target system ceases, years after the project was initiated. Such a *long transaction* has the following characteristics:

-- It is persistent, not going away when the associated OS process terminates.
-- It is not feasible to roll back to solve update conflicts.
-- Conflicts have to be reduced and controlled by high-level transaction planning facilities.

Long transactions start/terminate with check-out / check-in operations. Check-out creates a local sub-database (or a workspace WS) and makes private copies of the objects the transaction is going to operate on. Check-in returns the objects in the WS to the centered database.

In SPT, transactions represent tasks performed by a number of actors, making task decomposition both necessary and natural. Task decomposition produces a *nested transaction* hierarchy. With the check-out / check-in mechanism, nested transactions are implemented by nested sub-databases.

Nested transactions are *cooperating* in the sense that the owners of the transactions cooperate to solve a big task, using a common database. Substantial SPT systems (such as EPOS [CON95]) have some high-level transaction planning facilities to help the project manager to better divide and schedule the transactions, and to define high-level communication protocols among the leaf sub-transactions to drive the more low-level database mechanisms (e.g. data sharing, locking, propagation and negotiation policies). Given a proposal project partition, *impact analysis* techniques can be used to assess the connections between subprojects. The results of the analysis can be used to adjust the proposal partition to reduce the dependencies among subprojects, to schedule the identified subprojects, and to suggest suitable cooperation protocols between parallel subprojects.

6 Database Usage in SPT System

We said that almost all SPT systems use OODB as their centered data repository, this is true only logically. As matter of fact, most current SPT systems use ERA DBs extended with object-oriented features. We believe this is due to the fact that the most traditional SE databases were based on ERA model, and that the commercially available OO-DBMSs are very rare. Moreover, most existing OO-DBMSs do not pay special attentions to the needs of SPT. In terms of implementation, EPOSDB [CON95] is built on an underlying relational system; The underlying framework for ALF [CAN94] is PCTE (the ECMA standard); Marvel [KAI88] has designed its own active object base; Only SPADE [BAN94] uses an existing OO-DBMS O_2.

The central database is connected with several workspaces (WSs). In order to solve the problem of concurrently accessing the database, many SPT systems (such as MELMAC [DEI90], EPOS[CON95], etc.) introduce the *server* concept. Instead of using storage operations by each user, a special process called *server process* does so. Each WS gets a *client process* invoking the storage operations. There is a communication protocol between the client processes and the server. The different clients that request for data are served by the server according to a fair schedule.

The existing SPT systems are implemented in various languages (C, C++, Prolog, SmallTalk, etc.). The database must provides the proper language interface (sometimes several language interfaces). For example, EPOSDB [CON95] has a Prolog interface and a C++ interface. The interface should be as simple as possible, in order to increase the portability of the SPT system. Essentially, there are only two preliminary operations: *fetch* and *store*, and a small set of interface functions would be enough. Let us have a look at (part) of the Prolog interface of EPOS.

Prolog predicate	*semantics*
checkout_file(D, W)	to check out a file from database to workspace. D and W are the path-names of the file in database and workspace, respectively.
checkin_file(D, W)	to check in a file from workspace to database. D and W are the path-names of the file in database and workspace, respectively.

query_E(O, A1, ..., An) For entity type E, based on the instantiation of the arguments:

1. to retrieve attributes Ai for the given object O of type E; or
2. to test if the attributes of the given object O are Ai; or
3. to retrieve object with attributes matching Ai

query_R(O1,O2,A1,...,An) For each relation type R, based on the instantiation of arguments:

1. to retrieve O1 related to O2 by R, given O2 and attributes Ai
2. vice versa
3. to test if O1 and O2 are related by the matching relationship

create_E(O,A1,...,An) to create a new instance of type E, the identity is bound to O

update_E(O, A1,...,An) to update the attributes of object O to the values A1,...,An

insert_R(O1,O2,A1,...,An) to insert a relationship between objects O1 and O2, with attr. Ai

delete_R(O1,O2,A1,...,An) to delete the matching relationship between O1 and O2

convert_T(O) to convert object O to the type T (a supertype of the type of O)

7 Conclusions

Software Process Technology (SPT) systems need specially designed databases. Logically, these databases are OODBs, but because the lack of commercially available OO-DBMS, in most current SPT systems, they are really ERA DBs extended with object-oriented features to better support for versions, structuring and consistency control. SPT systems usually start from such a platform and then add process modeling facilities. To fully support process modeling and management, extensions in the following directions are important:

-- The purpose of a SPT system is not only to specify the software process, but also to enact the process. Hence the DBMS should be active, being able to react to events. This feature can be used for low-level change propagation, and integrated as part of the process engine (the mechanism to enact the software process).

-- Software process is long-lived, the process as well as its model are changing during the long lifetime of a software project. Hence the DBMS must be reflective, providing very flexible schema management, to support process evolution and process model evolution.

-- Most Software projects are team work, involving many people working for a common goal and sharing objects. From the DBMS point of view, this means nested, cooperating transactions, and the DBMS should support high-level cooperation strategies in addition to the traditional low-level mechanism such as data sharing and locking.

-- In SPT systems, different roles have different viewpoints to the process. Some SPT systems have two levels (MELMAC): on the top level, each viewpoint can be described in its own formalism and schema, while on the underlying level, all schemas from different views are transformed into a uniform one. Other SPT systems (Adele-TEMPO, SPADE) provide the kernel formalism first, and then extend the kernel with more process-specific features which can be defined in terms of the kernel.

-- In order to improve the software process, a SPT system must be able to describe and analyze the process in quantitative way. This means that software metrics must be integrated into SPT systems, and the information about product baselines, metrics, history, statistics, etc. must be stored and maintained in the database.

Obviously, traditional DBMSs (hierarchical, network, or relational) are hopeless to support these new requirements. We think OO-DBMSs are the most prominent candidate for this new application area, as demonstrated by existing SPT systems and the analysis of this paper. The designers of new OO-DBMS should keep these requirements in mind.

References

[BAN94] Bandinelli, S., etc.(1994). SPADE: An Environment for Software Process Analysis, Design, and Enactment. *Software Process Modeling and Technology*, pp. 223-248, *Research Studies Press LTD.*

[BEL94] Belkhatir, N., Estublier, J., Melo, W. (1994). Adele -TEMPO: An Environment to Support Process Modeling and Enaction. *Software Process Modeling and Technology*, pp.187-222, *Research Studies Press LTD.*

[CAN94] Canals, G., etc.(1994). ALF: A Framework for Building Process-Centered Software Engineering Environments. *Software Process Modeling and Technology*, pp. 153-186, *Research Studies Press LTD.*

[CON95] Conradi, R., Liu, C., Hagaseth, M.(1995). Planning Support for Cooperating Transactions in EPOS. *Information Systems*, Vol.20, No.4, pp. 317-336.

[DEI90] Deiters, W., Gruhn, V.(1990). Managing Software Processes in the Environment MELMAC. *Proc. SIGSOFT'90*, pp.193-205, Irvine, California, Dec, 3-5.

[KAI88] Kaiser, G.E., Feiler, P.H., Popovich, S.S.(1988). Intelligent Assistance for Software Development and Maintenance. *IEEE software,* May 1988, pp. 40-49.

[LIU91] Liu, C., Conradi, R.(1991). Process Modeling Paradigms: Evaluation. *Proc. of First European Workshop of Software Process Modeling*, pp. 39-52. AICA, Milan.

[SUT90] Sutton, S.M., Heimbigner, D.(Junior), Osterweil, L.J.(1990). Language Constructs for Managing Change in Process-Environments. *Proc. SIGSOFT'90*, pp.206-217, Irvine, California.

Using active rules to maintain the data consistency in heterogeneous database systems

Shi-Ming Huang and Jung-Kwi Liu
Database/Knowledge Base Research Group
Department of Computer Science and Engineering
Tatung Institute of Technology
Taiwan, R.O.C.
E-Mail: smhuang@cse.ttit.edu.tw

Abstract

The heterogeneous environment is emerging in the current information systems. Within this situation, it is desirable whenever maintain consistency across databases, i.e., to ensure that they do not contradict each other with respect to the existence or value of real-world entity. Maintaining data consistency is particularly difficult in heterogeneous database systems (HDBSs). This is due to the *schematic* and *operation* heterogeneity problem. Active rules have been used to deal with this complex data consistency problem. Unfortunately, much research is focused on the database systems with a unify data model and the schematic heterogeneity problem. In this paper, the authors extend the problem domain into the operation heterogeneity problem within the different data model' systems. The aim of our research is to see how the active rules can be used to maintain data consistency in HDBSs. We examine the active rules in the different types of autonomous local database systems with different integrity constraint mechanisms. We also describe new mechanisms that allow active rule processing to occur separately at each site and guarantee correctness.

Keywords: Heterogeneous Database Systems, Federated Database Systems, Active Database Systems, Active Rule, Integrity Constraint, and Data Consistency.

1 Introduction

Over the past three decades, there has been a tremendous improvement made in Database Systems (DBSs). Such new systems evolve hierarchy DBSs, network DBSs, relational DBSs, and object_oriented DBSs. Within these new situations, the integrating these different DBSs to become a HDBS is required in the information systems.

In the recent years, the integrating production rules (i.e., active rules) into a DBS to become an active DBS has become an emerging issue for the database research to maintain the data consistency and integrity. Several researchers have discussed that the integrating active rules into HDBSs will be a potential solution for the data consistency and integrity problem in HDBSs [DO95; CER92; HSU92]. Unfortunately, much research simplify the problem to maintain consistency on the different relational DBSs. In this paper, the authors extend the problem domain into integrating different data model systems. The aim of our research is to investigate the active rules in the different types of DBSs with different integrity constraint mechanisms. We integrated a relational DBS and an object oriented DBS in our experiment. The objectives of our research are:

- to maintain data consistency and integrity in HDBSs;
- to solve out the integrity constraint conflict problem between the different autonomous DBSs within a HDBS;
- to develop a new transaction management mechanism for HDBSs.

In this paper, the authors give an overview of an active database in next section. The authors, then, describe how the active rules maintain data consistency of a DBS in section 3. Section 4 shows an example of a HDBS which is used in this paper. Section 5 describes the problems of data consistency in HDBS. Section 5 also discusses new mechanisms that allow heterogeneous active rule processing to occur separately at each site and guarantee correctness. In final section, the authors make a conclusion and discuss future work.

2 Active Database Systems

The aim of an active database is to perform automatic monitoring of conditions which defined over the database state and the ability to take action (possibly subject to timing constraints) when the state of the underlying database changes (transaction-triggered processing). Most active database rules use definitions which are like a production rule. They are different to the AI pattern-based rule language in which a rule is triggered only when there is new data in the working memory that matches the pattern. They use the event-based rule language, in which a rule is triggered by an event such as the insertion, deletion or modification of data. The form of an active database rule is:

on event
if condition
then action

The rule is triggered when the event occurs. Once the rule is triggered, the condition is checked. If the condition is satisfied, the action is executed. POSTGRES [STO87], Ariel [HAN89], Ode [GEH91], and HiPAC [DAY88] are systems of this type.

3 Integrity Constraints for Data Consistency in Heterogeneous Database Systems

The preservation of the integrity of a database system is concerned with the maintenance of the correctness and consistency of the data. It has been suggested that the specification of integrity constraints could account for as much as 80 percent of a typical database definition; thus a system that supported such specifications would relieve application programmers of a significant burden [DAT86].

Integrity rules may be divided into four broad categories in the Database Management Systems (DBMSs) [HUG91; AND92]:

- Domain integrity rules, which are concerned with maintaining the correctness of attribute values within entities.

- Intra-relation integrity rules, which relate to the correctness of relationships among attributes of the same entity, and to the preservation of key uniqueness.
- Referential integrity rules, which are concerned with maintaining the correctness and consistency of relationships between entities.
- User-defined integrity constraints, which relate to the mechanisms of the rule declarative specification for the integrity constraint, such as triggers, active rules, etc.

3.1 Active Rules in the Relational Database Systems

Many traditional relational DBSs are typically rather weak on integrity. Most of their integrity checking is done by user-written in procedural code. It would obviously be preferable to be able to specify integrity constraints in some more declarative fashion and thereby have the system to do the checking instead. Active rules have been integrated into the traditional relation DBSs for the integrity constraints in much active database research [DAY95]. Many prototype systems have shown a great success in the data consistency by using active rules, such as POSTGRES [STO91], Ariel [HAN89], Starburst[WID91], etc. The following is an example in the POSTGRES[STO91]:

Assume a POSTGRES database system at a company with a relation *EMP*(emp#,name,sex,....) to keep employees' information. When we insert a new employee information to *EMP* or delete a employee information form *EMP*, we can easily keep the consistency between *EMP* and backup copy *EMP-COPY* by following *insertemp* and *delemp* rule.

define rule insertemp
on insert to EMP
then insert into EMP-COPY (*select* * *from* EMP *where* EMP.emp# = *new*.emp#)

define rule delemp
on delete EMP
then delete EMP-COPY *where* EMP-COPY.emp# = *old*.emp#

The benefit of the active rules for the integrity constraints in relational DBSs can be seen straightforward. Active rules can be seen as a declarative style language in relational DBSs. They enable database designers to declare the database integrity in the database design period but not in the application development time. Many database companies have tried to include the active rules into their next generation relational DBS products. The new SQL standard- SQL3, has also involved some of the active rules' mechanism.

3.2 Active Rules in the Object-Oriented Database Systems

Object-oriented DBSs have emerged in current information systems. They have a rich knowledge representation mechanism. They also contain stronger integrity constraint mechanisms than the mechanisms in relational DBSs. The integrity constraints in the object-oriented DBS can be seen as following [AND92]:

- key properties of attributes or uniqueness constraints;
- explicit consistency constraints;
- pre- and postconditions of methods;
- triggers or similar active elements.

Many current commercial object-oriented DBSs provide the capability to associate explicit constraints with a class definition, as well as triggers. Constraints are typically Boolean expressions that refer to the properties of the class and are checked for validity following execution of operations of the class. Triggers monitor the database at run-time and when a trigger condition become true, the associated trigger action is initiated.

Active rules have also been used in the object oriented database research for data consistency, such as HiPAC [ANW93], SEDSDT [HUA94], [BEE91], etc. The following is an example from the HiPAC system.

Assume a company use HiPAC to manage its warehouse management and include a class qunatity_on_hand to record product information. We can define a following rule to alert manager when the amount of product item is less than threshold number:

Event:	update quantity_on_hand (item)
Condition:	quantity_on_hand (item) < threshold (item)
Action:	alert (mgr)

Integrating the active rules into the object-oriented DBS is an obvious thing. Much active database research using the object-oriented technology [STO87; DAY88; HAN89; GEH91; CER93; HUA94; DO95]. It seems that the object-oriented technology will be the future to integrate active rules into DBSs.

3.3 Active Rules in Heterogeneous Database Systems

HDBSs manage several different databases which are designed by the different DBMSs. The different DBMSs may have the same data models or different data models.HDBSs can be classified into nonfederated DBSs and federated DBSs which are based on the autonomy of the DBSs. A nonfederated system is that the DBSs are not autonomous in the integrating environment. All databases are fully managed by a single global schema and all operations are performed uniformly. A federated DBS is a collection of cooperating DBSs that are autonomous. The autonomy is mean that each local DBMS has the ability to manage their own local databases which are integrated into a federated DBS [SHE90].

Heterogeneity in a federated DBS is primarily caused by the autonomy. The different DBSs have different characteristics and capabilities. This is the reason that an organization chooses different DBSs for different use. For example: the research and design department may choose an object-oriented DBS because its good efficiency in graph representation, but the personnel department may choose a relational DBS for convenient use and maintenance.

Schematic and operation heterogeneity are a crucial problem in building and using a HDBS. This is due to the different DBSs operate independently and the databases may include structural and representational discrepancies (i.e. conflicts). Schematic heterogeneity can takes form of [CER93]:

- naming conflicts: when different databases use different names to represent the same concepts;
- domain conflicts: when different databases use different values to represent the same concepts;
- meta-data conflicts: when the same concepts are represented at the schema level in one database and at the instance level in another;
- structural conflicts: when different databases use different data organization to represent the same concepts.

Operation heterogeneity can be seen as the integrity constraint difference, the functionality difference, and the association and sharing with other systems difference. Within these situations, it is desirable whenever maintain consistency across databases, i.e. to ensure that they do not contradict each other with respect to the existence or value of real-world entity.

The data consistency maintaining is particularly difficult in HDBSs. Active rules have been used to deal with this complex problem, such as [DO95; CER93; HSU92]. Their results have given a very positive opinion to use the active rules in the data consistency maintenance of HDBSs. The following is an example from Ceri and Widoms' research [CER93].

Unfortunately, much research simplify the problem to maintain the data consistency on the different relational DBSs with the semantic heterogeneity problem. In this paper, the authors extend the problem domain into the operation heterogeneity problem within the different data model systems. The aim of our research is to investigate the active rules in the different integrity constraints mechanisms of DBSs. To allow the reader to follow the problem, a new definition is presented.

Definition: A database system is called a *weak integrity constraint system*, if it does not include the user defined integrity constraints. Otherwise, it is a *strong integrity constraint system*.

Assume the Energy Department of Italy use a HDBS to describe the power distribution networks--power supplies, transportation, and use--and the data were actually recorded in two different relational databases. The first database, which we call MN, supports the design and maintenance of a regional power network for the area of Milan. MN use the following schema, where the first attribute of each table is a key for that table.

plant (plant-id, location, power)
user (user-id, location, power)
node (node-id, location, power-loss)
wire (wire-id, fr, to , type, voltage, power)
wire-type (type, max-voltage, max-power, cross-section)

The second database, which we call IN, supports national-level monitoring of the power network throughout Italy. IN uses the following schema:

node (id, region, location, function, power)
connection (connection-id, fr, to)
wire (wire-id, connection-id, type ,voltage, power, age)
wire-type (type, max-voltage, max-power, size)

We know that the tuples in MN.wire-type must also appear in IN.wire-type. We can define the following rules to maintain the data consistency between MN.wire-type and IN.wire-type:

```
define rule InsUp on MN.wire-type
when inserted, updated
then insert into IN.wire-type (select * from (inserted union new-updated)
                                where MN.wire-type.type not in
                                (select type from IN.wire-type))

define rule DelUp on MN.wire-type
when deleted, updated
then delete from IN.wire-type where type not in (select type from (deleted union old-
            updated) where <type,..,cross-section> not in (select * from
MN.wire-type))
```

4 An Example

Due to the design convenience and higher performance, the research and development (R&D) department of a company develops its DBS into an object_oriented DBMS which has a strong integrity constraint and its language is C++ like. In the other hand, the customer service (CS) department of the same company uses a weak integrity constraint relational DBS to manage its customer service data. These two different DBSs manage their data separately and independently. Their database subschemas are as bellow respectively (Fig 1):

The relational database, db1 in the customer service department (SQL-like schema)	In object-oriented database, db2 in the R&D department (C++ like schema)
Create table Fault_info (product_no char(10) not null primary_key, product_name char(10), fault_amount integer));	class product_fault { public: char *product_no ; char *fault_name ; int fix, fault_amount; } constraints if fix = 1 then fault_amount = 0; }

Fig 1. local database schemas

The CS department need to collect the complained information of fault from customers. When the amount of the same fault is larger than the threshold of the tolerance amount, the CS department must inform and request the R&D department to correct the fault. The R&D department will process this information and monitor this fault status. The two departments both use the databases to process these information. We assume that the company has built a HDBS to integrate these two local DBSs. The global schema is showed in Fig 2. The VCLASS is a virtual class to represent a global subscehma in our system. Our example is to append the active rule functionality into this heterogeneous environment. This will enable the system can automatic monitor the consistency of the fault information in these two local DBSs.

Heterogeneous database system global schema (UniSQL/M like schema)

```
CREATE VCLASS Fault
(
 product_no string;
 product_name string;
 fault_amount integer;
 fault_name string;
 fix        integer;
)
AS  SELECT  product_no, product_name, fault_amount, not_available,
            not_available
    FROM    db1.Fault_info
AS  SELECT  product_no, not_available, fault_amount, fault_name, fix
    FROM    db2.Product_fault;
```

Fig 2. The global schema of example

5 Data Consistency Constraints

5.1 Active Rules

To monitor the fault information and automatically change its status for data consistency and integrity between these two local DBSs. We append the following active rule into the HDBS. The syntax of the active rule is POSTGRES like:

define rule R1 for db1
on update to db1.fault_info
if fault_amount > tolerance_amount
then update db2.product_fault (fault_amount)

The rule will be triggered when the fault_amount on table fault_info of db1 is updated and the fault_amount is larger than the threshold of the tolerance amount. The action will update the fault_amount data in the product_fault class of db2. This will keep the fault_amount data consistency between db1 and db2.

5.2 Attributes of A Rule Activation

Active rules are combined with coupling modes to extend their semantic in most of active DBSs. The coupling modes define the execution attributes of active rules which determine how rule events, conditions, and actions relate to database transactions. Each global transaction contains triggering transactions and data transactions in active HDBS. The triggering transaction represents the process of the rule inference. The data transaction represents the original database transaction. There are five different execution attributes to determine semantic of an active rule (see Fig 3) in our active HDBS. Database designers have the flexibility of deciding whether or not the conditions and actions should be executed in the triggering transaction. Besides, database designers can also make a decision for priority and lifetime of active rules.

```
Activate rulename,
        Trans_coupling = Same | Separate,
        EC_coupling = Before | After,
        CA_coupling = Immediate | Deferred,
        Execute_model = Repeat | Once,
        Priority = <number>.
```

Fig 3. The Syntax of the Rule Activation Attributes

The execution attributes for a rule activation are described in the below:

- *Trans_coupling* The execution of a rule is treated as a transaction in our active HDBS, i.e. triggering transaction. The triggered rule seemed as a part of global transaction when Trans_coupling is set to *Same,* and it will be executed in sequence. On the other hand, the triggered rule seemed as another separate transaction and executed in parallel if the rule is specified to *Separate*.

• *EC_coupling* This is to define the evaluation sequence of the event and condition part of an active rule. The *Before* EC_coupling means that the rule condition is evaluated immediately when the rule is reasoned. The *After* EC_coupling means that the rule condition is evaluated after the data transaction committed.

• *CA_coupling* This is to present the execution sequence of the condition and action part of an active rule. The *Immediate* CA_coupling means that the rule action is executed immediately after the rule condition is evaluated. The rule action is executed after data transaction committed, when CA_coupling is specified with *Deferred.*

• *Execute_model* The triggered rule will automatically be deactivated after it is committed, when its execute_model is specified to *Once.* On the other hand, the rule are always active if Execute_model is specified to *Repeat.*

• *Priority* The priority of a rule will be used for the rule conflict resolution. The rule of higher priority will be executed before lower one.

For example, if we define the execution attributes of R1 rule as:

Activate R1,
Trans_coupling = Same,
EC_coupling =After,
CA_coupling = Immediate,
Execute_model = Repeat,
Priority = 2.

After the fault_amount of the fault_info table is updated in db1, the condition of R1 is evaluated. If the condition is true, the action will be executed immediately. Thus, the fault_amount of class product_fault is updated by R1. After the action is executed, the original database transaction is processed. Rule R1 is always active.

5.3 Rule Activation Mechanism

The activation of active rules determine how the rule is reasoned in DBSs. Much research for this problem is focused on the ECA (Event-Condition-Action) mechanism [STO87; DAY88; HAN89; GEH91; CER93; HUA94; DO95]. A rule is triggered when the event occurs. Once the rule is triggered, the condition is checked. If the condition is satisfied, the action is executed. The forward chaining control strategy is widely used in the inference engine of active DBSs to combine with this ECA mechanism.

The rule activation is much more complicated in HDBS than in the general single DBSs. This is due to the consideration of active rule activation in HDBS not only the conflict, termination, execution sequence, and repeating times; but also the global serializability, global progress, network failure, and rule dispatch.

Due to the decentralized global transaction management, rule must be dispatched to suitable sites after it is defined correctly. The rule need be dispatched to the site that contain the data item which specified in rule event. A global rule will be substituted to one or several local rules to each local DBSs. The task dispatched mechanism need to manage this problem.

Global serializability requires global rules to have the same relative serialization order at all local sites in which their local rules are executed. The histories of rule activation in each local site DBSs need to be used to maintain the global serializability.

The global rule activation may inference the other global rules. The local rules may be triggered more than once during the global rule triggering. The local rules may inference the other local rules. The global progress requires the global rules and local rules must to be terminated in a safe status to against the looping and conflict problems.

When network connection is broken down, continuing limited rules activation until the link is restored. All the rules activation that reference to a unreachable site will be aborted. A global rule may be dispatched to a unreachable site and a reachable site. The rule activation need to deal with this network failure problem.

In our research, the authors extend the ECA mechanism to involve different coupling modes to deal with this complex problem. Fig 4 shows the algorithm of the rule activation mechanism. Fig 5 shows the process flow of the rule activation mechanism. The process is separated into four different modules: event evaluation, condition evaluation, action execution, and data transaction. These four parts are combined with coupling modes to be process in different sequence. The network control mechanism, global serializability control mechanism, global progress mechanism, and task dispatched mechanism for rule and data are suitable placed into each module.

6. Conclusion

The paper presented a deeply investigation for the maintenance of data consistency in DBSs by using active rules. This paper also discussed how active rules can be used in HDBSs to maintain the data consistency. A new rule activation mechanism for active HDBSs has been discovered by authors.

Maintaining data consistency is particularly difficult and complex in HDBSs. Much research is focused on assertion-based approach[SPC92] and summary schema model approach[BRI94]. The assertion-based approach uses corresponding assertions and links to integrate local schemas and maintain the equivalent data items in multidatabase system. The summary schema model uses a global linguistic abstract data structure to allow users using imprecise query and maintain data consistency among synonymous data items. This paper has shown that active rules are also a solution to deal with this problem. Several issues need to be further explored in the context of our approach. These include extension of efficient condition evaluation, efficient detection of contradict rules, concurrency control of executing transactions, optimization of user defined rules, parallel execution of conditions and actions, a new transaction management, network failure control mechanism, global serializability control mechanism, global progress mechanism, and task dispatch mechanism.

```
Void main (T)          /* T is a global data transaction in HDBS */
{
 If ( a global transaction (T) occurs )
  {Transaction_Begin(T);
     Triggering_Transaction_Begin(T);
        Event_Detect(T);
        Rule_Inference(Before);
        /* Before: a rule set which rules ; ¦ EC_coupling is equal to Before */
        Data_Transacton_Begin(T);
                Dispatch_Transaction_to_LDBS(T); /* LDBS means local DBS */
                Execute_Data_Transaction(T);
        Data_Transaction_End(T);
        Execute_Action(TEMP);  /*TEMP is a queue to save un_executed actions */
        Rule_Inference(After);
         /*After is a rule set which rules ; ¦ EC_coupling is equal to After*/
        Execute_Action(TEMP);
   Triggering_Transaction_End(T);
 Transaction_END(T);
  } }

void Rule_Inference(Rule_set RS)
{
  Condition_Evaluation(RS);
  While Qualify              /*Qualify is a rule set which contains the rules of inference*/
  { R = Conflict_Resolution(Qualify); /*R is the highest priority rule in Qualify*/
    if (R.CA_coupling == immediate)
      Execute_Action(R)
   else AddQ_Action(R, TEMP);  /* Add a action into TEMP */
   DeleteQ_Rule(R, Qualify)             /* Delete a rule from Qualify */
  } }

void Execute_Action(Action_Set TEMP)  /* TEMP is a queue to store the actions */
{
        While TEMP
        { A = DeleteQ(TEMP);
          Action_Dispatch(A);         /*Dispatch actions to suitable local sites */
          Network_Failure;     /* Network failure control */
          Global_Serializability;             /*Global serializability control */
          Global_Progress;                     /*Global progress control */
          Action_Execute(A);
        } }
```

Fig 4. The Algorithm of the Rule Activation Mechanism

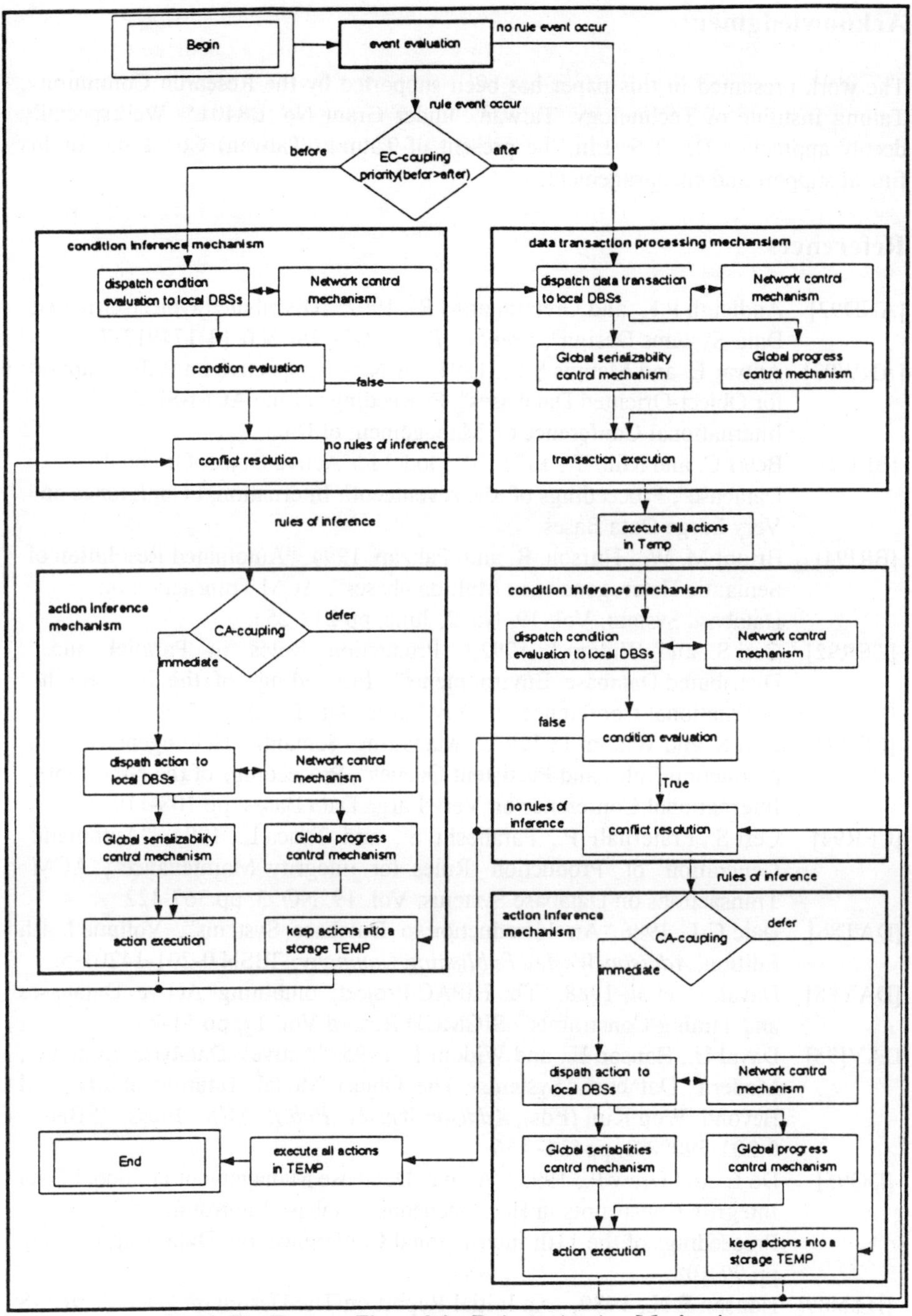

Fig 5. The Process Flow of the Rule Activation Mechanism

Acknowledgment

The work presented in this paper has been supported by the Research Community, Tatung Institute of Technology, Taiwan., under Grant No. B84015. We especially deeply appreciate Dr. T.S. Lin, the present of Tatung (Taiwan) Co., Ltd., for his finical support and encouragement.

References

[AND92] Andleigh P.K. and Gretzinger M.R., 1992, "Distributed Object-Oriented Data-Systems Design", *Prentice Hall (Pub)*, ISBN 0-13-174913-7.

[ANW93] Anwar E. and Maugis S.C., 1993, "A New Perspective on Rule Support for Object-Oriented Databases", Proceedings of the ACM-SIGMOD International Conference on Management of Data.

[BEE91] Beeri C. and Milo T., 1991, "A Model for Active Object Oriented Database", Proceedings of the seventeenth International Conference on Very Large Data Bases.

[BRI94] Bright M. W. , Hurson. R. and Pakzap, 1994, "Automated Resolution of Semantic Heterogeneity in Multidatabases", ACM Transaction on Database System, Vol. 19, No. 2, June, pp 212-253.

[CER92] Ceri S. and Widom J., 1992, "Production Rules in Parallel and Distributed Database Environments", Proceedings of the Eighteenth International Conference on Very Large Data Bases. pp 339-351.

[CER93] Ceri S. and Widom J., 1993, "Managing Semantic Heterogeneity with production Rules and Persistent Queues", Proceedings of the Nineteenth International Conference on Very Large Data Bases. pp 108-119.

[CER94] Ceri S., Fraternali P., Paraboshi S., and Tanca L., 1994, "Automatic Generation of Production Rules for integrity Maintenance", ACM Transactions on Database Systems, Vol. 19, NO. 3, pp 367-422.

[DAT86] Date C.J., 1986,"An Introduction to Database Systems", Volume I, 4th Edition, *Addison-Wesley Publishing Company*, IBSN 0-201-14201-5.

[DAY88] Dayal, U. et al, 1988, "The HiPAC Project: ombining Active Databases and Timing Constraints", SIGMOD Record Vol. 17, pp 51-70.

DAY[95] Dayal U., Hanson E., and Widom J., 1995, "Actives Database Systems", Modern Database Systems- The Object Model, Interoperability, and Beyond, Won Kim (Eds), *Addison Wesley (Pub.)*, ACM Press, ISBN-0-201-59098-0, pp434- 456.

[DO95] Do L. and Drew P., 1995, "Active Database Management of Global Data Integrity Constraints in Heterogeneous Database Environments", Proceedings of the 11th International Conference on Data Engineering, pp 99-108.

[HAN89] Hanson E.N., 1989, "An Initial Report on The Design of Ariel: A DBMS with an Integrated Production Rule System", SIGMOD Record , Vol. 18, No. 3, pp 12-19.

[HSU92] Hsu I.M., Singhal M. and Liu M.T, 1992, Distributed Rule Processing in Active Databases , roceedings of he Eighteenth International Conference on Data Engineering, pp 106-113.

[HUA94] Huang S.M.,Smith P., and Tait J.I., 1994, "Expert Database System: The Way Forward? "Database Management Horizons, 5th International Hong Kong Computer Society Database Workshop, Hong Kong.

[HUG91] Hughes J. G., 1991, "Object-Oriented Databases", *Prentice Hall (Pub)*, ISBN 0-13-629874-5.

[GEH91] Gehani N. and Jagadish H. V. , 1991, Ode as an Active Database: Constraints and Triggers , Proceedings of the Seventeenth International Conference on Very Large Data Bases. pp 327-336.

[SHE90] Sheth A.P. and Larson J.A., 1990, Federated Database Systems for Managing Distributed, Heterogeneous, and Autonomous Databases , ACM Computing Surveys, Vol. 22, NO. 3, pp 183-236.

[STO86] Stonebraker M. and Rowe L.A., 1986, The Design of Postgres , ACM Sigmod Record, pp 340-354.

[STO87] Stonebraker M. and Rowe L.A., 1987, "The Design of POSTGRES", University of California, Berkeley, Electronies Research Laboratory, Internal Memorandum UCB/ERL 85/95.

[STO91] Stonebraker M. and Kemnitz G., 1991, "The Postgres Next-Generation Database Management System", Communications of the ACM, Vol. 34, No. 10, pp 78-92.

[SPC92] Spccapietra S. , Parent C. and Dupont Y. , 1992, "Model Independent Assertions for Integration of Heterogeneous Schemas", VLDB journal, 1, pp 81-126.

[WID91] Widom J., Cochrane R.J., and Lindsay B.G., 1991, "Implementing Set Oriented Production Rules as an Extension to Starburst", Proceedings of the Seventeenth International Conference on Very Large Data Bases.

An Object-Oriented Approach to the Knowledge-based Scheduling Environment

John G Hughes, P Ye, Y Song, D Glass, MD Mulvenna
Faculty of Informatics, University of Ulster
Co. Antrim BT37 OQB, U.K.
E-mail: {JG.Hughes; P.Ye; Y.Song; D.Glass;
MD.Mulvenna}@ulst.ac.uk

Abstract. The combination of knowledge-based and operations research techniques is a promising approach to real world scheduling problems. In this paper an object-oriented approach to the knowledge-based scheduling environment is proposed. Three main issues in the approach, namely data modeling, knowledge modeling, and control modeling are discussed in the paper.

Keywords. knowledge-based scheduling systems, object-oriented approaches, knowledge modeling, operations management.

1. Introduction

Scheduling is an important part of today's society. The scheduling problem has been one of the major topics in Operations Research (OR) for many years. Recently, researchers in the area of Artificial Intelligence (Al) have paid a lot of attention to this problem as well (e.g. [STEF86], [GOEF90], [SMIT92]). Due to the dynamics of the scheduling process and its nature as a NP-hard problem, scheduling is still a difficult problem to tackle, and so far, no single approach can solve it effectively and completely.

Using Al techniques in conjunction with OR can often provide an enriched environment for problem modeling and solving. On the one hand, the key issues in Al are concerned with knowledge representation and reasoning. This offers the possibility of solving specific problems when representing these real world problems at the conceptual level and modeling human being's problem-solving knowledge into computerized software systems. On the other hand, operations research offers a set of algorithms and heuristics which help the developer consider global issues concerning a problem-solving process itself, such as performance analysis of solutions and optimization. To some extend, techniques in OR help to overcome our inability to handle large number of variables and inter-related performance criteria in complex and dynamic manufacturing environments simultaneously. Current research and development has revealed that the combination of knowledge-based techniques and operations research methods is a promising approach to real world scheduling problems ([RODA88], [KING89]).

In this paper, an object-oriented approach to the knowledge-based scheduling environment is proposed. The idea underlying this approach is that the principles of the Object-Oriented paradigm provide a good way of simplifying the application development process for scheduling problems by organizing relevant problem-solving knowledge and procedures together in terms of reusable software components. Based on this theme, three main issues in the approach are discussed in the paper, namely data modeling, knowledge modeling, as well as control modeling. The paper is outlined as follows: the scheduling problem is briefly described in section 2. In section 3, the object oriented approach is defined in terms of the knowledge base, the algorithm base, the object-oriented data model, the database linker, as well as the user interface. Their detailed descriptions are also given in the section. It follows the discussions and the summary in section 4.

2. The Scheduling Problems

Scheduling can be defined simply as a decision-making process for allocating resources over a period of time in order to accomplish some tasks, subject to a set of pre-defined performance criteria. Generally speaking, a lot of knowledge is required in solving real world scheduling problems, which can be practically classified into three groups, i.e. domain knowledge (jobs, machines, materials, products, etc.), problem-solving knowledge (status analysis, heuristics, inferences, etc.), and problem-solving procedures (simulation algorithms, OR algorithms, etc.). Although the knowledge-based approach has been applied in the scheduling area for some years, the number of operational scheduling applications based purely on knowledge-based techniques is limited ([RICK881, [ADIG93]). The main reason comes from people's inability to handle a large number of variables and constraints together with inter-related performance criteria involved in the decision-making process simultaneously in real world complex scheduling environments ([STEF86], [RICK88]). From the developers point of view, in addition, scheduling strategies and methods are not always readily available from human schedulers in many cases. Therefore, simply modeling the problem solving knowledge captured from human schedulers into knowledge-based scheduling systems may lead to so-called *local greedy solutions*. However, current work in relevant areas, especially in operations research (OR) and evolutionary computing (EC), offer a set of methods to approach the scheduling problem. These methods, such as branch and bound in OR and genetic algorithms in evolutionary computing, take global performance criteria and organizational objectives of the problem at hand into account. To some extent, satisfactory or even optimal solutions can be obtained for large and complex scheduling problems using these methods ([TSAN93], [GOLD89]). As suggested by many researchers, combining techniques from Al and OR together is a promising way of developing software systems to solve real world scheduling problems (e.g. [KING89], [WOLF94], and [ROLS94]).

Because of the lack of robust models for the problems [ADIG93], simply putting the techniques from OR and Al together is normally not enough for solving real scheduling applications. As pointed out by Kusiak [KUS187], architectures are needed so that the combination of OR algorithms with a knowledge-based system into an application could be used for solving the problems. The object oriented approach described in the next section provides a flexible and customizable way in which relevant problem-solving knowledge and methods from AI and OR could work in a complementary manner, providing feasible solutions for scheduling problems.

3. The Object-Oriented Approach

3.1 The definition of the approach

As denoted in Figure 1, the object-oriented approach consists of five components, i.e., the knowledge base, the algorithm base, the object-oriented data model, the database linker, as well as the user interface.

The object-oriented data model consists of the data objects which are classified into several inter-related classes. These objects may require all relevant data from the external databases belonging to different application systems within an organization, such as the MRP system and the marketing system, etc. The connection between the object-oriented data model and external databases is accomplished via the database linker. The data model gives the description of a generic scheduling domain, and the objects in the data model can invoke relevant objects in the knowledge base if needed. The knowledge base has two types of objects, namely the *template* objects and the *generic* objects. The former are the templates of problem-solving procedures which can be reconfigured or even replaced according to the characteristics of a specific scheduling domain being considered. The generic objects and the algorithm objects in the algorithm base are domain-independent problem-solving procedures and algorithms which are applicable for a set of scheduling domains. Finally, the user interface acts as a master control system in this framework, and the user can interact with either the knowledge base or the data model via the interface so that interactive decision-making processes can be carried out by the scheduling environment and the solutions are provided for the situations modeled in the object oriented data model.

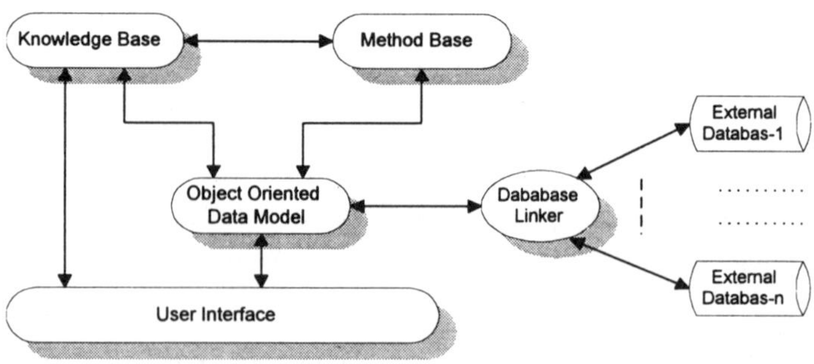

Figure 1. The Object Oriented Architecture

One of the main benefits of this object oriented approach for the scheduling environment is that it provides a consistent way to model the variety of related domain data and problem-solving knowledge within one framework. Secondly, reusability and extensibility of common software components for scheduling problems can be reached in terms of knowledge modeling based on the conceptual scheme described in Section 3.3. In addition, the control mechanism within this scheduling environment is reduced via message passing between the objects in the knowledge base, the algorithm base, and the data model. These issues will be discussed in the following sections.

3.2 Data Modeling

A lot of information is required for the scheduling process, such as material requirements for orders, manpower availability, and machine related information (setup times, processing rates, etc.). In an organization, these information are normally readily available from the databases belonging to different systems within it. For example, the information required by the shift pattern class could come from the database in the personnel department, and the information required by the product class may come from the MRP system. All required data are acquired via the *database linker*.

As the common ground for all problem-solving procedures and algorithms, the object-oriented data model provides required information for the decision-making process of a scheduling domain. Furthermore, all relevant data in the scheduling environment is organized in terms of inter-related classes and represented by a standardized conceptual representation. Figure 2 shows the inheritance relationship between these classes.

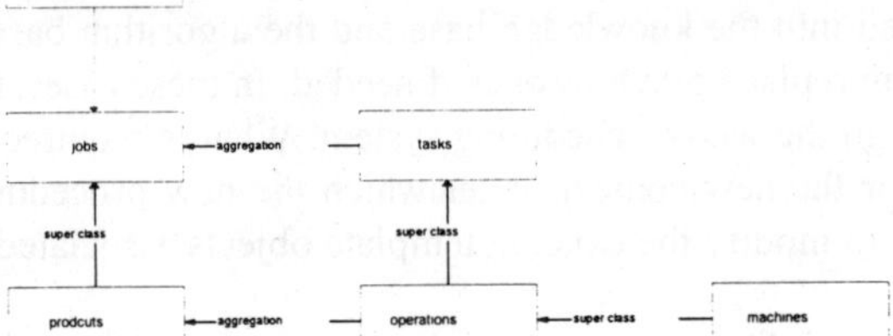

Figure 2. Inheritance Diagram of Data Classes

Taking the *product* class as an example, one *product obj*ect is actually a product specification corresponding to a specific product manufactured on a shop floor. Normally, a product specification consists of manufacturing description (the process routing) as well as material (raw materials and parts) description. The former corresponds to the *operation* class, and the latter corresponds to the *material class*. Each order is associated with a specific product. Hence, the *order* class is the subclass of the *product* class with additional attributes, such as 'due date'. 'quantity', etc.

This data model is serviced as a common ground not only for all problem-solving procedures and algorithms for a scheduling problem, but could also for other production related applications. In addition, it represents domain knowledge at different levels, thus increasing the model's facility for change and extension. For instance, if the process routing for a product is changed, what is required is to change the corresponding objects in the *operation* class, and the new orders for the product will follow the new process routing. Furthermore, the control mechanism for complex scheduling decision could be simplified. This will be discussed in Section 3.4. Any updating from external databases will be reflected in the relevant objects in the data model, which may invoke problem-solving procedures and/or algorithms by sending messages to appropriate knowledge objects in the knowledge-base and/or algorithm objects in the algorithm base. Finally, the data model can supply data responding the end user's inquiries via the user interface connected to it.

3.3 Knowledge Modeling

The knowledge base and the algorithm base in our architecture consist of a set of self-contained and co-operative objects. In the knowledge base, it is called the *knowledge object,* and in the algorithm base it is called the *algorithm object.* Each object is associated with one particular problem-solving task in the decision-making process of a scheduling environment. The required data for these knowledge objects and algorithm objects are provided by the data model. One or several objects in the knowledge base and the algorithm base can co-operate each other to provide the problem-solving strategies or solutions for a particular situation on a shop floor. Furthermore, the knowledge objects in the knowledge base are classified into two types, namely the template objects and generic objects. The former co-ordinates other knowledge objects and the algorithm objects for a problem-solving procedure required either by the data objects in the data model or by the end user via message passing. These template objects should be customized according to the characteristics of a scheduling domain at hand. New problem-solving procedures and algorithms could be continuously added into the knowledge base and the algorithm base as corresponding objects, or they can replace previous ones if needed. In these cases, the developer does not have to redesign the whole scheduling system. What is required is to create a new template object for the new context under which the new procedures and algorithms are introduced, or to modify the existing template objects associated with the context.

To facilitate the reusability and to reduce the complexity of the control mechanism of the systems based on our approach, a conceptual scheme denoted in Figure 3 is used to describe the objects in the knowledge base and the algorithm base. This conceptual scheme is similar to the autonomous planning cell (APC) given by Rolstadäs [ROLS941, within which the controller provides necessary control information to the planner. Each object has three different external connections, i.e., the decision goals, the control connection and the planning connection. The decision goals come from the template objects or data objects in the data model, which determine the object's local decisions. Planning connection is actually data exchange between an object in the knowledge base or the algorithm base and the data model within which the object gets required data for its process from the data model and returns the results to the data model (if applicable). Besides the decision goals, the controller of an object may need additional information from other objects in the knowledge base or the algorithm base as parameters to set up the tasks carried out by the planner for some specific problem situations, and the control connection provides this mechanism. For instance, suppose one object *evaluator* in the knowledge base is for evaluating shop floor performance. Its evaluation procedure is actually configured according to the performance criteria metric specified by some template object or other object in the knowledge base. Here the criteria metric is one of its decision goals. For carrying out its evaluating procedure, it may require some objects in the algorithm base to provide computational work according to the decision goal (the metric). This is accomplished via the control connection. Finally, the required data could be obtained from relevant data objects in the data model, and the evaluation results (planning information) could be sent to relevant objects in the knowledge base or in the algorithm base according to other decision goals provided by the template object that requires the evaluation service of the object *evaluator*.

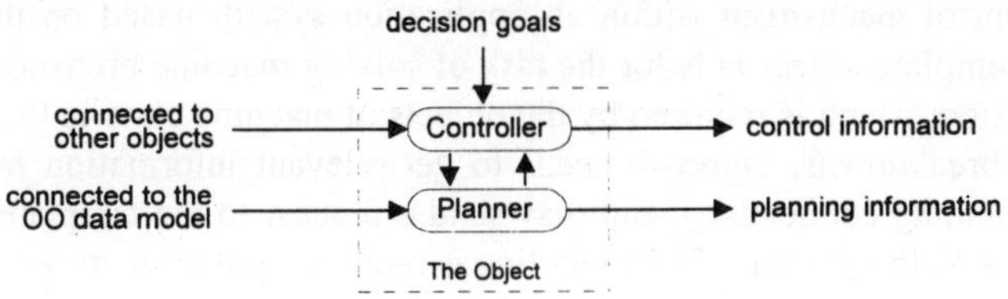

Figure 3. The Conceptual Scheme of the Objects

In this way, the domain specific problem solving modules (i.e., the template objects) are separated from the generic problem-solving modules (i.e., the generic objects and the algorithm objects). Therefore the generic problem-solving modules can be reused for different scheduling applications, and for each individual scheduling application the developer has only to reconfigure or replace the template objects in the knowledge base in accordance with the characteristics of the problem at hand. As the objects in the knowledge base and the algorithm base are actually co-operative and self-contained software components, the reusability of these components is increased, and the high level of extensibility and the low degree of maintenance of the final systems based on these components may be reached.

3.4 Control Modeling

The object oriented approach proposed in this paper is aimed at simplifying the application development process for scheduling problems. The reusability of generic software components is one aspect of the simplification. Another one is concerned with the control mechanism of the decision-making processes within scheduling applications based on this approach.

As described earlier, a template object in the knowledge base carries out a procedure, possibly coordinating other knowledge objects and/or algorithm objects, for a specific task requested by the end users via the user interface or data objects in the data model. It provides a basic template of a problem-solving component. As far as a specific scheduling system is concerned, if the problem-solving procedure provided by a template object is required, the object will be instantiated, or modified (reconfigured), or even replaced by a domain specific object, according to the characteristics of the problem being considered. Therefore, the decision-making process for a problem-solving task required within a specific application domain is constructed without changing the rest of objects in the system.

An instantiated template knowledge object specifies a problem-solving task in a scheduling system. This task is carried out either by the object itself, or by the interaction between the template object with other objects in the knowledge base and the algorithm base. The task requirements are given by the end user via the user interface (i.e., the procedure supplied in the planner of the object, see Figure 2), or by some data objects in the data base via message passing. An example given in Figure 4 shows the control mechanism within an application system based on the approach. Suppose the template *object-m* is for the task of solving machine breakdowns within a scheduling system which is required by the objects of machine class in the data model. For machine breakdowns, *object-m* needs to get relevant information from the data model (via planning connection), and may send a request to the template *object-j* for rescheduling task. In addition, if rescheduling is required, *object-m* may send a request to the generic *object-k* for evaluating the rescheduling results, or send a request to the algorithm *object-i* for capacity/demand analysis. During its problem-solving process, *object-m* interacts with the end user via the user interface to make its decisions. All these objects may require data from the data model which is done by the planning connection. Furthermore, *object-j (for* rescheduling) may consult the end user for its own rescheduling procedure, or send requests to other objects to get qualitative or quantitative intermediate results, so that the interactive decision-making process between the scheduling environment and the end user, as well as between a set of problem-solving modules, can be achieved.

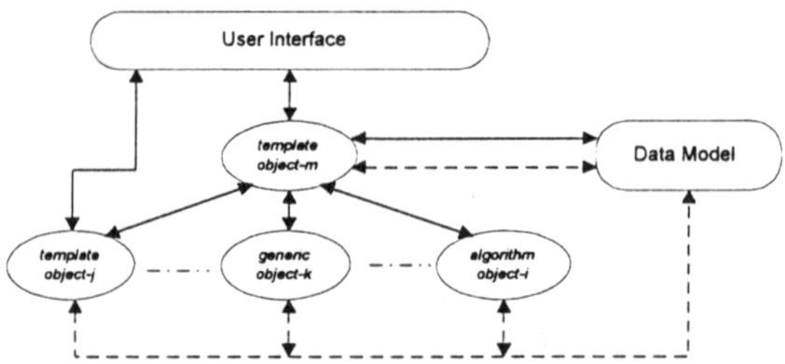

—— : *the control connection;* ········: *the planning connection*

Figure 4. The Interaction between the objects

4. Summary

In this paper, an object oriented approach to the scheduling problem is proposed, and each part is descried in some detail. Within this approach, relevant problem-solving knowledge and algorithms are represented as self-contained and interactive software components (the objects in the knowledge base and the algorithm base). Furthermore, the objects in the knowledge base are classified into two types, namely the template objects and generic objects. The former provides a set of problem-solving templates, and the latter corresponds to a set of domain-independent problem-solving components. For a specific scheduling application, the required template objects are instantiated or modified in accordance with the characteristics of the problem at hand. Finally, the object oriented data model serves as the common ground for all the software components.

One of the main benefits of the approach proposed here is the simplification of the development process for scheduling applications due to the reusability and extensibility of these software components. In addition, the complexity of control mechanisms among data, problem-solving procedures, as well as relevant algorithms may be reduced via message passing. Having studied several real scheduling domains and developed a prototype scheduling system, a scheduling library prototype currently is under development at NIKEL (Northern Ireland Knowledge Engineering Laboratory) which follows the approach. Microsoft Visual C++ is used as the development environment. During this development process, two issues have been found crucial for developing a reusable scheduling library. One is concerned with the scheduling ontology. A scheduling library (or development environment) should based on a suitable ontology which gives a set of core concepts and their descriptions in scheduling domains. This view is shared by other researchers, such as Smith [SMIT94] and Hori [HOR1941. The scheduling ontology actually provides a group of conceptual building blocks based upon them the reusable software components are constructed. Secondly, the object oriented approach proposed in this paper requires careful design considerations with generality and extensibility in mind. Because of the diversity of the scheduling problems, designing the template objects which could be dynamically reconfigured or modified for a set of scheduling applications is not an easy task. The conceptual scheme proposed provides a coherent view for constructing knowledge objects and algorithm objects in the knowledge base and the algorithm base, which plays a key role to coupling reusable software components together based upon the object-oriented data model. As an enabling technology, the principles of object orientation provide possibilities of organizing data, problem-solving knowledge and procedures within one framework, and reusing software components of a development environment for a set of scheduling applications.

References

[GEOF90] Geoffrey, AL, Britt, DL & Gohring, JR 'The role of artificial intelligence techniques in scheduling systems', Proc. Goddard Conf. In Space Application of Al, NASA, pp 29 - 41, 1990.

[GOLD89] Goldberg, DE: Genetic Algorithms in Search, Optimization, and Machine Learning, Addison-Wesley, 1989.

[HORI94] Hori, M, Nakamura, Y & Hama, T 'Configuring problem-solving methods: a CAKE perspective', Knowledge Acquisition, vol. 6, pp 461 - 488, 1994.

[KING89] King, CU & Fisher, EL 'Integrating simulation, optimization and knowledge-based techniques to identify and eliminate production bottlenecks', International Journal of Computer Integrated Manufacturing, vol. 2 (6), pp 317 - 328, 1989.

[RICK88] Rickel, J 'Issues in the design of scheduling systems', Proc. of the Conference on Expert Systems and Intelligent Manufacturing, pp 70-89, 1988.

[RODA88] Rodammer, FA & White Jr KP 'A recent survey of production scheduling', IEEE Transaction on Systems, Man, and Cybernetics, Vol. 18, No. 6, pp 841 - 851, 1988.

[ROLS94] Rolstadäs, A 'Beyond year 2000 - production management in the virtual company', IFIP Trans. B - Applications in Technologies, vol. 19, pp 3 - 10, 1994.

[SMIT92] Smith, SF 'Knowledge-based production management: approaches, results and prospects', Production Planning & Control, vol. 3, No 4, pp 350 -380, 1992.

[SMIT94] Smith., SF and Lassila, 0 'Configurable systems for reactive production management', IFIP Trans. B: Applications in Technology, vol. 15, pp 93 - 106, 1994.

[SNYD93] Snyder. A 'The essence of objects: concepts and terms', IEEE Software, pp 31 - 42, Jan. 1993.

[STEF86] Steffen, MS 'A survey of artificial intelligence-based scheduling systems', Fall Industrial Engineering Conference Proceedings, pp 395 - 405, 1986.

[TSAN93] Tsang, E: Foundations of Constraint Satisfaction, Academic Press, 1993.

[WOLF94] Wolf, G 'Scheduling management: an object oriented approach', Decision Support Systems, vol. 11, pp 373 - 388, 1994.

An Object-Oriented Approach to Interoperation of Heterogeneous Information Sources

Ling Liu[1] and Calton Pu[2]

[1]University of Alberta, Edmonton, Alberta T6G 2H1 Canada
email: lingliu@cs.ualberta.ca
[2]Oregon Graduate Institute, Portland, Oregon 97291-1000 USA
email: calton@cse.ogi.edu

Abstract. In the modern Internet environment, various types of data sources have become accessible, including multimedia data and web pages. Some of the fundamental assumptions in traditional databases, such as the existence of a global schema and data consistency maintained by a Data Base Administrator, are no longer true in many of the new data sources. We outline the DIOM [LP95b] object-oriented approach to build interoperable heterogeneous information systems despite the absence of global schema and the presence of data inconsistency. We describe the metadata catalog management component of DIOM, a key service in the support for interoperation among heterogeneous information sources. To support a flexible and customizable conection between information consumers and information producers, DIOM metadata catalog development utilizes the adaptive specification mechanisms, provided in DIOM interface description language, for explicit description of information consumers' domain query requirements and for object-oriented abstractions of information producers' information sources.

1 Introduction

One of the important contributions of database research is the carefully chosen set of assumptions made on the data in the database. For example, a relational database is described completely by the database schema, and data/schema consistency is maintained by the Data Base Administrator (DBA). Query processors and optimizers use database schema in critical ways. Similarly, atomic transactions [GR93] depend on data consistency assumption, since they are defined as programs that take a database from a consistent state to another consistent state. In the current generation of new information systems (or so called non-traditional database systems (NDBs) such as scientific data [BP93], multimedia databases, a variety of Internet data sources [LP95b], some of these important assumptions do not hold and classic database techniques may not apply directly. In this paper, we examine two decreasingly valid assumptions in nontraditional databases that strive to be interoperable: (1) data is consistent in the database, and (2) database schema is reasonably stable. Our focus is on the interoperability problems aggravated by inconsistency and rapid evolution. We restrict our attention to these two assumptions due to the complexity of the issue. We acknowledge the importance of other traditional database assumptions and anticipate much more work to be done in this direction.

We have proposed the Distributed Interoperable Object Model (DIOM) [LP95b] to address the problem of data inconsistency and dynamic system evolution in the integration of heterogeneous information sources. The main idea of DIOM is to define interoperability as a flexible and voluntary interfacing of heterogeneous information consumers and information producers. This interfacing is defined explicitly, by using abject-oriented abstractions to capture query requirements from the consumer side and the metadata of information sources from the producer side. Our main contribution in this paper is the design of a metadata catalog management system, a key service in DIOM for supporting transparent and customizable access across multiple disparate information sources. We demonstrate that, given the evolving and inconsistent nature of individual data sources, how object-orientation can be utilized in the DIOM metadata model construction to facilitate the integration and access of heterogeneous information sources.

2 Problems Analysis

Although obvious in retrospect, it is worthwhile to restate that traditional database assumptions do not necessarily hold simply because we call a data source a *database*. There is a strong temptation to apply database results to new data sources, since database theory and software are typically stronger than existing data access support. However, without examining the validity of traditional database assumptions we run the risk of introducing more problems than we solve. For example, if data is already inconsistent, then using atomic transactions will not produce a consistent database state. The inconsistency could be amplified by some transactions, for instance, one that makes multiplication involving a numerical field with inconsistency [RP95].

In this section we focus our analysis only on the traditional assumptions on data consistency and schema stability. By analyzing the validity of the data consistency and schema stability assumptions in traditional databases, we see that they are ensured by two basic factors: the central authority of DBAs, and the existence of a globally valid database schema. It is the role of DBA to run the programs that filter out inconsistent data, and be the arbiter in deciding which data is good when conflicts and contradictions arise. Usually, the syntactic aspects of data consistency can be decided automatically using the database schema and the semantic aspects of data consistency depend on custom/application programming or DBA intervention when everything else fails.

2.1 Data Inconsistency and Heterogeneity

One of the most important challenges in the interoperable database systems of the future, especially in a rapidly growing environment such as the Internet, is the handling of inconsistency when individual and heterogeneous databases are integrated into an interoperable database system.

By analyizing inconsistency, we start with the inherent inconsistency in an individual application-specific database. In some information systems, the inconsistency in data is well recognized, although not necessarily explicitly described. For example, most of scientific observational data, including much of satellite data such as the Earch Observation System, contain uncertainties inherent in the sensors. Sometimes these uncertainties are included as part of data (e.g., error bars). Other times, these uncertainties are considered part of the sensor description (e.g., model number and brand of an electronic microscope for digital images), or included in the metadata, as part of experimental setup description (e.g., in a Crystallographic Information File description of protein structures [NSF93]).

To complicate matters, the inconsistency may take several forms or contain several dimensions. For example, some inconsistencies are given by absolute bounds [RP95], as in bank accounts that allow limited withdrawals from Automatic Teller Machines, where the inconsistency is bounded by the daily cash withdrawal limit. In contrast, other inconsistencies depend on statistical and probabilistic models, such as the error bars in scientific data [BP93]. Analogously, in addition to value inconsistency, there is a time dimension to most data [PTWY94]. For example, even if we do not know the current value of a data item, knowing the last update time may be helpful. Another example of inconsistency involves the issues known as data quality. Without a DBA certifying the correctness and up-to-dateness of a data item, the judgment of its quality is much harder.

As we attempt to integrate information from multiple autonomous and heterogeneous data sources through interoperation, inconsistency is compounded, and in many cases, in an unpredictable way. Without a good handle on the inconsistency problem, these interoperable databases will become unreliable sources of data from the consistency viewpoint.

2.2 Dynamic System Evolution

A schema is often used as an interface between a data repository and programs. Once a schema changes, three levels of inconsistency may occur: (1)Incomsistency in schema itself; (2)Inconsistency between existing database and the modified schema; (3)Incompatibility of application programs in accessing data.

In traditional database systems, schemas were assumed to be reasonably stable. It is mainly because the cost of maintaining database consistency and program compatibility in the presence of schema modification can be too high to be affordable.

As the number of databases available via networks increases swiftly, Пeven when the changes in each individual component database schema are not frequent at all, the large number of component databases may add up to surprisingly frequent schema change events at the interoperable database system level. Assuming that there is only one change in two years for any component database schema, an interoperable system with two hundred databases as such will have to contend with one hundred changes every year, which corresponds to, on average, two changes every week!

3 Distributed Interoperable Object Model: An Overview

Distributed interoperable objects (DIOs) are objects that support a level of interoperability beyond the traditional object computing boundaries imposed by programming languages, data models, process address space, and network interface [Bet94].

Distributed Interoperable Object Model (DIOM) is developed mainly for incorporating system-wide scalability and evolution support as well as component composability into an interoperation framework. In an environment where multiple information sources are dynamically connected to the Internet, it is highly desirable for users and applications to be able to work with remote data sources and request services across networks as if they were working with a single database system. We have captured the requirements of these large-scale interoperable systems by USECA properties [LP95b] Uniform access to heterogeneous information sources, Scalability to the growing number of information sources, Evolution and Composability of software and information sources, and Autonomy of participants, both information consumers and information producers.

DIOM consists of an interface description language (IDL) and an interface query language (IQL). Rather than inventing yet another object-oriented data model, DIOM adopts the ODMG-IDL and ODMG-OQL object database standard [Cea94, Kim94] as the base model and adds a number of interface abstractions to allow new interfaces to be constructed in terms of existing ones, and to provide better support for the USECA properties. These incremental interface construction facilities include: *import mechanism, interface aggregation, interface generalization*, and *interface specialization*.

DIOM introduces base interface and compound interface concepts to separate the interface descriptions for information producers' source models and the interface descriptions for information consumers' domain usage models (personal views). Such a separation serves dual purposes: (a)It enables the system to automate the specification of base interfaces. (b)It allows information consumers to build dynamic and personal views, rather than monolithic and integrated snapshots, over the growing number of information sources. Other important features of the DIOM object model include:

- the incremental design and construction of compound interoperation interfaces through recursive application of abstraction and composition operators on the existing interfaces,
- the deferment of conflict resolution to the later stage of query evaluation in contrast to classical approaches that enforce conflict resolution by schema integration or at query formulation time,
- the support for application designers to define their own interoperation interface schema, independently of any system-supplied global schema.

A DIOM database consists of a collection of DIOs, which are composed through dynamically binding data from multiple data repositories provided by the underlying component systems. The DIOM interface definition language (DIOM-IDL) is used to the relevant portions of the information sources through object-oriented abstractions.

Consider an enterprise system that deals with book inquiry, sale, and purchase business in a distributed and heterogeneous environment such as the Internet. For concreteness, we assume that the relevant information sources that are currently available include BookStore database (Oracle), book club database (Sybase), publisher database (Informix), library database (ObjectStore), and bibliography file (in LaTeX `.bib` format). We refer to these information sources as component information sources of the given enterprise system. Fragments of the export schemas of these information sources are given in Figure 1, where the primary keys are underlined. Obviously, some of these information sources have similar data contents, but their representations are different. This is generally true for most of the information sources that are created and managed by separate organizations (information producers) with different business objectives or using different types of data repository managers.

```
Books(book#,subject,store#,language,publisherID,quantity)
Order(order#,book#,buyerID,data,quantity,price,status)
Buyer(buyerID,name,phone)
BookStore(store#,name,phone,location)

        DR1: BookStoreDB

Books(bookID,description,clubID,publisher,medium)
Member(member#,name,phone,address)
Order(orderID,bookID,member#,data,price,quantity,status)
BookClub(clubID,name,phone,address)

        DR2: BookClubDB

Books(bookID,title,language,medium,price,publisherID)
SaleDept(deptID,publisherID,bookID,manager)
Order(orderRef#,bookID,customerID,date,quantity,status)
PublishingDept(deptID,bookID,customerID,contract#,manager)
Customer(customerID,name,phone,address)
Publisher(publisherID,name,address,phone)

        DR3: USPublisherDB
```

```
Books(bookID,title,language,price,publisherID)
PurchaseOrder(order#,bookID,customerID,date,quantity,status)
Customer(customerID,name,phone,address)
Publisher(publisherID,name,address,phone)

        DR4: GMPublisherDB

Items(item#,category,libraryID,quantity)
Books(bookID,title,language,ISBN,publisher,year)
Journal(journalID,title,publisher,ISBN)
TechRep(TR#,title,author,institution,year)
BorrowRequest(readID,bookID,date,period)
Reader(readerID,name,phone,address)
Library(libraryID,name,address,phone)

        DR5: LibraryDB

Book(bibID,title,authors,publisher,year)
Article(bibID,title,author,journal,publisher,volumn,number)
InProceeding(bibID,title,authors,conf-name,publisher,year)
TechRep(bibID,title,authors,institution,year,month)

        DR6: Biblio.bib File
```

Figure 1: Fragments of the export schemas of example information sources

Suppose that a consumer wants to access the book information and the relevant supplier's information. She may describe her domain query model in IDL as follows:

```
CREATE INTERFACE Book
( extent books
  key    Book->ID )
{   GENERALIZATION OF
      select interface-name from Interface-Repository
      where  description = '*Book' OR description = '*Books';
    ATTRIBUTES
          String ID,
          String title,
          Supplier supplier,
          String medium,
```

```
            Double price,
            Order orderNo;    }

    CREATE INTERFACE Supplier
    ( extent suppliers
      key    Supplier->ID )
    {   GENERALIZATION OF
          select interface-name from Interface-Repository
          where  description CONTAINS
                 ['BookStore','BookClub','Publisher','Supplier'];
        ATTRIBUTES
              String ID,
              String name,
              String addr;   }
```

All queries and request for data and services may be formulated using DIOM interface query language (DIOM-IQL) against some IDL interfaces. For example, the query Q: "find titles, prices and supplier names of all the books that are related to 'SGML' can be expressed in IQL as follows:

```
SELECT Book->title, Book->price, Supplier->name
FROM   Book, Supplier
WHERE  Book->title CONTAINS 'SGML';
```

Figure 2: An example query

In DIOM, to process this query we first select relevant sources that should be used to answer this query. Then we reformulate this IQL query into a number of subqueries, each targeting at one single source before translating each subquery to the source-specific query expression that can be executable at the source. The metadata catalog generated based on IDL and IQL specifications plays a critical role in each step of the DIOM query processing.

In the following section we discuss how we construct and maintain the distributed metadata catalog in DIOM and what roles the metadata catalog management play in each phase of the DIOM query mediation process and in supporting USECA properties within the DIOM interoperation architecture [LP95b]. Examples are provided to highlight the benefits of object-orientated approach to the design of DIOM interface description language. For further detail about DIOM-IDL and DIOM-IQL, readers may refer to [LP95a, LPL96].

4 Metadata Support

In the Diorama project, metadata extracted from information consumer's interface schemas and information producers' export schemas are managed and maintained in the DIOM metadata catalog. In the following sections we will discuss three most important components of the metadata catalog: information source repository, interface repository, and implementation repository. Examples are provided based on the *Book-Sale* application scenario and the consumer's query given in the previous section.

4.1 Information Source Repository

Information source repository is created and maintained by the DIOM information source registration manager, which is responsible for recording all the available source producers' information, such as the information producer's name, the location pointer (e.g., the URL in WWW), the information source description (keywords), the export schema locator, the source type, and so on. A fragment of the DIOM information source repository is shown in Figure 3. Every application-specific mediator (App-mediator), once created, may also be registered as an information source to be available to the customer set of the DIOM system.

SourceName	PointerToProducerSite	SourceType	Description	ExportSchema
Harvest	harvest.cs.colorado.edu	Broker	PCSofware,CSTR,...	
Yahoo	yahoo.com	Broker	...	
CForder	diom.cs.ualberta.ca	AppMediator	Claim,DiagnosisRep,...	Diom_ClaimForder
DR1	dr1.com	RDB	Books,BookStore,...	DR1.BookstoreDB
DR2	dr2.com	RDB	Books,BookClub,...	DR2.BookClubDB
DR3	dr3.com	RDB	Books,Publisher,...	DR3.USPublisherDB
DR4	dr4.com.de	RDB	Books,PurchaseOrder,...	DR4.GMPublisherDB
DR5	dr5.org/	OODB	Books,Library,...	DR5.LibraryDB
DR6	ftp.cs.ualberta.ca	.bib file	Book,Article,TechRep	DR6.Bibliography
...	...	...	...	...

Figure 3: Fragment of DIOM information source repository

4.2 Interface Repository

Interface repository is another basic component of the DIOM metadata catalog. It is created and maintained by the IDL preprocessor and the DIOM base interface generator. Whenever a new information consumer's domain model is defined in DIOM-IDL, the interface repository will be extended. The first scan of the IDL preprocessor over a given IDL schema handles all the interfaces defined by means of the `import` and `hide` mechanisms. The base interface generator is invoked for each IDL interface defined using `import`. Figure 4 shows a fragment of the interface repository. For each consumer-defined (compound) interface or system-generated base interface, a pointer to the list of attributes, relationships, or methods associated with this interface definition is also maintained in the interface repository.

4.3 Implementation Repository

The DIOM servers (mediator level and wrapper level) provide a number of general services to facilitate the global query planning, the query reformulation, and the parallel execution of a multi-information source query. One of the most important services is the creation and maintenance of implementation repository metadata, which are used heavily by the DIOM query services provided by the mediators and their associated wrappers. The main issues to be addressed include: (1)how to establish a semantic correspondence between the types and

interface-name	interface-type	description	source-producer
Harvest	base	Security,PCSofware,CSTechReport,...	Harvest
Yahoo	base		Yahoo
ClaimForder	aggregation	Claim,Image,DiagnosisRep,...	Diom
DR1.Books	base	Books	DR1
DR1.BookStore	base	BookStore,Supplier,...	DR1
DR1.Buyer	base	Buyer,Customer,...	DR1
...	...	...	...
DR2.Books	base	Books	DR2
DR2.BookClub	base	BookClub,Supplier,...	DR2
DR3.Publisher	base	Publisher,Supplier,...	DR3
...	...	...	...
Diom.Book	generalization	Book, Books	Diom
Diom.Supplier	generalization	BookStore,BookClub,Publisher,...	Diom
Diom.Customer	generalization	Buyer,Customer,Reader,...	Diom
Diom.Order	generalization	Order,PurchaseOrder,...	Diom
...	...	...	...

Figure 4: Fragment of DIOM interface repository

relationships defined in the consumer's domain model with the classes and relations used in the producers' source models. (2)how to maintain the implementation metadata catalog in the presence of changes. The second issue will be addressed separately in Section 4.5.

The internal representation of relating an information source to a domain model for the `Book Sale and Purchase` application is illustrated in the Figure 5, Figure 6, and Figure 7. Each of these figures represents the attribute correspondence between mediated attributes defined in the consumer's domain model and source attributes defined in a particular information source model. The first column in each table contains the names of the mediated attributes and their type. The second column contains the corresponding information source level attributes, prefixed by the class or relation they belong to. For example, the attributes from database `DR1`, `DR2`, and `DR3` are described in the second column of the table in Figure 5, Figure 6, and Figure 7 respectively. A null value in a source attribute column denotes the non-existence of the attribute in the corresponding information source.

From the implementation point of view, the mediated attributes and their types are used as instruments to establish connections among similar attributes and their classes or relations defined in the relevant component information sources. These semantic links are central to the automation of global query planing, query refinement, query decomposition, and query result assembly (packaging).

Note that this type of metadata is mainly obtained by applying machine learning techniques to the metadata catalog and user profile (if any). For example, the knowledge about connecting term `Publisher, BookClub, and BookStore` to the term `Supplier` can be learned directly from the interface definition of `Supplier`, while the connection between the federated attribute `Book->price` and the source attribute `Order.price` in `DR1` can be learned by keyword-based partial matching. In order to build comprehensive domain-specific terminology matching rules and ontology, a sophisticated learning and knowledge discovery tool is needed. Appropriate interaction with the information consumer or domain expert may also be required. Our study on this topic will be reported in a

Mediated-attributes	DR1
Book→ID	Books.book#
Book→title	Books.title
Book→supplier	Books.store#
Book→orderNo	Order.order#
Book→medium	
Book→price	Order.price
Order→ID	Order.order#
Order→quantity	Order.quantity
Order→customer	Order.byerID
Customer→ID	Buyer.buyerID
Customer→name	Buyer.name
Customer→addr	
Supplier→ID	BookStore.storeID
Supplier→name	BookStore.name
Supplier→addr	

Figure 5: Fragment of implementation repository maintained at the wrapper to DR1

Mediated-attributes	DR2
Book→ID	Books.bookID
Book→title	Books.description
Book→supplier	Books.clubID
Book→orderNo	Order.orderNo
Book→medium	Books.medium
Book→price	Order.price
Order→ID	Order.orderNo
Order→quantity	Order.qty
Order→customer	Order.customerID
Customer→ID	Customer.customerID
Customer→name	Customer.name
Customer→addr	Customer.address
Supplier→ID	BookClub.clubID
Supplier→name	BookClub.name
Supplier→addr	BookClub.address

Figure 6: Fragment of implementation repository maintained at the wrapper to DR2

forthcoming paper.

4.4 Source-specific Metadata

In order to automate query translation and query result assembly, additional metadata are required. For example, for each attribute defined at an individual information source, the following information is needed: (1) the scale of the attributes, (2) the key constraint of the attributes (key, non-key, foreign key), and (3) the logical connection paths. The connection path assignment scheme varies for different types of information sources. For example,

- the connection path assignment scheme for the information sources managed by the relational systems is the following. A non-key attribute points to its key attribute(s). A key attribute points to their foreign keys, and

Mediated-attributes	DR3
Book→ID	Books.bookID
Book→title	Books.title
Book→supplier	SaleDept.publisherID PublishDept.publisherID
Book→orderNo	Order.orderRef#
Book→medium	Books.medium
Book→price	Books.price
Order→ID	Order.orderRef#
Order→quantity	Order.qty
Order→customer	Order.customerID
Customer→ID	Customer.customerID
Customer→name	Customer.name
Customer→addr	Customer.address
Supplier→ID	Publisher.publisherID
Supplier→name	Publisher.name
Supplier→addr	Publisher.address

Figure 7: Fragment of implementation repository maintained at the wrapper to DR3

each foreign key points to its home key. If a relation has no foreign key, the pointer field is null. This simple path assignment schema ensures that all the necessary joins can be constructed when translating a consumer-level query into a group of subqueries at information producer's source level, each against a single information source.

- The connection path assignment scheme for object-based information sources is even simpler. Each *oid* field corresponds to the key field of a given object class. The rest are non-key fields. The navigational path for the same attribute type may vary from query to query, depending on the specific structural pointers (object references) specified in each query.

These metadata are mostly related to a single data source. They can be obtained directly from the export schema of the given information source, and incrementally maintained by the corresponding DIOM wrapper. More importantly, the translation of subqueries into the component query expressions should be carried out at the wrapper layer to prevent query processing bottleneck at the DIOM distributed object server layer. Figure 8 shows the internal representation of the metadata catalog maintained by the corresponding DIOM wrapper, the local DIOM agent to the DR3 information source. Note that (1) the designated navigational paths in the above table only specify the logical dependency between the non-key attributes and the key attributes of the corresponding information source which are involved in the MDB consumer's interface description. During the subquery translation, these designated navigational paths will be re-examined based on the export schema in order to derive meaningful intra-database joins. (2) For each source attribute, a concrete structural pointer is derived at query execution time to replace the navigational path.

DR3.attribute	DR3.domain	DR3.scale	DR3.key	DR3.keyFD
Books.bookID	none	none	key	
Books.title	none	none	nonkey	Books.bookID
Books.medium	(CD-ROM, Paper)	none	nonkey	Books.bookID
Books.price	none	US$	nonkey	Books.bookID
Books.deptID	none	none	fkey	SaleDept.deptID PublishDept.deptID
SaleDept.deptID	none	none	key	
PublishDept.deptID	none	none	key	
Order.orderRef#	none	none	key	
Order.bookID	none	none	fkey	Books.bookID
Order.customerID	none	none	fkey	Customer.customerID
Order.quantity	none	none	nonkey	Order.orderRef#
Customer.customerID	none	none	key	
Customer.name	none	none	nonkey	Customer.customerID
Publisher.publisherID	none	none	key	
Publisher.name	none	none	nonkey	Publisher.publisherID

Figure 8: Fragment of source-sepcific metadata extracted from the export schema of DR3

4.5 Maintaining Metadata Catalog in the Presence of Changes

When a new information source is registered, to guarantee this new information source will be used to respond a query, updates to the existing metadata catalog is needed. Two strategies can be used for maintaining the metadata catalog up to date: (1) Immediate update or (2) Deferred update.

With immediate update approach, the maintenance proceeds in three steps: First, the DIOM server triggers the metadata catalog manger to perform an incremental recompilation on all the existing domain interface schemas to which this new information source may be related. Second, for each relevant domain interface schema, the implementation repository manager will be invoked to relate object types used in this new information source to the object types defined in the given domain model. Third, the source-specific metadata catalog manager, associated with the wrapper to this new information source, is invoked. The source-specific implementation metadata is extracted from the export schema of this new information source.

With deferred update approach, the incremental recompilation of existing domain interface schemas is delayed to the time when a query is issued. By using deferred approach, instead propagating changes to all the domain interface schemas, only those domain interface schemas that are frequently used by queries are updated accordingly.

When a change is made to the information consumer's domain model or the information producer's source model, a modification to the corresponding metadata is performed accordingly and transparently. For example, modifying the domain of attribute `medium` by adding `Postscript` format in the relation `Books` of the information source `DR3` requires a change of the metadata, at the column of `DR3.domain` and the row of `Books.medium` in Figure 8, from `(CD-ROM,Paper)` to `(CD-ROM,Paper,PostScript)`. Obviously, this change propagation can be done transparently.

5 Discussion

DIOM is being implemented in the Diorama project. Diorama presents the applications with a number of distributed query services in addition to the interface description language IDL and interface query language IQL. Information consumers may query the information from multiple heterogeneous information sources through a unified object-oriented view in terms of IDL, and executes requests (e.g., queries, updates on object links, and method invocations) at the relevant information sources. Diorama's components conform to client/server standards such as CORBA [For93] and are dynamically bound to individual information sources to support independent component evolution. For instance, DIOM interfaces to C++ applications may be a set of C++ classes that act as "surrogates" for the corresponding definition of the DIOM interface schema. Information consumers may define their domain query requirement without having any precise knowledge of the available underlying information sources. New applications may define their interoperation interfaces by aggregation or generalization of existing interfaces, or by refinement of pre-defined interfaces, rather than starting from scratch. When a component source evolves into a new version, to incorporate the changes at the component level into the interoperation interface level, some modification to the DIOM distributed metadata library may be necessary. To ensure the subsequent queries are processed against the up-to-date information sources, the incremental IDL/IQL recompilation will be invoked transparently. As a result, no manual rewriting of consumer's query interface schema and application programs is required. Furthermore, when the number of information sources that participate in the interoperation increases, the existing legacy applications may continue to work without source code changes.

6 Related Work

Representative projects in the area of integration of heterogeneous information sources [Wie92, Wie93] include TSIMMIS [GMea94, PGMW95], which introduces an object exchange model and a query language for integrated information access. The Context Interchange approach [SSR94, GMS94] represents data semantics explicitly using a shared ontology. Other projects include work at USC [DS93], HP Labs [Sha93], and IBM Almaden Research Center [CHea94]. The entire area of distributed object management [ODV93] has also important impact on this line of research.

In addition, much of the work on heterogeneous databases are also relevant. However, our viewpoint is somewhat different from the previous research on the integration of schematic and heterogeneity, such as [KS91, SK92, SL90, SM91, VH91]. Instead of trying to minimize the differences and make them disappear, we accept the differences and try to characterize them and utilize them as semantic annotation in the DIOM query evaluation process.

7 Conclusion

We have looked into two of traditional database system assumptions in this position paper: (1) data is consistent in the database, and (2) database schema is reasonably stable. These assumptions are severely strained in distributed interoperable data sources, such as multimedia databases, object-oriented databases, web pages and other information sources on the Internet. Due to autonomy of component data sources, an interoperable information system will contain inherent inconsistency, as well as frequent schema changes. As a starting point for discussion, we have outlined the DIOM approach as a possible technique to handle the schema evolution and the data inconsistency incurred by representational and semantic heterogeneity of data.

The main idea of the DIOM approach is mandating explicit and voluntary declarations of what are information consumer wants and what information producers' supplies are of most interest. These declarations are stored in the metadata management system and used for deriving the relevant portions of producers' source data and for connecting information consumers with information producers in a flexible and dynamic way. We have described how the DIOM metadata catalog is constructed, managed and maintained in a DIOM environment. Three groups of metadata repositories are discussed: (1)metadata related to information sources (information producers' source information), (2)metadata related to consumer's interface descriptions (information consumer's domain query requirements), and (3)metadata related to query implementations (establishing a flexible connection between consumer's queries and producers' source data). We also highlight the benefits of building distributed metadata catalog based on the object-oriented design of IDL.

Our work on the DIOM distributed catalog management continues. The proposal for distributed metadata catalog management and the utilization of object-oriented abstractions to IDL design is still in its early stage of development. The metadata model and catalog management present only a first step towards finding solutions for the interoperability problem. No doubt other ideas and techniques will arise in response to the breakdown of these traditional database assumptions. We contend that in large networks such as the Internet, interoperability among heterogeneous information sources requires a systematic reexamination of many of the assumptions made by traditional databases. The investigation of which traditional techniques still apply under the relaxation of a particular set of assumptions become an increasingly challenging area for research and development. For example, techniques such as Epsilon Serializability (ESR) [PL91, WYP92, RP95] have been developed to bound the amount of inconsistency in individual transaction processing systems. We are currently studying the application of ESR algorithms to control inconsistency in the Internet environment.

Acknowledgement

The work was supported partially by NSERC grant OGP-0172859 and NSERC grant STR-0181014 for the first author, and by ARPA under contract DABT63-95-C-0010 and NSF under grant IRI-9510112 for the second author.

References

[Bet94] Mark Betz. Interoperable objects: laying the foundation for distributed object computing. *Dr. Dobb's Journal: Software Tools for Professional Programmer*, (220), October 1994.

[BP93] R. Barga and C. Pu. Accessing imprecise data: An interval approach. *IEEE Bulletin of the Technical Committee on Data Engineering*, 16(2):12–15, June 1993.

[Cea94] R. Cattell and et al. *The Object Database Standard: ODMG-93 (Release 1.1)*. Morgan Kaufmann, 1994.

[CHea94] M.J. Carey, L.M. Haas, and P.M. Schwarz et al. Towards heterogeneous multimedia information systems: the garlic approach. In *Technical Report, IBM Almaden Research Center*, 1994.

[DS93] D.Mcleod D.Fang, S.Ghandeharizadeh and A. Si. The design, implementation, and evaluation of an object-based sharing mechanism for federated database systems. In *Proceedings of International Conference on Data Engineering*, Vienna Austria, 1993.

[For93] Object Request Broker Task Force. *The Common Object Request Broker: Architecture and specification*. Object Management Group, 1993.

[GMea94] Hector Garcia-Molina and et al. The tsimmis approach to mediation: data models and languages (extended abstract). In *Technical Report, Stanford University*, 1994.

[GMS94] C. Goh, S. Madnick, and M. Siegel. Context interchange: overcoming the challenges of large-scale interoperable database systems in a dynamic environment. In *Proceedings of International Conference on Information and Knowledge Management*, pages 337–346, 1994.

[GR93] J. Gray and A. Reuter. *Transaction Processing: Concepts and Techniques*. Morgan Kaufmann Publishers, 1993.

[Kim94] Won Kim. Observations on the odmg-93 proposal. *ACM SIGMOD RECORD on Management of Data*, 23(1), March 1994.

[KS91] W. Kim and J. Seo. Classifying schematic and data heterogeneity in multidatabase systems. *IEEE Computer Magazine*, 24(2):12–18, 1991.

[LP95a] Ling Liu and Calton Pu. The diom approach to large-scale interoperable information systems. Technical report, TR95-16, Department of Computing Science, University of Alberta, Edmonton, Alberta, March 1995.

[LP95b] Ling Liu and Calton Pu. The distributed interoperable object model and its application to large-scale interoperable database systems. In *ACM International Conference on Information and Knowledge Management (CIKM'95)*, Baltimore, Maryland, USA, November 1995.

[LPL96] L. Liu, C. Pu, and Y. Lee. An adaptive approach to query mediation across heterogeneous databases. In *Proceedings of the International Conference on Coopertive Information Systems*, Brussels, June 19-21 1996.

[NSF93] NSF with the cooperation of the Columbia University. *Proceedings of the CIF Tools Development Workshop*, Tarrytown, New York, November 1993.

[ODV93] T. Ozsu, U. Dayal, and P. Valduriez. *Distributed Object Management*. Morgan Kaufmann, 1993.

[PGMW95] Y. Papakonstantinou, H. Garcia-Molina, and J. Widom. Object exchange across heterogeneous information sources. In *Proceedings of International Conference on Data Engineering*, Taiwan, March 1995.

[PL91] C. Pu and A. Leff. Replica control in distributed systems: An asynchronous approach. In *Proceedings of the 1991 ACM SIGMOD International Conference on Management of Data*, pages 377–386, Denver, May 1991.

[PTWY94] C. Pu, M.K. Tsang, K.L. Wu, and P.S. Yu. Multiversion divergence control of time fuzziness. In *Proceedings of the Third International Conference on Information and Knowledge Management*, Gaithersburg, Maryland, November 1994.

[RP95] K. Ramamrithan and C. Pu. A formal characterization of epsilon serializability. *IEEE Transactions on Knowledge and Data Engineering*, June 1995.

[Sha93] M. Shan. Pegasus architecture and design principles. In *Proceedings of ACM/SIGMOD Annual Conference on Management of Data*, 1993.

[SK92] A. Sheth and V. Kashyap. So far (schematically) yet so near (semantically). In *Proceeding of the IFIP WG2.6 Database Semantics*, pages 283–312, Victoria, Australia, 1992. North Holland.

[SL90] A. Sheth and J.A. Larson. Federated database systems for managing distributed, heterogeneous, and autonomous databases. *ACM Transactions on Database Systems*, Vol. 22, No.3 1990.

[SM91] M. Siegel and S. Madnick. A metadata approach to solving semantic conflicts. In *International Conference on Very Large Data Bases*, pages 133–145, 1991.

[SSR94] E. Sciore, M. Siegel, and A. Rosenthal. Using semantic values to facilitate interoperability among heterogeneous information systems. *ACM Transactions on Database Systems*, Vol. 19, No. 2 June 1994.

[VH91] V. Ventrone and S. Heiler. Semantic heterogeneity as a result of domain evolution. *ACM SIGMOD RECORD on Management of Data*, 20(4), 1991.

[Wie92] Gio Wiederhold. Mediators in the architecture of future information systems. *IEEE Computer Magazine*, March 1992.

[Wie93] Gio Wiederhold. Intelligent integration of information. In *Proceedings of ACM/SIGMOD Annual Conference on Management of Data*, 1993.

[WYP92] K.L. Wu, P. S. Yu, and C. Pu. Divergence control for epsilon-serializability. In *Proceedings of Eighth International Conference on Data Engineering*, pages 506–515, Phoenix, February 1992. IEEE/Computer Society.

An Information Architecture to Support Modern Information Systems Development

Maria E Orlowska
The University of Queensland
Distributed Systems Technology Centre
Brisbane, Australia
E-mail: maria@cs.uq.oz.au

Abstract. This paper discusses the position of traditional databases, such as relational and object-oriented, in the context of growing demands for current and accurate information access within modern organizations.

We argue that independent development in all these areas may not be sufficient to guarantee steady progress in information management quality, dictated by open distributed computing environments. There is a large number of modern technologies which serve a good purpose if they are employed to perform tasks for which they have been designed and built. Recent advances in the systems integration area in general, and better awareness of networking environments, suggest the importance of thinking globally. A re-examination of data modelling technologies, and their suitability to separate operational data, data warehousing and departmental information requirements, may become beneficial. Additional factors prompting a global view are new, multiple-tiered architectures in client/server advances which dominate all larger information systems installations. This paper discusses these issues, and promotes a global view and a more open architecture for information management, rather than data management; architectures which should survive changes in an organization's business rules and new, growing data demand access to the outside world.

1. Introduction

An organization's success in information management strategies heavily depends on a global visionary approach to data management, and a good understanding of the consequences from potentially erroneous decisions. Developments and continuous improvements in relational technology, its combination with an object-oriented paradigm, and finally, interleaving with multi-tiered client/server architectures, are often very confusing, and, as such, difficult to deploy effectively. As a result, one of the technologies is blamed for failure, but often the problems are somewhere else - frequently in poor "information architectures" for the needs of the organization.

We begin this paper with brief reviews of three major technologies in information systems development: the relational technologies, object-orientation and the three-tier client/server computing. We try to capture the major reasons why they sometimes don't deliver as often expected. We will then present an information architecture which is more suitable for the combination/integration of current technologies, rather than investmenting in a web of isolated systems.

Codd's 1970 version of his famous paper on the relational model [COD70] begins with the words: ". . . users . . . must be protected from having to know . . . the internal representation (of data) . . . Activities of users at terminals and most application programs should remain unaffected when the internal representation . . . is changed."

This level of independence was a fundamental premise and a goal of the relational model. At that time, application code and control flow structure was tightly coupled to the implementation of data structures. Additionally, the data structure and access methods were often specific to applications. Such data processing arrangements resulted in a very high cost of system maintenance, and a relatively slow development process. The major problem was sharing data among applications; it was basically a file oriented process. The relational technology promised to solve these problems as well as provide other business benefits.

Relational technology is over 25 years old, and many applications still suffer from the same old problems. Legacy systems, heritage designs of applications, and poor methods of system migration to better data process platforms still place limitations on business information technology decisions. These categories of problems are well understood, though a large scale solution is unlikely to become available in the near future. Another more serious problem is associated with a poor understanding of the relational model in the vendor's world. Because just about every DBMS product today is labelled "relational" one might conclude that the relational model itself has failed to deliver. Despite putting a "relational" label on products, vendors continue to misunderstand and even misrepresent the technology. One serious consequence of the product's features is the fact that there is a common understanding between users that the relational model doesn't support the concept of objects. Debates along these lines, and problems with current, frequently used implementations of relational models are widely published in many sources [FRA95], [COD93]. On the other hand, features such as:

- Minimization of application code and improvements in code reliability
- Isolation of performance and resources management issues
- An active repository for business rules, processes and integrity constraints
- Guaranteed data consistency
- Guaranteed expressive completeness
- Freedom to distribute both data and processing
- The ability to grow
- Concurrent user support
- Complete recovery from any kind of failures
- Algorithmic database design
- High performance

have demonstrated that relational technology offers quite a big palette of desired database system attributes.

When commercial object oriented database management systems (ODBMS) emerged a few years ago, some proponents claimed that ODBMS technology would eventually dominate as the preferred database architecture. Some vendors decided to follow a moderate strategy and have gone as far as to merge the two approaches into integrated object-relational databases (ORDBMSs). ODBMSs are undoubtedly more suitable to certain application domains than RDBMSs, but they suffer from several deficiencies as well. The earliest ODBMS vendors emphasized flexible object definitions, high performance for non-relational object management and tight coupling with object-oriented languages such as C++ or Smalltalk. However, many users expected such DBMS features as querying, on-line backup and flexible concurrency control, but these were deferred to later releases. Most ODBMSs have these features, but the first impression still impacts on the market niche. There are several reasons why ODBMS didn't grow as quickly and as far as it was initially expected. The most frequent stumbling block is the lack of query support. Access to objects based on pointer navigation within C++ or Smalltalk programs is unfavourable compared with features offered by almost universally supported SQL. Expected extensions to SQL in the upcoming SQL3 standard [GAL94], [MEL94] are already promoted by ODBMS vendors. Despite the drawbacks in front-end systems to ODBMSs the object technology has recorded a great success. However, developers and organizations are still relatively low on the learning curve. Object orientation requires a different way of thinking, and it will take time before we get used to it.

Object technology uses three basic building blocks for systems development: classes, objects and messages. Classes are the templates that define objects. Objects are instances or run time versions of a class. Objects contain related data and methods, and messages are the means by which objects communicate. An object in a class can inherit attributes and procedures from higher classes. All objects are a member of a class, and an object's class membership determines the operations it can perform. Object technology promotes the ability to build applications from existing parts, i.e., instead of developing every program from scratch, one may assemble software out of standard objects that already exist in a similar way as most client/server development tools provide object libraries. Theoretically, developers could create applications by selecting and assembling objects from well supplied libraries, and if the developer must create a new object to meet the application requirements, it must be properly justified. Such a new object may be placed in a library for re-use in future application developments. According to Brodie [BRO95], these simple concepts of software development might be successfully applied to small and simple systems. A survey of large projects development has discovered that it is a complex concept. In particular, difficulties are associated with the very large sizes of object classes - a few thousand objects, and a very large number of object classes. Additionally, our inability to properly model - for the purpose of re-use - object semantic properties prevents this idea from general applicability. The repository technology for searching for a "right" object in such large sets, is not adequately developed. There are numerous examples of instances where "re-use" of software is less effective than its development from scratch.

This comment brings us to the issues and problems involved in large scale applications where numerous database systems of all kinds, must cooperate to satisfy application requirements. In order to monitor and improve the efficiency (performance) of such systems, additional levels in the traditional client/server architecture have been introduced.

A client/server architecture is based on the premise, as the object-orientation in general, that the key components of computing are loosely coupled, therefore, organizations can add and remove components without having to tear the structure apart. Implementing three-tier infrastructures is hard and more complex than a traditional two-level architecture. The major levels of consideration are: application logic, three-tier data and three-tier display. While much of the focus behind three-tier computing has been an application logic and its distribution across the network, there are certain principles that can be applied to data as well. Data itself should be separated from the data model or business rules that give meaning to raw data.

The client/server has changed the priorities of the information systems approach. The business and user-centric approaches now rule over the data-centric approaches that information engineering and structured methodologies have well supported. The context of development has shifted significantly. Traditional methodologies were not created to support technologies such as GUIs, object-oriented methods, rapid application development methods or concurrent engineering. Also, traditional methods focused on providing a great deal of information, and they are very complex, difficult to use and they require extensive modelling prior to the actual design and construction of the system. As Fig. 1 illustrates, often process modelling and data modelling are disjointed and can result in two different models.

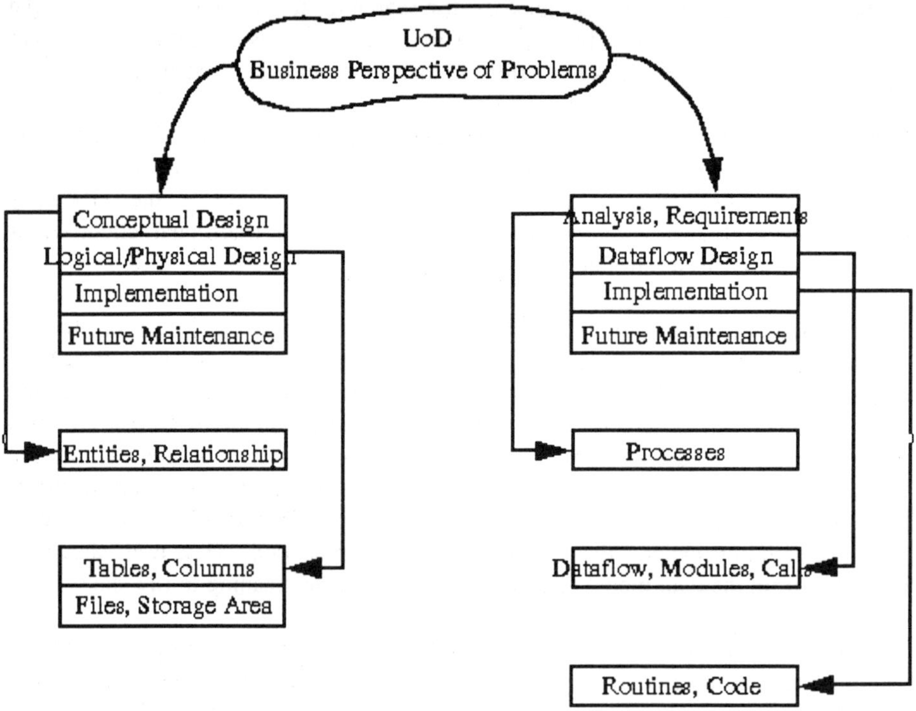

Fig. 1. Two modelling processes, data and process

It is useful to observe that most object modelling techniques are closely related to the entity-relationship modelling methods. The object model should however, combine process modelling and data modelling activities into a single model, as presented in Fig. 2. (This is one of the oldest topics in the area of conceptual modelling).

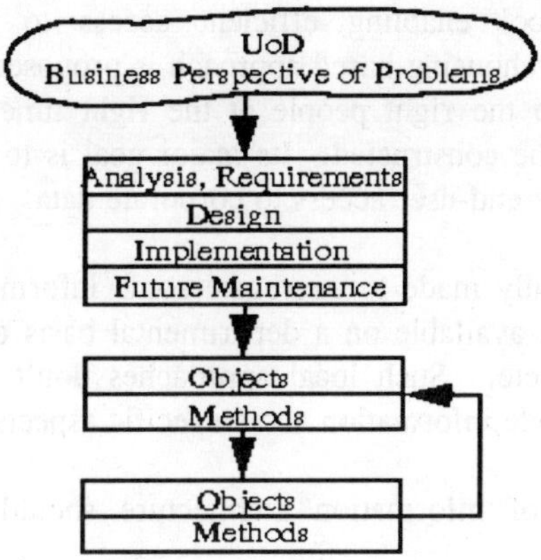

Fig. 2. Object modelling

In recent years, recognition of data warehousing, as a major principle to accumulate critical data for organizations, is growing. At the same time, this new term creates new levels of confusion, especially in combination with all mentioned technologies it is a complex construct, and often demands serious resources for implementation.

The data warehousing is not a new storage space for data within an organization. It is not an additional facility to store items that we don't really want to use right now, but are afraid to throw away. In fact, probably the last thing an organization should be doing with data is "warehousing" it. We should think pragmatically about the data we need to maintain and actively manage. Data warehousing is a mechanism for bringing different data sources together through a set of client/server tools as well as various enabling services. It is a complex environment and must be professionally designed, built and managed.

After examining the pros and cons of selected information systems technologies, we conclude this section with the following statement: If an organization whose information is tangled in a web of isolated systems, even implemented with state of the art technology, it will potentially experience problems with the advent of demands for expansion and collaboration across its own departments and in the outside business world.

2. Information Architecture

An information architecture, in a global sense, is necessary to integrate information across all products, supporting technologies and services. Such an architecture can help businesses understand, manage and foster better quality services (to their customers). As a tool enabling efficient access to information across an organization, a data warehousing based approach is proposed. To be able to deliver the right information to the right people at the right time and at cost, a global information view shall be constructed. Its major goal is to provide facilities to get faster and more accurate end-user access to corporate data.

Many attempts are usually made to aggregate some information sources. Most of them usually make data available on a departmental basis only. Often this data is inconsistent or incomplete. Such local approaches don't support enterprise-wide access nor do they provide information about specific aspects of business activities.

The major objectives of information architecture should include the following natural aspects:

- To secure data consistency - provide a single entry point for data
- To reduce/remove data redundancy - support
- To provide easy access to public data
- To accommodate legacy data
- To provide common application interface to all data
- To provide collection and loading process (data management facility) - transfer appropriate information from legacy applications to the data warehouse
- To provide a single point of storage for data knowledge

A key concept of this architecture is that all input and output are accomplished through objects, definitions and methods execution. User, read-only requests can be supported through view definitions, and to perform updates, there are predesigned methods. In the context of relational databases, Fig. 3 depicts database objects.

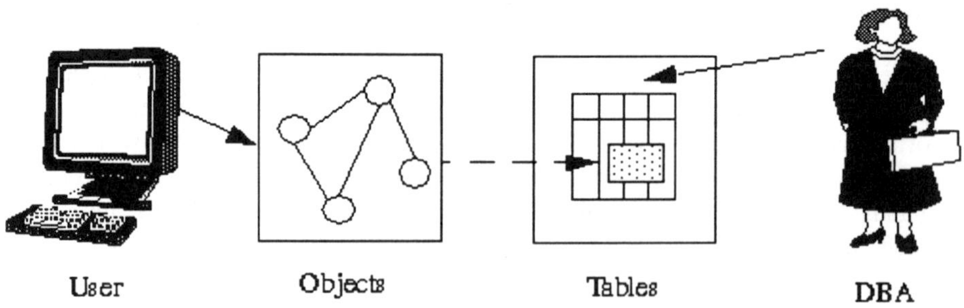

Fig. 3. Data objects

The first difficulty in adapting this idea is obviously associated with the "right" definitions of objects at the logical and physical level. To be able to approach this critical design problem, we need to be able to answer the following questions: What are the critical factors for successful operation by different people within an organization? What are the key things they need to track on a regular basis? What are the key activities supporting the success factors, and what data is required?

To build a proper infrastructure, an organization must identify the most important processes (MIPs), define the technical architecture, build the data model, validate the model and build and implement the supporting data warehouse. The information can be grouped into subject or the most important processes regions. These are the things that the organization is doing on a routine basis: tracking and analysing in order to achieve its major objectives.

The majority of the most important processes are cross-functional, thus it is critical for each information region to support the enterprise's common goals and objectives. However, analysing information regions does not necessarily require complete process modelling, such as data flow diagrams. A good understanding of data entities and their attributes for each business application is sufficient. We addressed these issues in [MUH95].

In general, the enterprise data model provides a high-level framework for constructing new applications across information regions and constructing future databases. Consolidation and integration of information across legacy applications must be supported by the model. It is often a hard requirement to satisfy. Many legacy systems don't have adequate documentation, and reconstructing their data model conceptualization of their application requires reverse-engineering procedures. As usual in data modelling practice, once the enterprise model is developed, the participants from the initial information region analysis shall review the most important processes and entities that support them. It is important that the data model must completely support all of the most important processes.

Another step in building information architecture is related to data identification through data mapping. The complexity of this process depends on the quality of knowledge about participating data sources. If systems are well documented, the resolution of some integration issues is not very hard, and validation of decisions can be provided by users. However, if there is a poor semantic description of a system's applications and the data itself, the problem is hard; especially when most organizations have redundant data entities that represent the same object but are defined differently. Application and business aspects must participate in identification and design sessions, and provide the necessary background to complete this process.

Another validation process is required. It is to ensure that data and information are going to the proper place in the data model. All effort should be taken to make all necessary modifications to the model.

Probably the most important aspect of setting up a new architecture is to define business rules consistent with the data modelled. For example, let us assume that we bring together information from two departmental databases. Both seem to have common fields, such as customer name, account number etc. If there are even subtle differences, combination potentially could become a disaster. One department, for example, may define a customer as the corporate entity, while another may define a customer as the local office or a large corporation. Putting this information together will not provide an accurate data entity.

Once the analysis phase is concluded one can move to create a long-term architecture for data warehousing. An infrastructure must be in place that supports sophisticated performance so that data can be moved quickly and transparently around an organization. Such infrastructure consist of repositories, data dictionaries, transaction management services, and tools that allow hierarchical and non-hierarchical information sources to be used together. Tools are also necessary for data query, reporting and management.

In general, the data warehouse is a physical collection of information from existing legacy systems which consolidates historical information and translates information into a uniform format that makes the data available for information sharing, analysis, decision support and everyday operational needs of the organization.

As we have mentioned earlier, all of the most important processes must link to the views of the data that support them. Processes are divided into business topics which are linked for presentation by the user access interface. Fig. 4 illustrates the high level architecture.

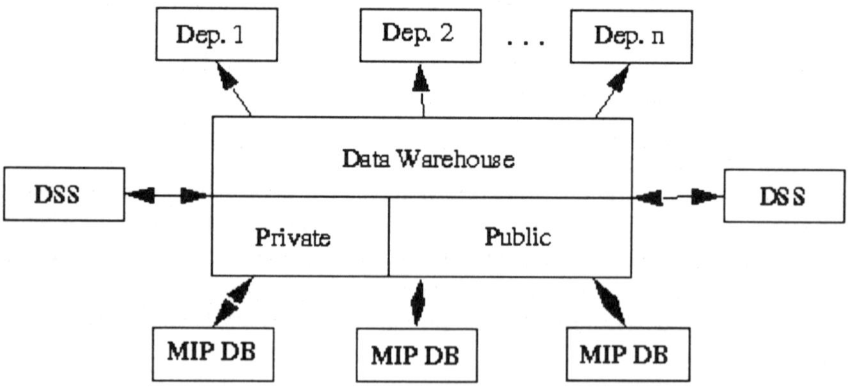

Fig. 4. Information architecture

At the departmental level the databases have read-only operations, defined by views. These databases can be updated on a daily basis to guarantee consistency and data integrity. Most updates are done at an operational level where the most important processes are connected to the data warehouse. The decision support systems basically use the transformed data, often from legacy applications in derived formats. The data should come from the operational level but not from the departmental system. Development of applications in such an environment may require different sources of data, a corporate data repository, data objects and methods, and views to the operational and data warehouse databases. The corporate data repository identifies all the data objects and their methods, the relationship between the methods and data objects, and the relationship between application components and methods. In the construction of client/server applications some guidelines can be provided to what extent the code should be positioned and allocated to a client site and to the server site. However, we don't cover this topic in this paper.

Deploying the right technology for the implementation of such architecture is very important if not critical. Mainframes and massively parallel processes may be used by large organizations for the retrieving, translating, loading and distributing of data. Parallel processors may be needed for storage and retrieval if efficiency has a high priority. An RDBMS is definitely an effective means for storing and retrieving vast amounts of data. Designed appropriately, the database can offer unsurpassed power for an organization to analyse and manage their business. The communication backbone must adequately support the information architecture. In many cases enhancements might be required for an existing network infrastructure. Finally, the client/server environment offers the power of the desktop, and LAN for data access and making presentation tools.

We finish these considerations with a few comments on the possible ways to introduce information architecture within an organization. It is a complex task. We suggest that first a relevant pilot project should be identified that can demonstrate the technical considerations and prove that such an approach can be productive. The pilot project should be relatively simple in terms of its scope and the amount of data involved. It's important to implement the architecture in an incremental fashion.

Another issue which deserves a concluding comment is a comparison of data warehousing with distributed databases. One may think that data warehousing and distributed databases are opposite strategies, when, in fact, the presented architecture may or may not imply a single, centralized data store. Even the centralized data store is a form of distributed data because no matter how we design a warehouse we may replicate some data from operational systems. Once this data is replicated we are deploying a distributed database technology. Therefore, many of the tools and problems generally associated with data distribution are also relevant to data warehousing.

3. Conclusions

We presented an information architecture as a global view of data and information required by an organization's operations. The characteristics of the proposed approach to our information structure are: there is only one point of data entry, departmental data is updated once a day (or an adequate period time), data to the middle level, data warehouse (centralized or distributed) are only transferred from the operational level, and decision support systems are supplied with data from the data warehouse. The approach discussed provides great flexibility for system development and overall data integration.

References

[COD70] Codd, E.F. (1970). "A Relational Model for Large Shared Data Banks", CACM 13(6).

[FRA95] Frank, M. (1995). "Object-Relational Hybrids", DBMS 8(8).

[COD93] Codd, E.F., Codd, S.B., Salley, C.T. (1993). "Providing OLAP to User-Analysts: An IT Mandate", DBMS.

[BRO95] Brodie, M. (1995). "Putting Objects to Work on a Massive Scale: The Emperor's Clothes are Object-Oriented (and Distributed)", IRAB Seminar, The University of Queensland.

[MUH95] Muhlberger, R.M., Orlowska, M.E. (1995). "A Business Process Driven Multidatabase Integration Methodology", Database Reengineering & Interoperability. (Proc of 6th Int Hong Kong Computer Society Database Workshop).

[GAL94] Gallagher, L. (1994). "Influencing Database Language Standards", SIGMOD Record 23(1).

[MEL94] Melton, J. Editor (1994). Database Language SQL3, ANSI, Database Committee (X3H2).

Why Users Cannot 'Get What They Want'†

Ray J Paul
Department of Computer Science and Information Systems
Brunel University
Uxbridge, Middlesex, UB8 3PH, U.K.
E-mail: Ray.Paul@brunel.ac.uk

Abstract. *The notion that users can 'get what they want' has caused a planning blight in information systems development, with the resultant plethora of information slums that require extensive and expensive maintenance. This paper will outline why the concept of 'user requirements' has led to a variety of false paradigms for information systems development, with the consequent creation of dead systems that are supposed to work in a living organisation. It is postulated that what is required is an architecture for information systems that is designed for breathing, for adapting to inevitable and unknown change. Such an architecture has less to do with 'what is wanted', and more to do with the creation of a living space within the information system that enables the system to live.*

1 Information Systems for Business

There are many forms of information systems (I.S.) in practice. This paper restricts itself to those I.S. that are used by human beings to assist them in their endeavours, the type of I.S. that are exemplified by business I.S.. I.S. for washing machines or computer driven machines in manufacturing may have a simpler structure for which the argument in this paper may not apply.

A textbook description of the development process for I.S. might go as follows:

- Strategic study, identification of problem
- I.S. planning - feasibility and requirement
- Business analysis - specification
- System design
- Construction design

---

† The paper is based on:

R J. Paul. Why Users Cannot 'Get What They Want'. first published in *The CRICT Workshop Papers* (J. Low and S. Woolgar, Eds.) (2 April 1993, Brunel University). CRICT, Brunel University, Uxbridge. pp. 1-10.

reprinted in *ACM SIGIOS Bulletin*, December 1993, Vol 14. No 2, pp 8-12.

reprinted in the *New Zealand Computer Society Quickface Newsletter*, 1994. pp. 1, 14-19.

reprinted in *International Journal of Manufacturing System Design*, December 1994, Vol 1, No 4, pp 389-394.

- Construction and workbench test
- Systems installation
- Test of installation
- Operation
- Implementation
- Evolution - maintenance
- Phase out

Of course, it is well recognised that such an I.S. development process requires iteration between tasks and the overlapping of tasks. Furthermore, it may even be appropriate to undertake development without treating them as distinct tasks at all. There is also some recognition that in the real world there is some uncertainty. For example, Avgerou and Cornford [AVG93] suggest that the lifespan of a system may be increased in uncertain environments by anticipating future changes such as:

- Technological trends
- Changes in legal and regulatory requirements
- Trends in the industry within which the organization operates
- Changes in the broader economic environment
- Changes in the attitudes, expectations, tastes, or climates of opinion
- Changes of structure and style of management within the organization

There is little doubt that if the above wish list could be fulfilled, I.S. development would be relatively simple. However, there is little evidence that such fulfilment is anything other than wishful! In the meantime, the literature is replete with proposals to improve on the current state of the art.

2 Problems

The most generous observation that one can make about current I.S. development is that most, if not all, systems disappoint. This disappointment is mostly with the customer, be that the user or the owner, but also with the analysts and developers. A good example which demonstrates this point is the sad case of the London Ambulance Service computer system that spectacularly failed and had to be disconnected on its first days of operation [WAT92]. On Monday and Tuesday 26 and 27 October 1992 between 10 and 20 people are alleged to have lost their lives because the emergency service failed them. Clearly in this case the customers were 'disappointed'. But what of other interest groups. The man in charge of the system is alleged to have said:

> *"The computer did not fail on that Monday - it was working exactly as it was designed to."*

The report goes on to observe that the people using the computer system - in the control room and in the ambulances - are "doing things wrong". That is, they are not doing what the computer has been designed to expect. The article further conjectures that the problem is that the London Ambulance Service staff are used to a system where people deal with people. Human beings can pick up potential problems in the inflexion of a voice - but they are not yet adept at pre-empting problems when dealing with computers.

Similar examples abound. Taurus, the collapsed automated system for share dealing in the City of London, is a more recent and financially spectacular failure. The question that one might ask is "are there any complete success stories?" This sometimes gets turned into the opposite question "why don't systems do what people want?" But perhaps the better question to ask does not concern whether people get what they want, nor even how can we find out what people want, but the more fundamental question of how people can know what they want. We shall return to this last question after the next section, where we examine attempts to alleviate disappointment by the offering of a palliative.

3 Palliatives

The analysis task mentioned in the I.S. development list of tasks above is intended to produce a logical specification containing information about what the new system is intended to do. Since there is some uncertainty about this, methods have been proposed that attempt to alleviate the difficulty of achieving this. Some of these palliatives are as follows.

One school of thought advocates the use of standards as a way of solving I.S. problems. This line of reasoning assumes that the cause of the problem is that the methods used are not applied with sufficient rigour, so that misunderstandings and poor communication between customers and developers, and between developers, creep in. Try harder. However, this optimistic approach, that there exists the 'optimal' solution, and all you have to do is seek it more carefully, belies the fact that optimality is a non-existent state of affairs in business I.S.. Furthermore, the rapidly evolving world of computer hardware, software, operating systems and environments, distributed and network developments, not to mention rapidly changing theories of management, organizational structures and behaviour, and socio-economic theories, defeat a solution based almost entirely on standards. Standards for what?

Cousins of standards are evaluation and review. These concepts are also based on the notion that if you try hard enough, you will get it right. Review enables you to look back and change your mind periodically, so that system requirements can be refined into a correct version. Evaluation is designed to constantly check that objectives are being met, a means of reinforcement and remembering.

A very popular palliative is prototyping [DEA83]. Prototyping is a method of quick systems component construction, which is adopted within the framework of a broader system development approach or methodology to solve contentions between analysts, users, software and hardware. Such optimism is based on the idea that everything can be got right in the end if you go around the problem enough times. This approach has advantages over the 'get it right first time' approach, but there is little evidence of any significant improvement in I.S. development.

Incremental development is based on the notion that you can creep towards where you want to be. This approach accepts that you cannot know what you want, well, not straight away. So far better to head off in the best direction by building part of the system, and then changing direction as necessary based on this experience for further development. This way you will get closer to where you want to be, wherever that is. The approach has the advantage that the customer(s) is taken along with it, and is therefore probably more agreeable with the system as it develops.

User Participation is another popular attempt to resolve the unresolvable [LAN83]. By getting user participation in decision making about the project, and/or in the actual analysis and design, the analyst is more likely to elicit the requirements of the system, and in the latter case, make it presentable to the user. End User Computing similarly attempts to involve the user, but now by handing over chunks of the system to the users to develop themselves, perhaps supported by I.S. professionals. Whilst generating user participation, the user is still in no better position to know 'what he wants', but is no position to complain about it, since it is his fault.

Flexibility Analysis for information requirements determination and systems analysis, seeks to forecast organizational changes which will necessitate changes of the information system, and then tries to provide adequate flexibility to meet them [FIT90]. This approach is likely to have limited success. It is in the nature of modern business that the future is uncertain - if it was certain, then courses of action based on the certainty would be adopted that would change the future! Only with the benefit of hindsight can we know the unknowable. Such approaches are very common (for example, finding a 'business mission', and designing the business in [MUM85]), and confuse the difference between planning for the future and planning the future. Since uncertain change is inevitable, planning for change would appear to be more appropriate. At the time of writing, who can predict the outcome of international trade negotiations? If a trade war develops, it is difficult to think of many businesses that will not be seriously affected relative to a free trade situation. The future is known by someone maybe, but how do you predict which person this is?

There are other strategic approaches to I.S. development, such as Critical Success Factors and Business System Planning [WAR90]. Such approaches may give insights, but the analyst must not be seduced by them - a better insight is not an 'answer'.

Formal methods are an attempt at eliminating the need for corrective maintenance of I.S. software by proving the correctness of its code, that is, the equivalence of the code to the specification. This of course is therefore highly dependent on the quality of the specification. Also, given the current difficulty in achieving such code correctness, it is not a very practical method for changing circumstances. In business I.S. it is not very practical because there are no formal models that capture the richness of the application domain, for example organizational behaviour.

All these palliatives attempt to take an existing way of thinking about I.S. development, and make it work by tinkering with it. It is the contention of this paper that the underlying way of thinking, or the paradigms used for system development, are themselves wrong for the reasons given in the next section.

4 Fixed Point Theorem

All of the discussion so far has been based on I.S. paràdigms that have one common fallacy. This fallacy is expressed through the following 'mock' theorem.

4.1 The Fixed Point Theorem of Information Systems

There exists some point in time when everyone involved in the system knows what they want and agrees with everyone else.

Why is this theorem assumed to be true? Because we want to build the system to an exact specification.

Proof of theorem:

Theoretical -none

Empirical - none

Counter examples - plenty

4.2 Extension to the Fixed Point Theorem

The fixed point in the theorem remains fixed for the project duration, or even longer.

Proof of extension:

Well, the theorem is false, so the extension is too.

4.3 Implications of the Theorem and Extension

The implications are clear. Systems are built for one (hypothetical) point in time, whereas the system must work over some time continuum. Hence, disappointment. Building I.S. with the implicit, or sometimes even explicit assumption that the Fixed Point Theorem is true is guaranteed to cause problems. Before discussing ways of thinking that might not be based on the Fixed Point Theorem, it might be further illuminating to look at the reasons why this state of affairs has occurred.

5 How Did This Happen?

Grindley [GRI86] gives an excellent resume of how we arrived at the current state of the art in I.S. development in the chapter entitled 'The History of a Mistake'. One major cause is the project based nature of development. A project based approach is inherently finite time horizon driven whereas the environment is infinite horizon. This generates a number of differences between the desire to build something, and the need to make it work. These include targets versus standards, the inspirational motivation of a project team versus 'the pride in a job well done' motivation of the personnel running the system, the temporary society of the project developers versus the permanent society of the users, building versus maintaining. There is no doubt that a project mentality inherently begs for the Fixed Point Theorem to be true. This is exemplified by the project 'sign-off' where the customer agrees with documents of questionable interpretation, to take that version of the system as something that is 'acceptable'.

Out of the project mentality, and the breaking down of the development into tasks, comes the notion of maintenance of the system after implementation, and in particular of enhancement maintenance. The very word maintenance suggests corrective action, as though somehow the need for change could have been avoided if somehow we had known better. The Fixed Point Theorem again.

One can conjecture that the reasons for this state of affairs lie in the character of the workers in I.S.. Computer scientists often appear blessed with myopic optimism, the belief that a computer can help with any problem with enough effort. The only restrictions on solving the problem are time and money. Technology is the saviour. I.S. professionals, whilst sceptical of this myopic optimism, often appear to be seeking a faith or belief, searching for new paradigms and new methodologies, attempting to restructure the world to fit the beliefs they hold, missionaries in a dark unbelieving world. Such zeal is being translated into new crusades, where grandiose claims about future business opportunities are based around I.S. restructuring of the business. A new breed of professional, classified under Information Management, is now stepping forward with the notion that business can be re-organised for I.S.. This specialist is looking at the strategic direction of the organization, wishing to participate in the overall development of the organization itself. Current approaches seem to concentrate on planning, regulation and co-ordination, the necessary structuring methods that help understand organizations, but should not be used as blueprints for running the organization. Creativity, the lifeblood of a business, has little chance in the latter type of environment.

Mixed with the I.S. professionals' motivations, we have the political motivations of all actors in the scenario. Building an I.S. in order to promote individuals within organizations is no different to other methods of achieving the same ends, but potentially more expensive when things go wrong. It is conjectured that the London Ambulance Service debacle is related to a political decision that the service must be computerised because that was the only way to make dependence on individuals less, and to reduce manpower in the service. This fits with Government and management philosophies or dogmas of the 1980s. Once again, this approach incorrectly perceives change as going from one fixed point to another fixed point.

Methodologies and software engineering are Fixed Point Theorem driven. Their terminology is of optimality, best solution, minimum cost, maximum functionality etc., all meaningless concepts in a human environment. In an attempt to get it right, many developments adopt a kitchen sink mentality, where everything you can think of must be included for completeness, albeit at the expense of complexity and its resultant mistakes and misunderstandings. Less can be more. Methodology Is No Substitute For Intelligent Thinking (MINSFIT).

6 Living Paradigms

So far we have discussed a major reason why I.S. disappoints. In this section, we shall look at possible ways of thinking (not solutions!) that might help. We have observed that the Fixed Point Theorem essentially leads us to the development of dead systems, systems designed to meet the needs of the business at one point in time. What is required for living businesses, however, are living systems. Systems should breathe, be designed to adapt to unknown change. Systems should grow, mature, and die (they do anyway!). Very few aspects, if any, of a businesses' operations are expected to be designed for life, static, so why should I.S.? A successful business is constantly adapting to change, and therefore so should the I.S.. The question of how this should be done must not be allowed to determine what it is that we want to do. Thinking of a living system development may be difficult, but without remembering that that is what is required, the Fixed Point Theorem will undoubtedly re-emerge consciously or unconsciously. The following discussion concerns some thoughts on living system development, but is not meant to be an/the answer. We have a long way to go yet.

It is worth mentioning another major factor in a living system paradigm. This is the question of right and wrong, the question of correct and faulty. A living system is neither right nor correct. It is a system that is adapting to need. In this sense, it is not wrong or faulty either. The expectation should be that the system is constantly undergoing change to meet the changing need. The opportunity to change the system has to be seen as a virtue in itself, not a point of negative criticism concerning a past lack of perspicacity. This is not to say that mistakes cannot be made, since individuals will continue to do that, but criticism of the system encourages cover-ups, a get it right mentality, and back to a dead system.

6.1 Evolutionary Development

Avgerou and Cornford [AVG93] discuss evolutionary development, where the process may start with a broad architecture of a set of desired systems, the various components of which will be developed gradually. This architecture, they claim, can be implemented initially with limited functional components, but retaining assigned slots and interfaces for further components. The concept of 'core' systems (networks, corporate databases etc.) may give a shape to an architecture, and allow the various groups in an organisation considerable flexibility as to how and at what pace they develop their own systems.

Whilst conceptually attractive, little is known that enables such development to take place successfully. There is, of course, a great temptation to return to the Fixed Point Theorem at any point in the system development.

6.2 The 'Environment' Paradigm

The environment paradigm takes the office block as its analogy. An office block has a basic structure which can be adapted to differing needs. It will have a sub-structuring (floor, part-floor) which may be sub-divided, but usually in some adaptable way (partitioning, walls etc.). Services are provided in general (water, telephones, electricity etc), and can often be supplied to any part of the building. Although the provision of such services can be expensive, it does not usually require the dismantling of the building. Partial disablement of the building does not stop the business continuing its operations, since functions can be moved to another part of the building.

Within an office environment, there is a great deal of individual control of personal space. Managers can decide within certain limits to organise their space to suit their managerial needs and style, and individuals can organise their personal workspace to provide an acceptable environment. Such individual control can be improved or made worse by the adequacy of funds for improving equipment and fixtures and by managerial skills, but these matters do not tend to rest with the building architecture. The implementation of the system is distributed, often with a view to subsidiarity.

Subsidiarity might enable proper end user computing. The basic systems structure is laid down, and within that, the user can implement the sub-systems required for his or her purposes. This might require some thought on which application packages and tools for restructuring should be made available, and how to avoid any sub-system locking information away from the organization in general (a general problem). DIY tools and kits might be the order of the day. These kits would also have to be adaptive if the individual end user is not to become a victim of the Fixed Point Theorem.

6.3 The Anatomy Paradigm

The anatomy paradigm suggests a skeletal structure to which a variety of muscle, nerve and flesh structures can be constructed as required. Information can flow as the blood of the system, being diverted and connected as and where required. The system reacts to outside responses and is adaptive accordingly. The brain(s) are of course, the users.

A sub-requirement of an anatomical or any other living system will be mechanisms for change. In an anatomical context, one can see I.S. doctors providing local help so that the user can get what he wants on a individual basis. More serious changes can be handled by hospitalisation, where the system continues to function, but some parts provide a restrictive service until adaptation has occurred.

Doctors and hospitals might be the wrong analogy, since this gives the ambience of mending things, patching up, treating sickness and disease. A better analogy might be renovators, people who come in to improve the system, which is working, but could work better. I.S. Quality Analysts?

6.4 The Gardening Paradigm

Gardens constantly change, evolve, grow. A basic architecture may be laid down - paths, trees, lawns. But the smaller plants come and go, can be moved to some extent, and everything is evolving with the seasons. Gardens require incessant attention - pruning, weeding, reduction of bugs and plant predators. Excessive action leads to temporary empty spaces, or islands of apparent inactivity. Lack of attention can lead to choking, overgrowth, the death of some plants at the expense of others.

The gardening analogy fits the needs of business systems very well. It also exemplifies the earlier point about success and failure. The latter can be quite obvious. But is a garden ever finished, complete, or successful (except at the Chelsea Flower Show!)? A garden may be adequate to please visitors, but the gardener is never satisfied. There is always something to improve upon, something to tend to as the rest of the garden moves on. In a dynamic, changing, uncertain world, this is what is required from a business information system as well.

7 Conclusions

First, living system development is a way of thinking, not a solution methodology. The latter leads straight back to the Fixed Point Theorem. Second, demanding 'success' will lead to failure. Third, in spite of the immense cultural and economic pressures, the project based approach has to be broken. Software engineering cannot be compared to any other engineering. It may be time to move on and away from Software Engineering altogether.

At Brunel we are investigating new ways of thinking (as are others). Gardner et al [GAR95] are looking at tailorable systems as a way of giving the user gardener control over his/her patch of the garden architecture (English, Italian, Japanese etc.). Some preliminary work by Crick et al [CRI95] is examining the work of Miller and Miller [MIL90] to see if biological constructs for living systems can contribute to better architectures for I.S. But the major improvements in I.S. development will occur when many if not most people involved take on the paradigm shift necessary.

References

[AVG93] Avgerou, C. and Cornford, T. (1993). Developing Information Systems. *Macmillan*, Basingstoke.

[CRI95] Crick, A., Kanellis, P. and Paul, R.J. (1995) Towards a flexible systems architecture capable of adapting to unforeseen and continuous change. Department of Computer Systems and Information Systems Research Report, *Brunel University*.

[DEA83] Dearnley, P.A. and Mayhew, P.J. (1983) In favour of system prototypes and their integration into the systems development cycle. In *The Computer Journal*, Vol.26, No.1, February, pp.36-42.

[FIT90] Fitzgerald, G. (1990) Achieving flexible information systems: the case for improved analysis. In *Journal of Information Technology*, Vol.5, No.1, March, pp.5-11.

[GAR95] Gardner, L.A., Paul, R.J. and Patel, N. (1995) Moving Beyond the Fixed Point Theorem with Tailorable Systems. Published in the *Proceedings of the 3rd European Conference on Information Systems* (Doukidis G, Galliers R, Jelassi T, Kremar H and Land F, Eds.) (1-3 June, Athens). pp. 183-192

[GRI86] Grindley, The Report (1986) Fourth Generation Languages: Volume 1, A Survey of Best Practice. *IDPM Publications Ltd*, London.

[LAN83] Land, F and Hirschheim, R. (1983) Participative systems design: rationale, tools and techniques. In *Journal of Applied Systems Analysis*, Vol.10.

[MIL90] Miller, J.G. and Miller, J.L. (1990) Introduction: the nature of living systems. *Behavioural Science*, 35, 3, 157-163.

[MUM85] Mumford, E. (1985) Defining System Requirements to meet Business Needs: a case study example. In *The Computer Journal*, Vol.28, No.2, April, pp.97-104.

[WAT92] Watts, S. (1992) Of mammon and the machines he employs. In *The Independent On Sunday*, 8 November, London.

[WAR90] Ward, J., Griffiths, P. and Whitmore, P. (1990) Strategic Planning for Information Systems. *Wiley*, Chichester.

A Grammar-Based Approach for the Integration of Text-Dominated Databases

Nabil Kamel
Information Systems Department
City University of Hong Kong
Tat Chee Avenue, Kowloon Tong, Hong Kong
Tel: (852)2788-8697
Fax: (852)2788-8694
Email: iskame@cityu.edu.hk

Abstract. This paper summarizes our work in building an advanced graphically-oriented software environment for the integration of remote databases and analysis tools. The environment is based on the idea of using a formal grammar to describe the content and syntax of the output reports generated by remote tools and/or database application programs. The syntax-described reports, which can also include entire relations from a relational database, are then used as self-described components in the integration. By defining a data manipulation language to manipulate the syntax-described reports, users can issue a variety of powerful inter- and intra-database retrieval and manipulation queries. A prototype system, called XBio, has been designed and built. The initial target application domain was the molecular biology domain, but applications in other areas, such as financial and sociaological research are equally valid.

1. Introduction and Motivation

Currently, there is a consensus among users of public databases that heterogeneity of available database systems and software tools, and the nonuniformity of their data formats, creates one of the most frustrating and time consuming situations obstructing effective research.

This paper describes our approach to build an advanced facility for interoperable access to multi-format remote databases and analysis tools. We refrain from describing system implementation details in the current paper, as this has been described elsewhere [Kame92a, Kame93, Song 92]. We focus on the data modeling and integration approach developed. The XBio system serves as a workbench with which a molecular biologist or other researcher can assemble complex reports containing items from multiple databases and analysis tools, some of which may be located at remote sites. The system is designed to be user-friendly (through the use of a GUI), to respect the heterogeneity and autonomy of the remote databases and analysis tools, to have a high degree of interoperability among existing systems with heterogeneous input and output formats, to be customizable by the user, and extensible by a system administrator.

The current implementation of XBio takes the unique approach of providing an integration of both remote databases and software tools. In order to provide powerful interoperability capability, we make use of a new paradigm for data integration (based on a context-free grammar) to describe the data in the databases as well as the reports generated by application programs and analysis tools.

As a vehicle for implementing the grammar, we have adopted the ISO standard Abstract Syntax Notation One (ASN.1) as a data definition and description language. In an effort to promote ASN.1 from a data description language to a data model, we have added to ASN.1 a Data Manipulation Language (ASN.1 DML). The ASN.1 DML can be thought of as a counterpart to the relational algebra, but one that operates on parsed text rather than on relations. This XBio language is used for writing application programs and as the basis of the query capability of the GUI . Since the tabular structure of relations can always be described using simple grammar specifications, this approach is capable of handling relational databases as a special case. Hence, XBio provides the ability to easily do inter-database operations, whether the databases are relational or in the form of flat text files with ad hoc formats.

In the sections that follow, we briefly discuss other approaches to heterogeneous database integration and compare it with ours. We go on to describe our approach in depth including a discussion of our data model in sections 3 and 4 respectively. In section 4.1, we begin a discussion of the ASN.1-based XBio DDL, including it's derivation and operators. Finally, in section 5, we offer our conclusions.

2. Prior Approaches and Background

In this section we review some of the existing approaches to database integration, and we contrast these approaches with our approach. We can identify two major classes of database integration approaches: tightly-coupled and loosely-coupled.

The tightly-coupled approaches advocate a unified schema that is assembled from individual schemas of component databases through the processes of schema merging and integration ([ELM89], [BUN93], [GEL93]). Additionally, this approach requires mapping the actual data from the local schemas to the global schema and mapping queries against the global schema to queries against the local schemas. Many tools and systems have been proposed to facilitate these tasks, including the work on the Object Protocol Model (OPM) and its associated tools ([CHE93a], [CHE93b], [MAR91], and [MAR93]). The tightly-coupled approaches are represented by the Federated Database Management System (FDBMS) approach ([HAM79], [HEI85], and [SHE90], in which "federations" of databases are formed by creating a global schema in some powerful data model. Despite the attractiveness of the uniformity provided by a global model, tightly-coupled approaches have been criticized for their extreme sensitivity to changes in the local schemas. Any such changes require re-merging of the schemas.

In the loosely-coupled approach there is no global schema; instead, a powerful query language is defined that can access multiple remote databases simultaneously. To obtain results from multiple remote databases, the user writes a program that explicitly queries each database and combines the results. The loosely-coupled approach is exemplified by multidatabase systems ([LIT86], [LIT87], [LIT90], and [KRI91]), in which linguistic (rather than architectural) features are the main focus.

The work in [BUN89] represents a compromise between the loosely-coupled and the tightly-coupled approaches in that the user specifies a simple set of "is-a" relationships to relate a higher conceptual view of the data to the underlying schemas, resulting in simpler schema merging.

Neither the FDBMSs nor multidatabases address the question of integrating software tools with the databases. In addition, none of these approaches offer a high-level way of uniformly operating on flat-file text databases and output reports having ad hoc formats.

In our approach, data and tool integration is done on two levels. First, there is a level where the data integrators have an opportunity to tightly couple subsets of databases and tools through low-level programming. The federations thus formed can also include sets of application programs (manipulation tools) that are considered to be an integral part of the federation. Remote application programs which can be directed to multiple databases are directed only to those in the current federation. This helps define a local query operational domian. Thus, temporary tight federations are formed among arbitrary database and tool subsets at this first level. (It is our view that a combination of tight and loose-coupling among databases is necessary in any realistic data/tool integration environment.) The second level provides more general interoperability in the loosely-coupled tradition; no global model is used, and a language-centered approach is followed. In order to have enough power to query both structured and unstructured text, we are using a new ASN.1 DML as our integration language at this level. Thus, a multidatabase language is used which is capable of integrating software tools (through their outputs) with databases. The databases are represented by formally described ASCII text flat files containing the data in the database (e.g. relation dumps), or containing the outputs of user-accessible application programs. In the latter case, the data is represented by formal syntax descriptions of the application program output reports.

The ASN.1 DML consists of a set of data operations analogous to embedded SQL statements, but ones that can operate on flat file databases also. This approach has the advantages of not being overly sensitive to schema changes, and of having the ability to combine tabular and flat-file databases with application tools within the same integration. The approach has many additional features, including the ability to customize the system easily by forming user-specified federations, the ability to build a generalized automatic format converter that will convert among different formats without having to write explicit format converters for each case (this can be done through the use of the formal grammar description of the inputs and outputs of each tool), and a few other features related to the Graphical User Interface (GUI) which we have developed for the prototype. The next section provides more details about the prototype system.

3. System Overview

XBio consists of a federation coordinator with a graphical user interface, an ASN.1 text parser, a high-level embeddable ASN.1 DML interpreter, an ASN.1 based graphical browser/manipulator, a central data structure representing ASN.1 parsed documents, and a set of libraries. These modules are shown in Figure 1, which gives a system overview.

The *Federation Coordinator* is the component for managing the networking aspects of the system. It maintains sufficient information for each database to allow users to invoke searches on particular databases or documents, and to invoke computational tools . This information is kept in the *System Encyclopedia*, which the user is not allowed to alter, and in the *User Catalog*, which is updatable by the user. By editing the user catalog, users can customize and extend their system.

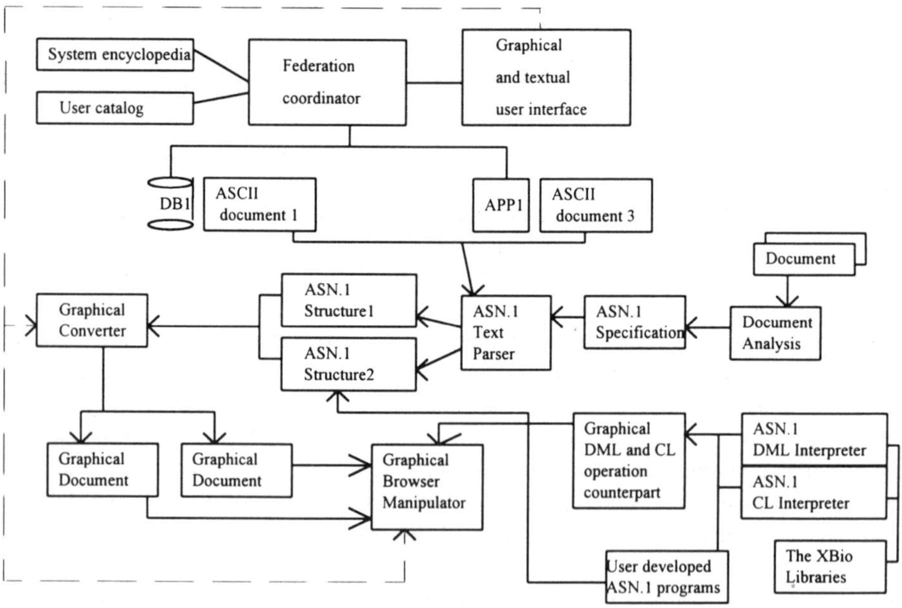

Fig. 1. An Overview XBio

Once some database search results (or analysis tool outputs) have been obtained, they are placed in *ASCII Documents*. To perform interoperability functions among these ASCII reports, the user invokes the *ASN.1 Text Parser* to parse each one, using pre-stored *ASN.1 Specifications*. The result will be in the form of a special data structure referred to as an *ASN.1 Structure*. Two of these are shown in Figure

1. ASN.1 structures can be operated upon through embedded DML programs (*ASN.1 Programs*), which rely on the DML interpreter and its associated *XBio Libraries*. Alternatively the user may perform the interoperability functions graphically , through the *Graphical Browser Manipulator*. The graphical representation of a document is obtained by converting instances of the ASN.1 structure to *Graphical Documents*, through a *Graphical Converter*.

4. The Data Model

Abstract Syntax Notation One (ASN.1) is selected as the basis of our proposed language. ASN.1 has been adopted by the National Institutes of Health (NIH) as a medium for exchange of data among heterogeneous architectures. The National Center for Biotechnology Information (NCBI) has also adopted ASN.1 as the formal description language for the important microbiology databases it manages, and has compiled and made public many important molecular biology databases in the form of ASN.1 described files. In addition, tools exist to verify the correctness of ASN.1 specifications, to convert ASN.1 specifications into C data structures, and to load ASN.1 encoded data into them.

Unfortunately ASN.1 is not completely satisfactory. It does not have a defined Data manipulation Language (DML) and it does not have the power to describe arbitrary Context Free Languages (CFLs). We therefore propose enhancement and modifications of ASN.1 to meet our requirements.

4.1 ASN.1 as DDL

The Abstract Syntax Notation One (ASN.1) is International Standards Organization Standard 8824 (ISO8824). ASN.1 is a formal syntax description language that was first proposed for use in networking applications where data structures are described using ASN.1 and exchanged among machines in this format. Locally, each machine has ASN.1 translators to convert the received data structures to local format for the local machine. ASN.1 has seen extensive and wide ranging application in this, the originally intended way of using it. Because of its general syntax description ability, it has found application in a variety of scientific circles for describing and exchanging their data. This includes NIH, NCBI, and more recently the Chemical Abstract Service (CAS). One may wonder, with the development of so many database models, why was there a need to adopt a language, ,not originally intended for databases, as a database model? The main reason behind this choice, appears to be the inability of the relational model to represent hierarchies and text formats. Many of the biologists who have developed the existing microbiology databases (over 100 such databases are reviewed in [KAM92b]) have implemented them as flat text databases, such as the well known GENBANK, a simplified fragment of which is shown below:

```
LOCUS       HCECUTICLE   6027 bp ds-DNA          INV      18-
AUG-1994
DEFINITION  Hyalophora cecropia cuticle protein 66 gene, complete cds.
ACCESSION   L13971
KEYWORDS    cuticle protein.
SOURCE      Hyalophora cecropia DNA.
  ORGANISM  Hyalophora cecropia
            Lepidoptera; Glossata; Bombycoidea; Saturniidae.
//
LOCUS       HUM3INGRN    4396 bp ds-DNA          PRI      18-
AUG-1994
DEFINITION  Homo sapiens integrin beta-3 subunit gene, promoter
region and partial cds.
ACCESSION   L28832
KEYWORDS    integrin; integrin beta-3 subunit; promoter; subunit.
SOURCE      Homo sapiens DNA.
  ORGANISM  Homo sapiens
            Primates; Haplorhini; Catarrhini; Hominidae.
//
```

In this flat text database, records are separated by a special delimiter: "//CRLF" and each record consists of a number of fields, beginning with a capitalized tag. Here, The tags LOCUS, DEFINITION, ACCESSION, KEYWORDS, SOURCE, and ORGANISM are shown. There are hierarchical relationships among some of these fields (e.g. ORGANISM is a subfield of SOURCE), and multi valued fields are permitted (e.g. KEYWORDS). Obviously, both these features are disallowed in the relational model. Table 1 shows an ASN.1 syntax description of the simplified GENBANK version given above.

<table>
<tr><th>Module 1</th><th>Module 2</th></tr>
<tr><td>ORG-module DEFINITIONS
::=
BEGIN
EXPORTS Organism;
Organism ::= SEQUENCE {
org VisibleString,
items SET OF
VisibleString }
END</td><td>GB-module DEFINITIONS ::=
BEGIN
EXPORTS GB-entry;
IMPORTS Organism FROM
ORG-module;
GB-set ::= SEQUENCE OF
GB-entry
GB-entry ::= SEQUENCE {
locus VisibleString,
definition VisibleString,
accession VisibleString,
keywords SEQUENCE OF
VisibleString,</td></tr>
</table>

	segment VisibleString **OPTIONAL**, source VisibleString, organism Organism } **END**

Table 1: ASN.1 specification of a simplified Genbank database

This specification is provided in two specification modules, each beginning with the module name (for example ORG-module in module 1) followed by the ASN.1 reserved word **DEFINITIONS** and the operator "::=". All the reserved keywords are capitalized and rendered in bold. The specification consists of a number of rules (productions) each having a nonterminal symbol on the left hand side, followed by the operator "::=" and the rule body. The rule body consists of simple or a composite data type. A simple data type is like integer, float, VisibleString; and a composite datatype is specified using one of ASN.1's type constructors. The most used ones are shown in Table 2, together with their meaning:

Constructor Name	Meaning
SEQUENCE	constructs a record of multiple fields of several heterogeneous datatypes. order is significant.
SEQUENCE OF	constructs a record of multiple fields of uniform datatypes. order is significant.
SET	constructs a record of multiple fields of several heterogeneous datatypes. order is insignificant.
SET OF	constructs a record of multiple fields of uniform datatypes. order is insignificant.
CHOICE	offers a choice of any one of several heterogeneous datatypes.

Table 2: ASN.1 type constructors

The keyword **OPTIONAL** specifies that a certain field in a any of the above constructs is optional, some databases conforming to the ASN.1 specs may have it, and some may not. Finally, the keywords **EXPORTS** and **IMPORTS . . . FROM** specify which rules can be exported, or must be imported from another module, respectively. Modularity is introduced in ASN.1 to control specification complexity.

4.2 ASN.1-Revised

A necessary, but unfortunately missing, component of ASN.1 is the ability to specify terminal symbols in the specification. This is absolutely necessary for using ASN.1 as a grammar. We have modified ASN.1, while retaining backward compatibility, to allow this feature, a modified version of the ASN.1 specs for module 1 of the simplified GENBANK using the new feature is given in Table 3:

Module 1

ORG-module **DEFINITIONS** ::=
BEGIN
EXPORTS Organism;
Organism ::= **SEQUENCE** {
orgtag ' ORGANISM',
org VisibleString,
'\n',
items **SET OF SEQUENCE** {
item VisibleString,
semi ';' } **OPTIONAL**,
lastitem VisibleString, '.' }
END

Table 3: Modified ASN.1 specification of module 1 in the simplified Genbank database

Note that we now have the ability to specify the organism more accurately by specifying a tag in the specs (e.g. ORGANISM') rather than describe it simply as the primitive datatype VisibleString. This allows us to build compilers to parse the database.

It is interesting to compare the representational power of this notation to the relational model. The main advantages of ASN.1 specifications over the relational model are that the whole structure can be named from within (the dichotomy of relation name versus attribute name of the relational model in non-existent here), and attribute hierarchies can be clearly represented. In addition, the following can be represented directly in our modified ASN.1 but not in the relational model: instance level delimiters, optional attributes, multi-valued attributes, the simultaneous representation of ordered and unordered attributes, and the ability to represent structured text with ease. Finally, tuples can also be defined as either ordered or unordered. Obviously, these features make the proposed language much better suited to integrating flat-file databases, with ad hoc structures, than the relational model and its languages.

4.3 The DML

In order to allow the user to issue high-level queries against ASN.1 documents, and to promote our modified ASN.1 from a data structure description language to a data model, we define a query language (DML) for it and define precisely the operations of this DML. Since the parsed ASN.1 text is a tree, many of the operators of the DML are tree operations. It is implicit here that "tree" and "subtree" refer to the parse tree and its subtrees. The results are always given in a textual representation of the parse tree.

4.3.1 Subtree Extraction

We define the operations GET FIRST and GET ALL to retrieve one subtree or all subtrees, bearing a certain label. GET FIRST retrieves a complete subtree defined as the first encountered subtree with a root labeled by a certain non-terminal symbol. The underlying order for traversing the tree is always assumed to be pre-order.

GET FIRST <*subtree*>
FROM <*tree*> [INCLUDE PATH]

where *subtree* is the nonterminal symbol labeling the root of the sought-after subtree and *tree* is the nonterminal symbol labeling the root of the tree subject to the search. The optional qualifier "INCLUDE PATH" specifies that the path to the subtree from the root should be shown with the subtree itself.

The operation GET ALL is similar to GET FIRST in syntax and function, except that it retrieves all encountered subtrees placed together in their natural place in the original parse tree. In addition, it is possible to eliminate duplicates by using the optional qualifier UNIQUE.

GET ALL [UNIQUE] <*subtree*>
FROM <*tree*> [INCLUDE PATH]

If INCLUDE PATH is not specified, then the result is placed in an artificial tree with a root labeled by either SET or SEQUENCE depending on whether UNIQUE is specified or omitted, respectively.

4.3.2 The Assignment Statement

Assignment can be specified by using either the keyword INTO or by using the equal sign (=). In the first method, an assignment is done by using the keyword INTO in the GET statement, followed by an identifier that acts as the external name of the receiving tree.

GET { FIRST | ALL [UNIQUE] } <*subtree*>
FROM <*tree*> [INCLUDE PATH]
[INTO <*identifier*>]

In the second method, the assignment operator "=" is used to directly copy one tree into another:

<external_tree_name> = *<external_tree_name>*

4.3.3 Specifying Conditions

We can qualify the GET FIRST and GET ALL operations to restrict the result based on the outcome of some Boolean condition. The condition is specified in a WHERE clause.

GET { FIRST | ALL [UNIQUE] } *<subtree>*
FROM *<tree>* [INCLUDE PATH]
[INTO *<identifier>*]
[WHERE *<condition>*]

Only those subtrees for which the condition is true are returned. *The variables specified in the condition may not be part of the requested subtree.* Matching the condition variable(s) with the appropriate sought-after subtree is done by determining the smallest subtree that contains all the condition variables *and* the sought-after subtree.

4.3.4 The Comparison Operators

We must clarify the meaning of the comparison operators (<, >, =, <>, <=, and >=) when used to compare subtrees. Two subtrees are equal (=) if and only if they have exactly the same structure, labels, and terminal symbols. This requirement extends to optional parts of the subtrees as well; the subtrees must be identical. Nonequality (<>) is defined as the negation of equality. In considering SEQUENCEs, order matters, whereas in SET's it does not. The 'truth' of the other operators (<, >, <=, and >=) is determined by considering terminals, or data values, associated with the condition variables. One string is considered 'less than' another if the first string lexically precedes the second.

4.3.5 The Coupling of Subtrees

This is a crucial operation of our DML and allows interoperability among different databases to take place. When two trees are joined, one (generally) wider tree is produced. The operation allows joining an arbitrary number of trees.

GET { FIRST | ALL [UNIQUE] } *subtree1* [, *subtree2*], ...
FROM *tree1* [INCLUDE PATH] [, *tree2* [INCLUDE PATH]], ...
[INTO *<identifier>*]
[WHERE *<condition>*]

We explain the operation in terms of two trees, however the explanation can easily be extended to an arbitrary number of trees. There are three steps:

1. All instances of *subtree1* are located in *tree1*. All nonterminal variables occurring in the left hand side of the comparison are located in *tree1*. A grouping (according to the least common subtree definition given earlier) is carried out among the subtrees and comparison variables.

2. All instances of *subtree2* are located in *tree2*. All nonterminal variables occurring in the right hand side of the comparison are located in *tree2*. A grouping (according to the least common subtree definition given earlier) is carried out among the subtrees and comparison variables.

3. A join process is then carried out in the relational JOIN style by pairing the instances of *subtree1* with those of *subtree2*, such that the Boolean condition is true for each such pairing. A new non-terminal variable name is automatically derived from the labels of the two components of each pair of subtrees and made into a new root for the pair. The whole set of thus obtained is place in a single tree with a new name, derived from the name of *tree1* and *tree2*.

This operation is illustrated below:

4.3.6 Importing and Exporting Data

In XBio, importing data is implicit in that XBio requires data, ASN.1 specification, DML statement(s), and StartSymbol as initial input. XBio then calls the Text Parser to produce a tree structure corresponding to this input, that represents within it the flat text file, parsed by the ASN.1 specification. The EXPORT operation is used to produce various kinds of XBio output.

EXPORT <*tree*> TO <*text_file*>
EXPORT <*tree*> TO <*abstract_specification*>

5. Conclusions

We have developed and prototyped an advanced approach to provide a high degree of interoperability among remote databases and application tools, that combines a tight-coupling component and a loose-coupling component. Loose-coupling is supported by the novel use of formal syntax notation to link arbitrary reports and file formats, in an interoperable fashion. The approach relies on formal syntax descriptions of the data in reports and files as an intermediate step. ASN.1 is used, after a backward compatible modification is made, as a DDL. A new DML was defined, partly implemented and presented in this paper as a companion to ASN.1. In effect promoting ASN.1 to a database model. Much work is still needed to extend and enhance the language in order to be able to apply the modern concepts of database management, such as constraint specification, integrity checking, support for time, and object-orientation to this model. In addition, many information retrieval functions can also be incorporated in the language.

References

[BUN89] O. P. Buneman, S. B. Davidson, and A. Watters, "Querying Independent Databases", Information Sciences, 49:3, Niv. 1989.

[BUN93] P. Buneman, S. Davidson, and A. Kosky, "Theoretical Aspects of Schema Merging", Proceedings of Extending Database Technology, March 1992.

[CHE93a] I-Min Chen, Victor M. Markowitz, Francis Pang, Ofer Ben-Shachar, "OPM Schema Editor 1.1, A Graphical Editor for Specifying Object-Protocol Structures", Lawrence-Berkeley Laboratory Technical Report LBL-33410, Jan. 1993.

[CHE93b] I-Min A. Chen and Victor Markowitz, "The Object-Protocol Model: Design, Implementation, and Scientific Applications", Lawrence-Berkeley Laboratory Technical Report LBL-33644, Feb. 1993.

[ELM89] Elmasri, R. and Navathe, S. B., "Fundamentals of Database Systems", Benjamin Cummings, 1989.

[GEL93] James Geller, Yehoshua Perl, Eric Neuhold, and Amit Sheth, "Structural Schema Integration with Full and Partial Correspondence using the Dual Model", Submitted to Information Systems.

[HEI85] Heimbigner D., and McLeod D., "A Federated Architecture for Information Management", ACM Trans. Off. Inf. Sys. 3, 3, July 1985.

[KAR91] Peter D. Karp, The ASN.1 Path-Manipulation Package, National Center for Biotechnology Information, National Library of Medicine publication, May, 1991.

[HAM79] Hammer M., and McLeod, D., On Database Management System Architecture", Technical Report MIT/LCS/TM-141, Massachusetts Institute of Technology, Cambridge, Mass.

[KAM92a] Nabil Kamel, Tao Song, and Magdi Kamel, "Incorporating GUI in Integration of Molecular Biology Databases", in: The Third IEEE Workshop on Future Trends of Distributed Computing Systems, Taipei, Taiwan, 404-410, April 14-16, 1992.

[KAM92b] Nabil Kamel, "A Profile for Molecular Biology Databases", Computer Applications in the Biosciences (CABIOS), Vol. 18, No. 4, pp. 311-321, 1992.

[KAM93] Nabil Kamel, Tao Song, and Magdi Kamel, "An Approach for Building an Integrated Environment for Molecular Biology Databases and Software Tools" in: The International Journal of Distributed and Parallel Databases, Vol. 1, No. 2, 1993.

[KRI91] Ravi Krishnamurthy, Witold Litwin, and William Kent, "Language Features for Interoperability of Databases with Schematic Discrepancies", Proc. of the ACM SIGMOD, 1991.

[LIT86] Witold Litwin and Abdelaziz Abdellatif, "Multidatabase Interoperability", IEEE Computer, Dec. 1986.

[LIT87] Witold Litwin and Abdelaziz Abdellatif, "An Overview of the Multi-Database Manipulation Language MDSL", Proceedings of the IEEE, Vol. 75, No. 5, May 1987.

[LIT90] Witold Litwin, Leo Mark, and Nick Roussopoulos, "Interoperability of Multiple Autonomous Databases", ACM Computing Surveys, Vol. 22, No. 3, Sep. 1990.

[MAR91] Victor Markowitz, "An Architecture for Identifying Objects in Multidatabases", 1st Int. Workshop on Interoperability in Multidatabase Systems, Kyoto, Japan, April 8-9, 1991.

[MAR93] Victor Markowitz and Arie Shoshani, "Data management Tools for Scientific Applications: An Overview", Lawrence Berkeley Laboratory, Feb. 1993.

[OSI91] Open Software Foundation, OSF/Motif R 1.1 Series, Prentice Hall, 1991.

[SCE86] R. W. Scheifler and J. Gettys, ``The X Window System'', ACM Transactions on Graphics, Vol 5, No.2, 1986.

[SHE90] Amit Sheth and James Larson, "Federated Database Systems for Managing Distributed, Heterogeneous, and Autonomous Databases", ACM Computing Surveys, Vol. 22, No. 3, Sept. 1990.

[SON92] Tao Song, "Design and Implementation of an Integrated Environment for Molecular Biology Databases and Application Tools", M.S. Thesis, University of Florida, Gainesville, FL 32611, 1992.

Modelling Transactions for Distributed Multimedia Database Systems

Weihai Yu
Department of Computer Science
University of Tromsø, Norway
E-mail: weihai@cs.uit.no

Abstract. This paper discusses the transaction modelling issues for distributed multimedia database management systems (MMDBMSes) and proposes an approach. The issues are related to the nature of media types and distributed multimedia processing, and to the way multimedia systems evolve. We believe the openness issues are the most essential to the modelling of transactions in distributed MMDBMSes. Our approach is object-oriented and primarily aimed at the openness issues. The behaviour of transactions is abstracted in *transaction ally* (TA) types and TA types are organised in hierarchies. Relationships between transactional behaviour are modelled explicitly with class inheritance. We show how this approach meets the various requirements.

Keywords. transaction, multimedia, interoperabilty, object-oriented, specification.

1. Introduction

With a distributed MMDBMS, information producers create multimedia information and manipulate the information over long periods of time; information consumers access the information to satisfy their needs at certain moments. On the one hand, the users of an MMDBMS, i.e., the information producers and consumers, must be isolated from each other in such a way that they do not interfere with each other's ongoing work. On the other hand, they should be able to co-operate as group when their activities require so.

DBMSes have been originally developed to support concurrent activities with the (ACID) transaction management subsystems [GRA93]. While the ACID transactions are successful in traditional database applications such as banking and air ticket reservation, they are too restrictive for advanced applications with specific requirements like long duration, co-operative activities, interoperability, and so forth. Over the years a number of extended transaction models have be proposed to meet these requirements [ELM92]. The challenge of an MMDBMS is many-fold. A multimedia system can be characterised as integration, variation and evolution. Furthermore, media data are different from the data traditional DBMSes process. In this paper, we discuss the new requirements on transaction models in distributed MMDBMSes and propose possible solutions. We will focus on transaction modelling issues rather than on supporting techniques.

The extended transaction models in the literature solve some problems in MMDBMSes. We will discuss some additional problems specific to multimedia data processing, such as QoS (quality of service) management. The main issue, however, is how the features of these different transaction models can be integrated in a consistent way in an MMDBMS and how evolution is facilitated. There is some related work dealing with transaction models in general (e.g., [CHR90] [BAR95]). Their focus is on the recognition of primitives common in many transaction models and the specification [CHR90] or implementation [BAR95] of different transaction models using these primitives. Our approach focuses on how new transaction features can be obtained from exiting transaction models and how different transaction models can be integrated to meet the requirements in MMDBMSes.

2. Requirements

The requirements for MMDBMS transaction models arise from the nature of multimedia data, the way multimedia information is produced and consumed, and the way MMDBMSes themselves are constructed and evolve.

2.1 Nature of Media Objects

Media objects often contain huge volume of data. Some media objects, such as audio and video streams, contain temporal constraints during their production and consumption. The temporal constraints can be either inside an object, e.g., sampling rate of an audio stream, or between different objects, e.g., between two audio channels of a stereo audio stream. The duration of capture and playback of such media objects is dependent on the nature of the media objects themselves and is often long.

Production of multimedia information is a complex and time consuming process. For example, descriptive information on raw video segments is produced manually.

Huge data volume, inherent temporal constraints and complicated authoring process, all these imply that transactions accessing multimedia objects are typically long.

> ***Requirement 1.*** *(Long-lived transactions) An MMDBMS should support long-lived transactions.*

The primary observation is that the isolation and atomicity properties of the ACID transaction model must be relaxed [ELM92].

A number of transaction models have been proposed to deal with issues typically for long-lived transactions by making use of the semantics of data and transactions, including compensation [GAR87], early release of locks when the access pattern of an transaction is known in advance [SAL94], splitting a long transaction into multiple smaller and/or shorter ones [PUC88], conflicting modes based on abstract data types [WEI89], ε-serializability [WUK92], etc. All these extensions can be applied to transactions in MMDBMSes.

Some transaction models are particularly applicable due to the characters of multimedia applications:

- Transaction models based on read-only access. Multimedia objects, once produced, are seldom updated, although some derivation such as cutting and fading is required during presentation.
- Transaction models based on access patterns. Patterns of access to continuous media objects are often predictable, e.g., sequential playback of a video segment.
- Transaction models that allow restricted inconsistency. The user is usually less critical to the inaccuracy of multimedia data than to data for banking or air flight reservation.

2.2 Authoring

As mentioned earlier, production of multimedia information is a complex process. Due to the heterogeneous nature of media types and diverse information associated with media objects (such as contents and descriptions), authoring multimedia information requires people with different expertise. Support of cooperation is therefore essential.

> ***Requirement 2.*** *(Ço-operation) An MMDBMS should support co-operative transactions*

Again, the isolation and atomicity properties of the traditional transaction model should be relaxed [ELM92].

A number of transaction models have been proposed in the literature that allow co-operative activities, either by checking-in/checking-out or by dynamically restructuring transactions [PUC88]. All these extensions can be applied to transactions in MMDBMSes.

The split-join facilities of dynamic transaction restructuring is a sound candidate. In MMDB authoring, cooperation is often in the form of previewing intermediate products of other authors. This can be done by joining the authoring transaction of the product that one wishes to preview. Also by the sequential nature of continuous media objects, splitting and committing the part of product that has done so far is meaningful.

Since consistency is often not so critical a requirement, a great degree of cooperation can be expected.

2.3 Resource Management

An important issue with multimedia systems is QoS management [VOG95]. We believe transactions are proper units for QoS control. In this context, ACID properties can be regarded as some particular QoS parameters. A transaction of a distributed MM application can be considered as composed of chains of components from sources to sinks. To guarantee QoS at certain level, resources required in all the components in the chain must be reserved for the whole duration of the transaction. Resource reservation is similar to data locking, but requires considerable extensions:

- Resource admission test such as schedulability test can be more complicated than a simple lock conflict test.
- The reserved resource for a transaction may be adapted upon QoS renegotiation.
- There should be mechanisms to monitor the usage of resources and to initiate exception events when QoS falls under the promised level. A transaction should be able to handle exception events coming from the components.

Requirement 3. *(Resource management) An MMDBMS should support transactions with general resource management facilities.*

No research work is seen that relates resource management to transaction management. QoS management is usually a task at the connection or session level, although transactions are units of processing more visible to the user. Transactions are originally units of concurrency control and recovery rather than of general QoS control. Basing conflict modes on ADT semantics [WEI89] seems to be the approach closest to generalised resource reservation.

2.4 Openness

Multimedia systems are characterised as variation, integration and evolution, so is transaction modelling. As discussed above, many extended transaction models can be applied. If several of them are to be supported in the system, the heterogeneity problem may arise: how can the features of these different transaction models be combined in a harmonious way and how can the user control the different features?

Requirement 4. *(Heterogeneity) An MMDBMS should allow heterogeneous transaction features and provide the user with the necessary facilities to handle them.*

An MMDBMS is usually built on top of an existing DBMS. An issue is whether the new transaction model for the MMDBMS works together with the transaction model of the existing DBMS. Moreover, since MMDBMSes are in the evolving phase, new transaction features may be added. A MMDBMS should allow the extension without significantly changing the parts that are already in use.

Requirement 5. *(Compatibility and extensibility) The transaction model of a MMDBMS must be compatible with that of the DBMS on top of which it is built and allow further extensions.*

Also, many MMDBMSes are now being developed in parallel and independently. A stronger requirement is that the transaction models of these MMDBMSes should be able to coexist in the future.

> ***Requirement 6.*** *(Interoperability) Different MMDBMS transaction models should be able to coexist to the greatest extend.*

We believe the openness requirements are the most profound to MMDBMS transaction models. A framework is needed to relate features of different transaction models in a structured way.

3. The TA Approach

Our primary goal is to model different transaction features in a way that is appropriate to meet the different requirements. We believe that object orientation is an appropriate approach to meet the *openness* requirements due to its strength in abstraction and polymorphism. In our approach, transactional behaviour is abstracted in transaction ally (TA) types. TA types are organised in hierarchies such that relationships between TA types can be modelled explicitly with class inheritance. This section describes the TA approach and discusses how it meets the different requirements. Correctness issues are informally discussed in [YUW95]. Formal reasoning is under way.

3.1 Encapsulating Transactional Behaviour

A transaction is a computational unit with certain transactional behaviour. That is, the transaction manipulates the effects on objects according to certain (concurrency control, recovery, resource management) rules. To deal with the diversified transactional behaviour in extended transaction models, we abstract the various behaviour into transactional types. TA types presented in this paper are such transactional types. A transaction model contains one or more transactional types. That is, in a transaction model, different transactions may have different transactional behaviour. For example, in the nested transaction model [MOS85], top-level transactions and nested-level transactions have different transactional behaviour.

In our framework, transactional behaviour is decoupled into two parts:

- Transaction-dependent behaviour, including termination management (commit or abort) and execution dependencies between transactions.
- Object-dependent behaviour, including object-level concurrency control, recovery, etc..

When transactions of a certain type T are used in an application, the application contains TActions and TMable objects (stands for "TAction-manipulable"). TActions are responsible for the transaction-dependent behaviour; TMable objects are responsible for the object-dependent behaviour. A TAction and the manipulated

TMable objects constitute a *transaction ally* (*TA*). A TA is an instance of a *transaction ally type* (*TA type*) T, which is a composition of the two types TAction and TMable.

Figure 1 shows how interactions occur through various interfaces when an Atomic TA (see Section 3.4) is used. Typically, an application calls `begin()` on an AtomicAction to start an Atomic TA. The application then calls `lock()` on AtomicMable data objects. These objects in turn call `register()` on the AtomicAction in order to "enter" the Atomic TA. When a data object is in the Atomic TA, the execution of all the operations, such as `op1()`, `op2()`, etc., complies with the rules of the Atomic TA. Finally, the application calls `end()` or `abort()` on the AtomicAction which ensures that all the objects in the Atomic TA execute `commit()` or `undo()`.

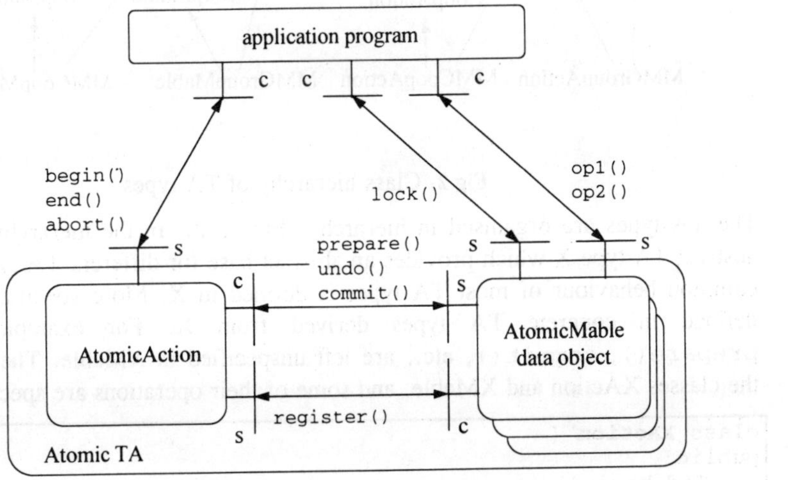

Interface types: s (server), c (client)

Fig 1. Interactions of an Atomic TA

3.2 Overview of the Example

The TA approach is described with an example throughout the paper. In the example, there are a number of transaction models, ranging from the traditional flat and nested transactions, split-join transaction groups, transactions for resource management, to an integration of all these facilities into a single transaction model. We will describe how a single TA type is specified, how a new TA type extends an existing one, and how different TA types can be used in a single application. Due to space limitation, not all TA types and operations are specified.

3.3 Specification of General Features

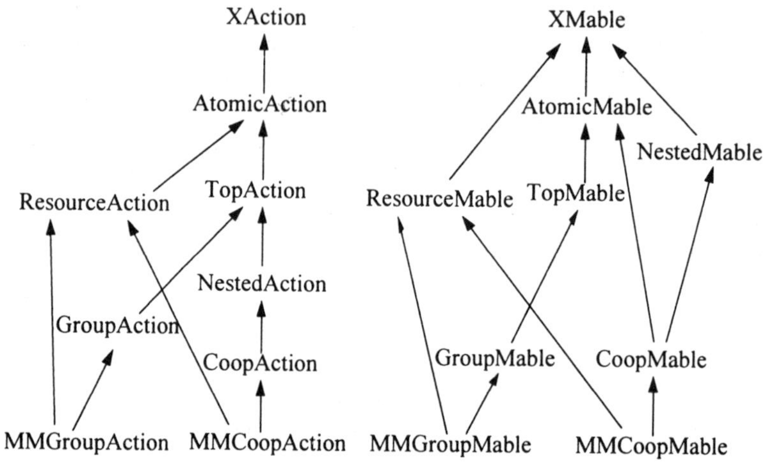

Fig 2. Class hierarchy of TA types

The TA types are organised in hierarchy (Figure 2). In the hierarchy, there is an abstract TA type X which provides an abstract base for different TA types. Only the common behaviour of most TA types is defined in X. More specific behaviour is defined in concrete TA types derived from X. For example, operations `prepare()`, `commit()`, etc., are left unspecified in XMable. The interfaces of the classes XAction and XMable, and some of their operations are specified below.

```
class XAction {
public:
    Tid begin();
    bool end();
    void abort();
restricted:
    virtual void register(XMable);
    void unregister(XMable);
    virtual Type mableType(XMable, XLock);
protected:
    bool end_1();
    void end_2();
    Tid tid;      // transaction id
    OidToType_map objs;
};

class XMable {
public:
    XMable();
    bool lock(XLock);
restricted:
    virtual bool prepare(Tid) = 0;
```

```
    virtual void commit(Tid) = 0;
    virtual void undo(Tid) = 0;
protected:
    virtual bool setLock(XLock) = 0;
    void releaseLock(XLock);
    void delegate(Tid, Tid);

    TidToType_map taType;
    XLock_set locks;
    Tid_set modified;
};

class XLock {
public:
    XLock(Tid, XLockMode); // XLockMode: Read < Write < WrRd
restricted:
    virtual XConfMode conflict(XLock);
                           // XConfMode: Conflict, Compatible
    void delegate(Tid);    // change owner
    void convert(Mode);    // change mode
protected:
    Tid owner;
    XLockMode mode;
};

Tid XAction::begin() {
effect result = self'.tid = (new Tid)  and  self'.objs = {}
}

bool XAction::end() {
effect if (end_1())
       then result = true and end_2()
       else result = false and abort()
}

bool XAction::end_1() {
effect if (∀obj in self.objs.domain:
                objs(obj)::prepare(self.tid))
       then result = true
       else result = false
}

XAction::end_2() {
effect ∀obj in self.objs.domain: objs(obj)::commit(self.tid)
}

XAction::register(XMable obj, Type type) {
effect self'.objs = self.objs.override(obj→type)
                       // map overriding: VDM terminology
}

Type XAction::mableType(XMable, XLock) {
effect result = <> // a ¨null¨ type
}

bool XMable::lock(XLock xl) {
effect result = mType::setLock(xl) and
       if (result)
       then self'locks = self.locks.merge(xl) and
            xl.owner.register(self, mType) and
```

```
            self'.taType =self.taType.override(xl.owner→mType)
            and
            if (xl.mode >= Write)
            then self'.modified = self.modeified.add(xl.owner)
                 and
                 self'.stable.tid = self.volatile
        where mType = xl.owner.mableType(self, xl)
}

XMable::delegate(Tid from, Tid To) {
effect ∀lk in self.locks:
            (if (lk.owner == from)
            then self'.locks =
                           self.locks.merge(lk.delegate(to))
                 and
                 if (lk.mode >= Write)
                 then self'.modified
                         = (self.modified.remove(from)).add(to)
                      and
                      self'.stable.to = self.stable.from)
        and
        to.register(self.tid, mType)  and
        from.unregister(self.tid, mType)  and
        self'.taType = self.taType.override(to→mType)  and
        self'.taType = self.taType.delete(from)
                              // map deletion: VDM terminology
        where mType = to.owner.mableType(self, xl)
}
```

We choose to use a specification mechanism similar to Larch/C++ [CHO93] and VDM [JON90] but more programming language oriented. Particularly, there is no precondition of an operation. Instead, the operation should be able to report undesirable effects via its returned values. However there is a `when` guardian which may block the execution. Also there is no additional tier as in the Larch family. The effect of an operation may include that of other operations as nested invocations. We also use some data types such as set and map that are not available in programming languages such as C++ but can be supported by a class library. Besides the public, protected and private operations as in C++, restricted operations can only be invoked within the same TA. `self` and `self'` are the states before and after execution respectively.

An object associated with multiple -Mable classes can exist in TAs of different types. The different classes need common information for concurrency control, such that the execution of an operation in one TA will not violate the enforced rules of other concurrent TAs. This common information is kept in the abstract class XMable. XMable maintains a list of abstract locks. Derived -Mable classes may use locks of concrete types derived from the abstract lock type. One requirement on the different lock types used by an object is that it should always be possible to determine whether two locks conflict. As a counter example, it is not possible to decide whether a lock using forward commutativity and a lock using backward commutativity conflict [WEI89]. So an object may not use forward commutativity in some TAs and at the same time backward commutativity in other TAs.

`lock()` acquires a lock by calling the type specific operation `setLock()` and does the necessary initialization. The stable state `self.stable.tid` (as well as `self.stable, self.stable.tid.prepare` in AtomicMable) is used for recovery. `delegate()` delegates an object from one TA to another. A TA commits in two phases (by calling the operations `end_1()` and `end_2()` respectively).

As we will see in Section 3.7, the actual -Mable type of a data object is dependent on the context when the object is used. The actual -Mable type of a data object is determined by the operation `mableType()` of XAction. -Action and -Mable objects also keep track of the actual -Mable types in the maps `objs` and `taType` respectively.

3.4 Specification of Concrete Features

The Atomic TA type encapsulates the behavior of flat transactions with strict two phase locking. The interfaces of the Atomic TA type are the same as the X TA type. Some operations are specified below. A data object behaves as AtomicMable when the manipulating action is AtomicAction and when the object is locked with an AtomicLock. Behaviour specific to the concrete TA type, i.e., locking, commit and undo, is specified.

```
Type AtomicAction::mableType(XMable xm, XLock, xlk) {
effect if (xm.isType(<AtomicMable>) and
                xlk.isType(<AtomicLock>))
       then result = <AtomicMable>
       else result = <>
}

bool AtomicMable::prepare(Tid tid) {
effect if (self.modified.contains(tid))
       then self'.stable.tid.prepare = self.volatile
       and result = true
}

AtomicMable::commit(Tid tid) {
effect if (self.modified.contains(tid))
       then self'.stable = self.stable.tid.prepare
       and
       (∀lck in self.locks:
            if (lck.owner == tid) then releaseLock(lck))
}

bool AtomicMable::setLock(AtomicLock lck) {
when   ∀lk in self.locks:
            lck.AtomicLock::conflict(lk) != Conflict
effect result = true
}
```

```
AtomicConfMode AtomicLock::conflict(lck) {
effect  if ((lck.owner == self.owner and lck.mode <= self.mode)
                or lck.mode == self.mode == Read)
        then result = Compatible
        else result = Conflict
}
```

3.5 Specification of Extensions

The split-join cooperative transaction model (modified from [BAR95]) is an extension to the nested transaction model. In the model, a cooperative transaction may join a transaction group, multiple transaction groups may merge into one, and a transaction group may split into multiple ones, all dynamically during execution.

A GroupAction behaves like a TopAction. Besides, a GroupAction may allow other CoopActions to become its new member; it may split into multiple independent GroupActions; and multiple GroupActions may merge into one. A CoopAction behaves either as an independent AtomicAction, or, when it joins a GroupAction, as a NestedAction. The TA types of the split-join cooperative transaction model is specified below.

```
class GroupAction: TopAction {
public:
    void mergeTo(Tid);
    Tid split(Tid_set, GroupMable_set);
    void joinFrom(Tid);
};

class GroupMable: TopMable {
};

class CoopAction: NestedAction {
public:
    Tid begin();
    Tid begin(Tid);
    void joinTo(Tid);
};

class CoopMable: TopMable, NestedMable {
public:
    virtual void commit();
protected:
    virtual bool setLock(CoopLock);
};

class CoopLock: NestedLock {
restricted:
    virtual CoopConfMode conflict(XLock);
};

GroupAction::mergeTo(Tid ga) {
effect  ∀ca in self.children: ca.joinTo(ga)
        and
```

```
        ∀obj in self.objs.domain: obj.delegate(self.tid, ga)
}

Tid GroupAction::split(Tid_set cas, GroupMable_set objs) {
effect  result = (new GroupAction).begin()
        and
        ∀obj in (objs * self.objs.domain): // * set union
                obj.delegate(self.tid, result)
        and
        ∀ca in (cas * self.children.domain): ca.joinTo(result)
}

GroupAction::joinFrom(Tid ca) {
effect  self.addChild(ca) // defined in NestedAction
}

Tid CoopAction::begin() {
effect  result = TopAction::begin() and self'.parent = nil
}

Tid CoopAction::begin(Tid ga) {
effect  result = NestedAction::begin(ga)
};

CoopAction::joinTo(Tid ga) {
effect  ga.joinFrom(self.tid) and self'.parent = ga
}

bool CoopMable::setLock(CoopLock lck) {
when    ∀lk in self.locks:
                (lck.CoopLock::conflict(lk) != Conflict)
effect  result = true
}

CoopMable::commit(Tid tid) {
effect  if (tid.getParent() != nil)
        then NestedMable::commit()
        else TopMable::commit()
}

CoopConfMode CoopLock::conflict(XLock lck) {
effect  if (self.owner.getParent() == nil)
        then result = TopLock::conflict(lck)
        else result = NestedLock::conflict(lck)
}
```

Notice that multiple inheritance is used for CoopMable. However, at a certain moment, a CoopMable object may only show the behavior of AtomicMable or NestedMable, but not both, although exactly which of the two may change over time (for example when a CoopAction joins a GroupAction). See the overloaded operation `begin()`, `commit()`, etc..

3.6 Specification of General Resource Management

Resources in distributed multimedia applications can be modelled as active objects [GIB95]. In particular, a resource must be monitored during a transaction to examine whether certain QoS level is maintained. If it is not, an exception event arises. An action must always be ready to handle the exception events it is aware of. The activeness of action and events are modelled with *threads*.

Moreover, resource reservation is different from locking in some respect. Upon request of resource, a target amount of resource and a lowerbound is given. A final amount is then admitted and reserved. More complicated tasks such as schedulability test are not discussed here. Recovery is in general not an issue, so stable states can be considered as having null values (or the locking mode is always read).

```
class ResourceAction: XAction {
public:
    Tid begin();
    void registerEvent(Event, Handler);
    void unregisterEvent(Event);
protected:
    thread listen();
    EventToHandler_map handlers;
};

class ResourecMable: XMable {
public:
    Resource adapt(Tid,Resource,Resource);
protected:
    virtual bool setLock(ResourceLock);
    void releaseLock(ResourceLock);
    thread monitor();
    Resource total, reserved, in_use;
};

class ResourceLock: Xlock{
restricted:
    virtual ResourceConfMode conflict(ResourceLock);
    void admit(Resource);
private:
    Tid owner;
    Resource amount, lower_bound;
};

Tid ResourceAction::begin() {
effect result = Xaction::begin() and fork(listen())
}

ResourceAction::registerEvent(Event ev, Handler hdler) {
effect self'.handlers = self.handlers.override(ev→hdler)
}

ResourceAction::unregisterEvent(Event ev) {
effect handlers' = handlers.delete(ev)
}
```

```
thread ResourceAction::listen() {
when    event(ev)
effect  handlers(ev) and listen()
}

Resource ResourecMable::adapt(
            Tid tid, Resource target, Resource lowerbound) {
when    self.reserved - lk.amount + lowerbound <= total
effect  self'.reserved = self.reserved - lk'.amount + res  and
        lk.admit(res) and result = res
        where
            lk.owner = tid  and
            res = min(target, total-self.reserved+lk'.amount)
}

bool ResourecMable::setLock(ResourceLock lck) {
when    self.reserved + lck.lowerbound <= self.total  and
        ∀lk in self.locks:
            lck.ResourceLock::conflict(lk) != Conflict
effect  self'.reserved = self.reserved + res  and
        lck.admit(res) and result = true
        where res = min(target, total - self.reserved)
}

ResourecMable::releaseLock(ResourceLock lck) {
effect  XMable::releaseLock(lck)  and
        self'.reserved = self.reserved - lck.amount
}

thread ResourecMable::monitor() {
when    self.in_use > total
effect  arise(Event("ResourceCongest", self, in_use - total))
        and
        monitor()
}

ResourceConfMode ResourceLock::conflict(ResourceLock lck) {
effect  if ((lck.owner == self.owner)
        then result = Conflict // cannot reserve twice
        else result = Compatible
}

ResourceLock::admit(Resource res) {
effect  self'.amount = res
}
```

A multimedia transaction can combine the features of various transaction models, such as general resource management and split-join cooperative transactions. An MMGroupMable resource, for instance, when manipulated by an MMGroupAction, may also be split into another MMGroupAction.

3.7 Over-manipulation

A TopAction can manipulate TopMable objects and AtomicMable objects at the same time since TopMable does not introduce any additional features to AtomicMable. We say a TopAction *over-manipulates* AtomicMable objects. Also, a

GroupAction over-manipulates TopMable objects. The restriction to the behavior of the over-manipulated objects is that the objects cannot be merged into another GroupAction or split from the GroupAction.

There are more examples of over-manipulation (with restricted behavior): a CoopAction over-manipulates AtomicMable and NestedMable objects; an MMGroupAction over-manipulates ResourceMable and GroupMable objects; an MMCoopAction over-manipulates ResourceMable and CoopMable objects.

Over-manipulation is also "transitive". An MMGroupAction over-manipulates GroupMable objects and a GroupAction over-manipulates TopMable objects, so an MMGroupAction over-manipulates TopMable objects as well.

4. Discussion

We have now discussed the requirements on transaction models for distributed MMDBMS and proposed an object-oriented approach to modelling transactional behavior. In this section we discuss how the approach meets the requirements.

The first set of requirements (Requirements 1, 2) concerns with the weakening of the ACID properties. A lot of transaction models have been proposed for this purpose. We have shown that the TA approach is general enough for modelling these extended transaction features. In particular, we have shown how split-join cooperative transactions can be modelled as an extension to the nested transaction model. Extensions can be modelled with new lock types, new stable states, new dependencies between transactions and new operations for transaction restructuring.

The approach is also capable of modelling general resource management (Requirement 3). Resources can be modelled as active objects with event handling facilities. Resource reservation can be modelled as a variation of data locking. This approach is a sound combination of ADT-based concurrency control and object-oriented multimedia programming [GIB95].

The openness issues (Requirements 4, 5, 6) are the most difficult to address. The soundness of the TA approach lies in that the features of transaction models are encapsulated in TA types and relationships between different features are modelled with class inheritance.

- Heterogeneity. A data object may show the features of different TA types and an action may manipulate data objects that are designed for different TA types. For example, a TopMable object can be manipulated by an AtomicAction (since TopMable "contains" the features of AtomicMable) and over-manipulated by an MMGroupAction; a GroupAction can manipulate MMGroupMable objects and over-manipulate AtomicMable objects.
- Compatibility and extensibility. Class inheritance makes explicit how extensions occur. With careful use of class inheritance (e.g., by following strict subtyping), backward compatibility can be guaranteed. For example, the split-join co-

operative transaction model is compatible with the nested transaction model. The rules of the nested transaction model will not be violated: the behaviour that is not allowed in the nested transaction model can only occur with split-join transactions by explicitly applying the new operations such as `split()` and `join()`.

- Interoperability. If two independently developed systems are to be included in an interoperable environment, what need to be done is to first encapsulate the local transactional behaviour into TA hierarchies and then export the hierarchies. By doing so, the different features of the two local systems may coexist, as we discussed with the heterogeneity requirement.

Note that our approach focuses on the modelling or specification of transactional behaviour rather than the implementation techniques. Yet the way we specify transactional behaviour is close to a prototype. Actually, a preliminary prototyping is done as a student project.

We haven't seen any closely related work so far. As loosely related work, ACTA [CHR90] is a formal framework that attempts to characterise the whole range of structural and behavioural properties of different transaction types. The behaviour of a transaction is specified with a set of operations known as significant events, and a set of axioms describing the dependencies between transactions and correctness criteria such as conflict serializability. The relationship between different transaction types is not explicit and therefore cannot be used for the openness issues.

5. Summary

Multimedia systems can be characterised as variation, integration and evolution, so is the transaction subsystem. Furthermore, we must take into consideration the other important aspects of distributed multimedia systems such as QoS and resource management. This paper discussed the requirements on transaction models and proposed an approach. The requirements include almost all those observed in the other advanced database applications such as long-lived and co-operative activities. Issues more specific to multimedia systems include transaction-based resource management. Besides all these requirements, we believe the openness requirements are the most profound. Our approach is therefore primarily aimed at addressing the openness issues.

The approach is object-oriented, thanks to its ability of abstraction and modelling polymorphism. The behaviour of a transaction is decoupled into actions and objects, and abstracted in TA types. TA types are modelled in hierarchies where relationships between different TA types are explicitly abstracted with class inheritance. We used an example throughout the paper to show how the approach can be applied to address the different requirements.

References

[BAR95] Barga, R. and Pu, C. (1995): A Practical an Modular Implementation of Extended Transaction Models. In: Proceedings of the 21st VLDB Conference.

[CHO93] Choen, Y. and Leavens, G. T. (1993): A Quick Overview of Larch/C++. Technical Report, Department of Computer Science, Iowa State University.

[CHR90] Chrysanthis, P. K. and Ramramritham, K. (1990): ACTA: A Framework for Specifying and Reasoning about Transaction Structure and Behaviour. In: Proceedings of ACM SIGMOD '90.

[ELM92] Elmagarmid, A. K., (editor) (1992): Dtabase Transaction Models for Advanced Applications, Morgan Kaufmann Publishers.

[GAR87] Garcia-Molina, H. and Salem K. (1987): SAGAS, In: Procedings of ACM SIGMOD'87, pp 249--259.

[GIB95] Gibbs, S. J. and Tsichritzis, D. C. (1995): Multimedia Programming: Objects, Environments and Frameworks. Addison-Wesley.

[GRA93] Gray, J. and Reuter A. (1993): Transaction Processing: Concepts and Techniques, Morgan Kaufmann Publishers.

[JON90] Jones, C. B. (1990): Systematic Software Development Using VDM. Prentice Hall.

[MOS85] Moss, J. Eliot B. (1985): Nested Transactions: An Approach to Reliable Distributed Computing. The MIT Press, Cambridge, Mass.

[PUC88] Pu, C., Kaiser G., and Hutchinson, N. (1988): Split Transactions for Open-ended Activities. In: Proceedings of the 14th VLDB Conference.

[SAL94] Salem, K., Garcia-Molina, H. and Shands J. (1994): Altruistic Locking. ACM Trans. on Database Systems. 19(1):117-165, March.

[VOG95] Vogel, A. et al. (1995): Distributed Multimedia and QoS: A Survey. IEEE Multimedia. Vol. 2, No. 1, pp 10--19.

[WEI89] Weihl, W. E. (1989): Local Atomicity Properties: Modular Concurrency Control for Abstract Data Types. ACM Trans. on Prog. Lang. Systems. Vol. 11, No. 2, pp 249--282.

[WUK92] Wu, K. L., Yu, P. S., and Pu C. (1992): Divergence Control for Epsilon-Serializability. In: Proceedings of 8th International Conference on Data Engineering.

[YUW95] Yu, W., and Eliassen, F. (1995): Flexible Transaction Management in an Interoperable Database Environment. In: Cheung, T., Fong, J., and Siu, B. (editor), Database Reengineering and Interoperability. Plenum Publishing Corporation.

Towards a Knowledge-based System for Data Base Re-Engineering

Irene S.Y. KWAN
Department of Computing Studies
The Hong Kong Polytechnic University
Hung Hom, Kowloon
Hong Kong
E-Mail: csirkwan@comp.polyu.edu.hk

Abstract. A rapid growth in Data Base (DB) and Software Engineering (SE) technologies to keep up with the ever increasing complexity of information requirements have become one of the fastest establishing research areas today. Data Modelling become not only modelling static data structures but also its semantics evolution and its dynamic behaviour. Information systems become not only supporting decisions but also be able to make critical decisions based on knowledge-base provided and to refine as well as transform knowledge by neural networks. Yet there are a vast amount of applications developed in the past few decades utilising conventional DB methodologies like Hierarchical, Network and Relational models. These applications have been operating in the companies for a while and have become too costly to totally re-develop but too important to discard! This leave to one feasible approach - Re-engineering! Data are the fundamental asset of a company. How would software engineers reuse these data design? To reverse from these existing data base systems back to its initial conceptual design by use of Re-engineering and Knowledge-base approaches, and then transform these conventional DB design to new Object-Oriented DB (OODB) and incorporate with new users' requirement are possible. The goal of this research paper is to explore the possibility to establish a generic knowledge-based system to automate this reverse procedure of mapping existing data schema from Data Dictionary (DD) to OODB and integrate additional dynamic semantics as well as, if any, incorporate users additional requirements to the new model. This system is expected to ease in enhancing the current DB system by upgrading its underlying DB technologies and extend the capabilities of the existing DB system in terms of its data semantics representation power.

1. Introduction

Databases re-engineering is still an evolving technology. In its related research and development, much emphasis have been placed in programs re-engineering and there is relatively less awareness in DB Re-engineering. In fact, as information is the fundamental asset of the software and company, DBRE is increasingly being recognised as an urgent issue to tackle for meeting the change of technologies and business needs.

Full design recovery for re-engineering complete Database from existing code and DD is not considered practically feasible yet. The Re-3 technologies - Restructuring, Reverse Engineering and RE-engineering are considered to be the key technologies for the next decade. Transformation is central to re-engineering. As we can see much expertise are now exist about re-engineering. A logical next step is to encapsulate these knowledge and expertise, transform and install into an expert system rule-base.

A procedure of reengineering existing relational databases to object-oriented (OO) ones is applied in the proposed system. An extended Entity-Relationship (EER) model is used as the intermediate representation means during the conversion. A set of translation rules from both relational to EER and from EER to a generic OO model of OMT methodology is devised[KWA95]. The specific goal of this paper is to extend this research and to explore the possibility to develop a knowledge-base to protect companies' investment in their DB systems reengineering and to look upon the possibility in automation of database re-engineering for recovering of dynamic data semantics. The major technical contribution of this paper is the proposed dynamic semantics recovery knowledge base, which has an objective to reengineer the existing relational DB systems by transformation to take advantages of new object-oriented technology while reusing all the old features that were proven to be useful in the original systems. Hence, the ultimate target of this research is to explore means to make existing databases systems more maintainable and evolvable through the re-engineering approach.

2. Related Works

The topic of Database Re-engineering by schema translation from one database model to another has been a "classic topic" ever since more than one data models were used in developing database systems. It has been much more intensively studied and more rigorously treated after the Entity-Relationship (ER) model became available. Well established translation rules and algorithms for transforming the ER model and its variants into other models have been presented in the literature. For example: [ELM89] considered the translation from the ER to the relational model. [PUT90] investigated on transforming relational schema back to extended ER model. [GET93] proposed to translate from an extended ER model to a generic OO model. [NAR93] considered the translation rules for mapping the ER and the relational models into an abstract OO model. There have also been efforts of combining the ER model and the OO approach. For examples, the Object-Oriented Entity-Relationship Model (OOERM)[GOR93], which is an extension of the ER model featuring dynamic aspects. The Behaviour Integrated Entity-Relationship (BIER) approach[KAP88] combines the ER model and the petri-net model. The Deductive Entity-Relationship Model[BAT93] that allows one model class hierarchies and to express certain types of assert (on classes) using first order logic. The Object Modelling Technique (OMT) which can be regarded as a extension of the ER model with complete OO features, or alternatively, a comprehensive OODB model enhanced with advanced semantic features.

3. The System Framework

The new OO approach in DB design has claimed its advantages on more DB semantics representation and less impact in terms of changing requirements. Companies might seek for re-engineer their existing DB to OODB for better maintainability and evolutionary ability. Hence, the need to upgrade the underlying DB technology without changing the systems original functionalities lead to software industries to perform DBRE.

The proposed DBRE process is consisted of three-phases :-

(1) a reverse engineering translation phase from relational schema to the EER model, (2) a forward engineering phase from EER model to an intermediate OO model and (3) a dynamic data sematic and additional data requirement elicitation phase to recover a complete OO model. In the reverse engineering phase, static data semantics are recovered through static analysis of the database data dictionary and represented in the EER model as defined in [5]; in the forward engineering phase, dynamic data semantics are discovered, perhaps coupled with end-users' inputs[FON93], through analysis of database programs, are represented in an OO model. In this process, static and dynamic data semantic abstractions are represented by the OO model called OMT ("Object Modelling Technique") as defined in[RUM91], which is a generic model representation that can be easily tailored to any OO language and system.

To translate an EER schema to OO schema, a direct translation can only map the data structure, its relationships and its basic dynamic behaviours but not all the dynamic semantics hidden in the original EER model. In recovering a complete dynamic semantics by recapturing these dynamic semantics, a knowledge-based system is useful as key users views relies mainly on domain knowledge instead of mechanistic algorithms. The Expert system could then fill in the extra semantics needed in schema translation by navigating users to make knowledgeable decision whenever semantics judgment is required[HEV89]. Hence, the contribution of this paper is the extension of [KWA95] with a more detail and rigorous studies of phase 3. A set of heuristic translation rules with a systematic sequence of interactive knowledge elicitation dialogue for recovering dynamic data semantics from existing relational databases to OODBs via EER is presented.

The following figure outlined the architectural framework of the DBRE knowledge-based system :-

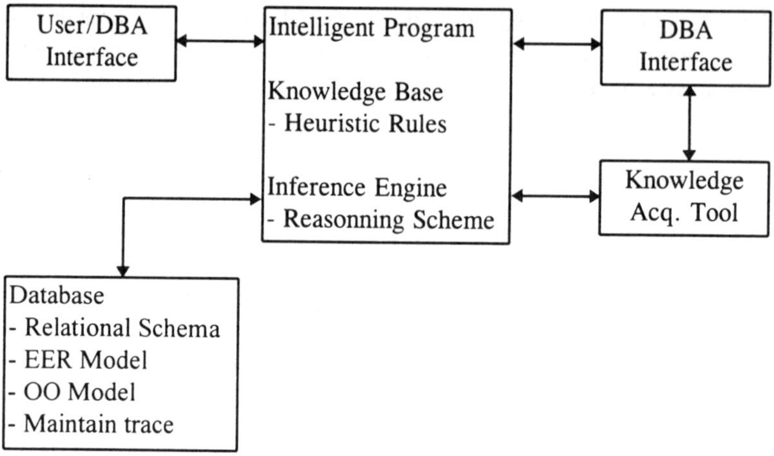

Fig. 1 The architectural framework of the DBRE knowledge-based system

The key users of this system is expected to be the Data Base Administrator (DBA) of the original relational DB system, who has a thorough understanding about the conceptual design, physical design and operations of the current DB system. Other users could assist in identifying new data requirements, if any, by incorporating additional data definition after the complete transformation of OMT object model and the dynamic Model is derived.

4. The Knowledge Derivation and Development of Heuristic Rule Set

The dynamic semantic could well be abstracted in dynamic model. The OMT Dynamic model consists of state diagrams and global event flow diagram, which specifies allowable sequences of changes to objects from the static object model. Thus, it forms a good representation in the reaction of objects to events and their behaviour over time. Upon the completion of schema translation performed in the first two phases in the DBRE process, phase 3 : dynamic semantic knowledge acquisition could then begin. Hence, the intermediate transformed OMT Object Model details such as object classes, associations and links should be readily available in the system database to assist in dynamic semantic knowledge acquisition.

Knowledge acquisition refers to the elicitation and internal representation of the knowledge discovered within the tool. In the proposed knowledge-based system, the vehicle for knowledge elicitation is a predefined sequence of dialogue between the DBA and the intelligent program of the knowledge-based system. The dynamic model could be best accomplished with the heuristic translation rules PLUS users'input via the designed dialogue in the knowledge-based system.

The process of knowledge derivation and development of the heuristic rule set could well be explained by use of "Heater System" case-study, which also assist in explaining the formation of a Dynamic model to recover the extra dynamic semantics.

In this section, the knowledge acquisition process is presented to demonstrate how control information can be elicited and represented as OMT dynamic model which consist of a global Event diagram and a set of State diagrams, one for each object showing the permissible patterns of events causing each change of state value within an object class.

4.1 Dynamic Data Semantic Elicitation

As for the "Heater System" case study, suppose we have recovered an intermediate OMT Object model as shown in following Fig. 2, obtained by following the previous translation steps in the proposed DBRE procedure [KWA95]. The next phase is to discover more dynamic semantics. The knowledge acquisition tool or so call the knowledge engineering facilitator is proposed in this paper. It is a program interact with DBA to help him/her to structure the hidden dynamic semantic in the original DB Systems, in a logical manner, thereby facilitating the generation of a set of domain specific rules. The users need to be asked the appropriate questions in a systematic way in order to discover the knowledge about the complete dynamic behaviour of the system. A set of steps with appropriate question(s) designed for each step are applied as knowledge acquisition tool. A set of heuristic rules are defined based on OMT dynamic model construction knowledge, to assist the reasoning scheme in the inference engine. These are presented by use of the "Heater System" case study below.

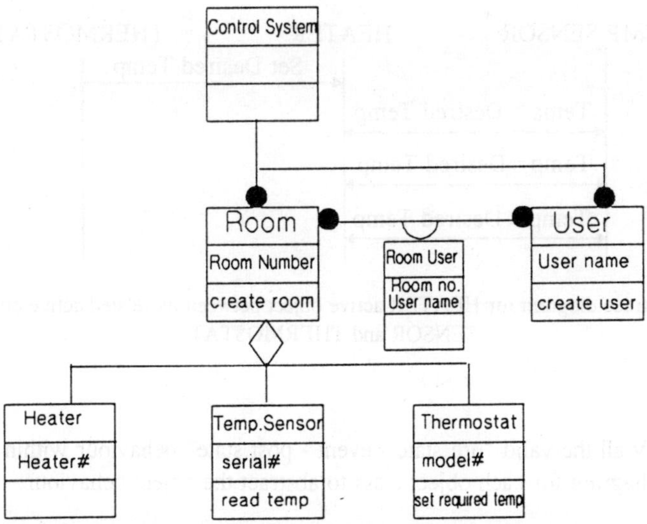

Fig. 2. An intermediate corresponding OMT Object Model of a Heating System

Step 1 Prepare typical scenarios of executing the system.

Question 1 In light of providing overall picture of the system, what are the expected 'Normal' behaviour in the system?

Answer: A Heater System Scenario by setting a Heater desired temperature by Thermostat and sense temperature by Temp.sensor

If temperature > desired temperature, switch heater off(event 1)

If temperature < desired temperature, switch heater on(event 2)

If temperature = desired temperature, no action to take (event 3)

Step 2 Identify events between objects and prepare an event trace diagram for each scenario.

Question 2 What are the causing and resulting event of change of state in each object class? (for example : Heater Object)

Answer:On -> E-1 -> Off -> E-2 -> On

where E-1 is Temp>Desired Temp. and E-2 is Temp<Desired Temp. Otherwise, E-3, that is no change of state value when Temperature=Desired Temperature.

These events or object behaviours can be abstracted in Fig. 3.

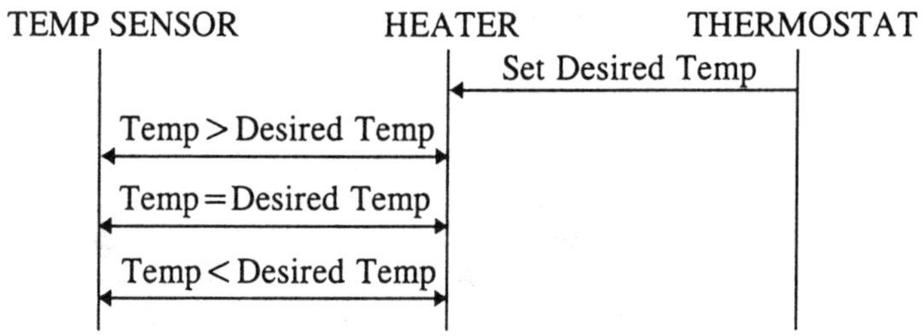

Fig. 3 Event-trace diagram for HEATER active object between its related active objects TEMP SENSOR and THERMOSTAT

Step 3 Identify all the valid "pre.state - event - post.state" behaviour within a class and build a state diagram for each object class to abstract the object behaviour.

Question 3: What are the valid state(s) of each object class? (e.g. Heater Object, ask object class one at a time)

Answer: On or Off, 2 state values only.

Question 4: What is the typical changing sequence for each active object? (e.g. Heater Object, ask one object class at a time)

Answer: On->Off->On subject to individual allowable event that stimuli the object state.

The attribute values and links held by an object are its "state" while an individual stimulus from one object to another is an "event". The pattern of states, events and state transitions, that is, the dynamic behaviour for a given class can then be abstracted as a State diagram. The captured states can then be described in Fig. 4.

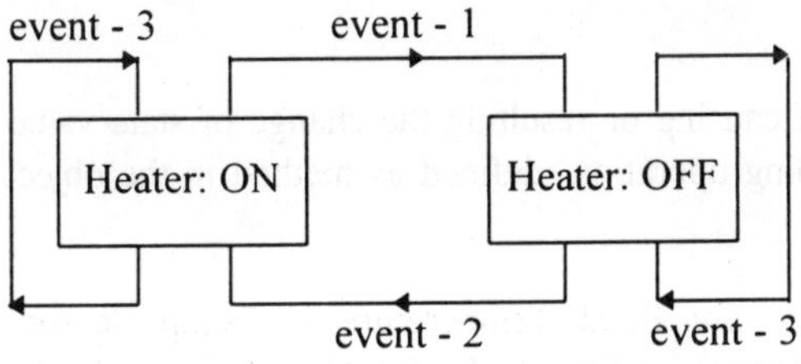

Fig. 4 A State Diagram of a Heater Object

4.2 The Heuristic Rule Set driven the reasoning path

Knowledge engineering involves much more than just translating the unstructured knowledge from human experts'terms to machine readable form. Its outmost important involvement is to recognize what knowledge is being used to solve a problem, categorizing this knowledge and deciding the optimised representation method[16]. The following is the set of heuristic rules draw upon the knowledge and experience of OMT dynamic model construction. This specific problem-solving knowledge are represented as rule-base within the knowledge-base of the system.

R1 : If there is State variable defined in an Object Class, then it is an Active Object.

R2 : If it is an Active Object, then there is one or more Operation(s) or Event(s) which caused reaction of itself AND changes its State value at each reaction.

R3 : If there is a change in State Value of an Active Object, then the Operation or Event that cause this change is encapsulated by packaging Method with data structure within the Object.

R4 : If the Operations or Events of an Active Object are all identified and defined as Methods within itself, then the behaviour of the Active Object over its lifetime is discovered.

R5 : If the each Operation or Event are defined with its per- condition State Value and its post-condition State value, then the sequence of the Object behaviour pattern could be discovered.

R6 : For each state diagram in the dynamic model, there is a corresponding state attribute definition in each Active Object Class in object model.

For example : Heater status in Heater, Temperature-reading in Temp Sensor and Required Temperature in Thermostat.

R 7 : For each event causing or resulting the change of state value of an object class, there is a corresponding operation defined as method in the object class in the object model.

For example : There are Read Temperature in Temp Sensor and Set Required Temperature in Thermostat, except no Switch On/Off Event in Heater Object. Hence, recover the hidden corresponding operational event in the related active object class and refine the complete object model as in Fig. 5.

With the previously described interactive dialogue supported by the above heuristic rule set, we could elicit the hidden dynamic semantic and ensure that only allowable operation(s) or event(s) are encapsulated in its corresponding object class, which will conclude the Object model is of consistent with the Dynamic model. As refer to the following Fig. 6 and compare it with the Object model in Fig. 2, we could see that more dynamic semantics are recovered through building the Dynamic model. Heater ON/OFF behaviours are identified through the interactive dialogue in elicitation process.

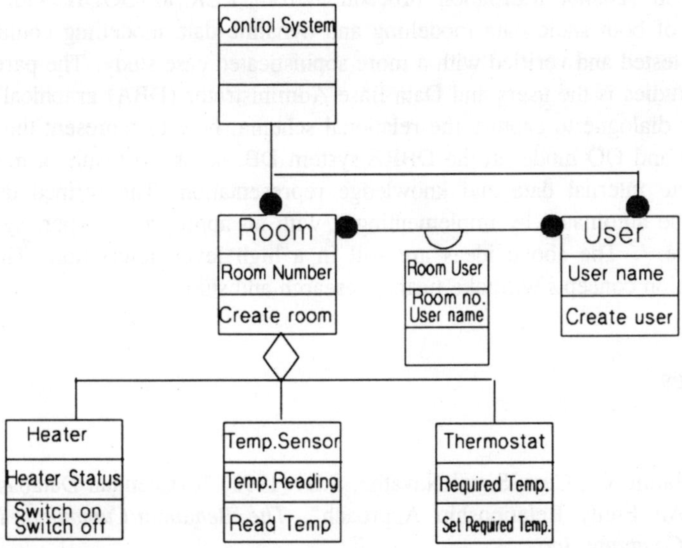

Fig. 5. Final OMT Object Model with more dynamic semantics

5 Conclusion and Suggestions for Future Enhancement

This paper proposes a knowledge-based framework to re-engineer a complete dynamic semantics represented in relational schema to OODB schema and ultimately form a complete OO model. A schema translation procedure with steps and mapping rules that consider the vital features (such as Entity as class, relationship as attributes, Cardinality of as object link/association, Weak entity as method, ternary relationship as multiple objects linkage) of the EER

models and the fundamental data abstraction concepts (eg multiple Inheritance as INHERIT mechanism, overlapping and disjoint Generalisation as CONSTRAINT mechanism, Categorisation, Aggregation and Association as METHOD) of OO data models are covered in author's previous published paper [kwa95]. In this paper, an exploring effort is made to recapture the control information and extra dynamic semantic that is not represented in original EER model. The elicited dynamic semantics are represented as state diagrams, event-trace diagrams in OMT Dynamic model. These have been explored with more formal approach to encapsulate the set of transformation knowledge into rule-base and predicate logic. This could set a feasible target to extend the existing CASE tools functionality to re-engineered RDB to OODB design.

The proposed schema translation procedure from EER to OODB with capturing capabilities of both static data modelling and dynamic data modelling could be semi-automated, tested and verified with a more sophisticated case study. The part that need to further studies is the users and Data Base Administrator (DBA) graphical interface, system/user dialogue to capture the relational schema, how to represent the translated EER model and OO model in the DBRE system DB, so as to result a more formal and complete internal data and knowledge representation. The refined design idea could then be automated by implementing it with an appropriate Expert system shell and software. The above ideas are still in a high level description. The detailed implementation concepts will take further research and study.

References

[BAT92] Batini, C., Ceri, S and Navathe, S.B. (1992) "Conceptual Database Design: An Entity Relationship Approach". *The Benjamin/Cummings Publishing Company, Inc.*

[BAT93] Battista, G.D. and Lenzerini, M., "Deductive Entity Relationship Modelling", *IEEE Transaction on Knowledge and Data Engineering*, 5(3), pp439-450, 1993.

[ELM89] Elmasri, R. and Navathe, S. "Fundamentals of Database Systems", *Benjamin/Cummings,* 1989.

[FON93] Fong J., Ho M. "Knowledge-Based Approach For Abstracting Hierarchical and Network Schema Semantics", *Proceedings of the 12th International Conference on Entity-Relationship Approach*, 1993, pp498-509.

[FON94] Fong J., Kwan I. "A Re-engineering Approach for Object-Oriented Database Design" *Proceedings of First IFIP/SQI International Conference on Software Quality and Productivity*, published by Chapman and Hall, 1994, pp139-147.

[GET93] Getta J. "Translation of Extended Entity-Relationship Database Model into Object-oriented Database",*Interoperable Database Systems(DS-5)'*, 1993, pp87-100.

[GON93] A Gonzalez, D. Dankel "The Engineering of Knowledge-Based Systems", *Prentice Hall International Editions* 1993.

[GOR93] Gorman, K. and Choobineh, J., "The Object-Oriented Entity-Relationship Model (OOERM)", *Journal of Management Information Systems*, 7(3), pp41-65.

[HEV89] A.R. Hevner, R. Linger (1989) " Method For Data Re-engineering in Structured Programs" *Proceedings of 22nd Annual Hawaii Int'l Conference on System Sciences,* 1989

[HUG91] Hughes J. "Object-Oriented Databases", *Prentice Hall*, 1991, pp102-106.

[KAP88] Kappel, G. and Schrefl, M., "A Behaviour Integrated Entity-Relationship Approach for the Design of Object-Oriented Databases", *Proceedings of 7th International Conference on Entity-Relationship Approach*, pp311-328, 1988.

[KWA95] I.Kwan, J. Fong & Q.Li "A Methodology for Reengineering Relational to Object-Oriented Database Systems Via an Extended E-R Model" *Proceeding of 6th International Conference of Database and Expert Systems Applications DEXA95*, 1995, pp152-161.

[Nar93] Narasimhan B., Navathe S., Jayaraman S. "On Mapping ER and Relational into OO Schemas" *Proceedings of the 12th International Conference on Entity-Relationship Approach*, 1993, pp397-692.

[PUT90] Put, F., "Schema Translation during Design and Integration of Databases" *Proceedings of 9th International Conference on Entity-Relationship Approach,* pp399-421.

[RUM91] Rumbaugh J. et al. "Object-Oriented Modelling and Design", *Prentice Hall*, 1991, pp183-185.

[SMI77] Smith, J. and Smith, D. (197 7) "Database Abstraction: Aggregation and Generalization", *ACM Transactions on Database Systems,* Vol 2, No 2, June, 1977, p105-133.

Multiple Granularity Locks for the KBMS Environment

Fernando de Ferreira Rezende and Theo Härder
Department of Computer Science
University of Kaiserslautern
P.O.Box 3049 - 67653 Kaiserslautern - Germany
Phone: ++49 (0631) 205 3274/4031
Fax: ++49 (0631) 205 3558
E-Mail: {rezende/haerder}@informatik.uni-kl.de

Abstract. As ever-larger knowledge bases (KBs) are being built, knowledge sharing becomes an aspect of paramount importance in Knowledge Base Management Systems (KBMSs). In this paper, we propose a way of controlling knowledge sharing by means of the LARS (**L**ocks using **A**bstraction **R**elationships' **S**emantics) approach for concurrency control in KBs. LARS synchronizes transactions through many different granules of locking, which are based on the semantics of the abstraction relationships commonly used in knowledge representation approaches. LARS supports a higher degree of potential concurrency in that it maintains different logical partitions of a KB graph, a means for representing KBs, and offers many lock types to be used on the basis of each one of the partitions. By such a way, LARS captures more of the semantics contained in a KB, through an interpretation of the (abstraction) relationships between objects, profits from such semantics for synchronizing the transactions, and thus makes feasible the exploitation of the inherent parallelism in a knowledge representation approach.

Keywords: concurrency control, knowledge bases, object-oriented databases.

1 Introduction

We begin this paper with the question: What exactly is a knowledge base? There is a lot of discussion on the meaning of *knowledge* or a *knowledge base*. Similarly, a variety of definitions of a knowledge base may be found in the literature. We present here a specific definition, widely accepted in the knowledge representation community, by Levesque and Brachman [LEV85]:

> *"A knowledge base has explicit structures representing the knowledge of the system which determine the actions of the system. It is not the use of a certain programming language or a data-structuring facility that makes a system knowledge-based."*

This definition views a knowledge base as a system with explicit structures representing the knowledge, and that is exactly the most important characteristic of such a system for our purposes. Any data model which explicitly represents the knowledge and, therefore, explicitly encodes the knowledge and the semantic structure of an application domain may use the results we present in this paper. We will see in a later section how our protocol visualizes such systems (as single-rooted, directed, and acyclic graphs). In other words, our approach for concurrency control

(CC) is general and applicable to a broad class of applications (e.g., object-oriented), and not only to knowledge-based systems.

In this paper, we present our approach for CC in KBs, an important research direction as ever-larger KBs are being built and the applicability of KBMSs grows [MYL90]. The main objective we have in mind is the provision of serializability for ACID transactions. With serializability we mean that our technique is governed by the *Serializability Theory* of Gray et al. [GRA76], which states that if an execution produces the same output and has the same effect on the database (DB) as some serial execution of the same transactions, it is correct, because serial executions are assumed to be correct. With ACID transactions we mean that the transactions running in our system have the properties of conventional ones, the ACID (atomicity, consistency, isolation, and durability) properties pointed out by Härder and Reuter [HÄR83]. In other words, our protocol neither treats the operations' semantics in order to allow non-serializable schedules to be produced, nor copes it with long-duration transactions (in fact, the transactions may span minutes and even hours, but are not anticipated in terms of days or months).

Among the most important classes of CC algorithms are *locking*, *timestamps*, and *serialization graphs* [BER87]. There is also a great body of variations of these classes based on multiple versions, multi-level, optimistic methods, etc. In particular, the class of locking-based algorithms has shown its practicality and performance. Additionally, locking-based algorithms have special solutions for graph structures, the abstractions for KBs that appear to be the most appealing [CHA92, MYL94]. Consequently, we have chosen to develop our CC technique for KBs based on locking. In particular, we consider multiple granules of locking for controlling the concurrent accesses in a KB. Granular locks are known to be meaningful, because they provide transactions the possibility of choosing, among different locking granules, the most appropriate one to accomplish their tasks. In addition, the use of implicit locks significantly minimizes the number of locks to be set by transactions. These are some of the reasons which lead us to hope to be able to use the power and elegance of granular locks also in KBs.

An initial version of the LARS protocol has been published in [REZ94]. In this paper, we present the evolution of our investigations on CC in KBs since [REZ94], which are here condensed in this much more robust version of LARS. Differently from [REZ94], here we have cut two lock modes (the conventional lock modes in the terminology of that paper), we analyze the representation of edges in KB graphs, we make some comments on inference engines, we analyze the problems of considering the semantics of methods for CC purposes, we expose in more details the problems of granular locks in a semantically rich structure like KB graphs, and we discuss in much more details the issues of insert and delete operations. This paper is organized as follows. After providing some particular KBMSs' issues (Sect. 2), we present an overview of granular locks and point out the main problems of its pure appliance in the KBMS environment (Sect. 3). Then, we introduce our approach for transaction synchronization in KBMSs (Sect. 4). Thereafter, we discuss related work (Sect. 5), and finally conclude the paper (Sect. 6).

2 Particular KBMSs' Issues

2.1 Abstraction Relationships

KBMSs manage complex and structured objects, and also different types of abstraction relationships. In fact, abstractions turned out to be fundamental tools for knowledge organization, and one of the most important aspects of KBMSs is that objects can play different roles at the same time [MAT88]. Consequently, the KBs' features can be visualized as a superposition of the abstraction hierarchies (in fact Directed Acyclic Graphs (DAGs)) of generalization, classification, association, and aggregation, building altogether the so-called *KB graph*. It is beyond the scope of this paper to begin a detailed discussion about the abstraction concepts, the reader is referred to [MAT88, MAT89] for more details on this topic. In order to illustrate one such a KB graph, in Fig. 1 we provide an example of a KB to support architects in the design of houses. Notice that the purpose of this scenario is merely to illustrate our solution for knowledge sharing, rather than schema design issues. This application scenario will serve as a running example for the rest of the paper .

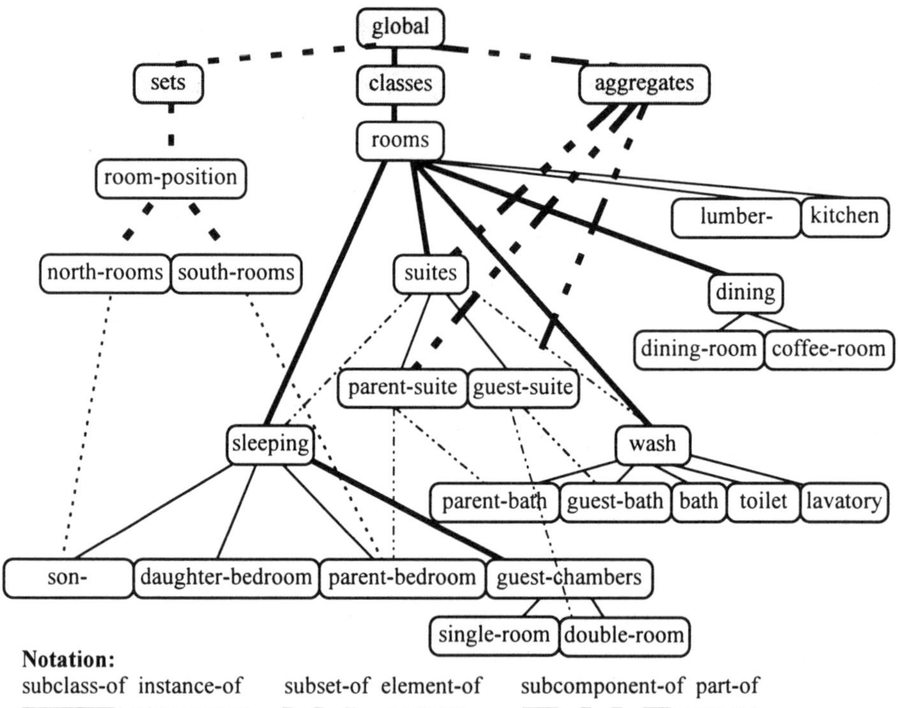

Fig. 1. An architecture knowledge base.

In order to restrict the KB to a rooted and connected graph, we have added the objects *global*, the only root of the whole graph, *sets*, the root of the association graph, *classes*, the root of the classification/generalization graph, and finally *aggregates*, the root of the aggregation graph. We provide such objects in order to have an adequate environment for the appliance of LARS. In addition, we assume that all objects (or schemas) are directly or indirectly related to *global*. When a schema is neither a class/instance, nor a set/element, nor a component/part, it is connected as a direct instance of *global*. In turn, all classes/instances, sets/elements, and components/parts are directly or indirectly related to the predefined schemas *classes*, *sets*, and *aggregates*, respectively. Moreover, we assume that the KB graph automatically stays in this form (rooted and connected) as changes undergo over time[1].

2.2 The Representation of Edges in KB Graphs

A point deserving a bit discussion is the representation of the edges in KB graphs. The edges in KBs may be represented either in a unidirectional way (one link, top-down) or in a bi-directional way (two links, top-down and bottom-up), depending on the implementation characteristics of a particular system. Representing the edges by unidirectional links has the clear advantage of less maintenance overhead, since maintaining one link up-to-date is less expensive than two links, of course. However, with a unidirectional representation of edges many significant queries may not be answered (at least at the same costs when bi-directional links are provided). Furthermore, questions involving the inheritance of attributes may be made much more difficult. To be more precise, we provide some examples (using the KB of Fig. 1) of such queries using a concrete knowledge base language, namely KOALA (KRISYS Object-Abstraction LAnguage) [DES90, MAT89]. Let us analyze the following KOALA query:

```
(ASK (?x  inherited-slots
          (supers guest-chambers   dining))
     (is-instance  ?x  rooms *))
```

This query retrieves all (*) the instances of the class *rooms* and shows their attributes inherited from the classes *guest-chambers* and *dining*. The first part of this query is a projection clause, which limits the results' presentation just to the attributes inherited (inherited-slots) from the classes *guest-chambers* and *dining*. The second part is a selection clause, which transitively retrieves the instances (?x) of the class *rooms*. In order to evaluate this query, first of all KOALA instantiates the class *rooms* (using the top-down links), retrieving all its instances. Secondly, KOALA goes from the instantiated objects to the classes *guest-chambers* and *dining* (using the bottom-up links), learns their structures, and by this way performs the projection. This is a common query, which may be evaluated very efficiently if bi-directional links are present. In the following, we provide a query now using both the classification and aggregation graphs:

```
(ASK (?x    ?y)
     (and  (is-instance     ?x rooms *)
           (is-instance     ?y suites *)
           (is-aggregation  ?x ?y    *)))
```

1. This representation and behavior are very similar to the ones used by KRISYS [MAT89] to represent KBs.

In simple words, this query retrieves all (*) the instances of *rooms* which take part in any *suites*. To evaluate this query, KOALA retrieves the instances of *rooms* (?x), then the instances of *suites* (?y), and thereafter it goes from the instances of *rooms* to the instances of *suites* via the aggregation relationships (bottom-up). This is also a very common query which may be evaluated efficiently by means of bi-directional links. In fact, whenever one wants to know which instances of a class take part in some aggregate, one uses the bottom-up links for finding the aggregates. Similar arguments may be used to justify bi-directional links in the association graph (for example, to efficiently answer simple queries like: Which instances of a class take part in some set?).

Therefore, bi-directional links may not be considered performance 'bottlenecks' in KBMSs, because the costs for maintaining them up-to-date are paid off when evaluating the queries much more efficiently. Smalltalk represents the edges for the abstraction concepts it provides by means of bi-directional links [GOL89]. C++ standard is being expanded to support bi-directional links, and in the next standard they are going to be available [HAR94, HÜS94]. KRISYS also supports bi-directional links [MAT89]. These are just some examples. Due to that, we assume that the edges in a KB graph are bi-directionally represented. Like the KBMSs' query evaluation components, we use the power of bi-directional links also in LARS. However, it is convenient to notice here that such bi-directional links are used in LARS just in the representation of the abstraction concepts, and **not** in the access paths (indices like B*-trees). This will become clear in the later sections.

2.3 Inference

In Artificial Intelligence, *inference* refers to the various processes by means of which programs (the so-called *inference engines*) drawn conclusions or generate new knowledge from facts and suppositions. There are several alternatives to knowledge representation aimed at performing inference, such as production rules, (full) first-order logic, Horn clauses, etc. In this section, we briefly discuss this topic and analyze the access and further lock requirements imposed by inference engines.

Production rules represent general knowledge about the problem domain, and can be used to represent a variety of different types of inference. Each rule is a simple program with the format [DAV77]:

(**IF** <condition>
THEN <action>)

where the condition is typically a conjunction of predicates, and the action activates other procedures which potentially change the KB state. A very important aspect of the inference process is the kind of control or guidance that is available to direct the process to the desired conclusion [HEU87]. Mechanisms used to identify applicable rules are denoted inference strategies [PUP86]. Among these, data-driven (or forward reasoning) and goal-driven (or backward reasoning) are the most common. In turn, the mechanisms used to determine the rule to be executed are called conflict resolution strategies (usually further divided into search strategies and conflict solving strategies).

Additionally to rules, first-order logic can also be used to represent procedural knowledge for the application domain. However, a major problem with general first-order logic for knowledge representation is the difficulty in expressing control structures that efficiently guide the use of a large KB [VAS85]. In order to reduce such problems, at the costs of also reducing the representation power, practical tools (e.g. Prolog) do not use full first-order logic, but only a subset known as definite (Horn) clauses. Horn clauses are interpreted in a procedural way reminiscent of the backward reasoning of production rules, leading to efficient search processes [FRO86].

All in all, the backward or forward reasoning mechanisms are processed following an object(or record)-oriented approach, and the paths that they use are the commonly available ones (indices, hash tables, abstraction graphs, etc.). Anyway, the search and/or (subsequently) update processes triggered by either production rules or Horn clauses may be mapped to the usual operators (like selection, projection, join, semi-join, etc.) supported by most data manipulation and knowledge languages. Therefore, the process of locking the objects that need to be accessed whenever the inference engine activates such production rules and/or Horn clauses does not generate any new problem to a CC mechanism operating in KBMSs where inference is supported.

2.4 Methods

Methods are used in KBMSs in order to describe the operational aspects of objects' attributes, i.e., they characterize the behavior of the real world entity. In the last few years, there have been considerable efforts in order to approach the limits of concurrency by exploiting the semantics of objects and their operations when synchronizing transactions. For example, a set object may allow simultaneous inserts, because the semantics of a set implies that the order in which concurrent inserts are performed does not matter, i.e., it makes no difference in the results of these operations, even though inserts would be classified as writes in a read-write scheme and therefore could not occur concurrently. The main idea behind the use of operations' semantics for transaction synchronization is to break the serializability of transactions, allowing non-serializable schedules to be produced, as long as they preserve the consistency and are acceptable to the system users.

Such an approach may be meaningful, since in some applications users may be satisfied with a schedule that preserves consistency, even though it is not serializable. It is well-known that allowing the transaction processing mechanism to run these schedules may result in higher parallelism and better performance in some cases [GAR83, CAS80, ESW76, KUN79, FIS82, GRA81, LYN83]. However, there is one drawback, among the main important ones, of such an approach [GAR83]: It is difficult for a general transaction processing mechanism to decide what schedules are semantically consistent. Although Badrinath and Ramamrithan [BAD88, BAD87] in their approach hold the opinion that the designer of an object type needs only to specify the semantics of operations, and their compatibilities ought to be (dynamically) determined from these specifications when the operations are requested to be executed on an object, it is more widely accepted that such a transaction processing mechanism must receive some help from the users of the system. The user (or objects designer) must provide a table indicating which operations conflict (cannot be executed concurrently). Hence, every time an object is created, besides describing the operations (or in the KB terminology, the methods) to be available for manipulating the object, the user must define a compatibility matrix for those operations (generally based on the commutativity of the operations). Such a 'commutativity matrix' is then used by the scheduler to synchronize the transactions executing those operations on the object.

In LARS, we do not exploit the semantics of methods to allow for non-serializable schedules due to several reasons. In the following, we discuss some of these reasons:

- One important question arising with such a methodology gives respect to schema evolution (or extensibility). That is, KBMSs and object-oriented database management systems (OODBMSs) allow the objects' definitions to be dynamically modified (concurrently) with the accesses to the objects defined by them. For example, a class can be modified by replacing an old method implementation by a new and perhaps more efficient one. Methods or even attributes may be added or deleted from a class. All of that has some impact on the use of methods' semantics for CC. Unfortunately, it is not yet so clear in such methodologies in how far schema evolution will be affected. It may become very hard to users, if every time one changes or inserts or deletes a method, one must analyze the semantics of all other methods of the object, in order to adjust the object's commutativity matrix. This is a drawback which may seriously confuse the extensibility property of such systems. In summary, the cost of serializable schedules may be unacceptably high in some applications, but it is really not a good idea to burden users with the classification and analysis of methods in order to define their commutativities.
- Another point worth of discussion is recovery. If commutative operations are allowed to be simultaneously performed on an object, a conventional (e.g., page-oriented) recovery mechanism does not work correctly. In such cases, logical logging must be performed and compensating transactions (or countersteps) must be provided. In turn, it could be very difficult in some cases to analyze transactions in order to write countersteps for their operations. The proper notion of commutativity depends upon the implementation and representation of the objects and all of that has impact on recovery. In particular, Weihl [WEI89] has shown that when operations on an object are executed by using the *update-in-place* policy [HÄR83] for recovery then the conflict (commutativity) relation must be derived from what he called *right backward commutativity*. On the other hand, if operations are executed with the *deferred-update* approach then the conflict relation is derived from *forward commutativity*. In general, the more semantics one uses in synchronization to improve concurrency, the more complex become the synchronization and, as a consequence, the recovery mechanisms.

- Most of the approaches for commutativity-based CC assume that each object provides operations that can be called by transactions to examine and modify the object's state, and additionally that these operations constitute the sole means by which transactions can access the state of the objects (among others, examples are [WEI88, BAD88, FAR89, GAR83, SCH84, RAK90, CHR91, HAD91]). However, we believe that in a real-life environment, some transactions may want to bypass the encapsulation of an object and rather access the object directly through a generic knowledge or data manipulation language. Therefore, the scheduler should in fact deal with the coexistence of methods and generic transactions that access objects directly. This may even more complicate the synchronization of transactions in such methodologies. Muth et al. [MUT93] present conceivable reasons for bypassing the encapsulation of an object and propose a protocol addressing this issue.

Finally, the most critical question is whether performance will really improve or not with the use of operations' semantics for transaction synchronization. Of course, in special applications performance may be definitively improved. However, there are applications where semantically consistent schedules may not be acceptable, because certain *anomalies* or *race conditions* [CAS80] may occur. As stated by Garcia-Molina [GAR83], it may be impossible to obtain the results of a semantically consistent schedule with any serializable schedule, and this may be undesirable to some users (refer to [GAR83] for some examples). In general, it is not yet known how practical these methodologies will be. Since the use of operations' semantics did not convince us so far, we designed the LARS protocol where methods compete for locks like any other transaction request. Hence, LARS copes with methods like ordinary read and write operations.

3 The Multigranularity Locking Protocol

Granular locks were first introduced by Gray et al. in [GRA76] by means of the *Multigranularity Locking Protocol* (MGL, for short). The basic idea of MGL comes from the choice of different lockable units, which are locked by the system to ensure consistency and to provide isolation. When choosing the lockable units for implementing this protocol, one will be always faced with the dichotomy: Concurrency versus overhead. On one hand, concurrency is increased by a fine lockable unit (e.g., a record or a field). Such a unit is appropriate for small transactions which access few units [GRA76]. On the other hand, a fine locking granule is costly for complex transactions which access a large number of granules. Such transactions would have to acquire and maintain a large number of locks [GRA93], which implies a larger overhead. Thus, a coarse locking granule (e.g., a file) would be more convenient for such transactions. However, a coarse granule discriminates against transactions which only want to lock a fine granule of the file [GRA76]. The main benefit of MGL is that it satisfies both of these situations, allowing lockable units of different granularities to coexist in the same system. Moreover, MGL created the notion of *implicit locks*, stating that by putting a lock on a granule, all descendants of it become implicitly locked without the necessity of setting further locks. Lastly, MGL introduced the so-called *intention locks* in order to prevent locks on the ancestors of a node which might implicitly lock it in an incompatible mode. Those locks are used to sign the intention of a transaction to set locks at a finer granularity. Thus, MGL has a basic set of locks composed of the IS (Intention Share), IX (Intention eXclusive), S (Share), SIX (Share Intention eXclusive), and X (eXclusive) modes, which are then applied to the nodes in a lock graph (a hierarchy or a DAG) (Fig. 2) [GRA76].

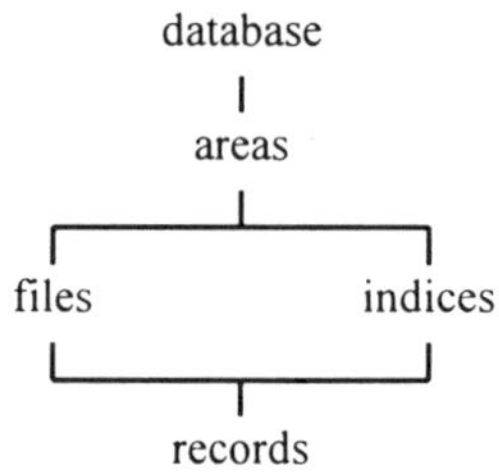

Fig. 2. A lock graph for granular locks.

Notwithstanding, a protocol like MGL is designed for a single organization hierarchy, extended to DAGs in case of index structures. Particularly in the case of DAGs, MGL requires that, before requesting an X mode access to a node, all parents of the node must be covered with IX (or greater) locks [GRA78, GRA76]. Consequently, all superiors of the node cannot be held by other transactions in incompatible modes. In the DAG of Fig. 2, to lock a particular *record* in X mode, one should lock in advance the corresponding *file*, *index*, *area* and *database* in IX mode. One question arises: How may transactions know which are the superiors of a node, in order to cover them with IX locks before requesting an X lock on it? This is possible because the data model, to which MGL may be applied, provides a strict separation between data and meta-data, a separate DB catalog. Hence, transactions may access, e.g., the DB catalog, and learn that (using Fig. 2) a *record* is always contained in a *file* and pointed to by an *index*, in turn a *file* and the respective *index* are contained in an *area*, and at last an *area* is contained in a *database*.

However, in data (knowledge) models provided by KBMSs, the object concept is completely symmetric, such that this separation data/meta-data (like, for example, in the relational model) no longer exists. The superiors of a node (an object in the KB graph) may be arbitrarily chosen, accordingly to the semantics of the application being modeled. More importantly, this information may be dynamically changed as a KB undergoes changes over time. Exemplifying, by means of the classification DAG of Fig. 3, how could a transaction know which are the superiors of any class, say $class_k$? A transaction, obeying MGL, does need such information in order to lock a class in X mode. This information is nowhere to find statically in KBMSs, as in usual DB catalogs in DB systems (DBSs). In addition, how could a transaction be sure that by putting an X lock on a class, no one of its subclasses would be accessed in a conflicting mode by another transaction? Using Fig. 3, a transaction putting an X lock on $class_k$ and IX on all its superiors (. . . , $class_i$, . . .) would have no guarantee that another transaction would not access $class_n$ by similarly putting an X lock on $class_j$ and IX on all its superiors (. . . , $class_i$, . . .). Therefore, transactions obeying MGL may get into troubles with implicitly locked objects, as long as they implicitly lock those objects in conflicting modes via different paths of the graph. As a consequence, the serializability of transactions may become violated.

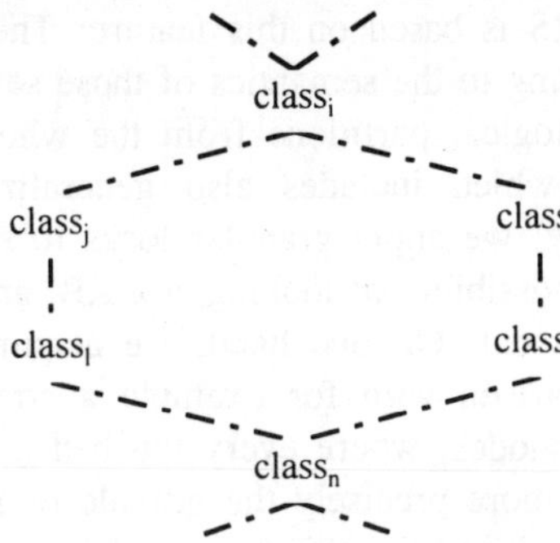

Fig. 3. A classification DAG.

Summarizing, if there would be just *strict* abstraction hierarchies in KBMSs, MGL would be adaptable and could work without problems. However, when *overlapping*, *multi*-abstraction hierarchies are possible, MGL fails due to the implicit locks on objects with multiple direct parents, because those objects might be implicitly locked in incompatible modes by different transactions using different paths along a single kind of hierarchy or different paths using different hierarchies. Finally, the richness of the KB structure makes the synchronization substantially more complicated in KBMSs.

Another problem of directly applying MGL in the KBMS environment is the unprofitable use of the semantically rich structure represented by KB graphs. If we would directly apply MGL to KB graphs, we would not at all be able to interpret their edges, which represent the abstraction relationships between objects (nodes). To put it another way, using MGL, when a shared/exclusive lock on a node is granted to a transaction, all descendants of this node are implicitly locked in the same mode, independently of the relationship the descendants have to the ancestor. A transaction changing an object's class properties puts an X lock on it and IX on its superiors, changes the object itself and all its subclasses and instances (due to the inheritance mechanism). However, if such an object is, at the same time, a set (component), all its subsets (subcomponents) and elements (parts) become also implicitly locked. This needlessly restricts the access to those objects by other transactions. Therefore, with such a behavior, many objects may be locked unnecessarily, because it is not possible to precisely specify which kind of descendants should be implicitly locked, and thus the overall concurrency may be affected negatively.

4 The LARS Protocol

4.1 The Basic Idea

The key feature of KBs is the presence of several semantic relationships. The basic idea which originates LARS is based on this feature: The KBs can be partitioned into several graphs, according to the semantics of those several relationships. Thus, we create three different logical partitions from the whole KB graph. These are called the *classification* (which includes also generalization), *association*, and *aggregation* graphs. Finally, we apply granular locks to each graph. By this way, we provide users with the possibility of looking at a KB, and abstracting from it just the partition to be worked out. On one hand, we acquire a minimization of the number of locks in comparison with for example a conventional approach with shared and exclusive lock modes, where every touched object must be locked. On the other hand, we define more precisely the granule of lock to be accessed by a transaction, allowing it to lock just the objects it really needs to access.

4.2 The Lock Modes

Following these logical partitions, we have created three distinct sets of lock types. Hence, similar to MGL, we have a *basic set* of lock modes, named: IR (Intention Read), IW (Intention Write), R (Read), RIW (Read Intention Write), and W (Write). However, we have this basic set of lock modes to each one of the logical partitions, i.e., to the classification (recognized by a subscript c ($_c$) following the lock mode), association ($_s$), and aggregation ($_a$) graphs. We named those locks as pertaining respectively to the sets of *C_type*, *S_type*, and *A_type locks* (in general, we call them *typed locks*). Table 1 presents, in a compact form, their semantics.

Table 1. Typed locks' semantics.

$IR_{c\|s\|a}$	gives intention shared access to the requested object and allows the requester to explicitly lock both direct **subclasses|subsets|subcomponents** of this object in $R_{c\|s\|a}$ or $IR_{c\|s\|a}$ mode, and direct **instances|elements|parts** in $R_{c\|s\|a}$ mode.
$IW_{c\|s\|a}$	gives intention exclusive access to the requested object and allows the requester to explicitly lock both direct **subclasses|subsets|subcomponents** of this object in $W_{c\|s\|a}$, $RIW_{c\|s\|a}$, $R_{c\|s\|a}$, $IW_{c\|s\|a}$ or $IR_{c\|s\|a}$ mode, and direct **instances|elements|parts** in $W_{c\|s\|a}$ or $R_{c\|s\|a}$ mode.
$R_{c\|s\|a}$	gives shared access to the requested object and implicitly to all direct and indirect **subclasses|subsets|subcomponents** and **instances|elements|parts** of this object.
$RIW_{c\|s\|a}$	gives shared and intention exclusive access to the requested object (i.e., implicitly locks all direct and indirect **subclasses|subsets|subcomponents** and **instances|elements|parts** of this object in shared mode and allows the requester to explicitly lock both direct **subclasses|subsets|subcomponents** in $W_{c\|s\|a}$, $RIW_{c\|s\|a}$, $R_{c\|s\|a}$ or $IW_{c\|s\|a}$ mode, and direct **instances|elements|parts** in $W_{c\|s\|a}$ or $R_{c\|s\|a}$ mode).
$W_{c\|s\|a}$	gives exclusive access to the requested object and implicitly to all direct and indirect **subclasses|subsets|subcomponents** and **instances|elements|parts** of this object.

4.3 The Lock Compatibilities

With respect to the compatibility of the above mentioned lock types, there are two distinct situations to be coped with by LARS. First, if the locks requested and granted give respect to the same set of objects (either C_type vs. C_type, or S_type vs. S_type, or A_type vs. A_type), then the compatibility matrix to be followed is the same of MGL known from the literature [GRA76, GRA78] (Table 2).

Table 2. Compatibility matrix for typed locks of the same type.

Granted Mode [c | s | a] (columns); Requested Mode [c | s | a] (rows)

	IR	IW	R	RIW	W
IR	☺	☺	☺	☺	
IW	☺	☺			
R	☺		☺		
RIW	☺				
W					

The second situation with respect to the compatibility of the typed locks is the one where both are of different types (either C_type vs. {S_type or A_type}, or S_type vs. {C_type or A_type}, or A_type vs. {C_type or S_type}). In this case, the compatibility of the lock modes is not the same as above, because distinct sets of objects are being dealt with. In [REZ94], a detailed discussion on this topic may be found. Here we limit to presenting the compatibility matrix (Table 3) and making some comments. The main point of this compatibility matrix is that conflicting lock modes applied to requests of the same abstraction hierarchy may become compatible when issued for different abstraction hierarchies, e.g., IW_c and W_a. In general, there are no conflicts between locks in different hierarchies if one of them is an intention lock. Only non-intention locks of different hierarchies conflict like ordinary R and W locks. The reason is simply that an intention lock in hierarchy *h* only 'protects' paths along hierarchy *h*. An R or W lock in another hierarchy *g* only implicitly locks objects reachable by hierarchy *g*. In the absence of multiple abstraction relationships to objects, one talks about disjoint sets of objects. Objects belonging to different hierarchies are implemented such that distinct parts of an object implement different hierarchies. Other object data can be accessed independently of the hierarchy that has been used to locate the object. This is the only chance for conflicts, and is covered by R/W and W/W conflicts. Multiple abstraction relationships to objects are discussed in the next section. In Table 3, the boxes marked with darker shadows are where LARS offers more concurrency, all of that due to the consideration given to the semantics of the edges in a KB graph.

Table 3. Compatibility matrix for typed locks of distinct types.

Granted Mode [c | s | a] (columns); Requested Mode [s *or* a | c *or* a | c *or* s] (rows)

	IR	IW	R	RIW	W
IR	☺	☺	☺	☺	☺
IW	☺	☺	☺	☺	☺
R	☺	☺	☺	☺	

RIW	☺	☺	☺	☺	
W	☺	☺			

4.4 Accessing Implicitly Locked Objects

Before passing on to the LARS' locking rules, there is a last important point to be coped with by LARS which deserves a little bit discussion. As a matter of fact, multiple abstraction relations involving an object in a KB may lead to problems with the implicit locks, so that the isolation property of transactions [HÄR83] may be seriously corrupted. Actually, an interference arises whenever an object with two or more parents (from now on called a *bastard*, in order to be differentiated from an object with only one parent, a *purebred*) is implicitly locked by one of them [REZ94]. The implicit lock on a child object is only visible if it is accessed through a specific path of the graph. In order to find out possible conflicts with implicitly locked bastards, all superiors or inferiors of an object may be accessed. For this purpose, all relationships have to be represented in a bi-directional way. In [REZ94], we have discussed many possible alternatives for avoiding conflicts in such situations.

We have chosen for LARS a kind of *lazy evaluation strategy* for lock conflict resolution with implicitly locked bastards. In this approach, a transaction may request and be granted an explicit lock without further proceedings. However, just before effectively accessing an implicitly locked bastard, it must verify whether this object is already locked in a conflicting mode by another transaction or not. If so, it must wait until this lock is released. If not, it sets an explicit lock on this object, signaling that it has accessed it. This lock acts like a tag in the object indicating that it has been already accessed via another parent of it. The key idea there is that a transaction needs to explicitly lock only those bastards which it actually accesses, leaving the others for the concurrent access by other transactions. This strategy may be better comprehended in the next section's example (Fig. 4).

4.5 The Locking Rules

Having presented the general guidelines of LARS, we are finally able to expose its complete rules to be followed by transactions when requesting locks on objects in a KB (see Table 4). Before explaining these rules, it is convenient to notice that transactions are allowed to directly set locks in the root object in any mode, and that LARS always produces *strict executions* [BER87], i.e., it requires the locks of a transaction to be released only at its termination (either commit or abort).

The first rule states that an IR lock (from the C_type, S_type, or A_type) on a non-root object must be preceded by either IR or IW locks (from respectively the C_type, S_type, or A_type) on at least one parent of this object, and so recursively until the root object is reached. The second rule has a similar meaning, but for the IW locks, requiring that they must be preceded by IW or RIW locks on at least one path from that object to the root object. The third rule states, first of all, that an R lock on a non-root object must be covered by IR or IW locks on at least one path from this object to the root object. Thereafter, it requires that a transaction must explicitly lock the bastard descendants[2]. This is implemented by LARS' lazy evaluation strategy thereby avoiding conflicts with implicitly locked objects. The fourth and fifth rules have a similar meaning, but for RIW and W locks, respectively.

Table 4. Locking rules.

1	Before requesting an $IR_{c\|s\|a}$ lock on an object, the requester must cover a path from the object to the root with $IR_{c\|s\|a}$ or $IW_{c\|s\|a}$ locks.
2	Before requesting an $IW_{c\|s\|a}$ lock on an object, the requester must cover a path from the object to the root with $IW_{c\|s\|a}$ or $RIW_{c\|s\|a}$ locks.
3	Before requesting an $R_{c\|s\|a}$ lock on an object, the requester must cover a path from the object to the root with $IR_{c\|s\|a}$ or $IW_{c\|s\|a}$ locks. In addition, before accessing any implicitly locked bastard descendant, the requester must set an $R_{c\|s\|a}$ lock on it.
4	Before requesting an $RIW_{c\|s\|a}$ lock on an object, the requester must cover a path from the object to the root with $IW_{c\|s\|a}$ or $RIW_{c\|s\|a}$ locks. In addition, before accessing any implicitly locked bastard descendant, the requester must set either a) an $R_{c\|s\|a}$ lock on it, if it is a leaf object, or b) an $RIW_{c\|s\|a}$ lock on it, if it is a non-leaf object.
5	Before requesting a $W_{c\|s\|a}$ lock on an object, the requester must cover a path from the object to the root with $IW_{c\|s\|a}$ or $RIW_{c\|s\|a}$ locks. In addition, before accessing any implicitly locked bastard descendant, the requester must set a $W_{c\|s\|a}$ lock on it.

We now provide an example (Fig. 4) using the architecture KB (Fig. 1). Suppose a transaction, say T1, wants to read the object *son-bedroom* as an element of the object *north-rooms*. To do that it must follow rules 1 and 3 for requesting, respectively, IR_s locks on the parents of *son-bedroom*, and an R_s lock on it. On the other side, another transaction, say T2, wants to write the object *sleeping* together with its subclasses and instances. In turn, it must follow rules 2 and 5 for requesting IW_c locks on the ancestors of *sleeping* and a W_c lock on it, respectively. However, when trying to access the objects *parent-bedroom* and *double-room*, T2 realizes that these objects are bastards, and, as stated by rule 5, it requests W_c locks on them, and is granted because they were free. The same may happen for the object *son-bedroom* as long as T2 tries to access it. When trying this, either T2 must wait, if the R_s lock on this object is still held by T1, or it may be granted, if T1 has already terminated.

An important point of explicitly locking bastard descendants, besides guaranteeing serializability, is the slackness of the original requirement of MGL of covering all paths from the node to the root, and as a consequence all ancestors, with intentions before granting an exclusive lock [GRA76]. This is a serious limitation when an object has several ancestors and is likely to be used via many of them. In such situations, it is very inefficient to set intention locks on all the parents [HER89], and as a consequence on all paths to the root, because too many locks are required, and a transaction may end up locking a large portion of the KB for a possibly simple

---

2 There may be situations where a descendant may have two edges pointing to the same ancestor. For example, when an object is at the same time instance and element of the same object. In such situations, the object is considered to be a bastard, no matter whether the parents are the same object.

operation, decreasing seriously the concurrency and increasing the overhead. Therefore, LARS significantly limits the overhead of the whole process of setting write locks, and still provides, to a limited extent, a minimization of the number of locks to be set by transactions, through the use of implicit locks.

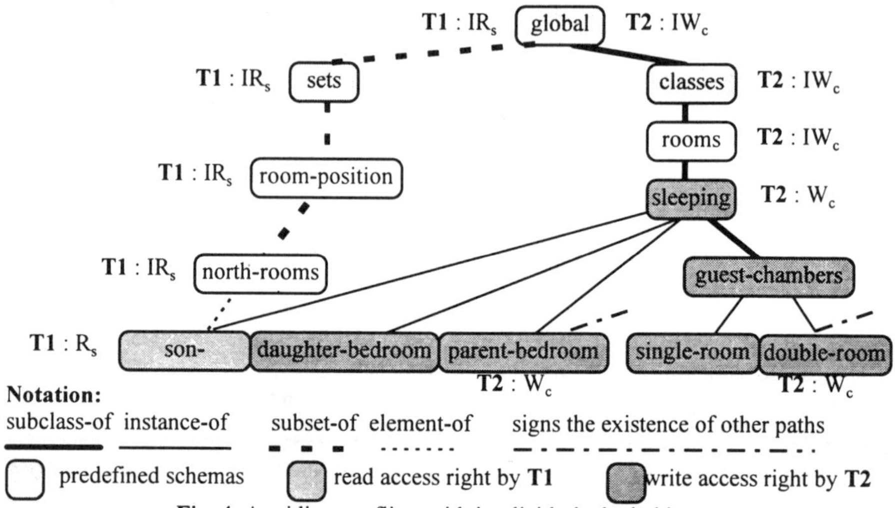

Fig. 4. Avoiding conflicts with implicitly locked objects.

4.6 Coping with Insert and Delete Operations

Thus far, we have considered a KB as a fixed set of objects, which can be accessed by reads and writes. Most real KBs can dynamically grow and shrink. Therefore, in addition to reads and writes, we must support operations to insert new relationships and objects as well as to delete existing relationships and objects. Before passing on to the explanation of the rules, we need to make some considerations in the way these operations are performed. We have assumed (Sect. 2.1) that a KB is represented by a rooted and connected graph and, additionally, that when an object does not participate in the defined abstraction relationships, it is treated as being an instance of the predefined root *global*. Further, we have assumed that the abstraction relationships between the objects are represented in a bi-directional way (Sect. 2.2). All of that has some consequences in the way each one of these insert and delete operations should be performed. In the following, we discuss inserts and deletes in detail. In particular, these operations may be arbitrarily complex, and we are interested in finding out the primitive operations by means of which any other complex operation may be realized as a composition of those. The essence of our idea is: There are four operations - insert node, insert edge, delete node, and delete edge; node operations are always accompanied by one edge operation; to operate on a node, it must be locked, and to operate on an edge, its end points must be locked.

Inserting an Object.

Since the KB graph is connected, the insertion of an object must be handled as an operation composed of two steps: The creation of the object itself and its connection to another existing object[3]. In turn, since two objects are involved in this operation, one could ask: Which is the object being inserted, the superior or the inferior object? The way LARS represents the KB graph (as a single-rooted graph) answers this question. It must be the inferior object, otherwise one would create another root in the graph when inserting an object as a superior. Hence, LARS considers the object being inserted as the inferior. Notice that this is not a restriction, but the establishment of a primitive case. If one states that an object O being inserted must be the superior, LARS can handle it as two operations. First, the insertion of O and its connection to a superior object (at least to the corresponding predefined object, and hence O is handled as an inferior), followed by the connection of O to the inferior object (coped with by the objects' connection rule).

Another important point in the insertion of an object gives respect to the roles of the superior object in the current KB state. We use the architecture KB (Fig. 1) in order to explain this point. Suppose we are designing our KB and that we have not yet defined the parts of the object *parent-suite*. Hence, *parent-suite* currently is just an instance of *suites*, and therefore takes no part in the aggregation graph. When inserting any part of *parent-suite*, one should acquire a lock of the A_type on it, since the aggregation concept is being applied. However, it is impossible to acquire an A_type lock on *parent-suite*, because it is not yet in the aggregation graph, and therefore one cannot navigate from the predefined object *aggregates* to it. Nevertheless, since the aggregation graph is rooted at *aggregates*, this operation must be accompanied by the connection of *parent-suite* to *aggregates* anyway. Hence, LARS treats such cases as first of all the connection of the superior object to the corresponding graph, followed by the insertion of the inferior object. In our example, LARS would connect *parent-suite* to *aggregates*, and thereafter insert any part of it. By this way, we have that the superior object is already connected to the corresponding graph when an inferior of it is being inserted. Particularly, we need this to synchronize the type of the locks to be requested in both objects.

At last, another important aspect is how many relationships (connections) are specified in the insertion of an object. For example, one can state that the object being inserted is an instance of a class and an element of a set (like *son-bedroom* in our architecture KB). In such a case, LARS decomposes such an operation and handles it as an insertion followed by as many connections as necessary (and so handled by the objects' connection rule). Hence, by the insertion of an object we are connecting it to a single superior object.

Finally, rule 6 in Table 5 presents the lock requests necessary to insert an object. It states that before inserting an object, its parent (the superior object) must be held in at least IW mode (and so recursively until the root object is reached). The type of such an IW mode is dictated by the abstraction relationship being inserted. Fig. 5 provides an example of the appliance of this rule. Suppose transaction T1 wants to insert the object *maid-bedroom* as an instance of *sleeping*. To accomplish this task,

[3] At least the predefined objects (*global*, *classes*, *sets*, and *aggregates*) will always be present in the KB graph.

T1 must request an IW_c lock on *sleeping*, the parent of *maid-bedroom*. In turn, this IW_c lock must be covered by IW_c locks on the parents of *sleeping* until the root *global*. Just after holding those locks, T1 is then able to insert the object *maid-bedroom*. As soon as *maid-bedroom* is inserted, T1 is granted a W_c lock on this object, and holds it until it terminates.

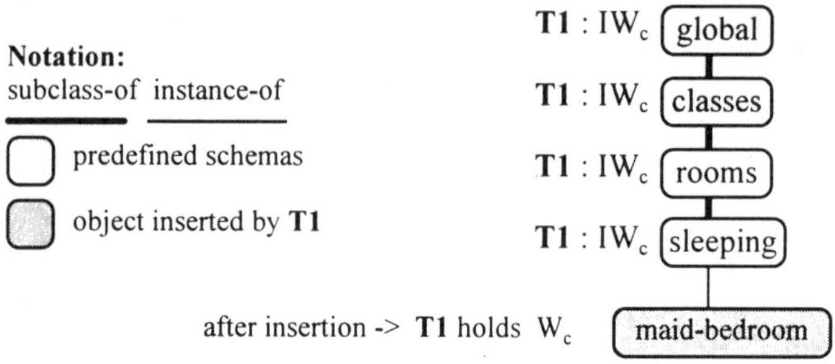

Fig. 5. Locks for the insertion of an object.

Deleting an Object.

We will profit from the above discussions about the insertion of an object and summarize our considerations about deleting an object. There may be several steps involved in this operation (the deletion of the object itself and several disconnections, depending on the current KB state). The primitive case comprehends the deletion of an inferior object and its disconnection from a superior object. Like above, the other more complex cases may be built upon this simple case, so that they may be composed of this primitive case and as many disconnections as necessary (thus handled by the objects' disconnection rule). Rule 7 in Table 5 deals with deletion of objects, similarly to insertions, with the extra requirement that the object itself (the inferior) must be held in W mode. Notice that such a W lock implies IW locks on a parent, on a parent of the parent, and so forth until the root is reached. Finally, the type of such W and IW locks is dictated by the abstraction relationship in question.

Connecting Objects.

Like before, also here two objects are affected by this operation, namely a superior and an inferior object, and the current state of both objects with respect to other objects in the KB may be arbitrary. The main difference here is that the inferior object may be either a bastard or a purebred. Rule 8 in Table 5 copes with the connection of objects. It states that in order to connect objects, the inferior object must be held in *any* W mode, and the superior object in at least IW mode (this one according to the abstraction relationship being applied). In Fig. 6, which complements the last example (Fig. 5), it becomes clear why any exclusive typed lock may be requested in this case, independently of the type. Suppose that T1 wants to connect the recently created object *maid-bedroom* as an element of *north-rooms*. Following rule 8, T1 must request a W lock on this object, normally a W_s lock, since it is applying the association concept. However, this object is not an element of any other object yet, what makes impossible the acquirement of a W_s lock on it (before the connection, there is no path from *sets* to it). Since *maid-bedroom* is an instance of *sleeping*, T1 requires a W_c lock on this object, and is granted because it in fact already holds such a lock due to the proceedings of the last example (if this were not the case, it should cover a path to the root with IW locks). Thereafter, T1 must require an IW_s lock on *north-rooms*, the new parent of it. In turn, this intention lock requires intention on the parents, recursively. Finally, after holding all the required locks, T1 connects the objects. Therefore, in the particular case of connecting objects, a transaction is allowed to acquire a W lock of any type in the inferior object. In general, such a W lock will in fact be of the C_type (W_c), because normally an object first receives its structure (type) by means of the inheritance mechanism of the classification concept, and thereafter it is connected to other objects using the association or aggregation concepts. As can be seen, the connection of objects is a bit more complicated operation, because the transaction does not know a priori which are the roles of both objects in the current KB state.

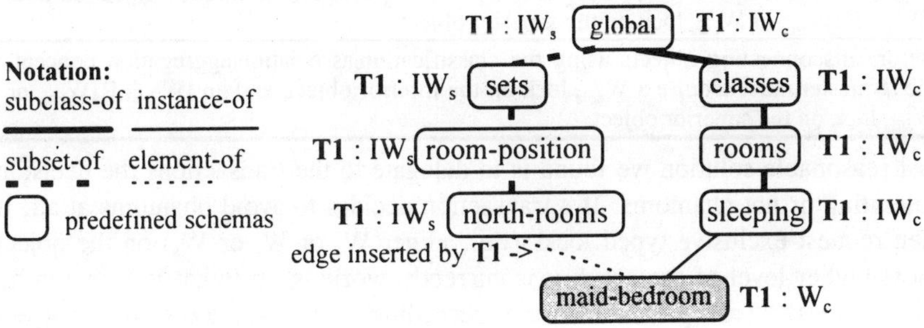

Fig. 6. Locks for the connection of objects.

Disconnecting Objects.

Profiting from all discussions so far, we shortly present the disconnection of objects. We shall only mention that we do not allow the disconnection of purebred objects, because if we disconnect a purebred (deleting its only edge, then), we are either disconnecting the KB graph or creating a new root of it. Hence, in the disconnection of a purebred, the transaction must choose between either deleting the object (and thus handled by the object's deletion rule), or connecting it firstly to another superior object (and hence handled by the objects' connection rule). Therefore, when disconnecting objects, the inferior object must always be a bastard object. Rule 9 in Table 5 presents the objects' disconnection rule. It is a simple case because the transaction does know the current roles of both objects, and by this way the path it must traverse for requesting locks. It must request a W lock on the inferior object, an IW lock on the superior, accordingly to the abstraction concept in question, and thus recursively cover a path to the root with IW locks.

4.7 The Phantom Problem

As stated by Bernstein et al. [BER87], the *phantom problem* is the CC problem for dynamic DBs. Granular locks provide physical locks, and being so we have problems with the so-called phantoms in LARS. Phantoms are characterized by inserted or deleted objects which may seem to appear or disappear to some concurrent transactions like a ghost. The phantom problem was first introduced by Eswaran et al. in [ESW76], which also proposed the *predicate locks* for elegantly coping with such situations. Since predicates do not seem applicable in an efficient way in the given KB structures [REZ95], we must deal with phantoms in some other manner.

Table 5. Locking rules for insert and delete operations.

6	Before inserting an object in the classification|association|aggregation graph, the requester must acquire an $IW_{c\|s\|a}$, $RIW_{c\|s\|a}$ or $W_{c\|s\|a}$ lock on the superior object. After the insertion, the requester is granted a $W_{c\|s\|a}$ lock on the object.
7	Before deleting an object from the classification|association|aggregation graph, the requester must acquire a $W_{c\|s\|a}$ lock on it, and an $IW_{c\|s\|a}$, $RIW_{c\|s\|a}$ or $W_{c\|s\|a}$ lock on the superior object.
8	Before connecting objects using the classification|association|aggregation concept, the requester must acquire either a W_c or a W_s or a W_a lock on the inferior object, and an $IW_{c\|s\|a}$, $RIW_{c\|s\|a}$ or $W_{c\|s\|a}$ lock on the superior object.
9	Before disconnecting objects using the classification|association|aggregation concept, the requester must acquire a $W_{c\|s\|a}$ lock on the inferior object, and an $IW_{c\|s\|a}$, $RIW_{c\|s\|a}$ or $W_{c\|s\|a}$ lock on the superior object.

The most reasonable solution we found is to delegate to the transactions the decision about tolerating or not phantoms. If a transaction decides to avoid phantoms at all, it must then request exclusive typed locks (i.e., either W_c or W_s or W_a) on the object in the next higher level of the graph it is currently working on (what is foreseen by the locking rules). Taking this measure accordingly, no phantoms may happen because other transactions are unable to access any inferior of such an object, or to create a new inferior, or to delete an existing inferior (all of that with respect to the working graph, of course). Exemplifying, if a transaction wants to read all instances of some class, it must request an R_c lock on the class (and **not** an IR_c lock on it and start locking its instances in R_c mode). Thereafter, any other transaction may neither create a new instance of this class, nor delete an existing one, due to the R_c lock hold by the reading transaction on it, and hence no phantom appears.

5 Related Work

As far as we know, the only other work addressing transaction synchronization in KBMSs is Chaudhri's Dynamic Directed Graph (DDG) policy presented in [CHA92, CHA94, CHA94a]. It is an extension of the locking protocol for hierarchical DBSs of Silberschatz and Kedem [SIL80]. Whereas the former is able to cope with cycles and updates in the underlying structure, this is not considered by the latter. The main distinction between LARS and DDG is that they address different problems. When transactions access a large number of objects there are two potential problems. The first problem is that the large number of locks held by a transaction can mean high locking overhead which can be potentially reduced by locking several objects at once (i.e., by using coarse granules of locking). The second problem, which is a consequence of using two-phase locking, is that the locks may be held for a long period of time, thus limiting the concurrency. DDG attempts to address the second problem and does not say anything about the first. In turn, LARS addresses the first problem and does not deal with the second problem. Nevertheless, among the main drawbacks of this protocol, we can cite: First, no difference is made between different abstraction relationships, i.e., it does not treat, for example, neither a class and its instances, nor an aggregate and its components, etc., as a single lockable unit. Hence, the semantics of the KB graph is not exploited to improve the concurrency. Second, no kind of implicit locks is defined. This may jeopardize the overall performance of this protocol, and, in addition, lead the lock system to run out of storage. Third, phantoms are not taken into consideration. A more detailed critical analysis of this protocol may be found in [REZ95].

Due to the lack of work on transaction synchronization in KBMSs, we have analyzed the suitability of some CC protocols from OODBMSs to the KBMS environment. The results of our analysis are reported in details in [REZ95a]. Due to space limitations, we are not going to discuss them here.

6 Conclusions

KBMSs are a growing research area finding applicability in many different domains. The higher its demand, the greater the necessity for knowledge sharing. In the near future, KBMSs will be applied more and more in real world applications. As a matter of fact, the research for CC techniques tailored to the KBMS environment plays a crucial role to this applicability. Moreover, it assumes a paramount importance as the demand for ever-larger KBs grows. Following this research direction, we have presented the LARS approach for CC in KBs. The most important characteristic of LARS is the partition of the KB graph into many logical ones, allowing by this way transactions to concurrently access such partitions through different points of view. Thereafter, to each one of these partitions, we have applied granular locks, providing thus many different lock types and taking the necessary precautions with respect to the dynamism of the KB graph. In this manner, LARS captures more of the semantics contained in a KB graph in the sense that it does not consider descendants of an object as being simply descendants of it, but, on the contrary, descendants with special characteristics and significance, which are based on the abstraction relationships of generalization, classification, association, and aggregation. This is the most important point of LARS, by means of which it can obtain a high degree of concurrency, exploiting the inherent parallelism in a knowledge representation approach.

In summary, the most important characteristics of LARS are: First, LARS offers different granules of locks and considers implicit locks, alleviating the task of managing too many locks due to the high number of objects in real world applications. Second, LARS copes well with multiple abstraction relationships to objects, by means of the requirement of explicitly locking bastards, which, in turn, relaxes the necessity of covering all paths to the root with intentions, reducing it to only one path. Third, LARS interprets the relationships between objects with respect to their semantics, providing typed locks for all abstraction concepts.

We have designed LARS to work with the three abstraction concepts that should be provided by KBMSs. However, LARS is flexible enough to be used by other object-oriented data models. In the case of a specific data model not supporting all the three abstractions, one should only cut off the corresponding lock modes of LARS, and handle bastards in the same way. Of course, the data model must be powerful enough to support bi-directional links in the representation of edges in KB graphs, because LARS uses them to easily find bastards. Representing the edges bi-directionally in KB graphs exclusively for the right functioning of LARS would probably not pay off. Finally, due to space limitations, we have not discussed issues like deadlocks, lock conversion, lock escalation, correctness concerns, and implementation aspects, although we have already addressed all of them. In particular, we have implemented LARS using as a running example the KBMS KRISYS.

References

[BAD87] Badrinath, B.R., and Ramamrithan, K. (1987). Semantics-based concurrency control: Beyond commutativity. In: *Proc. of the 3rd Int. Conf. on Data Engineering*, Los Angeles, USA, 304-311.

[BAD88] Badrinath, B.R., and Ramamrithan, K. (1988). Synchronizing transactions on objects. *IEEE Transactions on Computers* **37** (5), 541-547.

[BER87] Bernstein, P.A., Hadzilacos, V., and Goodman, N. (1987). *Concurrency control and recovery in database systems*. Addison-Wesley, USA.

[CAS80] Casanova, M.A., and Bernstein, P.A. (1980). General purpose schedulers for database systems. *Acta Informatica* **4**.

[CHA92] Chaudhri, V.K., Hadzilacos, V., and Mylopoulos, J. (1992). Concurrency control for knowledge bases. In: *Proc. of the 3rd Int. Conf. on Principles of Knowledge Representation and Reasoning*, Cambridge, USA.

[CHA94] Chaudhri, V.K. (1994). *Transaction synchronization in knowledge bases: Concepts, realization and quantitative evaluation*. Ph.D. Thesis, University of Toronto, Canada.

[CHA94a] Chaudhri, V.K., Hadzilacos, V., Mylopoulos, J., and Sevcik, K.C. (1994). Quantitative evaluation of a transaction facility for a KBMS. In: *Proc. of the 3rd Int. Conf. on Information and Knowledge Management*, Gaithersburg, USA.

[CHR91] Chrysanthis, P.K., Raghuram, S., and Ramamritham, K. (1991). Extracting concurrency from objects: A methodology. In: *Proc. of the ACM SIGMOD Int. Conf. on Management of Data*, Denver, USA, 108-117.

[DAV77] Davis, R., Buchanan, B.G., and Shortliffe, E.H. (1977). Production rules as a representation for a knowledge-based consultation program. *Artificial Intelligence* **8** (1), 15-45.

[DES90] Dessloch, S., Leick, F.-J., and Mattos, N.M. (1990). *A state-oriented approach to the specification of rules and queries in KBMS*. ZRI Report 4/90, University of Kaiserslautern, Germany.

[ESW76] Eswaran, K.P., Gray, J.N., Lorie, R.A., and Traiger, I.L. (1976). The notions of consistency and predicate locks in a database system. *Communications of the ACM* **19** (11), 624-633.

[FAR89] Farrag, A.A., and Özsu, M.T. (1989). Using semantic knowledge of transactions to increase concurrency. *ACM TODS* **14** (4), 503-525.

[FIS82] Fischer, J.M., Griffeth, N.D., and Lynch, N.A. (1982). Global states of a distributed system. *IEEE Transactions on Software Engineering* **SE-8** (3), 198-202.

[FRO86] Frost, R.A. (1986). *Introduction to knowledge base systems*. Collins, U.K.

[GAR83] Garcia-Molina, H. (1983). Using semantic knowledge for transaction processing in a distributed database. *ACM TODS* **8** (2), 186-213.

[GOL89] Goldberg, A., and Robson, D. (1989). *Smalltalk-80 - The language*. Addison-Wesley, USA.

[GRA76] Gray, J.N., Lorie, R.A., Putzolu, G.R., and Traiger, I.L. (1976). Granularity of locks and degrees of consistency in a shared data base. In: *Proc. of the IFIP Working Conf. on Modeling in DBMSs*, Freudenstadt, Germany, 365-394.

[GRA78] Gray, J.N. (1978). Notes on database operating systems. In: *Operating systems: An advanced course*, Springer.

[GRA81] Gray, J.N. (1981). The transaction concept: Virtues and limitations. In: *Proc. of the 7th VLDB*, France, 144-154.

[GRA93] Gray, J.N., and Reuter, A. (1993). *Transaction processing: Concepts and techniques*. Morgan Kaufmann, USA.

[HAD91] Hadzilacos, T., and Hadzilacos, V. (1991). Transaction synchronization in object bases. *Journal of Computer and Systems Sciences* **43** (1), 2-24.

[HÄR83] Härder, T., and Reuter, A. (1983). Principles of transaction-oriented DB recovery. *ACM Computing Surveys* **15** (4).

[HAR94] Hartinger, R. (1994). Syntax puzzle: The newest C++ extensions (in German). *c't* **9**, 184-190.

[HER89] Herrmann, U., Dadam, P., Küspert, K.M., Roman, E.A., and Schlageter, G. (1989). *A lock technique for disjoint and non-disjoint objects*. Technical Report TR.89.01.003, IBM Heidelberg Research Center, Heidelberg, Germany.

[HEU87] Heuschen, L. (1987). Reasoning. In: Shapiro, S.C. (Ed.), *Encyclopedia of Artificial Intelligence*, John Wiley & Sons, New York, USA, 822-827.

[HÜS94] Hüskes, R. (1994). Patience play: The forthcoming C++ standard (in German). *c't* **9**, 180-182.

[KUN79] Kung, H.T., and Papadimitriou, C.H. (1979). An optimality theory of concurrency control for databases. In: *Proc. of the ACM SIGMOD Int. Conf. on the Management of Data*, Boston, USA, 116-126.

[LEV85] Levesque, H.J., and Brachman, R.J. (1985). A fundamental tradeoff in knowledge representation and reasoning. In: R.J. Brachman and H.J. Levesque (Eds.), *Readings in knowledge representation*, Morgan Kaufmann, USA.

[LYN83] Lynch, N. (1983). Multilevel atomicity: A new correctness criterion for DB concurrency control. *ACM TODS* **8** (4), 484-502.

[MAT88] Mattos, N.M. (1988). Abstraction concepts: The basis for data and knowledge modeling. In: *Proc. of the 7th Int. Conf. on Entity-Relationship Approach*, Rom, Italy, 331-350.

[MAT89] Mattos, N.M. (1989). *An approach to knowledge base management - Requirements, knowledge representation, and design issues*. Doctor Thesis, University of Kaiserslautern, Germany.

[MUT93] Muth, P., Rakow, T.C., Weikum, G., Brössler, P., and Hasse, C. (1993). Semantic concurrency control in object-oriented database systems. In: *Proc. of the 9th Int. Conf. on Data Engineering*, Vienna, Austria, 233-242.

[MYL90] Mylopoulos, J., and Brodie, M. (1990). Knowledge bases and databases: Current trends and future directions. In: *Proc. of the Workshop on Artificial Intelligence and Databases*, Ulm, Germany.

[MYL94] Mylopoulos, J., Chaudhri, V.K., Plexousakis, D., Shrufi, A., and Topaloglou, T. (1994). *Building knowledge base management systems: A progress report*. Technical Report DKBS-TR-94-4, University of Toronto, Canada.

[PUP86] Puppe, F. (1986). Expert systems (in German). *Informatik Spektrum* **9** (1), 1-13.

[RAK90] Rakow, T.C., Gu, J., and Neuhold, E.J. (1990). Serializability in object-oriented database systems. In: *Proc. of the 6th Int. Conf. on Data Engineering*, Los Angeles, USA, 112-120.

[REZ94] Rezende, F.F., and Härder, T. (1994). A lock method for KBMSs using abstraction relationships' semantics. In: *Proc. of the 3rd Int. Conf. on Information and Knowledge Management*, Gaithersburg, USA, 112-121.

[REZ95] Rezende, F.F. (1995). Concurrency control techniques and the KBMS environment: A critical analysis. *RITA - Journal for Theoretical and Applied Computer Science* **2** (1), Brazil, 37-76.

[REZ95a] Rezende, F.F. (1995). *Evaluating the suitability of OODBMS concurrency control techniques to the KBMS environment*. Internal Report, University of Kaiserslautern, Germany. (submitted for publication).

[SCH84] Schwarz, P.M., and Spector, A.Z. (1984). Synchronizing shared abstract types. *ACM TOCS* **2** (3), 223-250.

[SIL80] Silberschatz, A., and Kedem, Z. (1980). Consistency in hierarchical database systems. *Journal of the ACM* **27** (1).

[VAS85] Vassiliou, Y., Clifford, J., and Jarke, M. (1985). Database access requirements of knowledge-based systems. In: Kim, W., Reiner, D.S., and Batory, D.S. (Eds.), *Query Processing in Database Systems*, Springer-Verlag, 156-170.

[WEI88] Weihl, W.E. (1988). Commutativity-based concurrency control for abstract data types. *IEEE Transactions on Computers* **37** (12), 1488-1505.

[WEI89] Weihl, W.E. (1989). The impact of recovery on concurrency control. In: *Proc. of the 8th ACM PODS*, 259-269.

Concurrency Control in an Object-Oriented DBMS by Exploiting Navigation

Mohsen Beheshti
Dept. of Computer & Mathematical Sciences
College of Sciences & Technology
University of Houston-Downtown
One Main Street
Houston, Texas 77002

Lois M. L. Delcambre
Comp. Sci. & Eng. Dept.
Oregon Graduate Institute
P. O. Box 44330
19600 NW Von Neumann Drive
Beaverton, OR 97006999

Abstract. Object Oriented transactions often imply the use of a large number of resources that are inaccessible to other incoming transactions if, traditional two-phase locking is used to support concurrency. The goal of this research is to improve the concurrency control performance by exploiting the navigational nature of long-running, transactions. The paper introduces a new concurrency control technique, *Group Protocol,* which is a combination of Two-Phase Locking (2PL) and Serialization Graph Test (SGT) techniques. Navigational Transactions may consist of two or more subtransactions. Depending on the nature of each subtransaction they may be executed using parallel processing. The performance evaluation done in this research indicates the applicability of this work for long-running navigational transactions.

1. Introduction

Conventional database systems deal with simple data types such as, integers and short character strings; they don't directly support applications with complex objects (data types) [11, 15, 31]. The new generation of database systems, provide traditional data management services, as well as support for long-running transactions with richer object structures [2, 3, 10, 13, 14, 16, 17, 18, 20, 21, 22, 23, 25, 26, 29, 30]. Here, a transaction often accesses and accumulates data by navigating through objects and classes. An *object* refers to a set of data definitions and their operations, and a *class* is a set of objects which have similar characteristics. For this reason there may be an opportunity to improve the concurrent performance for long-running transactions.

In order to provide a high-level description of a transaction, the *Navigational Transaction Language (NTL)* [4, 8] may be used to indicate how a transaction navigates from one object (class) to another. A transaction represented by NTL is a collection of one or more subtransactions which can be processed in parallel. Basically this research supports any transaction language that is powerful enough to give the following: 1) navigation path, 2) the order in which the objects are being traversed by the transaction, 3) how to add new objects to, or remove existing objects from a class, and 4) indicating where a *read* or *write* operation occurs.

Given the navigational transaction, a new locking protocol, the *Group Protocol (GP)* is proposed to group the operations in the transaction. Each group may release their locks before the other objects in the transaction are locked (not a pure *two-phase locking* protocol). Thus, more objects may become available for incoming transactions. The proposed protocol does not guarantee serializability in all cases, therefore, a verification test (*Serialization Graph Test*) is conducted whenever a transaction completes its execution. The *Group Protocol* is used to let the navigation path be traversed once. This is achieved by means of having at least two classes kept locked at any time to maintain the connection between them, and the effects of one class to the other. Navigating the path just once decreases the time needed for each transaction, and allows more parallelism thus, improves the performance

The data model presented in this research is a semantic data model because it supports navigational links. Section 2 introduces the *Navigational Transaction* concept, the *Navigational Transaction Language (NTL)*, and formally defines a navigational transaction. Section 3 explains the *Group Protocol*. Section 4 discusses the execution of multiple transactions. The performance evaluation is presented in Section 5 and, Section 6 covers the summary and future work.

2. Navigational Transactions (NT's)

As shown in Fig. 1, the procedures developed to prepare the transactions for concurrent processing are done statically. If the user provides a low level description of a transaction using a procedural language then the concurrency control using the *Group Protocol* is applied. However, if a high level description of a transaction (i.e., without procedural control over the order of DB operations) is provided by the user then there might be some opportunities for logical optimization before the concurrent execution is processed [4,5,6,7].

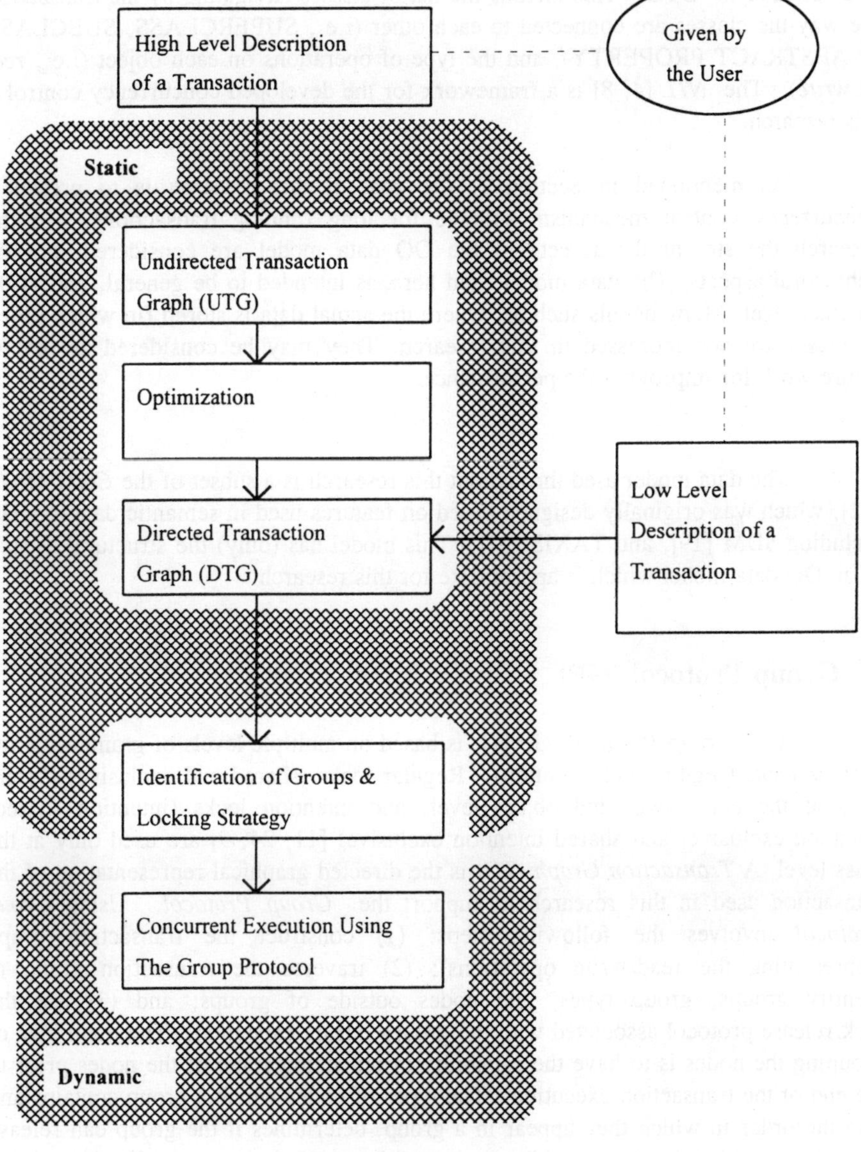

Fig. 1: Research Diagram

Here in Fig. 1 (inside the larger shaded block), a *Directed Transaction Graph (DTG)* developed in this research is used to represent the graphical representation of a transaction. It specifies the data access path of the transaction. The transaction language, *Navigational Transaction Language (NTL)* is introduced in this research also to represent the navigational properties of a transaction which is equivalent to its *DTG*. This include the list of classes navigating by the transaction, the way the classes are connected to each other (i.e., SUPERCLASS, SUBCLASS, or ABSTRACT PROPERTY), and the type of operations on each object (i.e., *read* or *write*). The *NTL* [4, 8] is a framework for the developed concurrency control in this research.

As mentioned in Section 1, the goal of this research is to present a concurrency control mechanism suitable for long running transactions. In this research the structural aspects of the OO data model are considered, not the behavioral aspects. The data model used here, is intended to be general, and at the abstract level. Many details such as, where the actual data is stored (in which object or class) are not addressed in this research. They may be considered as part of future work for improving the performance.

The data model used throughout this research is a subset of the *Class Model* [12], which was originally designed based on features used in semantic data models, including SDM [19], and TAXIS [27]. This model has (only) the structural aspects of an OO data model which is appropriate for this research.

3. Group Protocol (GP)

The *Group Protocol, GP* [4], is based on multiple levels of granularity and various locks (regular and intention). Regular locks (shared and exclusive) [9] are used at the class level and object level; and intention locks (intention shared, intention exclusive, and shared intention exclusive) [11, 24, 9] are used only at the class level. A *Transaction Graph (TG)* is the directed graphical representation of the transaction used in this research to support the *Group Protocol*. Using *Group Protocol* involves the following steps: (1) construct the transaction graph (representing the read/write operations); (2) traverse the transaction graph to identify groups, group types, and nodes outside of groups; and (3) use the lock/release protocol associated with the groups during execution. The main idea of grouping the nodes is to have the capability of unlocking some of the nodes prior to the end of the transaction execution. The types of nodes which a group contains and also the order in which they appear in a group, determines if the group can release its locks immediately after reaching its last node or if it has to wait. There can also be nodes that appear ahead of the first group which they release their locks immediately (like a group of size one).

The nodes of a *Transaction Graph (TG)*, are traversed one by one starting from the first node (which is marked by the directed transaction graph) to provide the following static information about each transaction:

1. Identifying the *Loose Nodes (LN)*, the nodes which do not belong to any groups; not all the *TG`s* have LN's however, if there are any, they appear starting at the beginning of the *TG* through out the end, or until the first group is identified. The *LN's* reflect navigational positioning (prior to the first update) and may be locked and unlocked individually.
2. Identifying the *Groups*, by marking the nodes which start the groups. A group is identified based on the type of nodes appearing in the group.

3. Based on the information given by the *TG* the type of locks and their granularity level may be established. A node may be used for update/display purposes on its local properties or just for navigational purposes. Different granularity levels may be assigned to different properties. Here, all the simple properties and each navigational property of a node in the *TG's* are considered as a unit of locking granularity.

To guarantee the one time pass through the navigation path, the *Loose Nodes* have locks on two classes at a time, and *Groups* keep the locks on all the classes belonging to that group to prevent loosing the connections. This way the correctness of each transaction by itself is guaranteed. The definition of each node in the TG is identified as follows:

I. Information given with the transaction:

A. Partition of nodes based on the transaction structure.

1. *Side Node (SN)*- A node connected to exactly one other node (i.e., a leaf node).
2. *Basic Node (BN)*- A node connected to exactly two other nodes (i.e., a node without branching).
3. *Compound Node (CoN)*- A node connected to more than two other nodes (i.e. a node with branching).

B. Additional labels placed on two nodes.

1. *Transaction Start Node (TSN)*- The first node in TG to be traversed (usually a side node).
2. *Transaction End Node (TEN)*- The last node in TG to be traversed (usually a side node).

C. Operations of nodes labeled by the user.

1. *Read Node (RN)*- A node where the data mentioned by the node will be fully or partially read.
2. *Update/Display Node (U/D)*- A node where the data mentioned by the node will be fully or partially updated or displayed.

II. Information established for the Group Protocol:

1. *Loose Node (LN)* - A node which does not belong to any groups.
2. *Group Start Node (GSN)*- The first node of a group (i.e. a SN, a CoN, or a U/D node).
3. *Group End Node (GEN)*- The last node of a group (i.e. a SN, a CoN, or a U/D node).

There are two types of groups, the *Update Group* and the *Read Group*, which are different because of the type of nodes they contain and the order in which they release their locks. They are discussed in more detail in subsequent sections.

3.1. Update Group (UG)

A group is called an *Update Group (UG)* if its GEN is a U/D node, (e.g., UG1, and UG2, shown in Fig. 2a). Node 3 in Fig. 2b is a CoN and RN, whereas node 1 in Fig. 2a is a CoN, a U/D node, a SN, the TSN, and a GSN for UG1 and UG2. The nodes of a UG are marked to be locked as they are being traversed. However, once all the groups in a TG are locked (at execution time), and the transaction is completed then the groups can release their locks. The following figures include *Read Groups (RG)* also. The definition of *RG* is given in the following subsection.

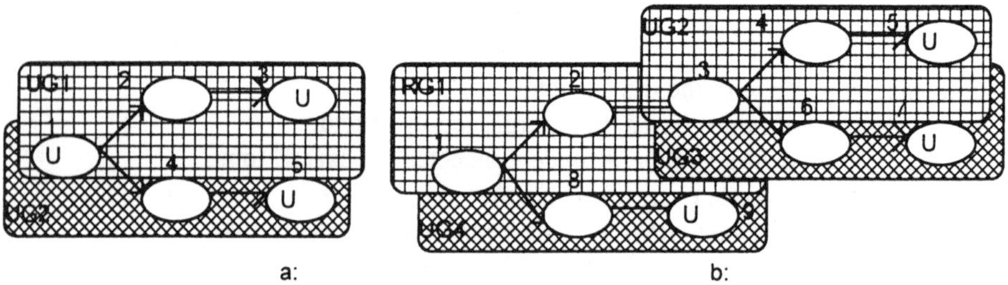

Fig. 2: Variations of Update Groups

Table 1 illustrates how update groups are marked to be locked and unlocked for the TG's given in Fig. 2. The entry U/D in the first column refers to the Update and/or Display process for a node.

LOCK	*UG1*	*(nodes 1, 2, and 3)*
LOCK	*UG2*	*(nodes 1, 4, and 5)*
U/D	*UG2*	*(node 5)*
UNLOCK	*UG2*	*(nodes 4, and 5)*

U/D	*UG1*	*(node 3)*
UNLOCK	*UG1*	*(nodes 2, and 3)*
U/D	*node 1*	
UNLOCK	*node 1*	

a. Locking and unlocking steps for Fig. 2a

LOCK	*RG1*	*(nodes 1, 2, and 3)*
LOCK	*UG2*	*(nodes 3, 4, and 5)*
LOCK	*UG3*	*(nodes 3, 6, and 7)*
LOCK	*UG4*	*(nodes 1, 8, and 9)*
U/D	*UG4*	*(node 9)*
UNLOCK	*UG4*	*(nodes 8, and 9)*
U/D	*UG3*	*(node 7)*
UNLOCK	*UG3*	*(nodes 6, and 7)*
U/D	*UG2*	*(node 5)*
UNLOCK	*UG2*	*(nodes 4, and 5)*
UNLOCK	*RG1*	*(nodes 2, and 3)*
UNLOCK	*node 1*	

b. Locking and unlocking steps for Fig. 2b

Table 1: Locking And Unlocking Update Groups

3.2. Read Group (RG)

A group is called a *Read Group (RG)* if its GEN is not a U/D node. There is no reason to keep an RG locked once its GEN is (a) traversed and, (b) is not locked by other groups in the TG. This allows other incoming transactions to be able to access the nodes sooner. Fig. 3 shows some examples of RG's. If the RG's GEN is the GSN of other groups in the TG, then it has to wait for the following groups to get unlocked first and release their GSN.

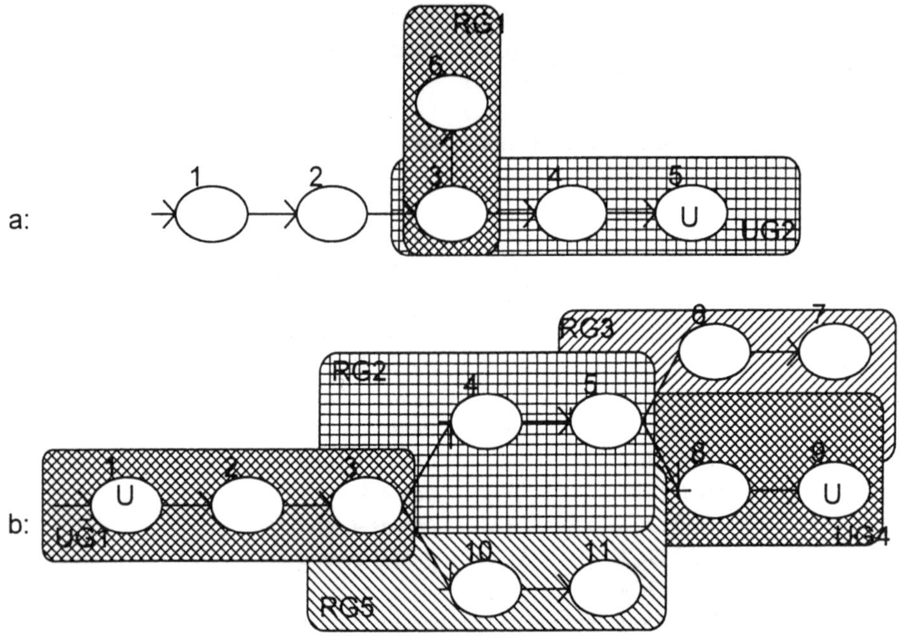

Fig. 3: Variations of Read Groups

For instance in Fig. 3b, node 5 is the GEN for RG2 and at the same time the GSN for RG3 (and UG4). Here RG2 which has RG3 and UG4 as its following branches, must keep all of its nodes locked, till RG3 and UG4 are released. The locking and unlocking steps using the Group Protocol for the groups shown in Fig. 3 are illustrated in Table 2.

LOCK	*node 1*	
LOCK	*node 2*	
UNLOCK	*node 1*	
LOCK	*RG1*	*(nodes 3 and 6)*
UNLOCK	*node 2*	
UNLOCK	*RG1*	*(node 6)*
LOCK	*UG2*	*(nodes 3, 4, and 5)*
U/D	*node 5*	
UNLOCK	*UG2*	*(nodes 4, and 5)*
UNLOCK	*node 3*	

a. Locking and unlocking steps for Fig. 3a

LOCK	*UG1*	*(nodes 1, 2, and 3)*
LOCK	*RG2*	*(nodes 3, 4, and 5)*
LOCK	*RG3*	*(nodes 5, 6, and 7)*

UNLOCK	*RG3*	*(nodes 6, and 7)*
LOCK	*UG4*	*(nodes 5, 8, and 9)*
LOCK	*RG5*	*(nodes 3, 10, and 11)*
UNLOCK	*RG5*	*(nodes 10, and 11)*
U/D	*UG4*	*(node 9)*
UNLOCK	*UG4*	*(nodes 8, and 9)*
UNLOCK	*RG3*	*(nodes 6, and 7)*
UNLOCK	*RG2*	*(nodes 4, and 5)*
UNLOCK	*RG1*	*(nodes 2, and 3)*
U/D	*node 1*	
UNLOCK	*node 1*	

b. Locking and unlocking steps for Fig. 3b

Table 2: Locking and Unlocking Read Groups

The following section presents the complete algorithm for the Group Protocol.

3.3. The Algorithm

Algorithm 1 gives the complete procedure to mark the *LN's*, generate the groups, establish the group type, and introduces the lock and unlock instructions, based on the groups. It takes a transaction graph as input, then statically specifies the groups. Then the order in which the locks are set and released for each group (update or read) is specified. In this algorithm, the *GroupIndex* is used to specify the order in which the groups are generated and locked. *CurrentNode* is the current node in the TG, which is being traversed. *NextNode()* is a function which returns the next node in the data access path to be traversed. The *GroupEndNode* and *GroupStartNode* specify the GEN and GSN of each group in the TG respectively. *GroupType* determines the type of the group which is set to either R*Group* for RG's or U*Group* for UG's.

Algorithm 1:
This algorithm is divided into three parts:

1. This block of code traverses the path to identify and mark the *Loose Nodes*. If the node to be read is supposed to start a group then *GenerateGroup* (another block of code) is called.

Main

```
1.        GroupIndex = 0
```

```
2.    CurrentNode = TSN
3.    WHILE (CurrentNode ≠ U/D OR CoN OR TEN)
4.                  MarkTheLooseNode
5.                  CurrentNode = NextNode (in the path)
6.    ENDWHILE
7.    IF            CurrentNode ≠ TEN
8.    THEN  CALL GenerateGroup
9.    ENDIF
```

Start from the Transaction Start Node (TSN, line 2), and order the groups by using the GroupIndex. Then traverse a node at a time, and check each node to see if it is a U/D node, a CoN, or a Transaction End Node (TEN, line 3). As long as no U/D node, Compound Node (CoN), or TEN is found in the course of traversing the nodes, mark the node as a Loose Node (*LN*) and get the next node (lines 3 through 6). A TEN encountered here (on line 3) marks the end of a (read-only) transaction with no groups. However, once a U/D node or a CoN is found then the grouping procedure starts, and from this point all the remaining nodes will be marked to be locked and unlocked as groups (lines 7 and 8).

2. This block identifies the Group Start Node (GSN), Group End Node (GEN) and also the type of each group. Here SN is a Side Node.

```
GenerateGroup
      GroupIndex = GroupIndex + 1
      GroupStartNode(GroupIndex) = CurrentNode
      CurrentNode = Next Node()
      WHILE CurrentNode ≠ U/D OR CoN OR SN
                  CurrentNode = NextNode()
      ENDWHILE
      GroupEndNode(GroupIndex) = CurrentNode
      IF          GroupEndNode(GroupIndex) = U/D
      THEN        GroupType(GroupIndex) = "UGroup"
      ELSE        GroupType(GroupIndex) = "RGroup"
      ENDIF
      IF          GroupEndNode(GroupIndex) = TEN
      THEN        CALL UnlockGroups
      ELSE        IF          CurrentNode = SN
                  THEN        CurrentNode = NextNode()
                  ENDIF
                  CALL GenerateGroup
      ENDIF
```

Depending on whether the group ends with a U/D node or not, the group will be specified as a UGroup or RGroup respectively (line 1 through 11). If the Group generated is a RG and its GEN is a Side Node, then the group is marked as one which at the time of execution may release its locks immediately after its GEN is traversed. If the group is an RG but its GEN is not a Side Node then this group is marked as one that at the time of execution stays locked till the group(s) that include(s) this GEN as its (their) GSN is (are) unlocked first. If the GEN of the current group is the TEN, the unlocking procedure (UnlockGroups) for the remaining groups (unlocked groups) in the TG starts (lines 12 and 13). If the GEN for a group is a Side Node then it can't be the GSN of another group. So to find the GSN of the next group, the next node in the TG path is traversed (lines 14 and 15).

3. This block of code marks release order of the locked UGroup's and RGroup's, once the TG is completely traversed. The UGroup's are marked to release their locks at execution time in reverse order. And finally the single remaining GSN is marked as the last node to be released.

```
UnlockGroups
    1.  WHILE GroupIndex < > 0
    2.        IF      GroupType(GroupIndex) = "UGroup"
    3.        THEN    MarkToUnlockCurrentGroup
    4.        ENDIF
    5.        MarkToUnlockEligibleRGroups
    6.        GroupIndex = GroupIndex - 1
    7.  ENDWHILE
    8.  MarkToUnlockNode
```

UG's are marked for release (in reverse order). Meanwhile, some RG's may become eligible for releasing their locks whenever their GEN's are released from other groups (line 5). As the process goes on, all the groups eventually are marked to become unlocked and all the nodes but one have released their locks. The last node (belonging to the last group being unlocked) is now marked to be unlocked (line 8).

4. Concurrent Execution

The information recorded statically for each transaction includes identifying the nodes in the transaction, the type of locks they require, and identifying the type of groups and how they lock and unlock the nodes. In this section, the dynamic execution of transactions is presented.

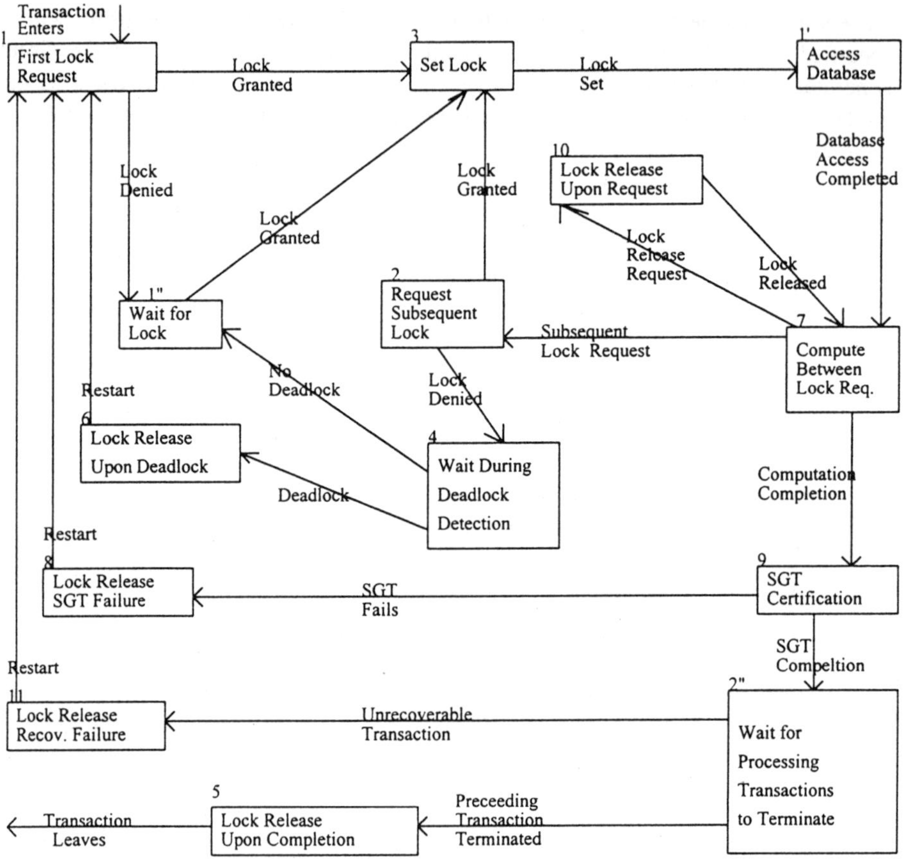

Fig. 4: State Transition Diagram

The behavior of a transaction using the proposed concurrency control here is illustrated in Fig. 4. A transaction enters the system by requesting its first lock. If the lock is already held by another transaction, the requesting transaction will be blocked. If the lock is available, the lock is set and the database is accessed to retrieve the requested data items. After this stage, the transaction cycles through the computation steps and makes subsequent lock requests as many times as needed.

Each subsequent lock request may be granted or denied in the same manner done for the first request. However, when a lock request is denied, the deadlock detection routine is invoked. If there is no deadlock, then the requesting transaction waits for the lock. Otherwise, the transaction is aborted, its locks are released and it is restarted. While transactions are requesting new locks, lock release requests are allowed, too. Lock release is based on the protocol proposed here, the *Group Protocol*, which indicates whether a lock release request is in order or not.

To guarantee the serializability of the transactions being executed, a certifier (i.e., SGT certifier) is applied to test a transaction after it has set all of its locks [9]. The object table required for the SGT certifier to keep track of the objects accessed by transactions is the lock table used for the *Group Protocol.* Thus, the overhead involved for SGT certification test here is less than the one needed for a regular SGT certification test used by itself. If the certification test fails (i.e., the execution is not serializable), then all the remaining locks for the requesting transaction are released and the transaction has to restart its execution. If the transaction passes the SGT test, it must wait for the successful termination of all the other transactions that have a conflicting operation(s) with it and have locked the conflicting object(s) before it. This is done to guarantee the transaction's recoverability. At this point the transaction releases all its remaining locks and leaves the system as a completed transaction.

In general, the concurrency control mechanism introduced here is different from an optimistic on reads and pessimistic on writes *(OrPw)* mechanism. This is because, other than the loose nodes (read nodes in front of transactions), there might be some other read nodes (belonging to update groups or read groups) which may stay locked till the end of transaction execution (not optimistic on reads). This is to guarantee the correctness of individual transactions using the navigational approach. Even for the loose nodes there are two classes being locked at one time to maintain the connection between the classes (to guarantee the one time navigation). In applications with high probability of conflicts between write and read operations, the OrPw mechanism has higher probability of undoing the transaction execution. This may be considered as a very costly process, specially for long-running transactions.

The next section discusses the performance of the proposed system by comparing the result against the two base line concurrency control mechanisms, i.e., Two-Phase Locking and a pure Serialization Graph Test.

5. Performance & Analysis

One of the major issues in introducing a new concurrency control mechanism is to analyze the trade-off between the disadvantages (overhead) versus the advantages of increasing concurrent access to the database. The amount of overhead is dependent on the characteristics of applications and the type of concurrency control mechanism used. In general, the characteristics are, the size of transaction in terms of the number of objects accessed, the size or granularity of locks, and how long the locks are held [28]. The goal here is to study the performance by: (1) characterizing the input, including the specification of characteristics of individual transactions, and the interaction among them, (2) choosing the performance metric(s), (3) establishing the base lines (i.e.,. TPL, and SGT), and (4) performing tests.

To evaluate the performance of the developed concurrency control, the metric *extra burden* is used which represents the overhead on the transaction [1]. This performance metric recognizes finite resources and it considers both the impact that the concurrency control has on the probability that the transaction will run to completion without conflicting with another transaction and the overhead imposed by the concurrency control technique on the transaction. Here the overhead is considered as those instructions/operations, both CPU and I/O, that would not need to be executed if the transactions were run alone on a computer without any concurrency control mechanisms.

The assumptions made for the simulation program are as follows:

1. All transactions have the same size (but the size can be changed for each simulation).
2. There is just one update group with a fixed size for each transaction.
3. The probability of conflicts and collisions are given as inputs.
4. No more than two transactions are involved in a conflict or collision.

Considering various sizes of transactions makes the model complex to use (assumption 1). One update group or multiple update groups have about the same effect on performance as long as the total number of update group nodes in a transaction is the same (assumption 2). This is basically because all the update group nodes hold their locks during the entire transaction execution. The probability of conflicts and the probability of collisions (where $Pcol \leq Pconf$), both have a direct effect on performance. Thus they are provided separately by the user to investigate their effects (assumption 3). Probability of conflicts and collisions involving more than two transactions is very low and not noticeable in the overall performance (assumption 4).

The parameters used in the simulation program are as follows:

1. *Transaction Size* (*TS*)- Number of nodes in each transaction.
2. *Multiprogramming Level* (*MPL*)- The number of transactions that may be active at the same time.
3. *Number of Update Nodes* (*Upn*)- The number of nodes in a transaction that update the database.
4. *Probability of Conflicts* (*Pconf*)- The probability of read-write and/or write-write conflicts among transactions.
5. *Probability of Collisions (Pcol)*- The probability of restarting the transaction upon deadlock detection (in the case of TPL), or failing the validation test (in the case of SGT).

6. *Probability of the Update Group* (*Pupg*)- The probability that nodes in a transaction belong to the update group. Also the percentage of nodes in the transaction which belong to the update group.

In the simulation model, a fixed number of transactions are generated and cycled continuously. After a transaction has completed and released all its locks, it is immediately sent back to the system and becomes a new transaction. The simulation model calculates the overhead involved for each transaction based on the assumptions and the parameters for each of the three techniques: TPL, SGT, and the developed algorithm. The simulation program was written in C.

The overall performance of the developed concurrency control mechanism indicates that, the technique is more suitable for applications which deal with *read* operations more often than *write* operations. However, in cases where *write* operations exists, as long as the Probability of the Update Group is within a certain range (i.e., less than or equal to .4) the developed technique is expected to perform better than the two base lines. Notice that *Pupg* is always greater than or equal to the probability of the number of *write* operations in a transaction.

6. Summary and Future Work

This research introduced a new concurrency control technique to improve the performance for long-running transactions. The grouping process of the *Group Protocol* is deterministic indicating the order in which the objects in a transaction are traversed. A directed acyclic graph is generated for each transaction. Therefore, no recursion, or looping is involved in each transaction graph.

The proposed mechanism works well when long-running navigational transactions are executed, assuming that, smaller update group nodes exist in long transactions. The Group Protocol may improve the performance up to 26% compared to optimistic or conservative schedulers. This is when the probability of conflicts and collisions are less than .7 and .25 respectively, and the transactions have 40 percent or less update group nodes. Based on the other performance models and the type of long-running transactions that have been tested, about 50% to 60% of transactions fall into this category [1]. This indicates that the developed technique is applicable to most of the existing applications in this area.

Another use of the proposed algorithm may offer a choice among TPL, SGT or the *Group Protocol*. This depends on the applications. That is, if the application uses read operations more frequently than write operations then the user may activate just the SGT part of the mechanism. The same applies when there are more write operations than read operations, and just TPL is activated (by defining the entire transaction as just one update group). Thus, different applications (optimistic, pessimistic, or mixed) may use the introduced concurrency control mechanism.

The data model used in this research is quite general and abstract. So, many details, such as where the actual data is stored (in which object or class), are not addressed here. These details may be considered as part of future work for improving the performance.

References

[1] Agrawal, Rakesh, and Dewitt, J. David, "Integrated Concurrency Control and Recovery Mechanism: Design ad Performance Evaluation", In ACM Transaction on Database systems, Vol., 10, o. 4, December 1985, Pages 529-564.

[2] Bancilhon, Francois, "Object-Oriented Database Systems", Proc. of the 1988 SIGMOD Conf., Washington, DC, March 1988, P. 152-162.

[3] Bancilhon, Francois, "The Design and Implementation of O2, and Object-Oriented Database System", Advances in Object-Oriented Database Systems: Second International Workshop on Object-Oriented Database Systems, Bad Munster am Sterin, West Germany. Also appears as Lecture Notes in Computer Science, No. 334, Springer Verlag, 1988.

[4] Beheshti Mohsen, "Improving Performance in Object-Oriented Database Systems by Exploiting Navigational Properties", Ph. D. Dissertation, The Center for Advanced Studies, University of Southwestern Louisiana, Lafayette, LA, May 1992.

[5] Beheshti Mohsen, and Delcambre Lois M. "A Logical Optimization Algorithm for an Object-Oriented DBMS", Arkansas Computer Conference - ACC'95, March 1995.

[6] Beheshti Mohsen, and de Korvin Andre. "Logical Optimization When Uncertainty Is Present", 6th International Conference and Workshop on Database and Expert Systems Applications, DEXA'95, September 1995.

[7] Beheshti Mohsen, and de Korvin Andre. "Applying Fuzzy Logic to an Object-Oriented Query Optimization Algorithm", 7th International Conference on Artificial Intelligence and Expert Systems Applications, EXPERSYS'95, November 1995.

[8] Beheshti Mohsen, and Delcambre Lois M. "A Navigational Transaction Language for an Object-Oriented DBMS", Arkansas Computer Conference - ACC '96.

[9] Bernstein,P. A., Haszilacos, V., and Goodman, N., "Concurrency Control and Recovery in Database Systems", by Addison Wesley Inc., 1987.

[10] Booch, Grady, "Object-Oriented Analysis and Design with Applications", 2nd Edition, The Benjamin/Cummings Publishing Company, Inc., 1994.

[11] Date, C. J., "An Introductin to Database Systems" by Addison Wesley Inc., Vol. II, July 1984.

[12] Davis, K. C., "The Formal Foundation for Object-Oriented, Algebraic Query Processing", Ph.D. Dissertation, The Center for Advanced Computer Studies, University of Southwestern Louisiana, Lafayette, LA, April 1990.

[13] Deux O., et. al., "The Story of O2", IEEE Trans. on Knowledge and Data Eng., Vol. 2, No. 1, March 1990.

[14] Dittrich, K. R., Dayal, U, and Buchmann, A., P., (eds.), "Topics in Information Systems: On Object-Oriented Database Systems", Springer-Verlay Berlin Heidelberg 1991, Printed in the United States of America.

[15] Elmagarmid, Ahmed K., "Database Transaction Models for Advanced Applications", by Morgan Koufmann Publishers, Inc., 1992.

[16] Fishman, D. H., et. al., "Iris: An Object-Oriented Database Management System", ACM Trans. on Office Inf. Sys., Vol. 5, No. 1, January 1987, p. 48-69.

[17] Ford, Steven et. al., "ZEITGEIST: Database Support for Object-Oriented Programming", Texas Instruments Incorporated, P.O. Box 655474, M/S 238, Dallas, Texas 75265.

[18] Garsa, Jorge F. and Kim, Won, "Transaction Management in an Object-Oriented Database System", Conf. Proc. on SIGMAD, Chicago Illinios, June 1988, P. 37-45.

[19] Hammar, M. and McLeod, D., "Database Description with SDM: A Semantic Database Model", ACM Transactions of Database Systems, Sept 1981, P.351-386.

[20] Kim, Won, et. al., "Composite Object Support in an Object-Oriented Database System", OOPSLA '87 Conf. Proc., Oct 1987, P. 118-125.

[21] Won, Kim et. al., "Features of the ORION Object-Oriented Database System", In KIM89.

[22] Kim, Won and Lochovsky, F. H. "Object-Oriented Concepts, Databases, and Applications", By Addison-Wesley Publishing Company, ACM PRESS, New York, New York, 1989.

[23] Kim, Won et. al., "Architecture of the ORION Next-Generation Database System", IEEE Trans. on Knowledge and Data Eng., Vol. 2, No. 1, March 1990.

[24] Korth, H. F., and Silberschatz A., "Database System Concepts", by McGrow-Hill Inc., 1986.

[25] Lecluse, Christopher et. al., "O2, an Object-Oriented Data Model", Proceedings of the ACM SIGMOS 1988 International Conference on Management of Data, Chicago, IL, 1988.

[26] Maier, D., et. al., "Development of an Object-Oriented DBMS", OOPSLA '86 Proc., Sep 1986, P. 472-482.

[27] Mylopolus, J., et. al., "A Language for Designing Database-Intensive Applications", ACM Transactions on Database Systems, June 1980, P. 185-207.

[28] Ray, Wayne Allen, "Concurrency Control Architecture in Distributed database Systems", Ph.D. Dissertation, Graduate School of Vanderbilt University, Nashville, Tennessee, December 1981.

[39] Stonebraker, M., "Object Management in POSTGRES Using Procedures", Proceeding of the 1986 International Workshop on Object-Oriented Database System, Pacific Grove, California, Sept 1986, P. 66-72.

[30] Stonebraker, M., "The Implementation of POSTGRES", IEEE Trans. on Knowledge and Data Eng., Vol. 2, No. 1, March 1990.

[31] Ullman, Jeffrey D., "Principles of Database and Knowledge-Base Systems", Volume I, By Computer Science Press, Inc., 1988.

Cost-Controlled OFL Rewriting Rules for Multiple Collection Traversals

Didier Chretien Fernando Machuca Puthirak Om ZhaoHui Tang

PRiSM Laboratory
University of Versailles/Saint-Quentin
45, Avenue des Etats-Unis
78035 VERSAILLES Cedex
France
email: <firstname>.<lastname>@prism.uvsq.fr

Abstract. The integration of path expression evaluations in an object-oriented cost-driven query optimizer is the subject of this paper. We present rewriting rules that transform path expressions into different object target programs (i.e., query execution plans). An analytical cost model is presented and used to compare the quality of various programs. We have used the OFL (Object Functional Language) traversal formalism to describe the rules. OFL is a target object language for OQL-like query compilers. By using the OFL formalism, the most efficient program corresponds to the best collection traversal. Experimental results when traversing multiple collections highlight the outperformance in some cases of ternary hash joins compared to classical binary hash join traversals. Binary and ternary joins are more responsive to the join selectivity than to the memory size. The results show that traversing path indexes are usually the most efficient traversals. Pipelined (i.e., one object at a time or depth-first pointer chasing) traversals can be highly efficient depending on the size of memory buffers.

Keywords
Target object language, cost model, path expression, performance measurements.

1. Introduction

The evaluation of path expressions is a crucial aspect in the optimization of object-oriented queries [BLA93, KIM95]. In fact, path expressions are the mechanisms most often used to query object bases [CAR88, GAR92, KIF92]. Path expressions describe multiple collection traversals — navigations in the deeply nested structures of objects. Path expressions may be *single valued* or *set valued,* and may appear in a query as part of a predicate, as a target of a query (when set valued), or as part of a projection list [OZS95]. Different techniques have been proposed to evaluate path expressions. The classical algebraic approach [COD70, SHA90, Vandelberg91, STE94] permits a decomposition of a long path in shorter binary paths. Efficient algorithms for traversing binary paths (i.e., join algorithms) are presented and compared in [SHE90]. A graph traversal approach [JEN90] enables a long path to be traversed *forward* and *backward*. A variant approach is the *typed algebra* [CLU92] which allows the Jenq et al. traversals to be described as binary algebra expressions. Another approach uses path indexes to directly achieve a whole navigation [KEM90]. A more general approach proposes using not only path indexes but also the physical information in linked objects to accelerate the navigation [ORE92]. This corresponds to pipelined (i.e., one object at a time or *depth-first pointer chasing*) traversals of multiple collections. Pipelined techniques have demonstrated their efficiency in main memory data base systems due to the fact that precomputed joins (i.e., *implicit* or *functional* joins) are always faster than other join methods [LEH86, VAL87]. In the best of all worlds, object identifiers (OIDs) can be converted to memory pointers (*pointer swizzling*) [KIM88, WHI92]. Unfortunately, these different techniques have never been captured in a single formalism. Moreover, they have never been compared against a cost model or an experimentation.

The goal of this paper is to show how to integrate different evaluations of path expressions in an object-oriented cost-driven query optimizer. We propose rewriting rules that transform path expressions into target object programs (i.e., execution plans). A cost model that evaluates the quality of the programs is given. The programs implement ternary and binary hash join traversals as well as path index- and pipelined- (i.e., n-ary pointer chasing) evaluations. We present experimental results that confirm the cost model and compare the efficiency of the programs. The rules are described by using the OFL (Object Functional Language) traversal formalism [GAR95b]. OFL is a target object language for OQL-like [CAT93] query compilers introduced in [GAR95a]. OFL programs describe the traversals of collections in the execution world. In the traversal, functional predicate and projection expressions can be applied. By using the OFL rewriting formalism the search space explored by the classic *query rewriting* and *query planning* phases of an object optimizer are uniformly described by OFL programs. Since the programs describe traversals of collections, equivalent programs correspond to equivalent traversals. Therefore, the primary objective of the optimizer process is to find the best traversal.

Experimental results when traversing multiple collections highlight the outperformance in some cases of ternary hash joins compared to classical binary hash join traversals. Binary and ternary joins are more responsive to the join selectivity than to the memory size. The results show that traversing path indexes are usually the most efficient traversals. Pipelined (i.e., one object at a time or depth-first pointer chasing) traversals can be highly efficient depending on the size of memory buffers.

We present in Section 2 the basic elements of the OFL rewriting formalism that we use to generate the target programs that evaluate path expressions. Section 3 introduces the equivalence rules to generate the different target programs for traversing path expressions. In Section 4, we present the analytical cost model that make it possible to analyze the quality of the programs. The experimental study that compares various target programs is addressed in Section 5. Section 6 concludes by indicating directions for further research.

2. Preliminaries

The major concern of this section is the description of the OFL (Object Functional Language) formalism [GAR95b] that permits the integration of the evaluation of path expressions in an object query optimizer. The formalism unifies the search space of classical *query rewriting* and *query planning* phases of an object query optimizer as OFL programs. OFL is an appropriate target object language for

OQL-like [CAT93] query compilers [GAR95a]. OFL programs describe the traversal of abstract collections (i.e., a functional description of collections in the execution world). To familiarize the reader with the basic concepts of the OFL formalism, we first describe the abstract collections, then the target object language, and finally the rewriting formalism itself.

2.1 Abstract Collections

Abstract collections model collections in the execution world of an OQL-like query compiler. The notion of *abstract collection* is introduced as a functional way to manipulate any kind of collection of objects, independently of the type of the collection instances and of the storage organization of the collection. An abstract collection is seen as a container of objects encapsulated by two specific sets of functions. The *behavioral functions* model the external collection definition. The *traversal functions* encapsulate the storage organization of the collection.

Definition 1: Abstract Collection

A container of objects encapsulated by a finite set of behavioral and traversal functions.

Indexes — essential in all optimization strategies [KEM90, ORE92, FIN94] — are integrated into the language as common abstract collections. Indeed, conventional indexes can be seen as collections where an object or a set of objects is related to an atomic value [KEM90]. In object-oriented databases, path indexes can be seen as collections providing a direct backward link [CLU92]; or collections supporting reference chains from one object instance to another or to a collection of instances objects [KEM90], in a way similar to multivalued attributes in user collections. Thus, these collections may be scanned using the aforementioned traversal functions.

Behavioral and traversal functions can be *monovalued* or *multivalued*. The *monovalued* functions map one or many abstract objects to a single abstract object. The *multivalued* functions return a collection of abstract objects. Functions may apply to a single object within a collection or to the whole collection (e.g., aggregate). We introduce now some notations that will be used in the rest of this paper. We denote ***C*** the universal set of collections and ***F*** the universal set of functions. For an abstract collection C_i, we denote its associated finite set of functions FC_i. We denote $C_i.f_j$ the jth function of FC_i. Figure 2.1 summarizes these notations.

FCi = { Ci.f1, Ci.f2, ... ,Ci.fn }
monovalued Ci.fj : Ci X ... ===>Ck
multivalued Ci.fn : Ci X ... ===>> Ck

$$C = \bigcup_{i=1}^{\infty} C_i \qquad F = \bigcup_{i=1}^{\infty} FC_i$$

Fig. 2.1: Summary of notations

2.2 OFL : The Language for Abstract Collections

OFL is based on a functional approach. OFL provides basic functions to traverse abstract collections and to evaluate predicates and projections on them. These basic functions are powerful enough to express different object evaluation strategies (e.g., set-oriented, pipelined, and hybrid evaluations). In addition, they can be used as building blocks to construct ad-hoc algebraic operators [GRA93].

OFL Elementary Function Constructors

OFL has the power of a complete functional language. It becomes possible to iterate on a function using a *while construct*. It also provides a *sequence construct* to sequentially apply functions. Moreover, as usual with functional programming, functions on abstract collections can be composed together. They can also be conditionally applied. Successive compositions yield functional expressions generally referred to as path expressions in object-oriented databases.

Definition 2: Path Expression

A finite sequence of function compositions of the form f0.f1....fn .

The function f_0 is the beginning of the path and f_n its end. If f_i, f_{i+1} are in the path, the abstract collection defining the first argument of f_i must be the abstract collection describing the result of f_{i+1}. A problem is the specification of path expressions mixing monovalued and multivalued functions. OFL proposes intermediate functions to apply monovalued functions to multivalued results. These intermediate functions are second order functions called quantifier functions.

OFL Quantifier Functions

The goal of quantifier functions is to provide tools to apply a function to all objects of a collection or to any object of a collection. It gives capabilities to construct complex collection path expressions. Quantifier functions have three arguments. The first argument is the collection to be traversed. The second is a predicate (Boolean function) indicating if the current instance has to be considered in the operation. The third is the function to apply when the evaluation of the predicate argument is true. OFL offers two quantifier functions ForAll and ForAny defined as follows.

Definition 3: Apply to all

A second order function of signature ForAll(C, p, f) that applies a function f to all objects of a collection C satisfying a predicate p.

Definition 4: Apply to any

A second order function of signature ForAny(C, p, f) that applies a function f to any object of a collection C satisfying a predicate p.

Quantifier functions apply functions to collections. Within a collection, objects are processed one at a time. To qualify the current instance of a collection Ci that is processed internally to a ForAll or ForAny function, OFL uses the function *Current* (Ci).

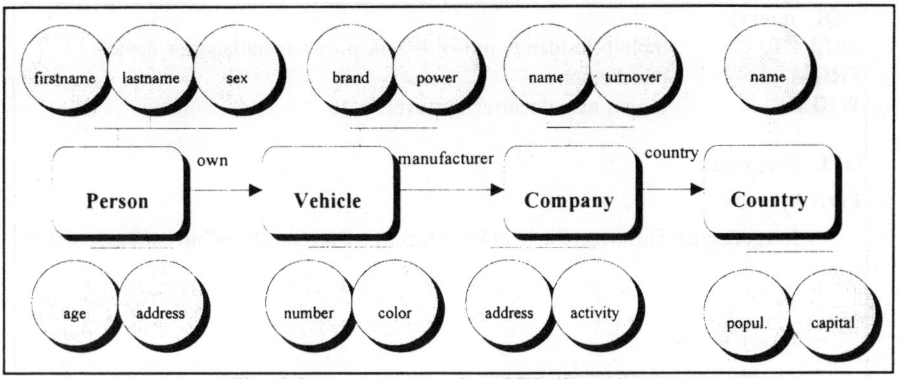

Fig. 2.2: An example of an ODL-like schema

To illustrate, let us assume the ODL-like [CAT93] schema presented in Figure 2.2. This ODL schema describes **Person**, **Vehicle**, **Company** and **Country** classes. Attributes of the **Person** class are `firstname`, `lastname`, `sex`, `age` and `address`; `brand`, `power`, `number` and `color` are attributes of the **Vehicle** class; `name`, `turnover`, `address` and `activity` are attributes of the **Company** class; *own*, *manufacturer* and *country* are class reference attributes; name, population and capital are attributes of the **Country** class.

Figure 2.3 illustrates an OFL program that evaluates an OQL query. Path expressions are used in the query in the description of the predicate and projection. The query retrieves the lastnames of persons and the brands of vehicles and company names of the vehicles they own. The OQL query is expressed on the ODL-like schema presented in Figure 2.2. The OFL program corresponds to a quantifier ForAll function. **Person'** is an abstract collection that refers to the class extents of the Person class. Methods associated to attributes become functions named in capital letters. **Tuple** (tuple construction) was used as the function to produce the results, as it is standard in complex object algebras [SHA90, CLU92]. To generate the results we use the **Insert** function that has as first argument the **Result** abstract collection.

```
OQL query:
SELECT      tuple(p.lastname, p.own.brand, p.own.manufacturer.name)
FROM        p in Person
WHERE       p.own.manufacturer.turnover = 10

OFL Program:
ForAll(Person',
    IntegerEqual(Turnover(Current(Manufacturer(Current(Own(Current(Person')))))
),
    10,
    Insert(Result,
    Tuple(LastName(Current(Person')),
    Brand(Current(Own(Current(Person')))),
    Name(Current(Manufacturer(Current(Own(Current(Person')))))))))
```

Fig. 2.3: Example of an OFL program evaluating a complex query

2.3 OFL Rewriting Technique

OFL rewriting rules are transformations applied on OFL programs that result in OFL programs. The search space explored by the classic *query rewriting* and *query planning* phases of an optimizer is uniformly described by OFL programs. Query rewriting is concerned with finding equivalent expressions to the one given by the user [HAA90]. In algebraic approaches, an algebraic expression represents a user query [SHA90, CLU92, BLA93]. Within the OFL formalism, an OFL program (a functional expression) represents the user query. Thus, equivalent expressions are equivalent OFL programs. Query planning explores the search space of *execution plans* to find the best one [VAL91, Lanzellote92, MIT93, FIN94]. Within the OFL formalism, query execution plans are OFL programs. Since the programs describe traversal of collections, equivalent programs correspond to equivalent traversals. The search for the best equivalent traversal includes the following transformations: reducing collection sizes by applying functional predicates; accessing directly collection instances (i.e., using indexes), which participate in results; and, factoring common and constant functional subexpressions to avoid complex duplicate evaluations.

To facilitate the description of the rules, the quantifier function notations [FIE88] were defined as follows:

- **ForAll**(C_i, lc_i p, f) where C_i (C_i in **C**) is an abstract collection, lc_i specifies the current instance of C_i, p (p in **F**) is a boolean function and f (f in **F**) is any function applied to c_i, or to $c_1, c_2, \ldots, c_i$ current instances in nested quantifier expressions; f can also be a quantifier function.
- **ForAll**(C_i, lc_i p, f) **[C_r]** is an annotated ForAll function where C_r (C_r in **C**) is the result abstract collection.

- **ForAny** or annotated ForAny quantifier functions have similar notations as those of ForAll.

While annotated quantifier functions permit the definition of set-oriented rewriting rules, non-annotated quantifier functions allow pipelined rules. A set-oriented equivalence usually has a symmetric pipelined equivalence, and vice-versa.
The equivalence of Figure 2.4 [GAR95b] shows how explicit join commutativity can be defined with OFL programs. This equivalence is valid both for set-oriented (the rule is then denoted **SEq1**) and pipelined (the rule is then denoted **PEq1**) programs. The rule uses the **DefCol** function to explicitly name abstract collections obtained dynamically. The importance of join commutativity was confirmed in [BLA93] for queries against a single target class [JEN90]. More than explicit joins, the quantifier expressions represent a sequence of select, join, and project operators, which can be evaluated as a whole [CLU92].

Equivalence P/SEq1
if Ck is not the result of a DefCol function DefCol(Ck,g(ci)) for some g in F:

ForAll(Ci, λci p1(ci), **ForAll**(Ck, λck p2(ck) and p3(ci,ck), f(ci,ck))) ≡
ForAll(Ck, λck p2(ck), **ForAll**(Ci, λci p1(ci) and p3(ci,ck), f(ci,ck)))

Fig. 2.4: Join Commutativity with OFL programs.

Since there are equivalences between algebraic operators and OFL quantifier expressions, all known algebraic equivalences can easily be redefined for OFL programs. [GAR95b] shows the following five equivalences among the operators of the algebra proposed in [CLU92] (similar to the ENCORE algebra of [SHA90]) and the OFL quantifier expressions.

i) **Select**(Ci, λci p(ci)) ≡ **ForAll**(Ci, λci p(ci), Tuple(ci)) **[Cr]**

ii) **Project**(Ci, λci f(ci)) ≡ **ForAll**(Ci, λci null, Tuple(f(ci))) **[Cr]**

iii) If the elements of Ci are tuple values and the elements of Ck are not:
Join(Ci, Ck, λci,ck p(ci,ck)) ≡
ForAll(Ci, λci null, **ForAll**(Ck, λck p(ci,ck),
Tuple(ci.a1, ...,ci.an,ck)))
[Cr]

iv) If the elements of Ci and Ck are tuple values:
Join(Ci, Ck, λci,ck p(ci,ck)) ≡
ForAll(Ci, λci null, **ForAll**(Ck, λck p(ci,ck),
Tuple(ci.a1,...,ci.an,ck.b1,
...,ck.bn))) **[Cr]**

v) If the elements of Ci and Ck are not tuple values:
Join(Ci, Ck, λci,ck p(ci,ck)) ≡
ForAll(Ci, λci null, **ForAll**(Ck, λck p(ci,ck),
Tuple(ci,ck))) **[Cr]**

Fig. 2.5: Equivalence of a Complex Object Algebra and OFL programs.

The Select operator selects the elements of the C_i collection that satisfy the predicate boolean function p. The Project operator applies a function f to all the elements of the collection C_i. The three join forms correspond to different types of input and result collections. **Cr** collection is the result collection.

3. Multiple Collection Traversals as OFL Rewriting Rules

In this section we propose equivalence rules that enable different evaluations of path expressions. The rules permit the generation of OFL programs that correspond to binary and ternary join traversals as well as path index and pipelined traversals. The cost model to evaluate the quality of the programs is given in Section 4, and the experimental results are discussed in section 5.
Since the pipelined OFL programs are directly generated from OQL-like queries [GAR95a], all the equivalence rules have as left terms pipelined programs.

3.1 From Pipelined to Binary Join Traversals

The objective of this equivalence is to use smart binary traversals well known as join operations. Many efficient implementations of join operators have been proposed in the literature for relational [SHA86, MIS92] and object [SHE90] databases. Two nested **ForAll** quantifier functions can be seen as the functional signature of a join operator. Thus, the equivalence **Eq1** described in Figure 3.1 permits the evaluation of path expressions by target programs that use faster binary join traversals.
Let us illustrate the application of the equivalence **Eq1** in Figure 3.2. The pipelined program evaluates the OQL query in Figure 2.3. The transformation enables a join traversal of the abstract collections Person' and Vehicle', corresponding to the class extents of Person and Vehicle classes, respectively. Company' is an abstract collection that stores the Company class extents. The result of the evaluation is held in the Result abstract collection.

```
Equivalence  Eq1:

ForAll(C1, λc1 ∃ c2, ..., cn (( c2 in C2, ..., cn in Cn) and
                        (c2 = c1.ai and c3 = c2.ak ... and cn = cn-1.ap) and
                        (cn.az = constant)),
       Tuple(c1.ar, c2.as, ...,cn.ah)) [Result] ≡
ForAll(ForAll(C1, λc1  null,
          ForAll(C2, λc2  c2 = c1.ai,
                 Tuple(c1,c2))) [Temp1],
       λc1 ∃ c3, ..., cn (( c3 in C3, ..., cn in Cn) and
                        (c3 = c1.a2.ak ... and cn = cn-1.ap) and
                        (cn.az = constant)),
       Tuple(c1.a1.ar, c1.a2.as, ...,cn.ah)) [Result]
```

Fig. 3.1: Pipelined and Binary Join Traversal Equivalences

```
ForAll(Person', λp ∃ (v, c) (( v in Vehicle', c in Company') and
                            (v = p.own and c = v.manufacturer) and
                            (c.turnover = 10)),
        Tuple(p.lastname, v.brand, c.name)) [Result] ≡
ForAll(ForAll(Person', λp  null,
          ForAll(Vehicle', λv  v = p.own,
                 Tuple(p,v))) [Templ],
        λc1 ∃ c ((c in Company') and
                 (c = c1.a2.manufacturer ) and
                 (c.turnover = 10)),
        Tuple(c1.a1.lastname, c1.a2.brand, c.name)) [Result]
```

Fig. 3.2: Example of a Pipelined and Binary Join Traversal Equivalence

```
Equivalence  Eq2:

ForAll(C1, λc1 ∃ c2, ..., cn ((c2 in C2, ..., cn in Cn) and
                              (c2 = c1.ai and c3 = c2.ak  and c4 = c3.cg... and cn =
cn-1.ap) and
                              (cn.az = constant)),
        Tuple(c1.ar, c2.as, c3.aj, ...,cn.ah))   [Result] ≡
ForAll(ForAll(C1, λc1  null,
          ForAll(C2, λc2  c2 = c1.ai,
             ForAll(C3, λc3  c3 = c2.ak,
                 Tuple(c1.ar,c2.as, c3.aj))) [Templ],
        λc1 ∃ c4, ..., cn (( c4 in C4, ..., cn in Cn) and
                          (c4 = c1.a3.ag ... and cn = cn-1.ap) and
                          (cn.az = constant)),
        Tuple(c1.a1.ar, c2.a2.as, c3.a3.aj, ...,cn.ah))  [Result]
```

Fig. 3.3: Pipelined and Ternary Join Traversal Equivalences

3.2 From Pipelined to Ternary Join Traversals

The prime object of the equivalence **Eq2** in Figure 3.3 is to integrate smart ternary traversals. Three nested **ForAll** functions can be seen as the functional signature of a ternary join operator. As shown in section 4 and 5, ternary joins outperform binary join traversals in some cases.

An example of the application of the equivalence **Eq2** is given in Figure 3.4. From the pipelined OFL program that evaluates the OQL query in Figure 2.3 we obtain a ternary join traversal of the abstract collections Person', Vehicle' and Company'. These collections correspond to the Person, Vehicle and Company class extents of the Person, Vehicle and Company classes, respectively. The result of the evaluation is held in the Result abstract collection.

```
ForAll(Person', λp ∃ (v, c) (( v in Vehicle', c in Company') and
                                      (v = p.own and c = v.manufacturer) and
                                      (c.turnover = 10)),
        Tuple(p.lastname, v.brand, c.name))  [Result] ≡
ForAll(ForAll(Person', λp  null,
            ForAll(Vehicle', λv  v = p.own,
                ForAll(Company', λc  c = v.manufacturer and c.turnover = 10,
                         Tuple(p,v,c)))) [Temp1], λr  null,
        Tuple(r.a1.lastname,r.a2.brand,r.a3.name)) [Result]
```

Fig. 3.4: Example of a Pipelined and Ternary Join Traversal Equivalence

3.3 From Pipelined to Path Index Traversals

The goal of the equivalence **Eq3** in Figure 3.5 is to integrate faster path index traversals. A complex path expression traversal can be precomputed and stored in a path index collection [KEM90]. Thus, a pipelined evaluation can be replaced by a supposed faster path index traversal.

```
Equivalence  Eq3:
if ∃ CPathIndex in C (c in CPathIndex) and (c.a1.ai=c.a2 and c.a2.ak=c.a3 ... and c.an-
1.ap=c.an):

ForAll(C1, λc1 ∃ (c2, ..., cn) ((c2 in C2, ..., cn in Cn) and
                                      (c2 = c1.ai and c3 = c2.ak  and c4 = c3.cg... and cn =
cn-1.ap) and
                                      (cn.az = constant)),
        Tuple(c1.ar, c2.as, c3.aj, ...,cn.ah))  [Result] ≡
ForAll(CPathIndex, λc c.an+1=constant,
        Tuple(c1.a1.ar, c2.a2.as, c3.a3.aj, ...,cn.ah))  [Result]
```

Fig. 3.5: Pipelined and Path Index Traversal Equivalences

An example of the application of the equivalence **Eq3** is given in Figure 3.6. The pipelined OFL program that evaluates the OQL query in Figure 2.3 is replaced by an OFL program that traverses the path index collection **PVCPathIndex**. The index collection holds the precomputed path expression *Person.own.manufacturer.turnover*. The result of the evaluation is held in the **Result** abstract collection.

```
ForAll(Person', λp ∃ (v, c) (( v in Vehicle', c in Company') and
                                      (v = p.own and c = v.manufacturer) and
                                      (c.turnover = 10)),
        Tuple(p.lastname, v.brand, c.name))  [Result] ≡
ForAll(PVCPathIndex λc  c.a4 = 10,
        Tuple(c.a1.lastname,c.a2.brand,c.a3.name)) [Result]
```

Fig. 3.6: Example of a Pipelined and Path Index Traversal Equivalence

The search space generated by these rewriting rules can be large. Quality of the OFL programs is measured by a cost model which is presented in the next section.

4. The Cost Model for Multiple Collection Traversals

In this section we propose a cost model (i.e., a set of math formulas) to estimate the cost of OFL programs which evaluate multiple collection traversals (i.e., path expressions). The formulas refer to operators (implemented as functions) that compose the programs. OFL rewriting formalism permits cost-driven transformations. In fact, OFL programs manipulate collections that are physical entities. There are several different components of the cost, for example, CPU_Cost, IO_Cost, etc. CPU cost is the cost of processing CPU instructions; IO_Cost is the cost of Input/Output between memory and disk. In the following, we present our analytical cost model for estimating the cost of executing a query. Table 1 lists some database parameters used in the cost analysis.

Parameter	Definition
Page	size of a disk page
IO	time to read/write a disk page
Mips	instruction execution rate
M	number of memory buffer pages
|C|	number of pages of collection C
||C||	cardinality of collection C
sel(C)	selectivity of a predicate on C
comp	compare two values in memory
$fan_{c1,c2}$	the average number of references from a C1 object to C2 objects
$D_{c1,c2}$	the average number of distinct references from a C1 object to C objects
O_c	average object size of collection C
Blevel	B-tree level of an index
b	B-tree fanout
hash	time to hash a value
$move(o_1)$	time to write an object in memory $move(o_1)=Oc_1/Mips$

Table 1: Database Parameters

Predicate evaluation

The cost of evaluating predicate P is eval_cost(P). We consider eval_cost(P) as pure CPU consummation.

Cost of Accessing an Index

Indexes are implemented with B tree structures. Suppose the B tree fanout is b, with Blevel levels, the CPU cost of index scan is

$$Index\_CPU\_Cost = \log_2(b) * Blevel * comp$$

The IO cost of accessing an index equals to the index tree level:

$$Index\_IO\_Cost = Blevel$$

Generate Temporary File
Both CPU cost and IO cost is proportional to the number of result objects(*card*):

$$OutPut\_CPU\_Cost(card, proj) = move(proj) * card$$

$$OutPut\_IO\_Cost(card, proj) = \frac{card * proj}{page}$$

Sequential Select
The CPU cost of Sequential Select is proportional to the number of objects to scan:

$$Sel\_CPU\_Cost(C, P, proj) = eval\_cost(P) * \|C\| + OutPut\_CPU\_Cost(\|C\| * sel(P), proj)$$
$$Sel\_IO\_Cost(C, P, proj) = |C| + OutPut\_IO\_Cost(\|C\| * sel(P), proj)$$

Index Select
If an index I is used to access the collection, the IO cost only takes into account the number of pages of C concerned by the index. We define the restricted collection C' by:

$$|C'| = \begin{cases} yao(\|C\|, |C|, \|C\| * sel(P)) & if \quad index \quad is \quad not \quad clustered \\ Selectivity(P) * |C| & if \quad index \quad is \quad clustered \end{cases}$$

$$IndexSel\_CPU\_Cost(C, P, I, proj) = Index\_CPU\_Cost(I) + OutPut\_CPU\_Cost(C * sel(P), proj)$$
$$IndexSel\_IO\_Cost(C, P, I, proj) = Index\_IO\_Cost(I) + |C| + OutPut\_IO\_Cost(C * sel(P), proj)$$

where yao(n,m,k)[YAO77] gives the estimation of number of block hits for selecting k records from a collection with n records grouped in m blocks. The predicate P can be a path expression like C.A1.A2.A2...An, in this case the I is an associated path index traversing these collections. We implement the path index using B tree data structure in the object server developed by PRiSM laboratory. We adapt the canonical extension of path index described in [KEM90], which contains only information about complete paths. The cost formulas for normal index access and path index access are the same since both of them are implemented using B tree structure.

Nest Join
The nested join algorithm considers the smaller collection as the inner operand. The nest join function charges m-1 pages of the inner operand into memory and pages of the outer operand one by one. Then it charges the next (m-1) pages of the inner operand to repeat the comparison. The comparison is done in a nest loop algorithm. The cost model for this function is the following(we suppose $|C_1| < |C_2|$):

$$NJ\_CPU\_Cost(C1,C2) = \|C_1\| * \|C_2\| * Comp + OutPut\_CPU\_Cost(N,proj)$$

$$NJ\_IO\_Cost = OutPut\_IO\_Cost(N,proj) + \begin{cases} |C_1| * Int(\frac{|C_2|}{m-1} + 1) + |C_1| & if \quad m <= |C_1| \\ |C_1| + |C_2| & if \quad m > |C_1| \end{cases}$$

Hash Join

The *hash-join-algorithm* which we implemented in the object server is based on the *GRACE-join-algorithm* [SHA86]. The goal of the hashing technique is to split the smallest collection (**C1**) in sub-collections of about one page. This can be done using an appropriate hash-function. In order to find a good hash-function, a complete scan of **C1** is mandatory. Then, the objects of these two collections are read and written into the buckets depending of the hash function. In a third phase, a classical *nested-loop-join* is computed on the matching sub-collections. We consider attribute with OID type as a normal attribute which can also be hashed on the OID value. This adaptation permits hash join algorithm to traverse two collections linked by OID references.

$$HJ\_IO\_Cost(C_1,C_2,P) = 4*|C_1| + |C_2| + 2*\lambda*|C_2|$$

$$HJ\_CPU\_Cost(C_1,C_2,P) = (\|C_1\| + \|C_2\|)*hash + \|C_1\|*write(C_1) + \lambda*\|C_2\|*write(C_2) + \lambda*\frac{\|C_1\|*\|C_2\|*comp}{|C_1|^2}$$

Some accelerators are supported in our algorithm. A technique named bit-filtering [BAB79, Dewitt85] can be used to reduce the cost of rewriting **C2**. The idea is to associate each bucket with a bit value in a vector. Those buckets with null value in the corresponding bit of the vector are thrown away directly after the partition so as to save CPU and IO cost. Moreover, for each bucket we manage a set of matching interval. This second hash filter is useful to reduce the size of **C2** (the larger collection) when the distribution of join values is discrete and not regular. In the above formula, λ represents the percentage of buckets whose associated bit is not null [SHA86]. In the case where the hash join attribute is the OID type (the logic link between these two collections), λ has the following value.

$$1 \geq \lambda_{a,b} \geq \frac{\|c_b\| - \|c_a\| * D_{C_a,C_b}}{\|c_b\|}$$

Ternary Hash Join

Binary hash join traversal algorithm needs to generate many intermediate results. These results are often voluminous and useless. To reduce this effect, we implement a new operator named *ternary-join-algorithm*. The algorithm is derived from the *hash-join-algorithm*. When a collection is read for the first time, a corresponding hash-function is computed (not for the last collection). When a collection is read for the second time, the hash-filters of the previous collection is applied (not for the first one) and the new hash-filters are computed (for the next collection). When all the collections are partitioned, the final join can be performed. A nested-loop is computed for the matching buckets of C1 and C2. For each couple of matching objects (cardinality: $fan_{C1,C2}\ \|C1\|$), a unique bucket (1 page) of C3 is scanned to determine the 3 matching objects. Similar to a binary hash join, a hash function can also be applied on attributes of OID type. The analytical cost of this function is the following:

$$TJ\_IO\_Cost(C_1,C_2,C_3,P) = 4*|C_1| + |C_2| + 2*\lambda_{1,2}*|C_2| + |C_3| + \lambda_{1,3}*|C_3| + fan_{C_1,C_2}*\|C1\|$$

$$TJ\_CPU\_Cost(C_1,C_2,C_3,P) = \|C_1\|*(hash + write(C_1)) + \|C_2\|*(hash + \lambda_{1,2}*write(C_2))$$

$$+\|C_3\|*(hash + \lambda_{1,3}*write(C_3))$$

$$+\lambda_{1,2}*\frac{\|C_1\|*\|C_2\|*comp}{|C_1|^2} + fan_{C_1,C_2}*\|C_1\|*\frac{Page}{O_{C_3}}*comp$$

$$\text{where } 1 \geq \lambda_{1,3} \geq \lambda_{1,2} * \lambda_{2,3}$$

$\lambda_{1,3}$ is the evaluation of the nested hash filters applied to C3. The efficiency of the ternary join depends on this parameter.

Binary Pointer Chasing

In an object database system, objects refer to each other through their object identities (OIDs), which generate an object network. Navigation among objects of different collections through OID references is called pointer chasing. In pointer chasing traversal algorithm implemented in our object server uses depth-first-fetch algorithm [GAR95c].

$$BPC\_IO\_Cost(C_1,C_2) = OutPut\_IO\_Cost(\|C_1\|*Sel_{C_1}*Sel_{C_2}*fan(C_1,C_2),proj)$$

$$+\begin{cases} |C_1| + yao(\|C_2\|,|C_2|,\|C_1\|*Sel_{C_1}*fan(C_1,C_2)) & if\ \ m >= yao(\|C_2\|,|C_2|,\|C_1\|*Sel_{C_1}*fan(C_1,C_2)) \\ |C_1| + (1-\frac{m-1}{|C_2|})*\|C_1\|*Sel_{C_1}*fan(C_1,C_2) & if\ \ m < yao(\|C_2\|,|C_2|,\|C_1\|*Sel_{C_1}*fan(C_1,C_2)) \end{cases}$$

$$BPC\_CPU\_Cost(C_1,C_2) = \|C_1\|*fan(C_1,C_2)*hash$$

$$+OutPut\_CPU\_Cost(\|C1\|*Sel_{C_1}*fan(C_1,C_2)*Sel_{C_2}*fan(C_2,C_3),proj)$$

The IO cost of binary pointer chasing consists of two parts: charging objects from C1 and C2 collections and, generating the result file on disk. Sel_{C1} is the selectivity of the predicate on C1 if it exists, otherwise it is equal to 1.

When the memory buffer size is m and $m >= yao(\|C_2\|,|C_2|,\|C_1\|*Sel_{C_1}*fan(C_1,C_2))$, there is almost no need of memory-disk swaps and the IO_Cost is equal to the total page number of C1 and the number of page block hits on C2.

When the memory is smaller, some pages need to be charged multiple times and for each reference from a C1 object to C2 object, there is $(1-\frac{m-1}{|C_2|})$ possibility that the C2 object is not in the memory, thus an IO operation is necessary.

The CPU cost also consists of two parts: the CPU cost of finding the memory address of each C2 object referred by C1 objects and, the CPU cost for attribute projection.

Nary Pointer Chasing

Nary pointer chasing is an efficient operator for traversing the path when the memory size is big, since it does not generate any temporary files.

$$NPC\_CPU\_Cost = comp * \|C_1\| * \prod_{i=1}^{n-1} fan(C_i, C_{i+1}) * Sel_{C_i}$$

$$NPC\_IO\_Cost = |C_1| + \sum_{i=2}^{n-1} yao(\|C_i\|, |C_i|, fan(C_i, C_{i+1}))$$

When the memory is small, the IO cost of pointer chasing can be very high since objects which are already charged into memory may be swapped into disk and then charged again during the navigation. For example, suppose the memory buffer size is so small that it can only hold one page of each collection along the path. Each time an object needs to be charged, it has to replace a page in the memory, and in the worst case, the number of IOs can be $\|C_1\| * \prod_{i=1}^{n-1} fan(C_i, C_{i+1})$.

5. Experimentation

The performance study focuses on the comparison among OFL programs which evaluate multiple collection traversals (i.e., path expressions). The programs are implemented on top of the object manager of the PRiSM laboratory. The programs use the algorithms that correspond to pipelined- (i.e., depth first pointer chasing), binary hash join-, ternary hash join-, and path index- traversals. We study the effect of the memory buffer size and the predicate selectivity of collections. The workstation used for the test is a Sun 4 with 32Mb of main memory.

5.1 Test Database

Figure 2.2 shows the test database schema. The average size of a Person object is about 120 bytes and a data page with 4Kbytes can store 32 objects. The attribute Age is uniformly distributed from 1 to 99. The cardinality of collection Person is 200,000. The links from objects in Person collection to Vehicle objects are randomly generated. Each data page can have 41 Vehicle objects inside and the total cardinality of Vehicle collection is 250,000. There are 5000 companies grouped in 167 disk pages and 200 countries grouped in 5 disk pages. The attribute Turnover of Company object has an integer value from 1 to 100 in millions dollars. Each value represents 1% of these companies which are uniformly distributed among all the data pages. Same distribution is done on the Age attribute of objects in Person collection. We create a path index on *Person.own.manufacturer.turnover*. The total size of the test database is about

50M. Before running each test, we clean up both UNIX buffer and the memory buffer of the object server.

5.2 Comparison of Sensitivity to Memory Buffer Size

The testing query is the following:

Select	*p.lastname, p.own.brand, p.own.manufacturer.name*
From	*p In Person*
Where	*p.own.manufacturer.turnover=10*

Fig. 5.1: Testing Query

We execute this query with different collection traversal algorithms including pointer chasing, two binary hash joins, ternary hash join and path index. On varying the memory buffer size of our object server from 100 pages (400Kbytes) to 2000 pages (8Mbytes), we get the following results:

Figure 5.2 shows that the path index algorithm has the best performance when the selectivity of the predicate is small (1%), and its response time is independent to the buffer size. The binary hash join between collections Company and Vehicle is applied first, and this generates a temporary result file. The result is then used to join with collection Person in the next step. Ternary hash join performs better compared to binary hash join, especially when the memory buffer size is small. The reason is that ternary hash join does not generate temporary file. When the memory buffer is small, the temporary file generated by the first binary hash join has to be materialized on disk. This makes a quite big different performance. When the memory buffer is about 250 pages (about 4% of the total of these two collections), ternary hash join gains 40% of performance over two binary hash joins. As the buffer size increases, the response times become closer.

Since there is no predicate on the first collection Person, the pointer chasing function has to charge the states of all the objects linked in these three collections into memory. Also, since the final result of the query is small (the selectivity on collection Company is only 1 percent), the intermediate result of the binary hash join between collection Company and Collection Vehicle is not large. In this case, pointer chasing doesn't show its advantage.

5.3 Comparison of Sensitivity to the Selectivity on Last Collection of a Path Expression

The next experiment uses the same query and the memory buffer size remains 1000 pages. The only difference is that the predicate selectivity on Company keeps on increasing. The predicate is still on the Turnover attribute, whose value is designed to guarantee the uniform distribution for a given selectivity.

From **Figure 5.3** we can see that the curves of binary hash join, ternary hash join and path index cross with the curve of pointer chasing function. The response time of binary hash join function is rising rapidly and we can see that when the selectivity is greater than 12%, the pointer chasing function is better than binary hash join. And the more the predicate selectivity, the more the difference between these two algorithms. Meanwhile, pointer chasing is quite independent to the selectivity on the last collection of the path expression *Person.own.manufacturer*. The main cost of executing pointer chasing is the IO cost.

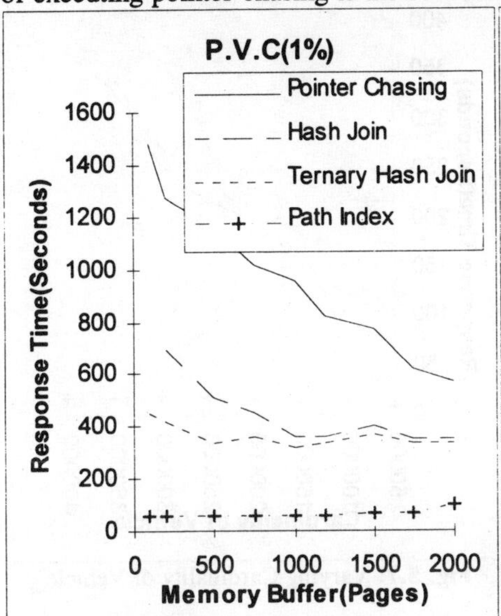

Fig. 5.2: Memory Dependencies of Different Access Functions

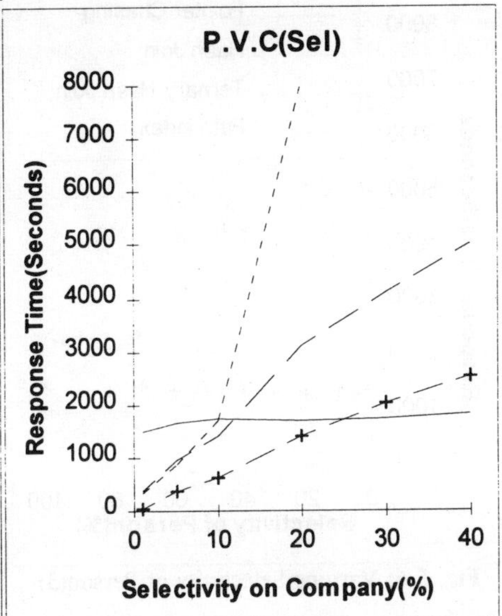

Fig. 5.3: Selectivity Dependencies of Different Access Functions

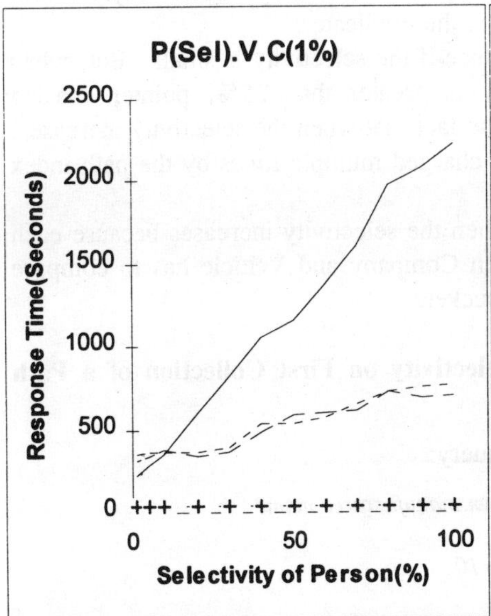

Fig. 5.4: Varying Selectivity of Person(1)

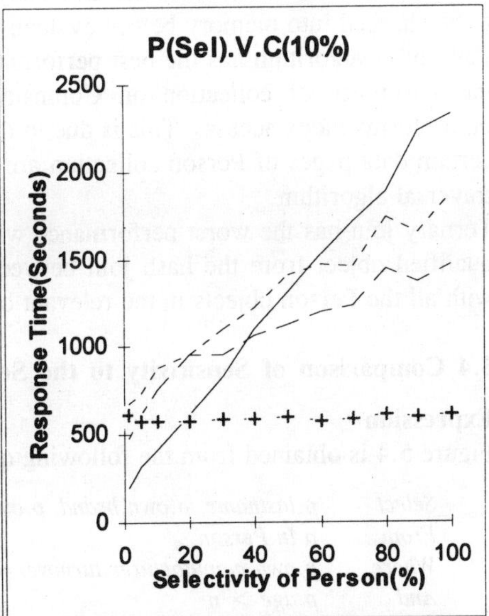

Fig. 5.5: Varying Selectivity of Person(2)

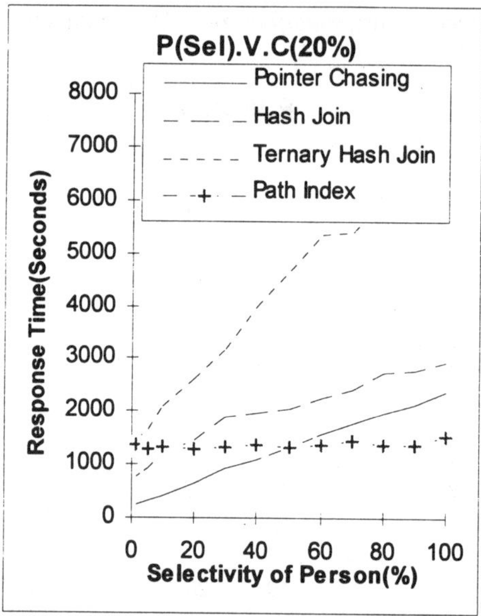

Fig. 5.6: Varying Selectivity of Person(3)

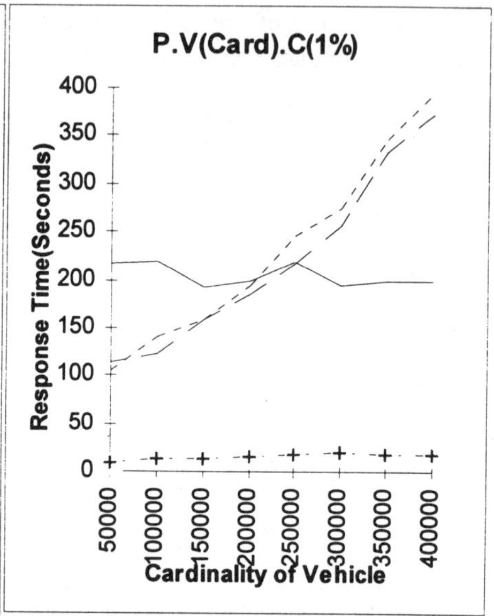

Fig. 5.7: Varying Cardinality of Vehicle

The CPU cost is negligible since pointer chasing follows pre-computed object links. The selectivity on Company has little influence on the response time of pointer chasing since the states of all the Company objects referred by Vehicle objects have to be charged into memory before evaluating the predicate.

Path index algorithm has the best performance if the selectivity is small. But, when the selectivity of collection on Company is greater than 25%, pointer chasing outperforms index access. This is due to the fact that when the selectivity increases, certain data pages of Person collection are charged multiple times by the path index traversal algorithm.

Ternary join has the worst performance when the selectivity increases because each qualified object from the hash join between Company and Vehicle has to compare with all the Person objects in the relevant bucket.

5.4 Comparison of Sensitivity to the Selectivity on First Collection of a Path Expression

Figure 5.4 is obtained from the following query:

Select	*p.lastname, p.own.brand, p.own.manufacturer.mame*
From	*p In Person*
Where	*p.own.manufacturer.turnover=10*
And	*p.age > **n***

Fig. 5.8: Path Expression Example

For running the above query, we vary the selectivity on Person collection while the selectivity of Company collection remains the same. From **Figure 5.4** we can see that pointer chasing algorithm is very sensitive to the position of predicate and its selectivity. When the selectivity of the first collection of the path Person increases, the response time of pointer chasing increases in a linear form, which is shown in the cost model. When the selectivity on Person is less than 10%, pointer chasing performs better than hash joins. But once the selectivity is greater than 10%, hash joins outperform pointer chasing. Compared to pointer chasing, hash joins are more stable when the selectivity of Person changes, since both ternary hash joins and binary hash joins start from a join between Vehicle and Company. Path index access function performs the best and its response time does not change on varying the selectivity on collection Person. This is because the predicate on collection Company remains the same and its selectivity is 1%.

When the selectivity on Company Collection is increased, the pointer chasing algorithm shows more advantages over hash joins. In **Figure 5.5**, we can see that the response time of binary hash join is almost double the rate in **Figure 5.4** while pointer chasing algorithm retains the same performance. We also see that the performance of path index access method has faster increased (more than 50 times) than the selectivity (1% to 10%). We can also see that when the selectivity on Person is less than 20%, pointer chasing even outperforms path index. This is due to multiple accesses of the same data pages of Person when using index access method. Meanwhile, index access is very stable when the selectivity on Person increases since the number of IOs to access the Person objects satisfying the predicate on *Person.own.manufacturer* remains the same. The same tendency is observed in **Figure 5.6** when the selectivity on Company is increased to 20%. We can see that in this case, pointer chasing is always better compared to binary hash join.

5.5 Comparison of Sensitivity to Size of Middle Collection of a Path Expression

In this experiment, we change the cardinality of collection Vehicle while Person and Company collections remain the same size. We fix the selectivity of Company as 1 percent and the memory buffer size for running this test is 1000 pages.

From **Figure 5.7**, we can see that the performance of pointer chasing remains relatively stable. This is because the cardinality of Person doesn't change and neither does the total number of references from Person to Vehicle. Although the cardinality of Vehicle increases, those who are not referred by Person objects are never charged into memory. Thus the response time of pointer chasing is not sensitive to the increase of Vehicle's cardinality. However, the costs of binary hash join and ternary hash join are increasing in a linear form. The formulas in our cost model give a good explanation for this result. Through this experiment, we propose a heuristic rule for query optimizer: *if in a path expression a small collection is followed by a large one whose objects are only partially pointed by objects of the previous collection, it is better to use pointer chasing to traverse these two collections.*

When Vehicle's cardinality increases, both binary hash joins and ternary hash join increase in a linear way.

6. Summary and Future Work

We have presented the integration of different evaluations of path expressions in an object-oriented cost-driven query optimizer. We have proposed rules that transform path expressions (i.e., multiple collection traversals) into target object programs. The quality of the programs is analyzed by a cost model. The programs use algorithms that implement ternary and binary hash join traversals as well as path index- and pipelined- (i.e., one object at a time or depth-first pointer chasing) traversals. We have also presented experimental results that confirm the cost model and compare the efficiency of the programs. The rules have been described with the OFL (Object Functional Language) traversal formalism which unifies the search space explored by the classic *query rewriting* and *query planning* phases of an object optimizer as OFL programs. OFL is a target object language for OQL-like query compilers. OFL programs describe the traversals of collections in the execution world. In the traversal, functional predicate and projection expressions can be applied.

The experimental study compares OFL programs that evaluate multiple collection traversals. We have studied the effect of the memory buffer size and the predicate selectivities of collections. The most significant results are:

- a cost-model is necessary;
- all the traversal algorithms are much related to the memory-buffer size and the collection sizes, and none of them is absolutely the best in all conditions;
- binary hash join traversals have been never shown as the most efficient, but they have usually been an appropriate evaluation;
- ternary hash join traversal can sometimes offer better performance compared to a traversal involving two binary hash joins, particularly when the memory buffer size is small compared to the collection sizes;
- pipelined (i.e., depth-first pointer chasing) traversals can be very efficient, but they are very sensitive to the memory buffer size;
- path index traversals are usually the best traversals since path indexes correspond to a materialization of a whole navigation.

The performance of the ternary join algorithm reminds us that certain operators (n-ary operators) abandoned in the research should be reinvested in an object environment. The cost-effectiveness of such operators is compromised by the complexity of a larger search space. We are working on looking for some heuristics (e.g., the one proposed in Section 5) based on both the cost model and the experimentation.

References

[BAB79] Babb E., "Implementing a Relational Database by Means of Specialized Hardware", ACM Transactions on Database Systems, Vol 4 n°1, March 1979.

[BLA93] Blakeley J., Graefe G., "Experiences Building the Open OODB Query Optimizer", Intl. ACM SIGMOD Conf. on Management of Data, 1993.

[CAR88] Carey M.J., Dewitt D., Vandenberg S.L., "A Data Model and Query Language for EXODUS", Intl. ACM SIGMOD Conf. on Management of Data, 1988.

[CAT93] Cattell R.G.G. Ed., "Object Databases: The ODMG-93 Standard", Book, Morgan & Kaufman, 1993.

[CLU92] Cluet S., Delobel C., "A General Framework for the Optimization of Object-Oriented Queries", intl. ACM SIGMOD Conf. on Management of Data, 1992.

[COD70] Codd E.F., "A Relational Model of Data for Large Shared Data Banks", Communications of the ACM, Vol 13 n°6, p377-387, June 1970.

[DEW85] DeWitt D., Gerber R.J., "Multiprocessor hash-based join algorithms", Int. Proceedings of Conference on Very Large Databases VLDB, p151-164, Stockholm, 1985.

[FIE88] Field A., Harrison P., "Functional Programming", chapter 11 and 12, Book, Addison Wesley 1988.

[FIN94] Finance B., Gardarin G., "A rule-based optimizer with multiple search strategies", Data & Knowledge Engineering 13, 1994.

[GAR92] Gardarin G., Valduriez P., "ESQL: An Object-Oriented SQL with F-Logic Semantics", Intl. Conf. on Data Engineering, Phoenix, February 1992.

[GAR95a] Gardarin G., Machuca F., Pucheral P., "OFL: A Functional Execution Model for Object-Oriented Languages", Intl. ACM SIGMOD Conf. on Management of Data, 1995.

[GAR95b] Gardarin G., Machuca F., "Query Optimization as Object Functional Language (OFL) Transformations", BDA, Nice, France, September 1995.

[GAR95c] Gardarin G., Gruser J.R, Tang Z.H., "A Cost Model for Clustered Object-Oriented Databases", Int. Proceedings of Conference on Very Large Databases VLDB, Switzerland, 1995.(to appear)

[GRA93] Graefe G., "Volcano, An Extensible and Parallel Dataflow Query Processsing System", Intl. Conf. on Data Engineering, 1993.

[HAA90] Haas L.M., Chang W., Lohman G.M., McPherson J., Wilms P.F., Lapis G., Lindsay B., Pirahesh H., Carey M.J., Shekita E., "Starbust Mid-Flight: As the Dust Clears", IEEE Transactions on Knowledge and Data Engineering, Vol.2, N.1, March 90.

[JEN90] Jenq B. P., Woelk D., Kim W., Lee W., "Query Processing in Distributed ORION", Intl. Conf. EDBT, Venice, Italy, March 1990.

[KEM90] Kemper A., Moerkotte G., "Advanced Query Processing in Object Bases Using Access Support Relations", Intl. Conf. on VLDB, Brisbane, Australia 1990.

[KIF92] Kifer M., Kim W., Sagiv Y., "Querying Object-Oriented Databases", ACM SIGMOD, USA, June 1992.

[KIM88] Kim W., et al., "Integrating an Object-Oriented Programming System with a Database System", International Conference on Object-Oriented Programming Systems, Languages, and Applications, SanDiego, 1988.

[KIM95] Kim W., "Object-Orientd Database Systems: Promises, Reality, and Future", in Modern Database Systems, Won Kim, Addison Wesley, 1995.

[LAN92] Lanzelotte R., Valduriez P., Zait M., "Optimization of Object-Oriented Recursive Queries using Cost-Controlled Strategies", ACM SIGMOD Int. Conf., 1992.

[LEH86] Lehman T., Carey M., "Query Processing in Main Memory Database Management Systems", ACM SIGMOD Int. Conf., Washington, D.C., May 1986.

[MIS92] Mishra P., Eich M.H., "Join Processing in Relational Databases", ACM Computing Surveys, Vol. 24, N°1, March 1992.

[MIT93] Mitchell G., Dayal U., Zdonik S.,"Control of an Extensible Query Optimizer: A Planning-Based Approach", Intl. Conf. on VLDB, Dublin, Ireland 1993.

[ORE92] Orenstein J., Haradhvala S., Margulies B., Sakahara D., "Query Processing in the ObjectStore Database System", Intl. ACM SIGMOD Conf. on Management of Data, 1992.

[OZS95] Ozsu M., Blakeley J., "Query Processing in Object-Oriented Database Systems", in Modern Database Systems, Won Kim, Addison Wesley, 1995.

[SHA86] Shapiro L., "Join Processing in Database Systems with Large Main Memories", ACM Transactions on Database Systems, Vol 11 n°3, p239-264, September 1986.

[SHA90] Shaw G., Zdonik S., "A Query Algebra for Object-Oriented Databases", in IEEE, 1990.

[SHE90] Shekita E.J., Carey M.J., "A Perfomance Evaluation of Pointer-Based Joins", in Proc. of the ACM SIGMOD Conference, 1990.

[STE94] Steenhagen H.J., Apers P.M.G., Blanken H., de By R.A., "From Nested-Loop to Join Queries in OODB", Intl. Conf. on VLDB, Santiago de Chile, September 1994.

[VAL87] Valduriez P., "Join Indices", ACM Transactions on Database Systems, Vol 12 n°2, p218-246, June 1987.

[VAL91] Valduriez P., Lanzelotte R., Ziane M., Cheiney J.P., "Optimization of non Recursive Queries in OODB", In Proc. DOOD, Munich, Germany, 1991.

[VAN91] Vandenberg S.L., DeWitt D.J., "Algebraic Support for Complex Objects with Arrays, Identity, and Inheritance", in Proc. of the ACM SIGMOD Conference, 1991.

[WHI92] White S., Dewitt D., "A Performance Study of Alternative Object Faulting and Pointer Swizzling Strategies", Intl. Conf. on VLDB, Vancouver, August 1992.

[YAO77] Yao S.B. "Approximating the number of accesses in database organizations", In Comm. of the ACM, 20(4):260, April 1977.

Translating Database Update Statements from Relational to Object-Oriented Database Systems for Database Reengineering

Joseph Fong
Department of Computer Science
City University of Hong Kong
Tat Chee Avenue, Hong Kong
Email: csjfong@cityu.edu.hk

Paul Chitson
Department of Computer Science
City University of Hong Kong
Tat Chee Avenue, Hong Kong
Email: cschitso@cityu.edu.hk

Abstract. In this paper we present a method to translate update transactions into equivalent transactions which can be executed over a reengineered version of a schema. The source schema is expressed in the relational data model and the target schema is a reengineered version expressed in the object-oriented data model. The translated transaction takes into consideration the enhanced semantics of the target schema, and the different inherent constraints of the two data models. The results of this work are applicable both to the construction of a relational interface to an object-oriented database and for a better understanding of the surrounding applications for application reengineering.

Keywords. Database Reengineering, Relational, Object-Oriented, Transaction Translation, Translation, Object Migration, Taxonomic Reasoning

1. Introduction

1.1 Database Systems Reengineering

Object-oriented systems offer improvements in productivity by providing direct support for complex highly structured data. Why then are so few companies adopting object-oriented database systems? The reasons include, a lack of trained personnel and a legacy of applications code. The former is gradually being catered for by numerous courses, but the latter poses many problems. The problem is not that companies do not see the benefits of object technology it is that they do not see the benefits of reengineering code which already works (unless maintenance costs are sufficiently high) when there are more "productive" tasks for its computer specialists to perform. Traditional database systems reengineering methodologies are best suited to large organisations with sufficient resources to reengineer the applications code within an acceptable time frame. For those companies which do not have the luxury of a large computer department, this style of reengineering (applications then database) is not suitable. How then can companies take advantage of the productivity benefits of object-oriented systems without the need to first redevelop the existing applications?

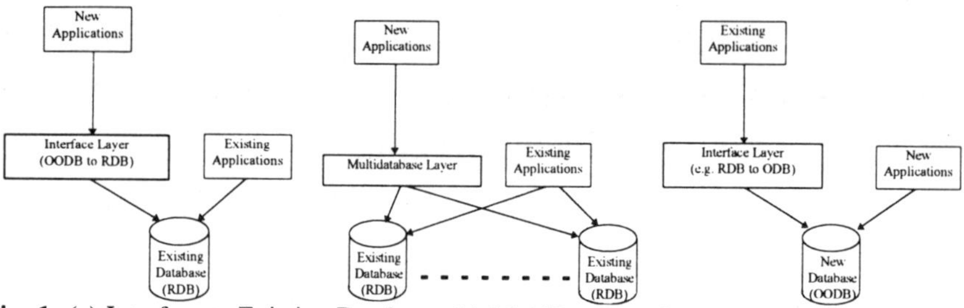

Fig. 1. (a) Interface to Existing Database, (b) MultiDatabase System, (c) Interface to New Database

Industry has provide two solutions to the problem, (1) an object-oriented interface to existing relational databases (see Fig. 1a), and (2) multidatabase systems (see Fig. 1b); the latter allows more than one database to be combined and provides query language support. The problem with these approaches is that they can not reliably provide the performance required by newer applications which use navigational access patterns to explore the data. However, they do provide a period of time over which existing applications can be reengineered. If the newer applications generally demand faster access times then it seems logical the we should consider designing a relational interface over the reengineered object-oriented database (see Fig. 1c). The performance impact of this interface on the existing applications would generally be unnoticeable as few applications perform set at a time processing instead they process the results of a query one at a time. It is with this in mind that we have begun to study techniques for translating between relational and object oriented data manipulation language expressions. In the following we are specifically looking at the translation of relational update expressions. The results of this work can be applied to (1) for the construction of an interface layer for the operation of existing relational applications, (2) the conversion of programs by code substitution, and (3) to provide a better understanding of the applications code for application reengineering.

1.2 Scope of This Paper

In this paper we address the process of update transaction translation for database reengineering. Our goal is to derive an equivalent object-oriented update transaction for a source relational transaction. To accomplish this we must take into consideration differences in the representation of the source schema's semantics resulting from the translation process, as well as the differences in the inherent semantics of the two data models. Because of the differences in semantics there does not normally exist a one-to-one mapping between the DML update expressions. The following example (where we ignore the relational database constraints) illustrates the types of problems encountered.

The relation Employee, shown in Fig. 2a, has been translated into the class hierarchy Employee-Manager shown in Fig. 2b. The instances of the class Manager are created from tuples in the relation Employee which are referenced by at least one other tuple in the relation through the mgr-id attribute. All tuples which are not managers become instances of the Employee class. The mgr-id field is changed into the object reference field *mgr* of type *Manager*. We have made the object identifiers (OID's) of the instances explicit in the Figure.

Employee

emp-id	mgr-id
1	2
2	NULL
3	2

(a)

⇒

Class Employee

OID	emp-id	mgr
001	1	003
002	3	003

+

Class Manager::Employee

OID	emp-id	mgr
003	2	NULL

(b)

Fig. 2. (a) Simple Relational Schema, (b) The Translated Object-Oriented Schema

Given the SQL INSERT statement,

INSERT INTO Employee VALUES (4, 3)

we might be tempted to translate this as (ignoring constraints and entity integrity):

```
E := Employee new.
E.emp-id=4.
E.mgr=select OID from Manager where emp-id=3.
```

The problem with this translation is that the select statement for the mgr field of employee will end up with a NULL value as there are no matching instances in the Manager subclass. The second temptation might be to use the deep extent of the class hierarchy derived from the relation Employee,:

```
E := Employee new.
E.emp-id=4.
E.mgr=select OID from All Employee where emp-id=3.
```

This translation finds the correct Employee but unfortunately it will be of the wrong type (Employee instead of Manager). In fact the translation for this insert statement should first find the matching employee by searching the deep extent of the class Employee (which contains all the tuples of the relation Employee). If the matching tuple is of the wrong type it should be migrated to the correct type, and then the OID value will be of the right type to be placed in the mgr field of the new employee.

```
M:= select OID from ALL Employee where emp-id =3;
if (M isa Employee) Migrate M to Manager.
E := Employee new. E.emp-id=4. E.mgr=M.
```

This simple illustration highlights just one of the many difficulties encountered in translating update transactions between data models. In fact, the correct translation of the above insert statement is further complicated by the inherent (data model) and explicit (stated) constraints which might be present in the source schema but which must be manually enforced in many of the existing object-oriented database systems.

1.3 Related Work

Several approaches to the run-time translation of queries between data models have been proposed [HOH89, KIE93, MEN93, MEN95, ROS84]. Models such as

[MEN93] and [ROS84] use a source schema (the schema over which the query is formed) which is derived by a rule-based translation process from the target schema. The uniform mapping between data model constructs allows a simple translation algorithm to be created. Unfortunately such mappings do not generally exist between the source and target schema's in reengineering projects, as the schema translation process (from source to target) recaptures the semantics of the data.

The translation of database update transactions between data models has not been studied in detail but a good statement of the problem can be found in [GAM88]. Related work on translating the effects of update transactions across views (and the inverse process of view maintenance) closely resembles the works described in [GAM88], however the majority of these papers address problems peculiar to the representation and materialisation of relational database views [e.g., DAY82, LAN90, FUR84]. The problems explored in these papers arise because of the value-based representation of associations in the relational database model. Such problems do not occur if the underlying database uses a reference based or pointer based model of associations, therefore the results of these papers have little influence on the work described here.

The effects of database updates on the position of an object in the class lattice have been studied by various authors [e.g., ABI85, ELS91]. In the latter of these papers predicates are used to determine class membership (this predicate positioning method is similar to the taxonomic reasoning method presented in [BER92]). If an object satisfies the predicates of a class it is consider a member of that class. An object can be a member of only one class at a time, an update which violates this principle is considered to be unsafe (a relaxation of this restriction and a simple set of migration operators can be found in [LI95]). Updates which cause an existing object to change its membership represent a potential migration, the update is accepted and the migration occurs if and only if a migration path has been specified between the source and destination classes. We have adapted the work discussed in these papers to construct methods suitable for the placement and migration of database entities resulting from a database update expression.

1.4 Overview

This paper is organised as follows. In section 2, we look at the relationship between the constructs in the source and target schemata. In this section we neither favour an existing translation methodology nor do we propose a new translation methodology, we only consider the results of the schema translation process. A classification of relations is defined based upon the role of the relations in the object-oriented database schema. In section 3, we look at the important topic of object instance migration. We highlight the necessity for instance migration to maintain the semantic integrity of the database and propose the use of migration paths and taxonomic reasoning to ensure that data is placed in the correct location in the database schema. In section 4, we describe the process of database update transaction translation. We look at the translation of single tuple SQL insert, update and delete statements using the information of the schema mappings and migration paths to ensure a correct translation is achieved. In section we summarise the work presented in this paper and give directions for future research efforts.

2. Schema Translation

2.1 Existing Methodologies

A large number of schema translation methodologies have been proposed in literature for reengineering and reverse engineering database schemata [e.g., MAR91, HAI93, ROS94]. In these methodologies, the user provides additional information necessary to re-establish the semantics of the data. This involvement of the user and the wide variety of mappings for seemingly similar source schema structures(e.g., weak entities and isa-relationships can be represented by the same constructs in the relational model) means that methods which go beyond the work of Meng et al [MEN93] must be created to deal with the translation of queries and updates.

2.2 Inter-Schema Relationships Framework

The data model constructs used in the source schema have a direct relationship with target schema constructs. By looking at the set of mappings which exist between constructs we can gain a better understanding of the difficulties involved in update translation. Below is a categorisation of the types of mappings which exist. Each relation will be assigned a category based upon its role in object-schema. For reasons of simplicity, we make the assumption that the source schema is normalised up to third normal form (3NF).

With a few noted exceptions the following general mappings hold:

1. All relationships represented by foreign keys in the relational model are maintained in the object model as associations, where the association is between the class of the relation holding the foreign key and the owner of that key. All associations will be considered bi-directional.
2. For simplicity only, we assume that all attributes have an identical names in both schemas.
3. An attribute or association which assumes a constant value for a specific class can be translated into meta-data (or a class constant) in the object schema.

Class Defining Relation (CDR)

A class defining relation is a relation whose data forms the basis of a class (not a class hierarchy, see below). There exists a 1:1 relationship between the tuples of the relation and the instances of this class. There are three types of relation that would satisfy this criteria, (1) a relation which does not have a foreign key as part of its primary key, (2) an M:N binary relationship relation which has attributes (or a ternary or higher order relationship relation), (3) a relation derived from a weak entity which does not semantically belong to the owner entity but merely depends upon its existence. The Employee relation in Fig. 2 is not a CDR as it maps into a hierarchy with its tuples being dispersed over the two classes in the hierarchy. Fig. 3 shows us some class defining relations of the types described above.

(a)

Product

pcode	name	revision
015	Radio	2
016	TV	4

Class Product

OID	pcode	name	revision
001	Paul	015	2
002	Peter	016	4

(b)

Order

supplier	product	qty
Sony	015	20
Phillips	016	30

Class Order

OID	supplier	product	qty
005	Sony	015	20
006	Phillips	016	30

Fig. 3. A Class Defining Relations (a) normal relation, (b) m:n binary relationship relation

Class Hierarchy Relation (CHR)

A class hierarchy relation is a relation which maps into a class hierarchy with a single root element. The tuples of the relation will be mapped into one or more instances of classes in the hierarchy, but each instance in the hierarchy will be derived from precisely one tuple. If a tuple can have more than one image under the mapping the class hierarchy represents an overlap generalisation. If the tuple can have only one image under the mapping then the hierarchy represents a disjoint generalisation, which is the more common variety in object oriented database systems. Where necessary we distinguish between the two sorts of generalisations by post fixing the subscripts "disjoint" for disjoint generalisations and "overlap" for overlap generalisations.

(a)

Project

id	mgr_id	priority	budget
1	2015	9	10000
2	2012	4	19000

\+

DesignProject

id	pcode
2	015

Class Project

OID	id	mgr	priority	budget
007	1	003	9	10000

\+

Class DesignProject::Project

OID	id	mgr	priority	budget	pcode
008	2	002	4	19000	015

(b)

Employee

emp_id	name	Sex	Skilled
2012	Paul	M	Y
2016	Peter	M	N
2015	Jane	F	N

Employee

OID	emp_id	name

Skilled::Employee

OID	emp_id	name
002	2012	Paul

Male::Employee

OID	emp_id	name
002	2012	Paul
009	2016	Peter

Female::Employee

OID	emp_id	name
003	2015	Jane

Fig. 4. Class Hierarchy Relations(a)Disjoint, (b)Overlap

The base class of a class hierarchy relation is the user defined relation at the root of the hierarchy derived from the relation. The relation employee in Fig. 2 is of type CHR . A number of other illustrative examples can be found in Fig. 4. We discuss the placement of tuples in these hierarchies in section 3.

Class Specialisation Relation (CSR)

Specialisation/generalisation hierarchies in the conceptual model are mapped into a series of relations in the relational model. If the chosen representation was that the additional attributes in the specialisation of a entity are stored in a separate relation then these relations will be classified as CSR relations. Inserting a tuple into CSR relations will cause an instance of one class to migrate to one of its subclasses. The base class of a CSR relation is the base class of the relation it refines. A CSR may specialise only class hierarchy relations. We do not consider multiple inheritance in this paper.

In Fig. 4b above, the relation DesignProject is a CSR which creates a single inheritance hierarchy when combined with the CHR Project. Without the relation DesignProject the relation Project would have been classified as a CDR.

Class Component Relation (CCR)

When a high level conceptual entity is mapped into the relational model it undergoes a process of normalisation. After normalisation a single entity will often be scattered over more than one relation. Of the relations generated from the normalisation of a single entity, one will be referenced by all the others, the base relation, and will be classified as either CHR, CDR or CSR. The remaining relations will have the classification of CCR.

There are two varieties of CCR's we will consider, the first has only 1 attribute other than the primary key of its base relation. This type of CCR will create a set of immutable object, that is objects without any OID's. The second type creates sets of mutable object. In the method description we have chosen to change CCR's of the second type into CDR type relations, simplifying the methods for translating the update expressions. The base class for a CCR relation is the base class of the base relation. Fig. 5 below shows an example CCR, the base relation in this example is the relation Employee. An Employee can have numerous Skills hence the set brackets in the skills columns of the resulting classes.

Employee

emp_id	name	age
2012	Paul	29
2016	Peter	30

+

Skills

emp_id	skill
2012	eletrical
2012	typing

⇒

Class Employee

OID	emp_id	name	age	skills
001	2012	Paul	29	{typing, electrical}
002	2016	Peter	30	{}

Fig. 5. A Class Component Relation Skills

Class Association Relation (CAR)

A class association relation is a special type of mapping for relations representing a binary M:N relationship where the relation has either no attributes, or the attributes semantically belong to one of the related entities. We assume in this paper that all CARs do not have additional non-key attributes, although we can easily accommodate them in the algorithms discussed below. A CAR will be mapped into associations between the classes derived from the relations participating in the relationship. CARs have two base classes, which are the base classes of the relations participating in the relationship. In the method for update translation only one of these base classes is required. Fig. 6 shows an example of a relation EmpProj which can be classified as a CAR.

Employee

emp_id	name	age
2012	Paul	29
2016	Peter	30

+

EmpProj

emp_id	p_id
2012	1
2012	2
2016	2

+

Project

id	mgr_id	priority	budget
1	2015	9	10000
2	2012	4	19000

⇓

Class Employee

OID	emp_id	name	age	projects
001	2012	Paul	29	{007,008}
002	2016	Peter	30	{008}

Class Project

OID	id	mgr	priority	budget	members
007	1	001	9	10000	{001}
008	2	002	4	19000	{001,002}

Fig. 6. A Class Association Relation

2.4 Assumptions

Several assumptions must be made for the results of a schema translation to be classified as successful. We use the following criteria for success (1) the schema can represent all the meaningful data held in the source database, (2) that there exists a translation of any source query which will extract the same information from the target schema using only the data and meta data stored in the target database. Given these criteria for success we can now state our assumptions about the schema and the data stored in the source database.

Assumption 1: The Target Schema Well-Defined

By well defined we imply that there are no missing semantic entities in the target schema. This means that for every semantically meaningful set of representable data in the source schema there exists a mapping of this information into the target schema so that no information is lost. A missing semantic entity could be a missing subclass in a class hierarchy. For example, if it is possible to insert an entity which can be placed in either class A or class B and the root class of the entity is not an overlap generalisation (or if multiple inheritance is allowed there does not exist a class which is both an A and a B) then the schema is not well-defined.

Assumption 2: All Foreign Keys are Total

According to the SQL standard a partial compound foreign key is not checked for a matching entity in the referenced (owner) relation, and therefore can contain meaningless data. Such keys will not map into a unique referencetherefore they can not be mapped into a single object reference. This assumption guarantees that data is not lost in the translation from a value-based to a reference-based association model, by ensuring all foreign keys are total.

Assumption 3: Distinct Classes formed from a single Relation must be associated

To guarantee that all the information in a relation is retained, when a single relation is mapped into more than one class these classes must be associated in some way. For relations of type CHR, this association is via the ISA link.

2.5 Example Schema and its Translation

The following example schemata will be used in all of the subsequent sections. This schema has been designed to illustrate some of the many types of mappings which can occur between two schemata. Where possible we have maintained the names of the attributes in the class model, and use the words 'Class' to identify the object-oriented concepts when the when the meaning is not clear from the context of the discussion. Fig. 7a, shows the source relational schema along with the classification and base classes for each relation. The derived object schema is shown in Fig. 7b.

(a)

Relation	*Classification*	*Base Class*
Employee <emp-d, name age>	CHR	Employee
Project <project-id, mgr, priority, budget>	CHR	Project
EmployeeProject <emp-id, project-id>	CAR	Employee,Project
DesignProject <project-id, product-code>	CSR	Project
Product <product-code, name, qty>	CDR	Product
Qualifications <emp-id, level, subject>	CDR	Qualification

(b)

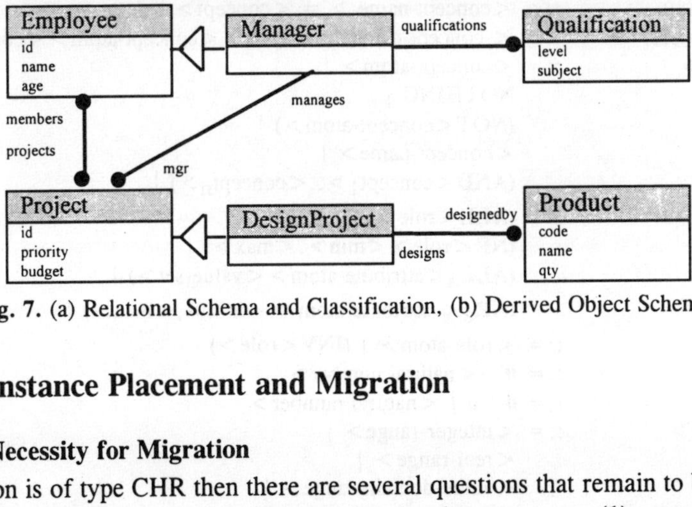

Fig. 7. (a) Relational Schema and Classification, (b) Derived Object Schema

3. Instance Placement and Migration

3.1 Necessity for Migration

If a relation is of type CHR then there are several questions that remain to be answered about the placement of tuples within the class structure: (1) annserted tuple should become an instance of which class in the hierarchy, and (2) if the data in the tuple is amended, or a related tuple is updated, how does this affect the position of the instance in the hierarchy. As we saw in the introductory example the initial placement of the tuple for employee 3 was as an instance of the Employee class. When a related tuple was added this forced the migration of the original tuple from employee to manager. In section 3.2 we review two techniques which when combined make it possible to determine where in the hierarchy a tuple should be placed and where after an update operation is its correct location, and the correct location of related instances.

3.2 Migration Graphs and Taxonomic Reasoning

3.2.1 Taxonomic Reasoning

The questions asked above about the initial placement and of possible displacements can be answered using the methods of taxonomic reasoning developed by member of the knowledge engineering community. Specifically we will use the results presented in [BER92]. In this paper Bergmaschi and Sartori present frame description language called FL* which is used to describe the differences and commonalties of *concepts*. A *concept* can be a primitive concept to the system or a defined concept. Each defined concept is described in terms of other more general concepts (its *genus)*, and locally defined structure (*differentiae*) which ascribe additional roles to a concept. A *role* is a defined relationship between instances of one concept and those of another (the *role filler*). Roles are further classified into two basic types attribute defining roles and association defining roles. Each role will have a definition line and a cardinality description. The definition line will also describe if the role is an inverse role of a role which already exists. Part of the grammar for this language is shown below, the complete grammar can be found in [BER92]:

<concept-decl>	::=	<def-decl> | <prim-decl>
<def-decl>	::=	<concept-name > = <concept>
<concept-decl>	::=	< concept-name > = (**AND** <concept-atom> <concept>)
<concept>	::=	<concept-atom> | **NOTHING** | (**NOT** <concept-atom>) | <concept-name> | (**AND** <concept$_1$>..<concept$_n$>) | (**ALL** <role> <concept>) | (**NR** <role> <min>, <max>) | (**ALL**$_a$ <attribute-atom> <value-set>) | (**NR**$_a$ < attribute-atom > <min>, <max>) |
<role>	::=	<role-atom> | (**INV** <role>)
<min>	::=	**0** | <natural number>
<max>	::=	**0** | **n** | <natural number>
<value-set>	::=	<integer-range> | <real-range> | <value-domain-range> | <value-domain-name>

<value-domain-decl> ::= <value-domain-name> = <value-atom$_1$>...<value-atom$_n$>

The following additional assumptions are required to ensure that the classification process is tractable, (1) a concept may not be cyclic, and (2)a concept can appear only once on the left hand side of a concept-declaration. A simple illustration will help to explain how this language can be used to classify the entities in our exple schema. For the Employee class in our schema its classification in FL* is as follows:

```
Employee =    ( AND e (NOT p) (NOT j) (NOT q)
              (ALLa id integer) (NRa id 1,1)
              (ALLa name string) (NRa name 1,1)
              (ALLa age integer) (NRa age 0,1)
              (ALLa qualifications Qualification) (NRa qualifications 0,n)
              (ALL projects Project) (NR projects 0,n)
              )
```

On the first line e is concept-atom, which is a definitive mark of the concept employee and can be used to distinguish it from other entities such as products(p), projects(j) and qualifications (q). The next four lines refer to attributes of the concept employee. The keyword ALL means that all the instances of the concept employee can have an id, a name and/or an age value recorded for them. The second half of these lines define the ratio of role owners to role fillers. Notice that an employee can have no qualifications thus qualifications is an optional attribute role. The last line of the definition describes the association role, projects, which describes the association between an employee and the projects for which they are members. Next we will look at how the concept of a manager is defined:

```
Manager    =  (AND Employee
              (ALL (INV mgr) Project) (NR manages 1,n)
              )
```

What distinguishes a Manager from an Employee is that they manage at least one project as is defined by the role projects which can have between 1 and n role fillers. Defining entities in this way provides us with a way in which to locate the correct location in the class lattice for a newly insert data item. We use the functions CONCEPTUALISE(o) and CLASSIFY(schema-def, conceptualised-object) from[BER92]. CONCEPTUALISE takes an object and produces a FL* description of the object. The function CLASSIFY takes the definition of the schema and the conceptualisation of a concept and returns a set of concepts which the new concept subsumes. When any change to the database is made it is necessary to check every object which might have been affected by the update and make the appropriate adjustments. Migration graphs (see 3.2.2) are introduced to reduce the scope of this search and to stop semantically undesirable migrations from occurring.

For each relation we can define an separate conceptualisation function which given a tuple (fully defined) returns a conceptualised version which replaces each foreign key by its corresponding OID value and defines the attribute by the value given. The function return false if any of the foreign keys in the relation cannot be expanded. We also define a method for each class to do the same for an object in a class.

3.2.2 The Migration Graph

Not every migration is semantically desirable and instances may not migrate even though when they are conceptualised they appear not to belong to the class in which they currently reside. A good example of this is the employee who become a manager. It may not make sense, based just upon the role in a project as a manager to banish a person from the status of manager when he no longer manages a project. Therefore we can semantically justify retaining an employee as a manager even though he does not fulfil the role of the manager completely. To aid in this decision process we have chosen a graph representation similar to that of El-Sharkawi and Kambayashi, [ELS91] who define a labelled directed graph of allowable migrations G = < V, E, L>. Each class in the object schema corresponds to a single vertex in the set V. Ordered pairs of classes between which migration is permitted make up the members of the set of edges E. Each edge in E is annotated with two separate annotations, the first annotation describes the attributes of the object at the beginning of edge or of related objects which if changed would cause a migration from the beginning of the edge to the end of the edge. This annotation reduces the amount of work that must be done each time an update is made to the database. The second annotation defines the type of migration which occurs down the edge, that is whether the migration is destructive of constructive. A Destructive migration means that the object ceases to be a member of the source class and becomes a member of the target class. A constructive migration is where the class remains a member of the source class and also becomes a member of the target class. We add additional edges to this graph which indicate migrations which are "not required",. These correspond to acceptable updates but allow the object to reside in a class even though it no longer satisfies the conceptual definition of that class. The figure below, Fig. 8a, augments the basic ISA hierarchy of our example schema with the migration paths indicated by the curved dotted lines. Each of these migration paths has an associated label which are defined in part b of the same figure.

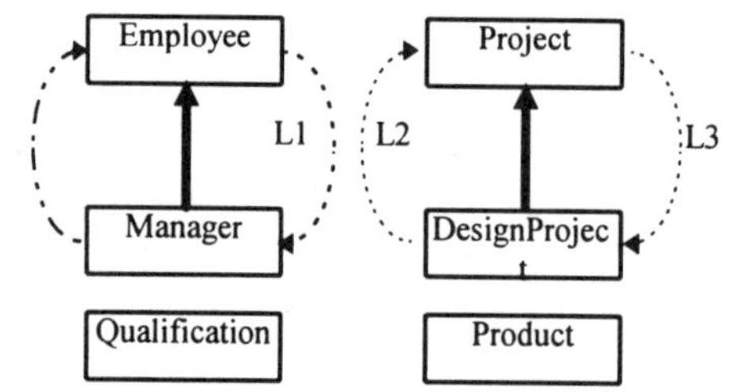

Label
L1 = Project.mgr = Employee, destructive
L2 = DesignProduct.designs is empty, destructive
L3 = Product. designedby = Project, destructive

←---- Not required ←...... Migration Path ← ISA

Fig. 8. (a) Migration graph (with ISA displayed), (b) Labels for the edges

You will notice that a migration from Employee to manager occurs when a project is inserted whose manager is a member of the shallow extent of the class Employee. The "not required" edge in the reverse direction tells us that if all the managers projects are removed the update can be accepted but a migration from the class manager is not required.

3.3 The Migration Functions

The actual migration operation has been discussed in some detail by Li and Dong [LI94]. In this paper they define three goals for migrations: identity preservation, behaviour transition and information conservation. These are summarised below:

Identity Preservation Goal: To preserve the identity of the migrating object during migration.
Behaviour Transition Goal: The ability to abandon the behaviour of the original class and adopt the behaviour of the target class.
Information Conservation Goal: To preserve as much of the information applicable to the destination class a possible.

Each object in their work can be a member of many classes, but for the purpose of initiating searches for attribute and methods one of the class is nominated as the base class for the object. The OID of the object is the same in all classes it occupies. A migration can be categorised into one of four types depending upon the type (constructive or destructive) and the cardinality (1:1 or 1:N) of the migration. Three operators sufficient to carry out all migrations were defined, *PROPAGATE, TRANSMIT* and *RETRACT*. The first two of these operations correspond to constructive and destructive migrations of an object whilst the latter enables an object to relinquish its membership from a list of classes

In this papers we define a function MIGRATION which given an object as a set of target objects decides the appropriate set of migration operators to perform:

MIGRATION(Object, DestClasses): BOOLEAN

The Migration function attempts to migrate the Object from its current state into the classes in the destination class set, DestClasses. If there are any classes in the list for which a migration or a "not required" path does not exist then function returns false, otherwise it performs the required migrations and returns true.

3.4 Migrating Related Entities

When an instance of a class is migrated, instances of other classes may also be affected. The migration graph tells us which objects might be sensitive to changes. Given an object and the list of changes made, we define a function which returns the set of objects affected by the change,

MGCHANGE(Object, Change): Set of Objects

where Change is a list of changes that have been made. This list will include the attribute value pairs for newly specified attributes, triplets, (attribute, oldvalue, new value), for modified attributes and changes in the class(es) that an object belongs too. Using the above function we define the following pseudo code algorithm for migrating related entities.

```
MIGRATERELATED ( object, change): Boolean
{
possiblyaffected = MCCHANGE(object, change)
while (possiblyaffected is not empty) do
```

```
        {
        remove any element O from the set possiblyaffected.
        newclasses = CLASSIFY(O.isa, CONCEPTUALISE(O))
        if (newclasses - O.isa is not empty)
            {
            if (MIGRATION(O, newclasses) == FALSE) return FALSE
            possiblyaffected=possiblyaffected ∪ MGCHANGE(O, typechanged)
            }
        }
        return TRUE
    }
```

This function migrates the related entities until no migrations are necessary. Objects are only added to the set, possiblyaffected, if they are affected by the changes made to the database as a result of the update transaction.

4. Transaction Translation

4.1 Transaction Translation Basics

From work on view maintenance we can described the problem of update translation as an equation:

$$T(U(I_R)) = V(T(I_R))$$

where T is a total function transforming the relational database state into its object-oriented equivalent, I_R is the state of the relational database before the update. Given the update U we need to find an update V such that the above equation holds. Implicit in this statement is that the constraints of the source relational database are also conserved in the object-oriented database. Therefore, before we look at the process of finding the equivalent update operation(s) we will look at the problem of constraint enforcement.

4.2 Constraint Enforcement

The support for arbitrary database constraints or even the simpler constraints are not supported in many of the existing object-oriented database systems. Constraints can be defined within the methods of the objects but if an update changes many values in the same object by calling several of these methods the same constraint may be checked a number of times. If we leave constraint checking until commit time and add the constraints to a special commit method then we are making a decision on when the constraints should be enforced. The choice of when to check should ideally reside with the user (or programmer). In this paper we will check constraints in the process of translating a single update expression, but do not make assumptions about where the constraints are kept or how they will be expressed. We have specifically chosen not to use the constraint enforcement methods that belong to a specific object-oriented database system.

Below, we classify the constraints of the relational schema into four basic types and discuss referential integrity constraint actions (we do not discuss the notion of triggered actions on ASSERT statements for simplicity).

Entity Integrity Constraints (or primary key constraints). We create an index object for each relation in the relational schema. This index stores primary key and associated OID values for all the tuples currently represented in the database. The index object provides methods to insert, delete and find entries in the index. This index can also be used to resolve foreign key values.

Referential integrity. Using the index created for each relation we can find the OID for each fully defined foreign key or updated foreign key in a relational tuple. The assumption that all associations are bi-directional means that enforcing this type of constraint is easily performed.

Local Constraints. Of the remaining constraints we define local constraints to be constraints which to be access data in the updated tuple only. In SQL2 expressions of this type could be written using the CREATE ASSERTION clause or more simply as a NOT NULL extension on an attribute definition. We define a function CHECKLCONS(relation, attribute-values):BOOLEAN which given the relation name and the value of the updated or inserted tuple returns true if no local constraint was violated and false otherwise.

Global Constraints. Global constraints include all those constraints, other than referential and entity integrity constraints, which reference data outside of the current tuple. For these types of constraints, which are specified using either the ASSERT statement or the UNIQUE clause are checked when the function CHECKGCONS(relation, Object):BOOLEAN is called. This function is similar to CHECKLCONS, returning true if no constraint was violated and false otherwise.

Referential Constraint Actions. Referential constrain actions are the actions triggered when a tuple referenced by a foreign key is deleted or has its primary key is updated. Their are four actions which can occur on either of these events DISALLOW(the default action), SET NULL, CASCADE and SET DEFAULT. The actions SET NULL and SET DEFAULT are unavailable for the foreign key in the primary key of CCR and CSR's as they are not semantically meaningful in these cases. In all other cases we have chosen to enforce these methods by placing a method in the primary key holding relations which checks all the references to itself and carries out the appropriate actions. We called this method *autoaction*. The *autoaction* method returns the boolean value true if all the actions have been taken successfully and false otherwise.

4.3 Input Requirements and Pseudo Code Description

The methods described below use the following functions and methods described above to perform there tasks. Below we have broken these into three different sets, auxiliary functions, relation functions, and class methods.

Auxiliary Functions

CLASSIFY(concept): CLASS SET A function returning the set of classes in the object schema that a new concept belongs to (see section 3.2.1).
MIGRATION(object, destclass): BOOLEAN Returns true if the object can migrate to the classes in destclass and perform the migration which can be either, constructive or destructive.
MIGRATERELATED(object, change): BOOLEAN returns true if all the migration of related objects that were necessary all completed successfully, and false otherwise.

Relation Functions
$INDEX_{REL}$ An index object is maintained for each relation in the source schema and is used for entity integrity constraint checks and for resolving foreign key values. An index object has the following three methods: *FIND(PKEY)* returns NULL if the item does not exist, OID otherwise *ADD(PKEY,OID)* returns false if already a member true + inserts entry otherwise *DEL(PKEY,OID)* returns false if already a member true + inserts entry otherwise
CHECKLCONS(relation, Tuple): BOOLEAN Checks local constraints for the relation given the data contained in the parameter tuple. Returns false if a constraint is violated and true otherwise.
CHECKGCONS(relation, Object): BOOLEAN Checks global constraints for the relation given the data contained in the parameter Object. Returns false if a constraint is violated and true otherwise.
CONCEPTUALISE(tuple): CONCEPT Given a tuple this function returns a conceptualisation of the data it contains. In creating the conceptualisation, the tuples foriegn keys are turned into object references. If any of the foreign keys could not be resolved the function returns the conceptualisation, NOTHING.
PKEY(tuple) returns the value of the primary key from the data in the tuple.
PKEYBASE(tuple) returns the primary key value of the base relation from using the tuples data (used for a CCR, CAR, and CSR's only).

Class Methods
PKEY : RELATIONPKEY Returns the primary key of an object base base relation.
AUTOACTION(operation) : BOOLEAN Performs the referential integrity actions that must be carried out when the primary key of an object is updated or the tuple is deleted. It returns true if no DISALLOW action were encountered and all updates to related classes could be performed. It returns false otherwise.
CONCEPTUALISE(object): CONCEPT Given an conceptualise returns a conceptual representation of it expressed in FL*. For objects in the database it is always possible to conceptualise the data.

The translation methods for update expressions described in the next three subsections are written in a version of pidgin C with each line consisting of a step number, and a set of actions. The actions are preceded by a set of square brackets containing the types of relations for which the action must be carried out. The operators ALL and NOT included with the type information have obvious meanings. Method invocations and attribute dereferencing is carried out using path expressions, i.e., O.attribute or O.method. We do not favour a particular object model and where DML commands of the object model are required we use English, to describe the actions. Comments are indicated by the comment marks "//".

4.4 Translating SQL Insert Expressions

Given an SQL expression of the form

INSERT INTO relation (variable-list) VALUES (value-list)

Using default values and NULL values we can expand the value list to contain data for the entire tuple, generating an insert statement with the following general form:

INSERT INTO relation VALUES (tuple)

We have broken the translation process into a set of 8 steps. In these steps if for any reason the transaction can not complete a ROLLBACK is called. This will terminate the transaction and undo any changes that may have occurred. The successful completion is marked by the insertion of the primary key of the newly inserted tuple into the index for the relation.

(1) *// Check Local Constraints*
[ALL] if (CHECKLCONS(relation, tuple) == FALSE) ROLLBACK

(2) *// Check entity integrity*
[ALL] if ($INDEX_{REL}$.FIND (PKEY(relation)) < > NULL) ROLLBACK

(3) *// For CHR's conceptualise the data in tuple.*
[CHR] OC= CONCEPTUALISE(tuple)

// For CSR, CAR and CCR's add the conceptualised tuple to the conceptualisation of the referenced object
[CCR, CSR, CAR] (a) O = $INDEX_{REL}$.FIND (PKEYBASE(tuple))
(b) OC = CONCEPTUALISE(tuple) U CONCEPTUALISE(O)

(4) *// For all but CDR 's , find the location for the updated or inserted object in the class lattice*
[NOT CDR] ClassSet = CLASSIFY(OC)

(5) *// For CDR 's insert the new object*
[CDR] O = INSERT entity

// For CHR's create an instance for each of the classes in ClassSet . All instances should have the same OID value.
[CHR] For all in ClassSet O =INSERT entity

// Migrate the object O to the classes in the class set. If it fails then rollback.
[CAR,CCR,CSR] if (MIGRATION(O, ClassSet)==FALSE) ROLLBACK

(6) *// Migrate related instances if necessary*
[ALL] if (MIGRATERELATED(O, changes) == FALSE) ROLLBACK

(7) // Check for general constraint violation
[ALL] if (CHECKGCONS(relation, O) == FALSE) ROLLBACK.

(8) *// Add the new (primary key, OID)pair to the index*
[ALL] $INDEX_{REL}$.ADD (O.PKEY, O)

4.5 Translating SQL Update Expressions

Given an update expression of the form,

UPDATE REL SET $var_i = val_i$ WHERE selection

where var refers to a variable in the relation REL, the index is used to identify the corresponding value in what follows. Like the translation of insert statements, the translation of update expression proceeds in a stepwise fashion. Before any constraints can be checked, the instance to be updated must be identified. The following 9 steps are sufficient for translating expressions between the two models whilst preserving the database constraints:

(1) *// Locate selected object using Query translation method (assumption is single object)*
[ALL] find object which corresponds to the selection, and create a tuple filled with the values taken from the object and from the var, value list. If the object cannot be found the ROLLBACK.

(2) *// Check Local Constraints*
[ALL] if (CHECKLCONS(relation, tuple) == FALSE) ROLLBACK

(3) *// If PKEY change check Entity Integrity and for CHR, CDR and CSR relation check referential Integrity actions are carried out.*
[ALL] if (pkey changed)
{
[ALL] if ($INDEX_{REL}$.FIND (PKEY(relation)) < > NULL) ROLLBACK
[CSR, CHR, CDR] if (O.AUTOTRIGGER(update) == FALSE) ROLLBACK.
}

(4) *// Update object*
[ALL] Update the values in the object

(5) *// Find the new location(s) for the updated object*
[NOT CDR] ClassSet = CLASSIFY(CONCEPTUALISE(O))

(6) *// Migrate if necessary the object O to the locations identified in step 5.*
[NOT CDR] MIGRATIONS(O, ClassSet)

(7) *// Migrate related instances if necessary*
[ALL] if (MIGRATERELATED(O, changes) == FALSE) ROLLBACK

(8) *// Check for general constraint violation*
[ALL] if (CHECKGCONS(relation, O) == FALSE) ROLLBACK.

(9) *// update the (primary key, OID)pair in the index if the primary key has changed.*
[ALL] if (Primary key has changed)
{
$INDEX_{REL}$.DELETE (O.PKEY, O);

$INDEX_{REL}$.ADD (O.PKEY, O);
}

4.6 Translating SQL Delete Expressions

Given an SQL deletes statement of the form,

DELETE FROM rel WHERE selection

The following 8 steps will translate the update expression into an equivalent set of operations on the object database:

(1) *// Locate selected object using Query translation method (assumption is single object)*
[ALL] find object which corresponds to the selection, and create a tuple full with values taken from the object and from the var,value list. If the object cannot be found the ROLLBACK.

(2) *// for CSR, CHR and CDR's check if allowable for autotrigger.*
[CSR, CHR, CDR] if (O.AutoTrigger(delete) == FALSE) ROLLBACK.

(3) *// Delete the object or remove its data.*
[CDR, CHR] delete object
[CCR,CSR,CAR] update data in object.

(4) *//Conceptualise updated object*
[CCR,CSR,CAR] ClassSet = CLASSIFY(CONCEPTUALISE(O))

(5) *//Migrate updated object*
[CCR,CSR,CAR] if (MIGRATIONS(O, ClassSet) == FALSE) ROLLBACK

(6) *// Migrate related instances if necessary*
[ALL] if (MIGRATERELATED(O, changes) == FALSE) ROLLBACK

(7) *// Check for general constraint violation*
[ALL] if (CHECKGCONS(relation, O) == FALSE) ROLLBACK.

(8) *// Delete form Relations Index*
[ALL] $INDEX_{REL}$.DELETE (O.PKEY, O);

5. Conclusion

In this paper we have discussed and presented one possible solution to the process of database update transaction translation. The rationale for proposing this method was to provide an alternative solution for companies wishing to migrate from a relational database systems to an object oriented database systems without having to wait until all the existing applications are made ready. With a method for the translation of database queries this creates a pathway for the gradual migration of existing applications between data models whilst allowing newer applications to be developed.

We are currently developing an interface system which will allow for the gradual migration of an application to the new database system by a stepwise replacement strategy. The new system will allow SQL and OQL to be mixed (noting that OQL is an extension to SQL) thereby facilitating the gradual reduction of the relational interface and greater freedom to make adjustments to the object schema.

References

[ABI85] Abiteboul, S., and Hull, R.,*Update Propagation in the IFO Database Model*, Proceedings of International Conference on the Foundations of Data Organisation, 1985, pp. 243-251.

[BER92] Bergmaschi, S., and Sartori, C., *On Taxonomic Reasoning in Conceptual Design*, ACM TODS, vol 17, No., 3, Sept. 1992, pp. 385-422.

[DAY82] Dayal, U., and Bernstein, P. A., *On the Correct Translation of Update Operations on Relational Views*, ACM TODS, vol 8, no. 3, Sept 1982, pp. 381-416.

[ELM93] Elmasri, R. A., Kouramajian, V., and Thalhiem, B. (eds.), Entity Relationship Approach-ER'93, Lecture Notes in Computer Science 823, Springer-Verlag, 1993.

[ELS91] El-Sharkawi, M., E., and Kambayashi, Y., *Object Migration Mechanisms to Support Updates in Object-Oriented Databases*, in [RIS91], pp. 80-94.

[FUR84] Furtadoa, A. L., and Casanova, M. A., *Updating Relational Views*, in [KIM84], pp. 126-142.

[GAM88] Gamal-Eldin, M. S., Thomas, G., and Elmasri, R., *Integrating Relational Databases with Support for Updates*, IEEE Data Engineering, 1988, pp. 202-209.

[HAI93] Hainaut, J-L, Tonneau, C., Joris, M., and Chandelon, M., *Transformation-Based Database Reverse Engineering*, in [ELM93], pp. 364-375.

[HOH89] Hohenstein , U., *Automatic Transformation of an Entity-Relationship Query Language into SQL*, in [LOC89], pp. 303–321.

[KIE93] Keim, D.A., Kriegel, H-P., and Miethsam, A., Object-Oriented Querying of Existing Relational Databases, in [MAR93], pp. 325-336.

[KIM84] W. Kim, D. S. Reiner, and D. S. Batory(eds), *Query Processing in Database System* , Springer-Verlag, 1984

[LAN90] Langerak, R., *View Updates in Relational Databases with Independent Scheme*, ACM TODS, vol. 15, No. 1, March 1990, pp. 40-66.

[LI94] Li, Q., and Dong, G., *A framework for object migration in object-oriented databases*, IEEE Data and Knowledge Engineering, vol 13, 1994, pp. 221-242.

[LOC89] F. H. Lochovsky, *Entity-Relationship Approach to Database Design and Querying*, Proceedings of the eigth International Conference on Entity-Relationship Approach, October 1989, Elsevier Science Publications, 1989.

[MAR91] Marinos, L., and Smit, R. A., From Relations To Objects: A Translation Methodology for an Object Oriented Front-End to RDBMSs, in [PAP91], pp. 148-167.

[MAR93] Marik, V., and Lazansky, J., Database and Expert Systems Applications, Lecture Notes in Computer Science 720, Springer-Verlag, 1993.

[MEN93] Meng, W., Yu, C., Kim, W., Wang, G., Pham,T., and Dao, S., *Construction of a Relational Front-end for Object-Oriented Database Systems*, VLDB'93, pp. 476-483.

[MEN95] Meng, W., Yu, C., and Kim, W., *A Theory of Translation from Relational Queries to Hierarchical Queries*, IEEE Knowledge and Data Engineering, vol 7, no. 2, April 1995, pp. 228-245.

[PAP91] M.P. Papazoglou, and J. Zeleznikow (eds*), The Next Generation of Information Systems: From Data to Knowledge*, Lecture Notes in Artficial Intelligence 611, Springer-Verlag, August 1991.

[RIS91] Rishe, N, Navathe, S., and Tal, D (eds), *Databases: Theory, Design and Applications*, IEEE Computer Society Press, 1991

[ROS84] Rosenthal, A., and Reiner, D. S., *Querying Relational Views of Networks*, in [KIM84], pp. 107-124.

[ROS94] Rosenthal, A., and Reiner, D., *Tools and Transformations --Rigorous and Otherwise--for Practical Database Design*, ACM TODS, v19, n2, June 1994, pp. 167-211.

Using Semantic Enrichment to Provide Interoperability between Relational and ODMG Databases

Uwe Hohenstein

Corporate Research and Development, Siemens AG, ZFE T SE 4, D-81730 München (GERMANY)
Email: Uwe.Hohenstein@zfe.siemens.de. Tel.: +49 89 636 44011.

Abstract. This paper deals with interoperability between relational and object-oriented database systems that support the emerging ODMG-93 database standard. In order to bring relational systems into line with the semantic and operational level of ODMG-93, we reap the benefits of ideas developed in the context of semantic enrichment: Semantics of relational data that is not reflected explicitly in relational tables is expressed directly by modelling it in the higher object-oriented model. Furthermore, ODMG operations are mapped onto relational ones in the other direction. Main emphasis is put on how queries related to object-oriented schemas are translated into relational SQL queries.

1 Introduction

During the 1990's, relational DBSs (database systems) dominated the database market for business data processing applications. Powerful query mechanisms and the simplicity of the relational model of data and have been accepted as vehicles for significant productivity enhancement in application development. However, the limitation of relational technology was exposed by the emergence of various classes of new applications such as multimedia systems, geographic information systems, engineering and design systems. Those applications manage complex object structures with a navigational kind of access, hangling from one object to others. Since relational DBSs lack specifying, querying and manipulating complex objects, such applications feel their needs not satisfied by relational systems. Especially, the performance turns out to be insufficient.
Tackling those problems led to the new generation of object-oriented DBSs, which aim at supporting complex structures efficiently. But object-oriented DBSs are no universal remedy either, as some important achievements of relational systems like powerful querying and data independence get lost for the most part. Hence, no changing of the guard is to be expected. Consequently, both technologies will peaceably coexist side by side in future.
In fact, new types of advanced applications such as computer-supported cooperative work and scientific information management can greatly benefit from the respective goodies of both technologies by using relational DBSs for simple structures with query-intensive parts, and object-oriented ones for complex data

and navigational parts. Object-Relational systems such as UniSQL [KIM92] enrich relational technology with object-oriented concepts to this end. Moreover, the research field of federated DBSs (also called interoperability or multidatabases) [SHE90, KAM91, HSI92, IMS93] attempt to provide an integrated access to data stored in several DBSs. A federation framework could provide not only access to relational and object-oriented systems. It can additionally take care of *transparency* in several respect: The user can be given a unified, database spanning, and transparent access to all the integrated data. In particular, users are protected from system-specific data models, access interfaces, query languages, paradigms etc. Indeed, the uniform interface should support navigational access (as in object-oriented DBSs) as well as powerful queries in order not to lose the power of relational systems. A unified and consistent view of the integrated data stored serves as a basis. With all that, the *autonomy* of the constituent systems is preserved. Each DBS still exists as before, especially existing data and running applications are not affected.

The field of federated DBSs has brought up several results and prototypes that tackle fundamental problems [FAN91, KAM91, HSI92, IMS93, BER94]. But most effort was dedicated to relational, network, and hierarchical DBSs. Only few approaches incorporate object-oriented systems, and if they do, they use an own system instead of arbitrary commercial ones (cf. Pegasus [RAF91]). Indeed, there are also vendors of object-oriented DBSs working on gateways to relational databases, but they provide only system-specific, and no general solutions.

Our project FIHD (**F**lexible **I**ntegration of **H**eterogeneous **D**atabase Systems) aims at providing a federation framework that is open wrt. commercial relational and object-oriented systems. The main idea consists of taking the emerging industrial standard ODMG-93 [CAT94] for object-oriented DBSs as a general interface to the federation. ODMG-93 is an adequate basis, because it defines definition and manipulation facilities. Most vendors of DBSs are committed to support this standard soon. Hence, a federation framework relying on ODMG-93 will be able to plug in those ODMG conforming DBSs easily (other systems in fact need an ODMG layer upon them). What we still have to do is to bridge the gap between ODMG-93 and relational DBSs, i.e.,

1. to represent the information defined by relational tables adequately in ODMG-93 concepts,
2. to implement the ODMG object manipulation and query language on top of the system, and
3. to assist the schema integration process and to provide transparent access.

Here, we focus on the first two topics, how to plug in relational DBSs in an ODMG-based federation framework. The first point is no principal problem. Tables can be transformed to object types that possess the same 'flat' structure. This is rather bad as there are no relationships between objects, no subtype hierarchies, etc. But Step 3, schema integration, is a difficult, complex, and ambitious task. An integrated access to DBSs requires a deep knowledge of the semantics of data so that interdatabase semantic relationships can be detected. Any support that can be provided previously is useful to let the integration concentrate on its real task. Consequently, it is reasonable to have a concise description of the relational data as much as possible. The often proposed solution is *semantic enrichment* [CAS91, CAS93]: Implicit knowledge is discovered by means of reverse engineering techniques [HAI93, CHI94, PRE94] and made explicit by using higher modelling concepts [DAV87, NAV87, YAN92]. Even more, the semantics is usable in form of high-level operations (cf. Step 2), manipulating objects and relationships instead of isolated tuples.

Our approach to semantic enrichment is tailor-made to these aspects. We use a powerful specification language that enables one to specify semantics given in relational data precisely. A specification defines how tables are linked to shape object types. It is our overall goal to make explicit any semantics that is implicitly given in tables, by using object-oriented concepts extensively.

The price we pay for comprehensive remodelling capabilities is that semantic enrichment must be specified *explicitly*. We consider this matter not so bad due to the following reasons: The information in demand is often available in form of database design documents that provide a good basis for semantic enrichment. Furthermore, there has been a flurry of activities in the field of data reverse engineering to propose algorithms, methodologies, and heuristics [HAI93, CHI94, PRE94]. This work as well as knowledge acquisition approaches [CAS91, MAR90], which analyze the contents of databases, do a valuable job to detect semantics. Hence, our approach is complementary and can benefit from this work. Furthermore, those automatic approaches do not always produce satisfactory results, there is a danger of expressing wrong semantics, a fact we definitively want to avoid.

The rest of the paper is structured as follows. Section 2 presents the ODMG-93 database standard [CAT94], its object model, object definition, object manipulation, and object query language.

Section 3 is then concerned with semantic enrichment. We present a logic-based specification language to remodel tables in the ODMG-93 object model. We demonstrate the power of the language by remodelling "relational" subtype hierarchies designed by different, mixed strategies. Although the specification of semantic enrichment must be done manually, the process of generating the ODMG interface is carried out automatically due to a *generative* approach: Given an enrichment specification, a complete database interface including query facilities is generated automatically. This interface implements an ODMG-93 conforming access to relational databases.

We single out the aspect of querying in Section 4. Non-procedural query languages are the essence of the relational database technology. There is no reason to abandon these cornerstones. The data model mapping from the relational to the ODMG-93 model implies a translation of queries in the other direction: Queries that are expressed in the object model must be mapped into relational queries, depending on the specified semantic enrichment. We concentrate on one important aspect, computing the extent, i.e., the set of all objects of an object type. Our ideas build the basis for any form of query processing/translation. We define this part of query evaluation in a formal way.

In the conclusions, we outline some future work we are planning to do.

2 The ODMG-93 Database Standard

2.1 Object Model and Object Definition Language

ODMG-93 [CAT94] is principally independent of programming languages. An object model provides concepts to model objects in a neutral manner. The object model defines a common object-oriented data model. Figure 3 presents an ODMG schema modelling a company database. There are *object types* like DEPT (with object identity) that possess attributes such as DId, Name, and Branches. Each attribute has a domain, which may be primitive like Float, or predefined like Date. Object types are also valid domains. For example, Address may have domain ADDRESS which is another type. Constructors like Set, Bag, List and Array are available to build complex domains by using already defined ones. Hence, Set<String> is a complex domain. A department has a staff, i.e., a set of employees. This is modelled by a *set-valued* relationship Staff from DEPT to EMP (double-headed arrow). The other way round, an employee WorksIn at most one department, expressed by a *single-valued* relationship (simple arrows). The directions Staff and WorksIn model the same semantic relationship from different perspectives. They are called *bi-directional*; both directions are kept consistent and referential integrity is guaranteed. In contrast, Head is just a *uni-directional* relationship, directed from DEPT to MGR only.

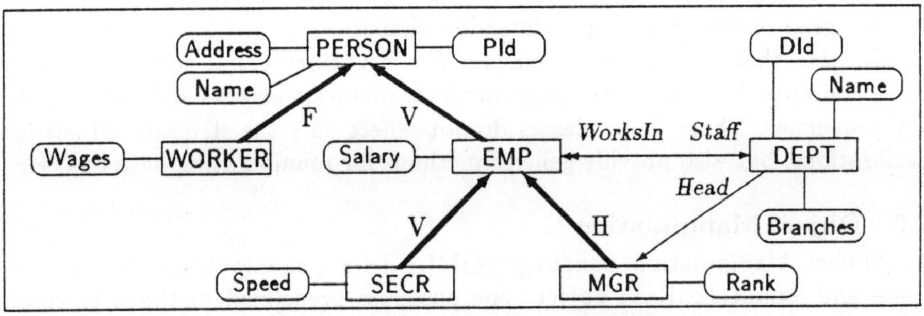

Fig. 1. Sample ODMG Schema

Object types can be organized in *subtype hierarchies*. Type PERSON has two subtypes, (blue-collar) WORKER and EMPloyee, and EMP in turn has subtypes, SECRetary and MGR (manager), graphically indicated by broad arrows. Each subtype inherits all the properties of its supertype(s), attributes as well as methods and relationships. ODMG-93 supports multiple inheritance. Hence, an object type can have several supertypes. Subtypes are disjoint wrt. instances. Non-disjoint subtypes must be modelled by means of multiple inheritance.

An *Object Definition Language* ODL reflects the concepts of the object model in a syntactic form. The ODL is still independent of any language-specific concerns. Figure 2 defines object types EMP and DEPT as interface declarations in ODL. Supertypes are specified behind a colon. An extent clause defines a variable to access the objects of a type: Hence, Depts is necessary to constitute an entry point in DEPT for querying data; only then can instances of a type be queried in an associative manner. A key-clause contains key attributes that care for uniqueness. For example, the DId-values of departments are requested to be unique.

```
interface EMP : PERSON                interface DEPT
  ( extent Emps                         ( extent Depts
  )                                       key DId )
  { attribute Float Salary;             { attribute Long DId;
    relationship DEPT WorksIn             attribute String Name;
                 inverse Staff;           attribute Set<String> Branches;
  }                                       relationship Set<EMP> Staff inverse WorksIn;
                                          relationship MGR Head;
                                        }
```

Fig. 2. Interfaces for EMP and DEPT in ODL

The part in curly brackets specifies attributes and relationships. Set-valued relationships are indicated by means of Set<...>. Keyword inverse marks a relationship as bi-directional, thus relating WorksIn in EMP to Staff in DEPT.
ODMG-93 defines *C++* and *Smalltalk bindings*. This means that ODL specifications can be transformed into C++ and Smalltalk representations. Corresponding preprocessors may perform the mapping. In case of C++, every interface declaration is transformed into a C++ class. Attributes and relationships are mapped to data members of corresponding C++ domains or predefined classes. Indeed, relationships result in pointer-like shapes.
Please note that key and extent clauses get lost, since C++ does not provide those concepts. It is up to the programmer to maintain extents and to guarantee key properties. Those C++ classes do not reflect only the structure of interface declarations, but also provide generic methods for manipulating data in C++.

2.2 Object Manipulation

An Object Manipulation Language (OML) defines manipulation features for C++ and Smalltalk. Each object type possesses predefined methods to create and delete objects, methods for navigating along relationships, for transaction management, querying, etc. The following piece of code presents a short C++ application program using the OML.

```
Database db;   db.open("myDB");
Transaction t; t.start();
Ref<EMP>       e = new(db) EMP  (3, "Lucky Luke", 3000);
Ref<DEPT>      d = new(db) DEPT (10, "Cowboys");
e->WorksIn = d;   cout << e->WorksIn->Name << endl;
...
d->Staff.delete_element(e);
Set<Ref<EMP>> empSet = d->Staff;
t.commit();
db.close();
```

Database and Transaction are predefined classes that manage database and transaction handling. After opening a database "myDB", a transaction is started. The basis for handling objects are so-called *references* given by a Ref template. They behave like C++ pointers in a certain sense, however, they are able to refer to transient *and* persistent objects. Particularly, attribute access and method invocation is done via '->'. Here, an object of type EMP with a PId 3, a name "Lucky Luke" and a salary of 3000 is created by applying operator new. The operator new requires a parameter db, the database the object is to be stored. Similarly, a department "Cowboys" is created. The employee e is hired by this department: d is assigned to the WorksIn relationship. Since the WorksIn/Staff relationship is bi-directional, the employee is implicitly inserted into the staff of department d. This can explicitly be done by d->Staff.insert_element(e), too. The employee is fired by d->Staff.delete_element(e). Additional methods are available to process the staff as a set of employees (Set<REF<EMP>>), e.g., iterators can be created to handle a collection element by element. All modifications to data are temporary, until a commit is made to the transaction. Any changes to objects and relationships are then stored persistently in the database.

All these methods are predefined for performing database operations. It is important to note that *user-defined* methods can be defined in C++ and attached to classes in order to provide object behaviour.

2.3 Querying

A special method oql(result, query) allows invoking associative queries. The parameter query contains a string that defines the query in an Object Query Language (OQL); variable result obtains the query result. OQL enhances SQL in an orthogonal manner with object-oriented features like inheritance and traversal along relationships.

OQL queries support the well-known SQL structure: Select t_1, ..., t_n from δ_1,..., δ_k where ϕ. Terms t_1, ..., t_n compute the target information, δ_1, ..., δ_k are declarations of the form var in ρ that restrict the values for variables var to a finite range ρ, and ϕ is a qualifying formula. The following OQL query computes *for each department d (in the extent Depts of DEPT) its Name and the average of its employees' salaries, provided d is headed by 'Lucky Luke'*:

```
select Name, avg(select Salary
                 from e in d.Staff)
from d in Depts
where d.Head.Name = 'Lucky Luke'
```

Terms t_i can be path expressions [KIM92] built by applying relationships. For example, d.Head.Name computes the manager's name of department d. Inheritance is respected, e.g., attribute Name can be applied to that manager, although it belongs to type PERSON. Subqueries Select-from-where and other terms like d.Staff that return a set are called set-valued. Aggregate functions like count, min, and avg can be applied to them, e.g., count(d.Staff) or avg(select e.Salary from e in EMP). Set-valued terms and extent names are valid ranges.

Formulas ϕ are built by using predicates like t in t_{set} and comparisons t_1 θ t_2 between terms ($\theta \in \{=, <, >=, ...\}$). By using logical connectives not, and, or, and quantifications exists $\delta : \phi$ and for all $\delta : \phi$, complex formulas can be composed.

3 Semantic Enrichement of Relational Databases

In order to bridge the semantic gap between ODMG-93 and relational databases, the basic principle of our approach consists of establishing a "real" object-oriented view of relational data. This is achieved by remodelling relational schemas in the ODMG model in a semantic enrichment process [CAS91, HOH95].

3.1 Related Work

A lot of work has been spent on transforming relational schemas into a high-level data model, almost Entity-Relationship (ER) based or object-oriented. We cite only few examples briefly, because they do schema mappings in a different context, intending to perform automatic transformations. Methodologies, heuristics, and algorithms have been developed to analyze data semantics in the context of semantic enrichment [CAS91], data reverse engineering [DAV87, NAV87, MAR90, HAI93, NAR93, CHI94, PRE94], and knowledge acquisition [CAS93]. [NAV87] propose a systematic approach for the reverse engineering of relational databases into extented ER models. [MAR90] focus on the more theoretical aspects of reverse engineering, and [PRE94] use an object-oriented design and analysis for the reverse engineering of relational data. A general framework is introduced by [HAI93]. It can be used not only for relational schemas, but also for other logical models, as it is based on schema independent transformations. Most approaches have in common that they expect a relational schema and a list of formal constraints, and then automatically construct corresponding entity/object types. Typical forms of constraints that are taken into account are primary keys and equality of names [DAV87], candidate keys [NAV87], functional dependencies, and (key-based) inclusion dependencies [MAR90, YAN92]. Other work like [CAS93] goes one step beyond with a previous *knowledge acquisition* phase in order to find those constraints by analyzing extensions of the databases.

Here, we present a new approach to semantic enrichment that is complementary to the above ones. Our approach has a different starting point: We assume that the semantics of tables has already been recognized, for instance, by using the algorithms mentioned. Instead of detecting the semantics, we direct our attention towards *expressiveness* of specification. We propose an approach that is capable of precisely remodelling any relational situations in object-oriented terms by using all the concepts of ODMG-93. To achieve this goal, connections between relational schemas and object-oriented ones are described explicitly: Tables are linked to shape object types by means of a *specification language*. This language takes into account several enrichment concepts in an orthogonal manner. Specifications are less formal than functional and inclusion dependencies.

This proceeding of explicit specification is motivated by the context of interoperability: To provide a good basis for schema integration, it is necessary to have a concise description of the relational data. But it is rather difficult to detect all the inherent semantics correctly in an automatic manner. For example, it is very complicated to rebuild correct subtype hierarchies from tables. Indeed, subtype hierarchies are often not recognized properly by automatic approaches:

Some work simply do not attempt to rebuild subtypes [DAV87], others (e.g., [CAS91, YAN92]) use inclusion dependencies between tables to detect just one of several possible strategies. Moreover, most algorithms work only for single-level hierarchies. Consequently, not all kinds of subtype hierarchies are recognized, the advantages of semantic enrichment get lost.

3.2 Generative Approach

In spite of specifying semantic enrichment manually by means of a specification language, the object schema is produced automatically due to a generative principle ([HOH93]): Given as input any enrichment specification, a generator produces an equivalent ODMG schema, given as a pile of C++ classes according to the language-specific ODMG C++ binding (cf. Subsection 2.2). Those classes provide an ODMG conforming database interface including query and manipulating facilities. Figure 3 illustrates the process of generation.

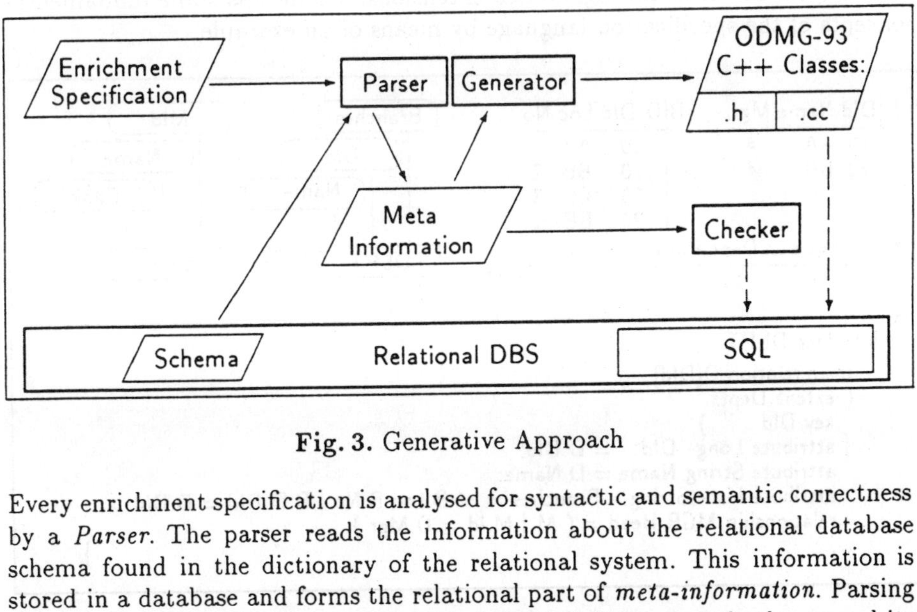

Fig. 3. Generative Approach

Every enrichment specification is analysed for syntactic and semantic correctness by a *Parser*. The parser reads the information about the relational database schema found in the dictionary of the relational system. This information is stored in a database and forms the relational part of *meta-information*. Parsing the specification, information about the derived object-oriented schema and its connection to relational tables is added to the meta information.

A *Generator* takes the meta information as input and generates the ODMG-93 conforming classes. The outcome consists of C++ header files (".h"), which contain the C++ class definitions including the signatures of methods, and implementation files (".cc") implementing those methods. Naturally, the implementation of methods must call SQL. All those generated classes provide a C++ database interface, implemented on top of the relational system. Application programs need only compile and link these classes into application programs.

Specifying semantic enrichment in an explicit way, obviously, not every specification makes sense. In principle, the user *supposes* that the semantics is present, but the database does not know that it has to satisfy that semantics. An *Inte-*

grity Checker has the task to prevent one from specifying nonsense by checking constraints on the relational data. Please consult [HOH95] for more details.

3.3 Principles of the Specification Language

Our specification language provides syntactic constructs that allows one to remodel relational tables in an object-oriented manner. Applications are given "real" object-oriented views of data. All the concepts of the ODMG-93 object model are extensively used to express semantics directly.

The syntax of the specification language bridles the horse from the back: It is specified what object types are the outcome and how they correspond to tables. This is advantageous, because an object type is generally made up of several tables. Moreover, the syntax remains intuitive and easily understandable, since the object types are immediately visible. We adopt the ODL of ODMG-93 and extend it to capturing explicit remodelling information. That is, interface declarations form the basis for logic-based extensions. We discuss some fundamental concepts of the specification language by means of an example.

D	DId	Name	Mgr
	10	AA	4
	20	BB	4

B	D_DId	Loc	No
	10	AA	1
	10	BB	2
	10	CC	3
	20	BB	1

M	Id	Name ...	Dept	Rank
	4	D	10	1

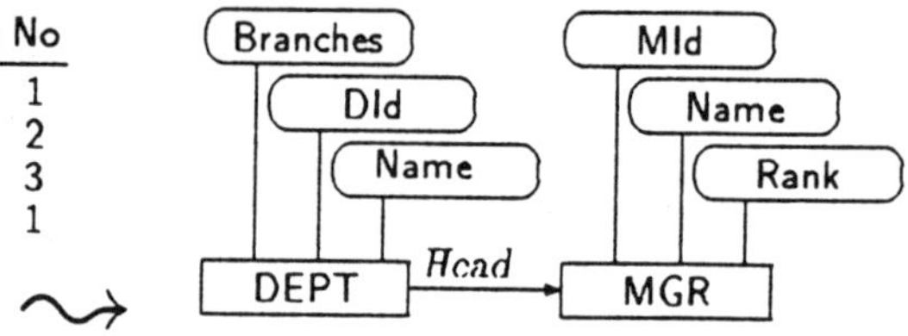


```
interface DEPT
  from relation D[DId]
  ( extent Depts
    key DId      )
  { attribute Long  DId   = D.DId;
    attribute String Name = D.Name;
    attribute List<String> Branches = < B.Loc:B.No | B.D_DId = D.DId >;
    relationship MGR Head = ( M | M.Id = D.Mgr );
    ...                                                              }
```

Fig. 4. Sample Enrichment

Let us consider the relational schema given in Figure 4. Table M represents managers (MGR), while table D contains departments (DEPT). The branches of departments are stored in table B (DId, Loc, No) the tuples of which contain the branches for each department DId value by value; each branch receives a number enumerating the branches of a department. The Mgr column in table D is a foreign key, it refers to the manager in M who is the *Head* of that department.

The enrichment specification in Figure 4 combines the tables D and B to one object type DEPT. A corresponding interface is defined as usual in ODL. However, there are some extensions. The clause from relation relates the object type DEPT to its *base* table D. It specifies in what table the *elements* of a type are found.

DEPT from relation D[DId] means that the type DEPT is built from table D directly. DId is the relational key of D. Each tuple, which is uniquely identified by its key value, refers to one object. We presuppose a key for each table, because it is necessary to constitute object identifiers in the database interface. Composite keys are possible.
Equations '=' occurring behind the attributes relate object type attributes to relational attributes. The simplest form is Long DId = D.DId and connects an object type attribute DId to a relational attribute DId directly. Attributes can be renamed by specifying different names on the left hand side of the equations.
A list constructor <...> can be used to make explicit the list-valued attribute Branches by Branches = < B.Loc : B.No | B.D_DId = D.DId >: Compute the Loc values for each tuple in B that possesses a D_DId equal to the DId of the department D. In this case, the attribute No is used to define an order on the locations. Similarly, a set constructor could have been applied to build a *set* of branches: Branches = { B.Loc | ... }.
In this way, it is possible to *cluster* any tables to one object type [YAN92].
Similarly, the Head of a department is made explicit by relationship MGR Head = (M | M.MId = D.Mgr): The head consists of that tuple in M (identified by the respective key) that has the manager's MId as value of Mgr. Round brackets convert a tuple in M into a corresponding object of type MGR. If relationship Head were represented by a table H(DId,MId), containing the Id's of the participating tables, then the specification would look like relationship MGR Head = (M | M.MId = H.MId, H.DId = D.DId). In both cases, the relationships can be expressed by composite attributes, too.

3.4 Remodelling Subtype Hierarchies

The "implementation" of subtypes offers a wide spectrum of possibilities. There are essentially four strategies called vertical (V), horizontal (H), flag (F), and complete materialization (M). Most approaches [MAR90, CAS91, YAN92] take into account only one strategy (the vertical one) and lack the handling of multi-level subtype hierarchies. However, these representations of subtype hierarchies are orthogonal and can be applied in a mixed manner. We discuss those strategies and show how to specify semantic enrichment.
We refer to the subtype hierarchy given in Figure 1, however, we disregard relationships for a moment. Let us assume in the following that PId 1 is a real person, 2 an employee, 3 a secretary, 4 a manager, and 5 and 6 are workers.
We distinguish between instances and elements. The set of *elements* comprises the objects of a type and all its subtypes. In contrast, the objects of a type itself are called *instances*. Thus, EMP possesses one instance 3, but a set { 2,3,4 } of elements.

- **Vertical Partitioning (V)**

Possibly the most common way of representing subtype hierarchies is a *vertical* partitioning. In Figure 5, each table refers to one object type in the hierarchy, and contains all the *elements* of the corresponding type. Only the specific attributes of the type are found in the table; attributes inherited from supertypes are

available in the tables associated with that supertype. To access the attributes of supertypes, tables must be joined over the Id attributes. The following inclusions hold between supertype's and subtype's tables: P.Id $\supseteq$ W.Id, P.Id $\supseteq$ E.Id, E.Id $\supseteq$ S.Id, and E.Id $\supseteq$ M.Id. Indeed, the literature about semantic enrichment uses these inclusions to identify vertical subtypes. Please note that those Id attributes may have different names and do not need to be keys, but they must guarantee uniqueness of attribute values. Furthermore, each table may use other attributes to relate to subtypes than it uses to relate to its supertype. Composite attributes can also be used.
Figure 5 demonstrates how to rebuild the subtype hierarchy. The elements of PERSON are found in table P, as usual (from relation), elements of subtype EMP in E, etc. Since each table contains only the specific attributes of that object type, the connection to the supertype table must be established. This is done by EMP : PERSON from relation E[Id = P.Id]: Tables E and P are related by Id (of table E) and Id (of P): A person is an employee if its Id occurs in E as a value of Id. Composite attributes are again possible. The handling of attributes is done as usual.

P	Id	Name	Addr
	1	A	A_town
	2	B	B_city
	3	C	C_village
	4	D	D_village
	5	E	E_city
	6	F	F_town

E	Id	Salary
	2	2000
	3	3000
	4	4000

S	Id	Speed
	3	133

M	Id	Rank
	4	1

W	Id	Wages
	5	555
	6	666

```
interface PERSON from relation P[Id]
   { attribute PId = P.Id;
     attribute Name = P.Name;
     ... }
interface EMP     : PERSON from relation E [Id=P.Id] ...
interface WORKER: PERSON from relation W[Id=P.Id] ...
interface SECR    : EMP      from relation S [Id=E.Id] ...
interface MGR     : EMP      from relation M[Id=E.Id] ...
```

Fig. 5. Vertical Partitioning of Subtypes

• Horizontal Partitioning (H)

Figure 6 shows a horizontal partitioning of types into tables. There is again one table to hold the information of one object type in the hierarchy. The structure of each table comprises the specific information of its corresponding type and, unlike vertical partitioning, the attributes of supertypes, too. Hence, the attributes inherited from supertypes are directly available in each table. But each table contains only the *instances* of a type. On instance level, exclusion conditions are fulfilled between super- and subtype's tables: P.Id $\cap$ E.Id $= \emptyset$, P.Id $\cap$ W.Id $= \emptyset$, E.Id $\cap$ S.Id $= \emptyset$, and E.Id $\cap$ M.Id $= \emptyset$.

The enrichment specification in Figure 6 should be understood as follows. Each from relation clause defines how to compute the *elements* of a type. The elements of PERSON, spread over the tables P, W, E, S and M, are obtained by computing the union ('+') of tuples. As objects are made of tuples of different tables, the key values of those tuples must be used to build object identifiers. The parts [...] indicate the identifying attributes. Attribute correspondences are specified in the same way: PId = P.Id + W.Id + E.Id + S.Id + M.Id; the persons' Id is stored in all those tables in possibly differently named attributes!

P	Id	Name	Addr
	1	A	A_town

E	Id	Name	Addr	Salary
	2	B	B_city	2000

W	Id	Name	Addr	Wages
	5	E	E_city	555
	6	F	F_town	666

S	Id	Name	Addr	Salary	Speed
	3	C	C_village	3000	133

M	Id	Name	Addr	Salary	Rank
	4	D	D_village	4000	1

```
interface PERSON from relation P[Id] + W[Id] + E[Id] + S[Id] + M[Id]
   { attribute Long PId = P.Id + W.Wid + E.Id + S.Id + M.Id; ...
     attribute String Name = P.Name + W.Name + E.Name + S.Name + M.Name; ... }
interface EMP : PERSON from relation E[Id] + S[Id] + M[Id]
   { attribute Float Salary = E.Salary + S.Salary + M.Salary; }
interface WORKER : PERSON from relation W[Id]
   { attribute Float Wages = W.Wages; }
interface MGR : EMP from relation M[Id]
   { attribute Long Rank = M.Rank; }
interface SECR : EMP from relation S[Id]
   { attribute Long Speed = S.Speed; }
```

Fig. 6. Horizontal Partitioning of Subtypes

- **Flag Approach (F)**

In contrast to the first strategies, one single table P can represent the whole hierarchy as well. Flags like Emp? etc. determine the specific subtype. Flags can denote elements or instances. They represent elements in Figure 7: Tuples having Emp?=true correspond to elements of EMP. Naturally, only sensible flag combinations must occur. For example, Secr?=true and Emp?=false is not valid, a secretary must also be an employee. Furthermore, non-applicable attributes must be NULL so that Emp?=false implies Salary=NULL, and so on.
If flags denote instances instead, then Emp?=true holds for *real* instances of EMP only. SECR instances still have Secr?=true, but now Emp?=false. Then, at most one flag is allowed to be true for each tuple in P.
Some variants of the flag approach are conceivable. In place of flags, an enumeration type type of domain { Emp, Secr, Mgr, Worker } can serve the same purpose. For example, the instances of EMP get a type-value Emp. The subtype specification can also be done by condition, e.g., Salary!=NULL could detect EMP instances. However, there will be no possibility to distinguish between "value is unknown" and "value is inapplicable (no subtype attribute)", because both are represented

by NULL. Even more general expressions could be used.

P	Id	Name	Addr	Emp?	Salary	Mgr?	Rank	Secr?	Speed	Worker?	Wages
	1	A	A_town	false	NULL	false	NULL	false	NULL	false	NULL
	2	B	B_city	true	2000	false	NULL	false	NULL	false	NULL
	3	C	C_village	true	3000	false	NULL	true	133	false	NULL
	4	D	D_village	true	4000	true	1	false	NULL	false	NULL
	5	E	E_city	false	NULL	false	NULL	false	NULL	true	555
	6	F	F_town	false	NULL	false	NULL	false	NULL	true	666

```
interface PERSON from relation P[Id] ...
interface EMP : PERSON from relation P[Emp? = true]
    { attribute Float Salary = P.Salary; }
interface WORKER : PERSON from relation P[Worker? = true] ...
interface SECR : EMP from relation P[Secr? = true] ...
interface MGR  : EMP from relation P[Mgr? = true] ...
```

Fig. 7. Flag Approach

These kinds of flag approaches can again be handled in the from relation clause. As usual, the part in [...] defines how to compute elements. The specification given in Figure 7 defines that any tuple in table P with Emp? = true refers to an object of type EMP. These objects are identified by Id, as arranged in PERSON. Other flag approaches are handled by different forms of conditions, for example, P[Emp? = true or Secr? = true or Mgr? = true] in case of instance flags.

• **Complete Materialization (M)**

Another relational representation of subtype hierarchies uses the schemas of horizontal, but the instances of vertical partitioning. For example, type EMP is represented by a table E(Id, Name, Addr, Salary) and contains three tuples with Ids 2, 3 and 4. This leads to redundancy, as the table P(Id, Name, Addr) contains the Name and Addr information for all tuples 1 to 6: The name 'B' of Id 2 is stored in P and E. Since each table contains the whole information of a type, all the elements and all the attributes, we call it *complete materialization*.

A specification again defines the correspondences between tables and types:

```
interface EMP : PERSON from relation E[Id=P.Id]
    { attribute Float Salary = E.Salary = S.Salary = M.Salary; }
```

The form from relation P[Id=P.Id] is similar to vertical partitioning, as each table contains elements. But in contrast to vertical partitioning, redundancies must be reflected: Employees' Salaries are stored in E, M and S. This is made clear in EMP by means of Salary = E.Salary = S.Salary = M.Salary.

3.5 Special Concepts

Additional forms are available to handle further aspects which are important for building object-oriented views of tables. We round off the specification language by briefly summarizing them.

Several relational attributes may correspond to a predefined ODMG data type. For example, three Integer-valued attributes Day, Month, and Year can be combined to form a date of foundation. Similarly, several relational attributes can make up an object type that is nested into another.

New object types may be introduced, e.g., if tables possess common attributes, in order to concentrate those attributes in a *generalized* object type. That supertype does typically not contain instances of its own (it is a so-called *abstract type*).

Owing to optimization reasons, tables are often unified on performance grounds after design, in order to avoid costly join operations. Hence, it is important to allow for *splitting up tables* into several object types.

Subtypes are disjoint w.r.t. instances in the ODMG object model. On the other hand, this is not true for tables, since they can contain tuples with the same Id. For instance, referring to Figure 5, an employee with Id 3 may occur in S and M, if 3 is a secretary and a manager at the same time. Non-disjoint types can be modelled by multiple inheritance: MGR:EMP and SECR:EMP are extended with an "artificial" subtype MGR_SECR : MGR,SECR that represents the intersection. MGR_SECR is necessary to be able to insert elements that are both manager and secretary; they become *instances* of MGR_SECR. The type EMP enables accessing all the elements, no matter whether managers, secretaries, or both.

One important point has been neglected so far. Relational DBSs possess modelling constructs such as not null that are provided neither in C++ nor in ODL. In order to reflect the relational semantics entirely, we introduced corresponding restrictions. Keywords like not null can be specified for attributes (in the relational sense), and relationships can be defined as mandatory: Any object must participate in a relationship of that type.

3.6 Complex Example

In order to demonstrate the full power of the specification language, we are presenting a complex relational schema that comprehends several concepts in combination. Particularly, we use a relational representation of Figure 1 that incorporates different subtype strategies within one subtype hierarchy. Reasons for that might be to speed up access for applications, which have different preferences for each level of the hierarchy. We apply a vertical strategy to PERSON–EMP and EMP–SECR, a horizontal one to EMP–MGR, and a flag approach to PERSON–WORKER (cf. annotations V, H, F to subtype edges in Figure 1). We obtain the tables given in Figure 8.

The tables reflect the characteristic inclusions $E.Id \subseteq P.Id$ and $S.Id \subseteq E.Id$ of vertical partitioning. According to horizontal partitioning, an exclusion condition $E.Id \cap M.Id = \emptyset$ holds: M contains additional employees who possess different Ids and have the complete PERSON and EMP attributes. Workers, finally, do not have a table of their own, but are part of P with a discriminant flag Worker?.

The WorksIn and Head relationships are represented by foreign keys Dept and Mgr, respectively. The Dept column in E refers to the department's DId, the employee works in, and similar for Mgr. Please note that horizontal subtypes receive all the properties of their supertypes. Hence, M also has an attribute Dept, since EMP's relationship to DEPT is valid for managers, too. Even the attributes of indirect supertypes are repeated. M obtains the attributes of P, although it is not a direct horizontal subtype of P. This is necessary, because M cannot "inherit" the attributes of PERSON otherwise by means of joins!

P	Id	Name	Addr	Worker?	Wages
	1	A	A_town	false	NULL
	2	B	B_city	false	NULL
	3	C	C_village	false	NULL
	5	E	E_city	true	555
	6	F	F_town	true	666

E	Id	Salary	Dept
	2	2000	10
	3	3000	20

S	Id	Speed
	3	133

B	D_DId	Loc
	10	AA
	10	BB
	10	CC
	20	BB

D	DId	Name	Mgr
	10	AA	4
	20	BB	4

M	Id	Name	Addr	Salary	Dept	Rank
	4	D	D_village	4000	10	1

```
interface PERSON    // no supertype
  from relation P[Id] + M[Id]
  ( extent Persons
    key PId       )
  { attribute Long PersId = P.Id+M.Id;
    attribute String Name = P.Name+M.Name;
    attribute String Address = P.Addr+M.Addr;
  }

interface EMP : PERSON
  from relation E[Id=P.Id][Id]+M[Id];
  ( extent Emps )
  { attribute Float Salary = E.Salary+M.Salary;
    relationship DEPT WorksIn inverse Staff
         = (D | D.DId = E.Dept+M.Dept); }

interface MGR : EMP
  from relation M[Id]
  { attribute Long Rank = M.Rank; }

interface DEPT    // no supertype
  from relation D[DId]
  ( extent Depts
    key DId       )
  { attribute Long DId = D.DId;
    attribute String Name = D.Name;
    attribute String Address = D.Addr;
    attribute Set<String> Branches =
       { B.Loc | B.D_DId = D.DId }
    relationship MGR Head =
       (M | Id = D.DId);
    relationship Set<EMP> Staff
       inverse WorksIn =
       { E+M | E.Dept+M.Dept=D.DId };
  }

interface SECR : EMP    // vertical
from relation S[Id=E.Id]
  { attribute Long Speed = S.Speed; }

interface WORKER : PERSON    // flag
  from relation P[Worker?=true]
  { attribute Float Wages = P.Wages; }
```

Fig. 8. Complex Specification of Semantic Enrichment

Figure 8 presents a specification that regains the schema given in Figure 1. PERSON from relation P[Id] + M[Id] specifies a horizontal strategy. The elements of PERSON are obtained by computing the union ('+') of tuples in P and M. Horizontal strategy is also reflected in attribute equations: Name = P.Name + M.Name specifies that people's names occur in P and M.

WORKER : PERSON from relation P[Worker? = true] indicates a flag approach: Type WORKER is subtype of PERSON represented by a flag Worker? in table P.

The form EMP : PERSON from relation E[Id = P.Id][Id] + M[Id] represents a vertical strategy first of all: E[Id = P.Id] means that E is vertical subtype of P. The tables E and P are related by attributes Id. E[...][Id] + M[Id] specifies that EMP objects are stored in the tables E and M due to horizontal partitioning. Please note different attributes could have been used for vertical and horizontal strategy!

Set<EMP> Staff = { E + M | E.Dept + M.Dept = D.DId } expresses a set-valued relationship. Remember, the relationship is relationally represented by a foreign key Dept in E and M. Staff consists of those tuples in E and M that have the department's DId as value of Dept. The inverse relationship WorksIn is analogously computed by (D | D.DId = E.Dept + M.Dept). Head and Branches are specified as in Figure 4.

4 Query Processing in Subtype Hierarchies

4.1 Embedding in the Runtime System

The output produced by the generator is an object-oriented *runtime system* that provides an ODMG-93 conforming access to relational data. The runtime system consists of C++ classes that represent relational tables, however, covering more semantics like relationships and subtypes. Moreover, methods define means for manipulation. Application programs, such as given in Subsection 2.2, can be written on an object-oriented level, not worrying about the representation of relationships and subtypes in the relational database. A programmer has nothing to do, since all the ODMG-93 methods are automatically implemented on relational SQL. Particularly, object-oriented queries can be invoked by using an oql method. In fact, the implementation of methods is done in direct correspondence to a specification of semantic enrichment.

The runtime system contains a special component, a *Query Manager*, handling OQL queries. It is up to the Query Manager to translate the OQL into SQL. The query transformation is internally done by means of operator trees. Any OQL query is transformed into an object-oriented operator tree that defines a procedural execution plan. This tree is mapped into a relational counterpart, optimized, and finally interpreted by executing SQL statements. We do not want to dive into technical aspects. We concentrate on some basic principles instead. Leaves of the object-oriented operator tree perform access to extents. Hence, the basis for queries is the notion of *extent*, the set of objects of a given type. From a logical point of view, the set of objects has two different understandings: The set can consist of elements (all the objects of the type and its subtypes) or instances (only the objects of the type itself). Differentiating between elements and instances is a general feature of query languages: Special concepts [KIM92, HOH92] to distinguish them are often available. Retrieving object type extents, the context objects are used is important. In some cases, only the Id's of objects are needed, because the operations are performed on just Id sets. This is particularly useful, if the query result is not materialized immediately, but later on, when objects are processed. In case of subtype objects, there are again two possibilities for fetching: Getting the specific attributes of an object only, or retrieving all the information about an object including the attributes of supertypes.

We present some query scenarios that take into consideration these important aspects of querying in the context of subtype hierarchies. Hence, we specify rela-

tional queries for selecting *instances* and *elements* with values of key attributes only (^{k}) or all all attributes (including those of supertypes) (^{a}). These query scenarios are mapped to relational queries. Using these scenarios, complete query evaluation can be done either by manually performing the query in memory, or by incorporating the mechanisms into general query transformations.
Please note the query transformation is heavily affected by the applied enrichment rules. In contrast to similar work ([MAR93, YU93]) that maps object-oriented to relational schemas and translates object-oriented to relational queries, we must take into account all the possibilities for enrichment!

4.2 Preliminaries

Generally, we take for granted that the enrichment specification is sensible, i.e., the table contents do not contradict the enrichment specification. Moreover, we assume some simplifications just for the ease of demonstration.

- If X is an object type, then T_X denotes the corresponding base table. Referring to Figure 8, we obtain $T_{EMP} \equiv$ E and $T_{WORKER} \equiv$ P, for instance.
- We assume that hierarchies are built over one common key attribute named Id (as in our examples), which has the same name in all tables. We thus consider only the form from relation T_{EMP}[Id=T_{PERSON}.Id] with one attribute Id. Consequently a natural join between T_{EMP} and T_{PERSON} can be used instead of explicit joins. Analogously, the required form of horizontal partitioning is T_{EMP}[Id] + T_{MGR}[Id] + ..., using again one commonly named attribute Id.
- Furthermore, we assume that relational attributes are directly transformed to equally named object-oriented ones of compatible domain. In particular, we assume that semantically equivalent attributes have the same name in horizontally partitioned tables: Name = T_{PERSON}.Name + T_{EMP}.Name + ... Otherwise, projections will need renaming.
- Flags in the flag approach are named according to object types: A subtype X implies a flag X? in its corresponding table.
- We here take into consideration only the strategies H, V, F due to space limitations. But complete materialization M does not bring up problems: The treatment is very similar to V, as both store elements, however there is no need performing joins to access the attributes of supertypes.

We introduce some notations that give access to meta-information, i.e., information about the mapping of the relational schema to the ODMG schema (cf. Figure 3 in Subsection 3.2).

- $\mathcal{P}_X^\alpha \uparrow$ (*predecessors*) should denote the path from object type X towards the root of the hierarchy following only subtype edges of type α, $\alpha \in \{$ V, H, F $\}$. The path ends if either the root of the hierarchy is reached, or an edge different to α occurs. X itself is not part of the path. The result consists of a list of object types. Those lists are represented by <...>; an empty list is denoted as <>. Lists have an order, which can be made visible by an operation [i] to select the i-th element. [*] selects the last element in the list. This is useful to

determine the end of a path given by $\mathcal{P}_X^\alpha\uparrow$.
Analogously, $\mathcal{P}_X^{\alpha,\beta}\uparrow$ accepts edges of both types $\alpha, \beta \in \{ V, H, F \}$.

- $\mathcal{S}_X^\alpha\downarrow$ specifies the *α-successors* of a given object type X, i.e., the set of those subtypes of X (except X) that possess an outgoing edge of type $\alpha \in \{ V, H, F \}$. The result is a set of object types.
- $\mathcal{D}_X^\alpha\downarrow$ is a special case of $\mathcal{S}_X^\alpha\downarrow$, yielding the set of *direct successors* of X that possess an outgoing edge of type $\alpha \in \{ H, V, F \}$.
- Finally, $\mathcal{R}$ denotes the root of the subtype hierarchy.

Referring to Figure 8, we obtain for instance: $\mathcal{P}_{SECR}^V\uparrow = <$ EMP, PERSON $>$, $\mathcal{P}_{SECR}^V\uparrow[*] =$ PERSON, $\mathcal{P}_{MGR}^V\uparrow = < >$, $\mathcal{S}_{PERSON}^H\downarrow = \{$ MGR $\}$, $\mathcal{S}_{PERSON}^V\downarrow = \{$ EMP, SECR $\}$, and $\mathcal{D}_{PERSON}^V\downarrow = <$ EMP $>$. $\mathcal{S}_{\mathcal{R}}^H\downarrow$ is the same as $\mathcal{S}_{PERSON}^H\downarrow$.
In addition to that, we agree on the following notations: $\oplus$ denotes a natural join, σ_ϕ is a select operator filtering tuples that satisfy the condition ϕ. π_a is a projection on the attribute a, and $\pi_X(T_Y)$ is a projection on all attributes of the object type X (including the inherited ones, as far as they are available in the table T_Y). Consequently, $\pi_{EMP}(E)$ is equivalent to $\pi_{Id,Salary}(E)$, because attribute Name (in spite of being inherited to PERSON) is not available in table E.

4.3 Queries in Subtype Hierarchies

In the remainder of this section, we present the queries that compute whole objects (^{a}) or key attributes (^{k}) of *inst*ances and *elem*ents for each type in a subtype hierarchy. To make the presentation more compact, we specify queries in relational algebra. Nevertheless, equivalent SQL statements can be derived effortless. At first, we consider hierarchies that are built by applying only one strategy. This will give us a better understanding of querying hierarchies and the mechanisms required by the various strategies.

- **Uniform hierarchy using strategy V:**

Having a homogeneous V-hierarchy, elements of a type X are computed in a simple way by accessing the corresponding table T_X, since each table contains exactly the elements of a type. Attributes of supertypes become available by joining the result with tables T_Z, $Z \in \mathcal{P}_X^V\uparrow$.
The computation of instances requires a set difference between table T_X and those tables related to direct subtypes of X. Technically speaking, we project T_X and its subtypes' tables on the common key attribute. Then the difference of Id-values can be computed. In the case of (^{a}), the result is joined with T_X and supertype tables T_Z in order to get the attributes of X and attributes inherited from supertypes.

$$inst^k(X) = \pi_{Id}(T_X) - \bigcup_{Y \in \mathcal{D}_X^V\downarrow} \pi_{Id}(T_Y)$$
$$inst^a(X) = (\pi_{Id}(T_X) - \bigcup_{Y \in \mathcal{D}_X^V\downarrow} \pi_{Id}(T_Y)) \oplus T_X \oplus \bigoplus_{Z \in \mathcal{P}_X^V\uparrow} T_Z$$
$$elem^k(X) = \pi_{Id}(T_X)$$
$$elem^a(X) = T_X \oplus \bigoplus_{Z \in \mathcal{P}_X^V\uparrow} T_Z$$

Obviously the formula for $inst^a$ can be optimized: If $\mathcal{D}^{\mathsf{V}}_{\mathsf{X}}\downarrow = \emptyset$, then no set difference is necessary. Hence no join with T_{X} is needed, since we can directly project on the X attributes: $\pi_{\mathsf{X}}(T_{\mathsf{X}}) \oplus \bigoplus_{\mathsf{Z}} T_{\mathsf{Z}}$.

Example: (related to the enrichment in Figure 5)

$$\begin{aligned}
inst^a(\mathsf{PERSON}) &= \big(\pi_{\mathrm{Id}}(\mathsf{P}) - (\pi_{\mathrm{Id}}(\mathsf{E}) \cup \pi_{\mathrm{Id}}(\mathsf{W}))\big) \oplus \mathsf{P} \\
inst^a(\mathsf{EMP}) &= \big(\pi_{\mathrm{Id}}(\mathsf{E}) - (\pi_{\mathrm{Id}}(\mathsf{S}) \cup \pi_{\mathrm{Id}}(\mathsf{M}))\big) \oplus \mathsf{E} \oplus \mathsf{P} \\
elem^k(\mathsf{PERSON}) &= \pi_{\mathrm{Id}}(\mathsf{P}) \\
elem^a(\mathsf{SECR}) &= \mathsf{S} \oplus \mathsf{E} \oplus \mathsf{P}
\end{aligned}$$

- **Uniform hierarchy using strategy H:**

Computing the instances is simple in this case, because each table contains exactly the instances of a type. Furthermore, the attributes of supertypes are already available in contrast to strategy V, so that no joins are necessary.
But we have to pay for the easy handling of instances with a more complex computation of elements. We have to build the union of subtypes T_{Y}, $\mathsf{Y} \in \mathcal{S}^{\mathsf{H}}_{\mathsf{X}}\downarrow$. Obviously, a projection on key attributes will give the variant (^{k}) in both cases.

$$\begin{aligned}
inst^k(\mathsf{X}) &= \pi_{\mathrm{Id}}(T_{\mathsf{X}}) , & elem^k(\mathsf{X}) &= \pi_{\mathrm{Id}}(T_{\mathsf{X}}) \cup \textstyle\bigcup_{\mathsf{Y}\in\mathcal{S}^{\mathsf{H}}_{\mathsf{X}}\downarrow} \pi_{\mathrm{Id}}(T_{\mathsf{Y}}) \\
inst^a(\mathsf{X}) &= T_{\mathsf{X}} , & elem^a(\mathsf{X}) &= T_{\mathsf{X}} \cup \textstyle\bigcup_{\mathsf{Y}\in\mathcal{S}^{\mathsf{H}}_{\mathsf{X}}\downarrow} \pi_{\mathsf{X}}(T_{\mathsf{Y}})
\end{aligned}$$

Example: (related to the enrichment in Figure 6)

$$\begin{aligned}
inst^k(\mathsf{PERSON}) &= \pi_{\mathrm{Id}}(\mathsf{P}) , & elem^k(\mathsf{EMP}) &= \pi_{\mathrm{Id}}(\mathsf{E}) \cup \pi_{\mathrm{Id}}(\mathsf{M}) \cup \pi_{\mathrm{Id}}(\mathsf{S}) \\
inst^a(\mathsf{PERSON}) &= \mathsf{P} , & elem^a(\mathsf{EMP}) &= \mathsf{E} \cup \pi_{\mathrm{Id,Salary}}(\mathsf{M}) \cup \pi_{\mathrm{Id,Salary}}(\mathsf{S})
\end{aligned}$$

- **Uniform hierarchy using strategy F:**

The flag approach uses one table $T_{\mathcal{R}}$ to represent the whole hierarchy ($\mathcal{R}$ is the root of the hierarchy). Selection conditions determine elements and instances in the table. Selecting the keys is controlled by means of projections.

$$\begin{aligned}
inst^k(\mathsf{X}) &= \begin{cases} \pi_{\mathrm{Id}}(\sigma_{\phi_1}(T_{\mathcal{R}})) & \text{if } \mathsf{X} \equiv \mathcal{R} \\ \pi_{\mathrm{Id}}(\sigma_{\phi_2}(T_{\mathcal{R}})) & \text{otherwise} \end{cases} \\
inst^a(\mathsf{X}) &= \begin{cases} \pi_{\mathsf{X}}(\sigma_{\phi_1}(T_{\mathcal{R}})) & \text{if } \mathsf{X} \equiv \mathcal{R} \\ \pi_{\mathsf{X}}(\sigma_{\phi_2}(T_{\mathcal{R}})) & \text{otherwise} \end{cases} \\
elem^k(\mathsf{X}) &= \begin{cases} \pi_{\mathrm{Id}}(T_{\mathcal{R}}) & \text{if } \mathsf{X} \equiv \mathcal{R} \\ \pi_{\mathrm{Id}}(\sigma_{\phi_3}(T_{\mathcal{R}})) & \text{otherwise} \end{cases} \\
elem^a(\mathsf{X}) &= \begin{cases} \pi_{\mathsf{X}}(T_{\mathcal{R}}) & \text{if } \mathsf{X} \equiv \mathcal{R} \\ \pi_{\mathsf{X}}(\sigma_{\phi_3}(T_{\mathcal{R}})) & \text{otherwise} \end{cases}
\end{aligned}$$

Here, we use the following selection conditions:

$\phi_1 \equiv \bigwedge_{\mathsf{Y}\in\mathcal{S}^{\mathsf{F}}_{\mathsf{X}}\downarrow} (\mathsf{Y?{=}false})$, $\phi_2 \equiv (\mathsf{X?{=}true} \wedge \bigwedge_{\mathsf{Y}\in\mathcal{S}^{\mathsf{F}}_{\mathsf{X}}\downarrow} (\mathsf{Y?{=}false}))$, $\phi_3 \equiv (\mathsf{X?{=}true})$

Formula ϕ_1 specifies the instances of the root $\mathcal{R}$: All flags must be false. For any other type X in the hierarchy, the instances are characterized by flag X? being true, and the flags of successor types (in $\mathcal{S}^{\mathsf{F}}_{\mathsf{X}}\downarrow$) being false ($\phi_2$).
Table $T_{\mathcal{R}}$ already contains all the elements of $\mathcal{R}$, hence no conditions are necessary. Elements of other types X are computed by ϕ_3, i.e., X?=true.

Example: (related to the enrichment in Figure 7)

$$\begin{aligned} inst^k(\mathsf{EMP}) &= \pi_{\mathsf{Id}}(\sigma_{\mathsf{Emp?=true} \wedge \mathsf{Mgr?=false} \wedge \mathsf{Secr?=false}}(\mathsf{P})) \\ inst^a(\mathsf{EMP}) &= \pi_{\mathsf{Id,Salary}}(\sigma_{\mathsf{Emp?=true} \wedge \mathsf{Mgr?=false} \wedge \mathsf{Secr?=false}}(\mathsf{P})) \\ elem^a(\mathsf{EMP}) &= \pi_{\mathsf{Id,Salary}}(\sigma_{\mathsf{Emp?=true}}(\mathsf{P})) \end{aligned}$$

• **Arbitrary hierarchies:**

We now turn to the complex case of hierarchies built by mixing strategies. Investigating hierarchies with a uniform strategy so far, we recognized the general principles of querying instances and elements. These mechanisms are now combined to handle arbitrary hierarchies like the one presented in Figure 8 before. Queries are now formalized in the following equations:

$$inst^a(\mathsf{X}) = \begin{cases} (\pi_{\mathsf{Id}}(\sigma_{\phi_1}(T_\mathsf{X})) - \bigcup_{\mathsf{Y}\in\mathcal{D}^{\mathsf{V}}_{\mathsf{X}}\downarrow} \pi_{\mathsf{Id}}(T_\mathsf{Y})) \oplus \pi_\mathsf{X}(T_\mathsf{X}) \\ \quad \oplus \bigoplus_{\mathsf{Z}\in\mathcal{P}^{\mathsf{F,V}}_{\mathsf{X}}\uparrow, \mathsf{Z}\in\mathcal{S}^{\mathsf{V}}_{\mathcal{R}}\downarrow\cup\{\mathcal{R}\}} \pi_\mathsf{Z}(T_\mathsf{Z}) \\ \quad \text{if } (\mathsf{X}\equiv\mathcal{R} \text{ or } \mathsf{X}\notin\mathcal{S}^{\mathsf{F}}_{\mathcal{R}}\downarrow) \text{ and } \mathcal{D}^{\mathsf{V}}_{\mathsf{X}}\downarrow \neq \emptyset \\ \pi_\mathsf{X}(\sigma_{\phi_1}(T_\mathsf{X})) \oplus \bigoplus_{\mathsf{Z}\in\mathcal{P}^{\mathsf{F,V}}_{\mathsf{X}}\uparrow, \mathsf{Z}\in\mathcal{S}^{\mathsf{V}}_{\mathcal{R}}\downarrow\cup\{\mathcal{R}\}} \pi_\mathsf{Z}(T_\mathsf{Z}) \\ \quad \text{if } (\mathsf{X}\equiv\mathcal{R} \text{ or } \mathsf{X}\notin\mathcal{S}^{\mathsf{F}}_{\mathcal{R}}\downarrow) \text{ and } \mathcal{D}^{\mathsf{V}}_{\mathsf{X}}\downarrow = \emptyset \\ (\pi_{\mathsf{Id}}(\sigma_{\phi_2}(T_\mathcal{F})) - \bigcup_{\mathsf{Y}\in\mathcal{D}^{\mathsf{V}}_{\mathsf{X}}\downarrow} \pi_{\mathsf{Id}}(T_\mathsf{Y})) \oplus \pi_\mathsf{X}(T_\mathcal{F}) \\ \quad \oplus \bigoplus_{\mathsf{Z}\in\mathcal{P}^{\mathsf{F,V}}_{\mathsf{X}}\uparrow, \mathsf{Z}\in\mathcal{S}^{\mathsf{V}}_{\mathcal{R}}\downarrow\cup\{\mathcal{R}\}} \pi_\mathsf{Z}(T_\mathsf{Z}) \\ \quad \text{if } \mathsf{X}\in\mathcal{S}^{\mathsf{F}}_{\mathcal{R}}\downarrow \text{ and } \mathcal{D}^{\mathsf{V}}_{\mathsf{X}}\downarrow \neq \emptyset \\ \pi_\mathsf{X}(\sigma_{\phi_2}(T_\mathcal{F})) \oplus \bigoplus_{\mathsf{Z}\in\mathcal{P}^{\mathsf{F,V}}_{\mathcal{F}}\uparrow, \mathsf{Z}\in\mathcal{S}^{\mathsf{V}}_{\mathcal{R}}\downarrow\cup\{\mathcal{R}\}} \pi_\mathsf{Z}(T_\mathsf{Z}) \\ \quad \text{if } \mathsf{X}\in\mathcal{S}^{\mathsf{F}}_{\mathcal{R}}\downarrow \text{ and } \mathcal{D}^{\mathsf{V}}_{\mathsf{X}}\downarrow = \emptyset \end{cases}$$

$$inst^k(\mathsf{X}) = \begin{cases} \pi_{\mathsf{Id}}(\sigma_{\phi_1}(T_\mathsf{X})) - \bigcup_{\mathsf{Y}\in\mathcal{D}^{\mathsf{V}}_{\mathsf{X}}\downarrow} \pi_{\mathsf{Id}}(T_\mathsf{Y}) & \text{if } \mathsf{X}\equiv\mathcal{R} \text{ or } \mathsf{X}\notin\mathcal{S}^{\mathsf{F}}_{\mathcal{R}}\downarrow \\ \pi_{\mathsf{Id}}(\sigma_{\phi_2}(T_\mathcal{F})) - \bigcup_{\mathsf{Y}\in\mathcal{D}^{\mathsf{V}}_{\mathsf{X}}\downarrow} \pi_{\mathsf{Id}}(T_\mathsf{Y}) & \text{otherwise} \end{cases}$$

$$elem^a(\mathsf{X}) = \begin{cases} (\pi_\mathsf{X}(T_\mathsf{X}) \cup \bigcup_{\mathsf{Y}\in\mathcal{S}^{\mathsf{H}}_{\mathsf{X}}\downarrow} \pi_\mathsf{X}(T_\mathsf{Y})) \oplus \bigoplus_{\mathsf{Z}\in\mathcal{P}^{\mathsf{F,V}}_{\mathsf{X}}\uparrow, \mathsf{Z}\in\mathcal{S}^{\mathsf{V}}_{\mathcal{R}}\downarrow\cup\{\mathcal{R}\}} \pi_\mathsf{Z}(T_\mathsf{Z}) \\ \quad \text{if } \mathsf{X}\equiv\mathcal{R} \text{ or } \mathsf{X}\notin\mathcal{S}^{\mathsf{F}}_{\mathcal{R}}\downarrow \\ (\pi_\mathsf{X}(\sigma_{\phi_3}(T_\mathcal{F})) \cup \bigcup_{\mathsf{Y}\in\mathcal{S}^{\mathsf{H}}_{\mathsf{X}}\downarrow} \pi_\mathsf{X}(T_\mathsf{Y})) \oplus \bigoplus_{\mathsf{Z}\in\mathcal{P}^{\mathsf{F,V}}_{\mathcal{F}}\uparrow, \mathsf{Z}\in\mathcal{S}^{\mathsf{V}}_{\mathcal{R}}\downarrow\cup\{\mathcal{R}\}} \pi_\mathsf{Z}(T_\mathsf{Z}) \\ \quad \text{otherwise} \end{cases}$$

$$elem^k(\mathsf{X}) = \begin{cases} \pi_{\mathsf{Id}}(T_\mathsf{X}) \cup \bigcup_{\mathsf{Y}\in\mathcal{S}^{\mathsf{H}}_{\mathsf{X}}\downarrow} \pi_{\mathsf{Id}}(T_\mathsf{Y}) & \text{if } \mathsf{X}\equiv\mathcal{R} \text{ or } \mathsf{X}\notin\mathcal{S}^{\mathsf{F}}_{\mathcal{R}}\downarrow \\ \pi_{\mathsf{Id}}(\sigma_{\phi_3}(T_\mathcal{F})) \cup \bigcup_{\mathsf{Y}\in\mathcal{S}^{\mathsf{H}}_{\mathsf{X}}\downarrow} \pi_{\mathsf{Id}}(T_\mathsf{Y}) & \text{otherwise} \end{cases}$$

with $\phi_1 \equiv \bigwedge_{\mathsf{Y}\in\mathcal{S}^{\mathsf{F}}_{\mathsf{X}}\downarrow} (\mathsf{Y?=false})$, $\phi_2 \equiv (\mathsf{X?=true} \wedge \bigwedge_{\mathsf{Y}\in\mathcal{S}^{\mathsf{F}}_{\mathsf{X}}\downarrow} (\mathsf{Y?=false}))$, $\phi_3 \equiv (\mathsf{X?=true})$ and $\mathcal{F} = \mathcal{P}^{\mathsf{F}}_{\mathsf{X}}\uparrow[*]$.

We do not want to formally prove the queries. Let us state some general considerations about the queries instead. We only consider the variant (^{a}). The other variant (^{k}) is a special case that does not require joins with supertype tables T_Z. To compute instances, a set difference between T_X and its direct V-successors ($\mathcal{D}^{\mathsf{V}}_{\mathsf{X}}\downarrow$) must be performed due to strategy V. Since T_X may contain elements of F-subtypes, the formulas ϕ_1 (if X is no F-subtype) and ϕ_2 (if X is F-subtype) select the corresponding instances as for strategy F. In the latter case, X has no corresponding table so that the uppermost table following F-edges, i.e., $T_\mathcal{F} = \mathcal{P}^{\mathsf{F}}_{\mathsf{X}}\uparrow[*]$, must be used. Since the difference operates on key values, (^{a}) demands for joining T_X with tables that correspond to V-supertypes in $\mathcal{P}_X^{V,F}\uparrow$. For example:

- X is no F-subtype:
  $$inst^a(\text{PERSON}) = \left(\pi_{\text{Id}}(\sigma_{\text{Worker?=false}}(\text{P})) - \pi_{\text{Id}}(\text{E})\right) \oplus \pi_{\text{PERSON}}(\text{P})$$
- X is F-subtype: $inst^a(\text{WORKER}) = \left(\pi_{\text{Id}}(\sigma_{\text{Worker?=true}}(\text{P}))\right)$

Please note that the path must include V- and F-supertypes to handle hierarchies like that correctly: Suppose a constellation $\text{D} \to^V \text{C} \to^F \text{B} \to^V \text{A}$. The problem is how to make the attributes of supertypes accessible. In case of $\text{X} \equiv \text{D}$, joining with $\mathcal{P}_X^V\uparrow = <\text{C}>$ is not sufficient since the attributes of A will not be reachable. A join with all V-nodes in $\mathcal{P}_X^{V,F}\uparrow$ and the root, i.e., $\mathcal{P}_X^{V,F}\uparrow \cap (\mathcal{S}_\mathcal{R}^V\downarrow \cup \{ T_\mathcal{R} \}) = <\text{C,A}>$, is necessary.
If there are no direct V-subtypes, i.e., $\mathcal{D}_X^V\downarrow = \emptyset$, then the attributes of X are computed directly, not requiring a join with T_X.
Queries computing elements are similar. Elements, spread over different tables (in $\mathcal{S}_X^H\downarrow$) due to strategy H, are collected by '∪'. Formula ϕ_3 is used to select elements in tables that possess flags. The flag approach uses the table $T_\mathcal{F}$, corresponding to $\mathcal{F} = \mathcal{P}_X^F\uparrow[*]$, to refer to the uppermost table following F-edges. To compute the (^{a})-information, again a join with V-supertypes is necessary.

$$elem^a(\text{PERSON}) = \pi_{\text{PERSON}}(\text{P}) \cup \pi_{\text{PERSON}}(\text{M})$$
$$elem^a(\text{EMP}) \quad = \left(\pi_{\text{EMP}}(\text{E}) \cup \pi_{\text{EMP}}(\text{M})\ \right) \oplus \pi_{\text{PERSON}}(\text{P})$$

Please note the queries still work if a hierarchy is not built over *one* key attribute! We just have to perform explicit joins via attributes instead of natural joins.

5 Conclusions

In this paper, we described an essential part to provide interoperability between relational databases and object-oriented ones that support the emerging standard ODMG-93 [CAT94]. The idea is to upgrade relational schemas to ODMG schemas in order to obtain a common semantic and operational level. Our approach is *user-driven*, because enhancing the semantics of relational schemas, i.e., specifying how tables are combined to object types, must be done explicitly by means of a powerful and intuitive specification language. Specifying the enrichment directly has the advantage that any kind of data semantics in tables can be expressed, building a real object-oriented view of relational data.
A concrete specification is then input to a generator that produces a corresponding ODMG schema automatically. This schema provides a complete object-oriented database interface similar to [JUN95, HOH93]. Generic methods allow operating on objects instead of tuples. Both the signatures of methods as well as their implementations on top of a relational system are generated. Relational data is operated in an object-oriented manner, using inheritance and relationships, and avoiding the impedance mismatch. Hence the door is opened to smoothly migrate from relational systems to object-oriented ones.
The presented generative approach has been implemented on SUN4 workstations in AT&T C++ on top of the relational system INFORMIX. The implementations make use of a compiler-compiler to produce the generator.

The process of semantic enrichment prepares the integration of database systems. Future work will be dedicated to the successive integration step. The main concern of the integration is to identify conflicts between several schemas belonging to different database systems, to resolve them and to merge the schemas to federated schema(s) in order to provide a uniform and transparent access to several databases. The federated, integrated schema is nothing but an additional software layer, the implementation of which is based upon the ODMG layers of the participating DBSs. Similar principles will be applied to define a federated schema, but different concepts are needed due to the different kind of problems to be solved. Hence, there will be a specification language for integration, now dissolving semantic heterogeneity between schemas. Syntactic constructs can handle typical problems of schema integration such as:

- Different units of measurement ($ vs. £), incl./excl. tax, etc.
- Naming conflicts like homonyms and synomyms.
- Complex restructurings to overcome structural differences ([KIM91, SPA91, KRI91, SCG92] between schemas.
- Generalisation to bring together objects of same type, but from different, heterogeneous databases [KAU90].
- Vertical fragmentation to "join" objects from different databases.
- Introducing new relationships between so far disjoint databases.

Having an integration language that provides corresponding syntactic constructs, we want to further apply our generative principle. Object classes that represent the federated schema are automatically generated and provide a uniform interface for the federation. In fact, query processing is again necessary with new challenging aspects. Up to now, a prototype that integrates INFORMIX with the object-oriented database systems VERSANT and Objectivity/DB has been implemented, but a lot of work is still necessary.

References

[BER94] E. Bertino, M. Negri, G. Pelagatti, L. Sbattella: Applications of Object-Oriented Technology to the Integration of Heterogeneous Database Systems. In: Distributed and Parallel Databases 1994, Vol. 2

[CAS93] M. Castellanos: Semantic Enrichment of Interoperable Databases. In [IMS93]

[CAS91] M. Castellanos, F. Saltor: Semantic Enrichment of Database Schemas: An Object-Oriented Approach. In [KAM91]

[CAT94] R. Cattell (ed.): The ODMG-93 Standard for Object Databases. 2nd edition, Morgan-Kaufmann Publishers, San Mateo (California) 1994

[CHI94] R. Chiang, T. Barron, V. Storey: Reverse Engineering of Relational Databases: Extraction of an EER model from a Relational Database. Data&Knowledge Engineering 12, 1994

[DAV87] K.H. Davis, A.K. Arora: Converting a Relational Database Model into an Entity-Relationship Model. In [ERA87]

[ERA87] S. March (ed.): Proc. 6th Int. Conf. on Entity-Relationship Approach, 1987

[ERA93] Proc. 12th Int. Conf. on Entity-Relationship Approach. Karlsruhe 1993

[FAN91] D. Fang, D. McLeod: Seamless Interconnection in Federated Database Systems. In Y. Kambayashi (ed.): Database Systems for Next-Generation Applications: Principles and Practice. World Scientific 1993

[HSI92] D.K. Hsia, E.J. Neuhold, R. Sacks-Davis (eds.): Proc. 5th IFIP WG 2.6 Database Semantics Conference (DS-5) on Interoperable Database Systems, Lorne (Australia), 1992

[HOH92] U. Hohenstein, G. Engels: SQL/EER : Syntax and Semantics of an Entity-Relationship Based Query Language. Information Systems 1992, 17 (3)

[HOH95] U. Hohenstein, C. Körner: A Graphical Tool for Specifying Semantic Enrichment of Relational Databases. Proc. 6th IFIP WG 2.6 Work. Group on Data Semantics (DS-6) "Semantics of Database Applications", Atlanta 1995

[HOH93] U. Hohenstein, E. Odberg: A C++ Database Interface Based upon the Entity-Relationship Approach. In M. Worboys, A. Grundy (eds.): Proc. of 11th British National Conf. on DBSs (BNCOD11), Keele (England) 1993

[HUC94] G. Huck, P. Fankhauser, R. Busse, W. Klas: IRO-DB: An Object-Oriented Approach towards Federated and Interoperable DBMS. In: Advances in Databases and Information Systems (ADBIS'94), Moscow 1994

[HAI93] J.-L. Hainault, C. Tonneau, M. Joris, M. Chandelon: Schema Transformation Techniques for Database Reverse Engineering. In [ERA93]

[IMS93] Proc. of Conf. on Research Issues in Data Engineering: Interoperability in Multidatabase Systems (RIDE-IMS'93). Vienna 1993

[JUN95] Y. Jun, S. Yoo: Design and Implementation of the spareC++ OODBPL. In: 6th Int. Conf. on Data and Expert Systems Applications (DEXA'95)

[KAU90] M. Kaul, K. Drosten, E. Neuhold: ViewSystem: Integrating Heterogeneous Information Bases by Object-Oriented Views. In: Proc. 6th Int. Conf. on Data Engineering, Los Angeles 1990

[KIM92] W. Kim: On Unifying Relational and Object-Oriented Database Systems. In O.L. Madsen (ed.): Europ. Conf. on Object-Oriented Programming 1992

[KIM91] W. Kim, J. Seo: Classifying Schematic and data Heterogeneity in Multidatabase Systems. Proc. IEEE Computer 24(12) 1991

[KRI91] R. Krishnamurthy, W. Litwin, W. Kent: Language Features for Interoperability of Databases with Schematic Discrepancies. In: [KAM91]

[KAM91] Y. Kambayashi, M. Rusinkiewicz, A. Sheth (eds.): Proc. of 1st Int. Workshop on Interoperability in Multidatabase Systems, Kyoto (Japan), 1991

[MAR90] V. Markowitz, J. Makowsky: Identifying Extended ER Object Structures in Relational Schemas. IEEE Trans. on Software Engineering 16(8), 1990

[MAR93] V. Markowitz, A. Shoshani: Object Queries over Relational Databases: Language, Implementation, and Applications. Conf. on Data Engineering 1993

[NAV87] S. Navathe, A. Awong: Abstracting Relational and Hierarchical Databases with a Semantic Data Model. In [ERA87]

[NAR93] B. Narasimhan, S. Navathe, S. Jayaraman: On Mapping ER and Relational Models into OO Schemas. In [ERA93]

[PRE94] W. Premerlani, M. Blaha: An Approach for Reverse Engineering of Relational Databases. Communications of the ACM 37(5), May 1994

[RAF91] R. Rafii, R. Ahmed, P. DeSmedt, B. Kent, M. Ketabchi, W. Litwin: Multidatabase Management in Pegasus. In [KAM91]

[SCG92] F. Saltor, M. Castellanos, M. Garcia-Solaco: Overcoming Schematic Discrepancies in Interoperable Databases. In [HSI92]

[SHE90] A. Sheth, J. Larson: Federated DBSs for Managing Distributed, Heterogeneous and Autonomous Databases. ACM Comp. Surveys 1990, 22(3)

[SPA91] S. Spaccapietra, C. Parent: Conflicts and Correspondence Assertions in Interoperable Databases. ACM SIGMOD-RECORD 1991, 20(4)

[YAN92] L.-L. Yan, T.-W. Ling: Translating Relational Schema With Constraints Into OODB Schema. In [HSI92]

[YU93] C. Yu, Y. Zhang, W. Meng, W. Kim, G. Wang, T. Pham, S. Dao: Translation of Object-Oriented Queries to Relational Queries. In: Int. Conf. on Data Engineering, Taipei (Taiwan) 1995

A Production Rule Approach to Modeling Complex Objects

Weijia Jia
Department of Computer Science
City University of Hong Kong
Tat Chee Avenue, Hong Kong
E-mail: wjia@cs.cityu.edu.hk

Abstract. This paper presents a novel approach to modeling structures of complex objects, class hierarchy and method behaviors of object-oriented databases. The approach uses Object-Identifier Grammars and its production rules to express a complex object into a tree and the nodes within the tree are set as the object/class identifiers. This approach is simple and efficient in processing a complex object via the rules. Restructuring the structures of objects and classes are flexible, efficient and transparent. Mechanisms of concurrency control and partitioning schemes for distributed object-oriented database systems using the rules are also presented.

1. Introduction

Object-oriented databases (OODBs) are receiving significant attraction as many of the systems become commercially available, such as GemStones [BRE89], O_2 [BAN91]. Objectivity/DB [OBJ90], ObjectStore [LAM91] etc.

[ATK89] indicated that an OODB must satisfy two criteria: it should be a DBMS, and it should be an object-oriented system. The second criterion translates into eight features which are treated as mandatory: complex objects, object identity, encapsulation, types or classes, inheritance, overriding combined with late binding, extensibility and computational completeness.

In the design of OODBs, complex objects (classes) and their operations constitute the system components. Operations on complex objects such as storing, accessing and restructuring are very costly. A simple method for modeling the complex objects for engineering of OODBs is desirable. There are many researches on modeling of object data such as calculus and algebra of complex objects [BAN89, ZAN85]. However, these approaches are complicated and do not support parallel/distributed OODBs.

This paper presents a very simple and powerful approach to modeling structures of complex objects, class hierarchy and method behaviors. The approach called Object Identifier Grammar (OIG) uses notions of grammar and production rules of [HOP79] to structure the complex objects. The grammars take advantage of identifiers of objects (classes) and expresses their structures as trees which capture semantics of object compositions and inheritance hierarchy. With the grammatical rules, processing of class hierarchy and complex objects can be transformed to the processing of corresponding rules, i.e., various operations on a complex object such as component accessing, storing, sharing, restructuring, concurrency controlling and distributed partitioning can be applied on the trees to gain efficiency and transparency for OODBs. Particularly, in designing a distributed OODBs, in order to achieve system availability, objects and classes are replicated and partitioned into groups and accessed concurrently in which serializability, consistency and transparency must be obtained.

The paper is structured into 6 sections. Section 2 gives the definitions of complex objects and grammar rules. Modeling of complex objects, class hierarchy, inheritance and behavior of methods are also presented. Operations on complex objects using the production rules are given in Section 3. Section 4 discusses design of concurrency control and its rule representations. Distributed object/class partitioning rules are given in Section 5 and we conclude in the final section.

2. Complex Objects and Identifier Grammars

In this section, we define the structures of complex objects. The OIG production rules to modeling the complex objects, classes inheritance hierarchy and behaviors.

2.1 Complex Objects

Definition 2.1: An atom object is an object with simple types of *Character* (String), *Number* (Integer, Fraction and Floating Number), *Boolean* (True, False), one pixel in a image and one phoneme of voice.

Definition 2.2: Two kinds of special objects are defined as: The upper-bound of all objects is denoted as *Top*, the low-bound of all objects (bottom) is written as *Null*.

[ATK89] has defined the minimal set of object constructor as *set, list* and *tuple*. *Sets* are natural way of representing collections from the real world. *Tuples* are natural way of representing properties of an entity. They are important because they have gained wide acceptance as object constructors through relational model. *Lists* (or *arrays*) capture order, one property of the real world which arise in many applications.

Definition 2.3: A set object is defined as $O = \{o_1, \ldots, o_n\}$, where o_i, $i = 1, \ldots, n$, are different component sub-objects in O.

Definition 2.4: A list object is defined as $O = (o_1, \ldots, o_n)$, where o_i, $i = 1, \ldots, n$, are indexed and (ordered) sub-objects in O.

Definition 2.5: A tuple object is defined as $O = [A_1: o_1, \ldots, A_n: o_n]$, where o_i are sub-objects, and $A_1, \ldots, A_n$, $i = 1, \ldots, n$ are distinguishable attribute names, the names are taken as atom objects. o_i can be denoted as $O.A_i$. For some attribute A, if A is not in $\{A_1, \ldots, A_n\}$, then $O.A = Null$;

Definition 2.6: A complex object is defined as an object constructed by applying above constructors in a finite steps.

Example 1. Following object is regarded as a complex object:

[r₁: {[name: John, age: 25], [name: Mary, sex: F]}
r₂: {[name: Tad, address: New_York], [name: Smith, address: London]}]

One object containing other objects as its components results in sub-object relation, As proved by [BAN89] that sub-object relation forms a lattices. The following definitions of depth and weight of complex objects are useful in judging of object processing complexity.

Definition 2.7: Depth of an object is defined as d:

1. For every atom object o, $d(o) = 1$ and $d(Null) = 1$.
2. Empty *Set/List/Tuple* objects: {}, ( ) and [ ], $d(\{\}) = d(()) = d([]) = 2$.
3. For a *Set/List/Tuple* object O, $d(O) = max\{d(o) \mid o \hat{I} O\} + 1$, where $o_i \in O$.

Definition 2.8. Weight of an object is denoted as w:

1. If O is an atom object, then $w(O) = 1$;
2. For an empty *Set/List/Tuple* objects, $w(\{\}) = w(()) = w([]) = 2$;
3. For a *Set/List/Tuple* objects $O = \{O_1, \ldots, O_n\}/(O_1, \ldots, O_n)/[r_1: O_1, \ldots, r_n: O_n]$,
   $w(O) = \Sigma_{i=1,\ldots,n} w(O_i) + 1$.

The weight function is useful for analyzing the operation overhead and complexity in certain cases, especially for distributed complex object processing (see Section 6). Note that the attribute names A_i ($i = 1, \ldots, n$) are only regarded as the properties of sub-objects (or instance variables). Thus, they are not counted in the weight function.

2.2 Object Identifier Grammars

Assume system-wide identifiers are set for each object as well as its sub-objects (components). Thus a complex object is uniquely defined and determined by its structure and value. With this in mind, we can easily associate the object structure with a tree. The internal nodes of the tree are identifiers and the leaves are atom objects. Note that attributes or instance variable names are attached to the nodes and not regarded as the identifiers. In this way, a complex object structure can be uniquely represented by an OIG which is defined as follows:

Definition 2.9: An object identifier grammar for one complex object O is denoted as $OIG(O) = (I, T, P, S)$ where I is a finite set of identifiers of sub-objects (non-atom objects) within O; T is a finite set of all atom (valued) objects within O and $T \cap I = \varnothing$. P is a finite set of production rules as defined in *Definition 2.9* below, and S, S Î I, is a starting identifier of OIG, it never appears on right-hand side of any production rule.

Definition 2.10: Production rules of $OIG(O)$ are constructed as follows:

1. For any atom object and special objects, i.e. *Top* and *Null*, the corresponding identifier and production rule are defined as themselves.
2. For a set object: $O = \{o_1, \ldots, o_n\}$ / $(o_1, \ldots, o_n)$ / $[A_1\!: o_1, \ldots, A_n\!: o_n]$, and its identifier I_O, the production rule is defined as
   $I_O \rightarrow \{o_1, \ldots, o_n\}$ / $(o_1, \ldots, o_n)$ / $[A_1\!: o_1, \ldots, A_n\!: o_n]$
   where o_i are atom objects and $o_i \neq o_j$ if $i \neq j$.
3. A finite steps of composition of (2) is a production rule. It has a new (unique) identifier on its left-hand side.

For example, Grammar rules of Example 1 follow below:

$S \rightarrow [r_1\!: A_1, r_2\!: A_2]$, $A_1 \rightarrow \{B_1, B_2\}$, $A_2 \rightarrow \{C_1, C_2\}$,
$B_1 \rightarrow$ [name: John, age: 25], B_2 ® [name: Mary, sex: F],
$C_1 \rightarrow$ [name: Tad, address: New_York],
$C_2 \rightarrow$ [name: Smith, address: London]

where $\{S, A_1, A_2, B_1, B_2, C_1, C_2\}$ are identifiers, T = {John, Mary, Tad, Smith, 25, F, New_York, London} are terminals (atom objects).

Theorem 1. *A complex object O is equivalent to its OIG.*

Proof: By induction on the object's depth. Denote the complex object as O and its grammar as OIG = (I, T, P, S).

Basis: When d(O) = 1 or 2, O is either an atom object, {}, () or []. According to the definition of OIG which is equivalent to O.
Induction: Assume the theorem holds for d(O)<k. For d(O)=k and k>2, consider $O=\{O_1, \ldots, O_n\}$, and the depth of O such that $d(O)=\max\{d(O_i) \mid O_i \in O\} + 1$ where $i=1, \ldots, n$. By Definition 2.7, for each O_i in O, depth of O_i is less then k. By induction, all the sub-objects of O are equivalent to its OIG_i

where i=1,..., n. Replace sub-objects in O with identifiers I_i (starting symbols of OIG_i), we have $\{I_1, \ldots, I_n\} <=> \{O_1, \ldots, O_n\}$.

Now we create a grammar for O. Define an identifier S to be the starting symbol for OIG(O). A production rule is created: $S \rightarrow \{I_1, \ldots, I_n\}$ and combined with that of OIG_i into a new OIG. Clearly, OIG is equivalent to O.

The proofs for $O = (O_1, \ldots, O_n)/[r_1: O_1, \ldots, r_n: O_2]$ can be similarly established by creating rules $S \rightarrow (I_1, \ldots, I_n)/[r_1: I_1, \ldots, r_n: I_n]$.

Definition 2.11. Select operation: $O = <O_1, \ldots, O_n>$ means that O selects one of O_i as its value.

Theorem 2. *OIG*s are closed under the constructor of *Set/List/Tuple* and *Select*.

Proof: Suppose $OIG_1=(I_1, T_1, P_1, S_1)$ and $OIG_2=(I_2, T_2, P_2, S_2)$ represent complex objects O_1 and O_2, respectively. We prove this theorem by explicitly constructing an OIG for constructors Set / List / Tuple and operation Select.

(1) A Set / List / Tuple for O_1 and O_2 results in $O = \{O_1, O_2\} / (O_1, O_2) / [A_1: O_1, A_2: O_2]$ and its associated grammar is constructed as $OIG = (I_1 \cup I_2 \cup \{S\}, T_1 \cup T_2, P, S)$, where $P = P_1 \cup P_2 \cup \{S \rightarrow \{S_1, S_2\}\} / P_1 \cup P_2 \cup \{S \rightarrow (S_1, S_2)\} / P_1 \cup P_2 \cup \{S \rightarrow [A_1: S_1, A_2: S_2]\}$.

(2) Selection of O_1 and O_2, for $O = <O_1, O_2>$, the corresponding grammar is built as $OIG = (I_1 \cup I_2, T_1 \cup T_2, P_1 \cup P_2 \cup \{S \rightarrow S_1 | S_2\}, S)$.

Theorem 3. An object O is achieved by applying *Set/List/Tuple* or *Selection* operation on O_1 and O_2, any sub-object of O_1 and O_2 is reachable if and only if it is reachable in either O_1 or O_2.

Proof: Consider the set constructor. If o is a sub-object of either O_1 or O_2, it will appear in a sub-trees either derived from G_1 or G_2. By Theorem 2, there is rule in OIG(O) such that S®$\{S_1, S_2\}$. This indicates that o appears in a sub-tree derived from OIG(O), thus o is also a sub-object of O. Since o is reachable from either S_1 or S_2 thus it is also reachable from S. Conversely, if o is a sub-object of O and it is reachable, then it can be derived from either S_1 or S_2. The proofs of List/Tuple and Select can be similarly established.

Note that *Theorem* 3 guarantees that there exists no orphan components after applying *Set/List/Tuple* or *Selection* operations to complex objects.

2.3 Support for Class/Type Hierarchy

Consider a class:

```
Class Class_name
  {
   A1: Type1/class1,
   ...
   An: Typen/classn
  }
```

where A_i are distinguishable instance variable names (i.e., the attributes). Denote the identifiers of *Class_name* as I_C and $class_i$ as I_i, the corresponding production rule is:

$$I_C \rightarrow [A_1: I_1, \ldots, A_n: I_n].$$

For example, consider the composition classes Employees-Dept-Proj below:

```
Class Employees:
{  Eid: Int
   Ename: String
   ESal: Float
   DepInfo: Dept
   ProjInfo: Proj
}

Class Dept:
{  Did: Int
   Dname: String
   Dhead: String
}

Class Proj:
{  Pid: Int
   Pname: String
   Budget: Int
}
```

The class Employees is a compositional class in which two instance variables: *DepInfo* and *ProjInfo* refer to two different classes. The classes above are translated straightforwardly into the following rules:

$I_E \rightarrow$ [*Eid: Int, Ename: String, ESal: Float, DepInfo:* I_D*, ProjInfo:* I_P]
$I_D \rightarrow$ [*Did: Int, Dname: String, Dhead: String*]
$I_P \rightarrow$ [*Pid: Int, Pname: String, Budget: Int*].

2.4 Inheritance

Inheritance has two advantages; it is a powerful modeling tool, because it gives a concise and precise description of the world and it helps in factoring out shared specifications and implementations in applications and enhancing software reuse. In our approach, a special attribute *IS-A* is used to link super-sub classes in the grammatical representations. An example will help to illustrate the idea. Consider the Employees and Manager classes. A manager is a kind of employees and the class Manager inherits all properties of Employees. Let I_M be the identifier of class Manager, rule of Manager is shown below:

$$I_M \rightarrow [IS\text{-}A\text{: } I_E, \ldots, (other\ components)].$$

2.5 Object Sharing

With the OIG grammar, it is easy to express two objects sharing a component. An example below is adopted from [ATK89]. Assume Peter and Susan both have a 15-year-old child named John. In real life, two situations may arise: Susan and Peter are parent of the same child or there are two children involved. In the first situation, the rules are:

$I_{Peter} \rightarrow$ [*name: Peter, age: 40, has_child:* I_{John}]
$I_{Susan} \rightarrow$ [*name: Susan, age: 41, has_child:* I_{John}]
$I_{John} \rightarrow$ [*name: John, age: 15*].

whereas in the second case, the rules become:

$I_{Peter} \rightarrow$ [*name: Peter, age: 40, has_child:* I_{John}]
$I_{Susan} \rightarrow$ [*name: Susan, age: 41, has_child:* I'_{John}]
$I_{John} \rightarrow$ [*name: John, age: 15*]
$I'_{John} \rightarrow$ [*name: John, age: 15*] where $I'_{John} \neq I_{john}$.

2.6 Behavior (Method) Modeling

So far we have discussed OIG approach to modeling the static structure of complex objects, class inheritance and composition hierarchy. This section focuses on the dynamic behavior modeling of methods.

From the perspective of methods defined in a class $M(C) = \{m_1, m_2, \ldots, m_n\}$, we further distinguish a set of methods in a class as "creator", that create objects, "updator" that change the state of the objects and "retriever" that report the state of the existing objects without any side-effect. This is analogous to the treatment of [Zodnick 94]. For simplicity, we here only consider "updator" and "retriever" methods of class C and they are denoted as $M_u(C)$ and $M_r(C)$, respectively. Therefore, the set $M(C)$ is partitioned into $M_u(C)$, and $M_r(C)$. In order to make the model uniform, we set an identifier for each method (use the same name). The behavior rules are shown below:

$$M(C) \rightarrow \{m_1, m_2, \ldots, m_k\},\ M_u(C) \rightarrow \{m_{u1}, \ldots, m_{ul}\},$$
$$M_r(C) \rightarrow \{m_{r1}, \ldots, m_{rp}\} \text{ where } l \leq k \text{ and } p \leq k.$$

Combine the rules with that of class in Section 2.4, we denote:

$$I_C * M \rightarrow [A_1: I_1, \ldots, A_n: I_n] * \{M_u, M_r\}$$

in which the notion $I * \{M_u, M_r\}$ means that methods in M_u (M_r) access (update or retrieve) the object identified by I. Set M_u and M_r can be further partitioned and applied to each instance variable (see Section 4).

3. Relational Operations

This section discusses examples how relational operations are applied to a complex object. Because a complex object and its OIG are equivalent, the operations are applied to the corresponding OIGs.

Definition 2.12: Substituting a component of an object O or its OIG with another component (identifier) is called a *Substitution*. Let r be the substitution function, we have:

1. $r(Top) = Top,\ r(Null) = Null.$
2. $r(X) = Y$, where X is an identifier within OIG, and Y is any identifier, but for any identifier $Z\ ^1 X$, $r(Z) = Z$.
3. If $I \rightarrow [A_1: I_1, \ldots, A_n: I_n]$ then $r(I)$ implies:
   $r([A_1: I_1, \ldots, A_n: I_n]) = [A_1: r(I_1), \ldots, A_n: r(I_n)]$.
4. If $I \rightarrow (I_1, \ldots, I_n)$ then $r(I)$ implies $r((I_1, \ldots, I_n)) = (r(I_1), \ldots, r(I_n))$.
5. If $I \rightarrow \{I_1, \ldots, I_n\}$ then $r(I)$ implies $r(\{I_1, \ldots, I_n\}) = \{r(I_1), \ldots, r(I_n)\}$.

If every atom object in O is replaced by another object (atom or complex one), then r is called a full-substitution of O. For a given well-formed formula F with n variables $\{X_1, \ldots, X_n\}$, if we can find a substitution function r such that $r\{v_1/X_1, \ldots, v_n/X_n\}$ where $v_1, \ldots, v_n$ are objects/identifiers, then r replacing all variables in F results in an object which is called a derived object from F (denoted as $r(F)$). Inverse substitution r^{-1} can be similarly established.

For example, a complex object (A relational object base) is in the form of:

$$ODB = [r_1: \{[A: o_a, B: o_b]\},\ r_2: \{[C: o_c, D: o_d]\}]$$

where r_1, r_2 are relations; A, B, C and D are attributes; o_x ($x = a, b, c, d$) represents any atom object. Without losing generality, assuming X, Y, X_1, Y_1 and Z are variables and S, I_p ($p=1,..,n$) are identifiers. The OIG(ODB) is defined as:

$$S \rightarrow [r_1\colon I_1,\ r_2\colon I_2],\ \ I_1 \rightarrow \{I_{11}, I_{12}, \ldots\},\ I_2 \rightarrow \{I_{21}, I_{22}, \ldots\},$$
$$I_x \rightarrow [A\colon o_a,\ B\colon o_b] \text{ (where x = 11, 21, ...)},$$
$$I_y \rightarrow [C\colon o_c,\ D\colon o_d] \text{ (where y = 21, 22, ...)}.$$

Following defines a *well-formed formula* before discussions other operations. Similar definitions can be found in [BAN89]:

Definition 2.13: (*Well-formed formula*)

1. A variable is a *well-formed formula.*
2. An atomic object is a *well-formed formula.*
3. If F_1, F_2, ..., F_n are *well-formed formulas*, then $(F_1,\ F_2, \ldots, F_n)$ / $\{F_1,\ F_2, \ldots, F_n\}$ / $[A_1\colon F_1,\ A_2\colon F_2, \ldots, A_n\colon F_n]$ is a *well-formed formula,* where A_1, A_2, ..., A_n are distinct attribute names.

Definition 2.14: For a production rule, if its right-hand side contains a *well-formed formula*, it is called a *formula rule* (*FR*).

Following examples illustrate the *FR* and their operations in which *X*, *Y* and *Z* are variables.

Example 3:

(1) $I \rightarrow [r_1\colon \{[A\colon X,\ B\colon b]\}]$ implies that for the relation r_1, it selects all the items in which their attribute B's values are b(s);

(2) $I \rightarrow [r_1\colon \{[A\colon X,\ B\colon Y]\},\ r_2\colon \{[C\colon X,\ D\colon Y]\}]$ projects r_1's attributes A and B, r_2's attributes C and D. The values associated with A are the same as that of C and that of B are same as that of D;

(3) $I \rightarrow [r_1\colon \{X\},\ r_2\colon \{X\}]$ is the intersection of relations r_1 and r_2.

Definition 2.15: A rewriting rule is an order pair $<FR => FR'>$, where *FR* and *FR'* are formula rules and all variables of *FR'* are subset of *FR*.

Example 4.

(1) $I \rightarrow [r_1\colon\{[A\colon X,\ B\colon b]\}] => I' \rightarrow [r\colon \{[C\colon X]\}]$ ("< >" is omitted here), Select r_1 and associated value b for attribute B; project A and assign the corresponding values of A to the relation r's attribute C.

(2) $I\rightarrow [r_1\colon \{[A\colon X,\ B\colon Y]\},\ r_2\colon \{[C\colon X_1,\ D\colon Y_1]\}] => I'\rightarrow [r\colon \{[A\colon X,\ B\colon Y,\ C\colon X_1,\ D\colon Y_1]\}]$

The Cartesian product of relation r_1 and r_2 into a new relation r.

(3) $I \rightarrow [r_1\colon \{[A\colon X,\ B\colon Y]\},\ r_2\colon \{[C\colon Y,\ D\colon Z]\}] => I'\rightarrow [r\colon \{[A\colon X,\ D\colon Z]\}]$

Conjoin r_1 and r_2, the condition is the associated values of B must equal to that of C, then project A and D into a new relation r;

(4) $I \rightarrow [r_1: \{[A: X, B: Y]\}, r_2: \{[B: Y, D: Z]\}] \Rightarrow I' \rightarrow [r: \{[A: X, B: Y, D: Z]\}]$, natural conjunction of r_1 and r_2.

4. Concurrency Control

It is desirable that high performance OODBs should be facilitated with incorporate concurrent invocations of methods on the complex objects. Due to the complexity and possible accessing conflicts, mechanism of concurrency control is required in the design of parallel/concurrent OODBs. This section explores a concurrent control engine for complex object by analysis of method-data dependency and combine them with OIG.

[CAM74] defined path expressions to specify concurrent (synchronization) activities among processes. The typical use of a path expression is in explicit parallel program languages, in which constructs are provided for designing "processes" that run in parallel. Path expressions constrain parallel activities. [WUL90] proposed a paradigm of intra-object parallelization through path expressions. There are two kinds of parallelism encapsulations described, i.e., dynamic and automatic parallelization. The former requires dynamic conflict resolution by rather low wait/signal primitives in the start and depart operations of object control engine. Those introduce extra runtime overhead. The latter needs data dependence analysis which is to associate each statement with a set of methods that are called in the statement. With dependence analysis, one has to determine the compatible path expressions and indirectly called procedure associating with the statement.

A new scheme is devised in this section by analyzing the dependency of the methods in terms of instance variables they access. To build such a dependency, a set of methods which conflict with each other should be detected. In the set, the methods that have conflict are not allowed to execute concurrently. Other methods with no interference are allowed to execute in parallel with *one* method in this set.

To find out the set which allows concurrent execution, let $\{v_1, v_2, \ldots, v_k\}$ be the instance variables of class C. Following the description of Section 2.6 that $M(v_i)$ is a set of methods that access variable v_i and $M(v_i) = M_u(v_i) \cup M_r(v_i)$ while $M_u(v_i)$ and $M_r(v_i)$, $i=1, \ldots, k$ are sets of methods which update and read variable v_i, respectively. Take two distinct variables v_i and v_j into consideration, it can be seen that if conditions:

$$M_u(v_i) \cap M_r(v_i) = \varnothing \wedge M_u(v_j) \cap M_r(v_j) = \varnothing \wedge M_u(v_i) \cap M_u(v_j) = \varnothing \wedge$$
$$M_u(v_i) \cap M_r(v_j) = \varnothing \wedge M_r(v_i) \cap M_u(v_j) = \varnothing$$

are satisfied, for any two methods $m \in M(v_i)$ and $m' \in M(v_j)$, m and m' can execute concurrently because m does not conflict with m' in terms of v_i and v_j. With this analysis in mind, we further define

$$M_{conflict}(v_i, v_j) = (M_u(v_i) \cap M_r(v_i)) \cup (M_u(v_j) \cap M_r(v_j)) \cup (M_u(v_i) \cap M_u(v_j)) \cup (M_u(v_i) \cap M_r(v_j)) \cup (M_r(v_i) \cap M_u(v_j))$$

Consequently, $M_{conflict}(v_i, v_j)$ is the set in which one method conflict with another if they run concurrently in terms of v_i and v_j. We extend this notion of conflict method set to all the instance variables of class C and denote it as $M_{conflict}(v_1, \ldots, v_k)$, the set in which the methods interfere with each other. Denote M_{con} as a set of methods that do not conflict with any other methods, we have

$$M_{con}(C) = M(C) - M_{conflict}(v_1, \ldots, v_k)$$

where $M(C)$ are methods that access the instance variables in class C. It can be seen that the methods in M_{con} can run in parallel with *one* method in $M_{conflict}$. Therefore, two methods m and m' are allowed to execute concurrently if and only if

$$(m \in M_{con}) \vee (m' \in M_{con}).$$

Similarly, any two methods in $M_{conflict}(v_1, \ldots, v_k)$ must execute serially.

Without losing generality, in the following, we do not differentiate the method (set) id with its name. Suppose M_{con} has been achieved, the concurrency control notion is encapsulated in OIG(C) as:

$$I_C * M_{con} \mid M_{conflict} \rightarrow [A_1: I_1, \ldots, A_n: I_n] * M_{con} \mid M_{conflict}$$

With the rule, mechanism of concurrency control is imposed when an instance object of class C is accessed by many methods concurrently.

From above discussions, we can see that achieving M_{con} requires static method-data dependence analysis. If one method invokes many other methods, the analysis becomes complicated and sometimes it is impossible to determine the precise set of variable accessed for the indirectly called methods.

5. Distributed Partitioning Schemes

OODBs technology has been applied in distributed environments such as client-server and federated multiple-databases [KIM91, OZS94]. The OIG representation is simple and useful in engineering design of databases, especially for distributed OODB systems (OODBs). Because users accessing a complete complex object do not want to traverse through multiple classes to extract all the relevant instance variables. OIG approach provides a short-cut for such kinds of applications. In designing the distributed OODBs, it is required that the objects to be fragmented into groups. The partitioning (fragmentation) schemes following the relation model can be classified as *horizontal* and *vertical* partitioning that divide the instance objects of a global classes into subsets. This section proposes several simple and efficient partitioning schemes with the OIG representations. For simplicity, we do not consider issues of *completeness, reconstruction* and *disjointness* for the partitioning schemes.

5.1 Horizontal Partitioning

A condition or a predicate that restricts the domain of a partitioning instance variables is known as a qualification [CER85]. Similar to the relation model, for a class C, rules of *OIG(C)* can be horizontally fragmented as $\{I^H_1, I^H_2, \ldots, I^H_n\}$ and each horizontal fragment has a qualification q_i defined for one instance variable. Following the descriptions of Section 2.3, define I_C as starting symbol of *OIG(C)*, the fragment rules of I_C are given as

$$I_C \rightarrow I^H_1 \mid I^H_2 \mid, \ldots, \mid I^H_k;$$
$$I^H_i \rightarrow (\textit{the same as that of } I_C \textit{ but with } q_i \textit{ applied}),\ i=1, \ldots, k$$

The original rules of I_C are embodied by I^H_i that applies with the qualification q_i on the instance variable. I_C selects I^H_i when q_i is necessary. For example, a class of *Supplier* is defined:

```
Class Supplier
{   Snum: Int;
    Name: String;
    City: String;
}
```

The corresponding rule of OIG(Supplier) is denoted as

$$I_S \rightarrow [\textit{Snum: Int, Name: String, City: String}].$$

If the domain of the instance variable *City* is limited to {"LA", "SF"}, then we have the qualifications q_1: *City = "LA"* and q_2: *City = "SF"* and the partition of *OIG(Supplier)* is:

$$I_S \rightarrow I_{S1} \mid I_{S2} \ \text{(selection of OIG)}$$
$$I_{S1} \rightarrow [\textit{Snum: Int, Name: String, City= "SF"}].$$
$$I_{S2} \rightarrow [\textit{Snum: Int, Name: String, City= "LA"}].$$

5.2 Vertical Partitioning

Instance variables of a class is divided into groups of fragment classes. The vertical fragment classes are $\{V_1, \ldots, V_k\}$ such that each class fragment V_i has a nonempty subset of instance variables. This can be easily represented by rules of *OIG*(*C*):

$$I_C \rightarrow [A_1: I_1, \ldots, A_n: I_n].$$

The vertical partitioning rule of I_C is thus written as

$$I^V_C \rightarrow [I^V_1, I^V_2, \ldots, I^V_k];\ I^V_i \rightarrow [\{A^i_j: I^i_j\}]$$

where $i=1,\ldots, k$, $j = 1, \ldots, k_i$ and k_i is the number of the instance variables in the fragment of V_i. The vertical partitioning of OIG(C) reflects the fragmentation of *IS-A* and composition hierarchy of a class.

Consider the classes Employees-Dept-Project in Section 2.3 and Manager in Section 2.4, vertical partitioning rules are shown below:

$I_M \rightarrow$ [*IS-A:* I_E, I_O].
$I_E \rightarrow$ [*Eid: Int, Ename: String, ESal: Float, DepInfo:* I_D, *ProjInfo:* I_P]
$I_O \rightarrow$ (*other components of Manager*)
$I_D \rightarrow$ [*Did: Int, Dname: String, Dhead: String*]
$I_P \rightarrow$ [*Pid: Int, Pname: String, Budget: Int*]

where identifiers I_E, I_O, I_D I_P are the identifiers representing the vertical partitioning of I_M.

5.3 Path Partitioning

The grammar can be internally represented as a structural index for the complex (composite) objects. The concept of grammatical (structural) index is different from the "normalized representation" of composite objects as a hierarchy of independent component objects in [TEE93], wherein, an access to the complete composite object requires navigating through the hierarchy by using the component object references. Whereas, an OIG itself forms a tree and its internal nodes (identifiers) can be taken as the references of the component (sub-) objects/classes, respectively. This eliminates the need to traverse the entire class or object hierarchy. This treatment is similar to the path partitioning of [KAR95]. But our representation is much more simple for the representation and design of complex objects and composition class hierarchy in OODBs.

6. Conclusion

We have presented a simple grammatical approach to modeling complex objects and class hierarchy for the design of OODBs. Modeling the complex objects and class hierarchy as production rules enables the objects to be handled with efficiency. The rules can be implemented as a structured references to the objects classes and methods. We have shown the availability of production rules on various DB operations, concurrency control and distributed partitioning. Future work requires a formal investigation of the rules and an inclusion of reliable communications for distributed/parallel OODBs.

References

[ATK89] Atkinson, M., Bancilhon, F., debit, D., Ditch, K., Mailer, D., Zdonik, S. (1989): The Object-oriented Database System Manifesto. In: Proc. of the 1st Int'l Conf. on Deductive Object-Oriented Database, pp.40--57.

[BAN89] Bancilhon, F. and Khoshafian S. (1989): A Calculus for Complex Objects. In: J. of Computer and System Science, 38, pp.326--340.

[BAN91] Bancilhon, F. et al. (eds) (1991): Building an Object-oriented Database System: the story of O_2,, Morgan-Kauffman Publishers.

[BRE89] Bretl, R, et al. (1989): The GemStone Data Management System. In: Kim, W., and Lochovsky, F.H. (eds.): Object-oriented Concepts, Databases, and Applications; Addison-Wesley (ACM Press), pp.283--308.

[CAM74] Campbell, R.H. and Habermann, A.N. (1974): The Specification of Process Synchronization by Path Expressions. (Lecture Notes in Computer Science Vol.16.) Springer-Verlag, New York, pp.89--102.

[CER85] Ceri, S. and Pelagatti, G. (1985): Distributed Databases: Principles and Systems. McGraw Hill, New York.

[HOP79] Hopcroft, J. E. and Ullman, J. D. (1979): Introduction to Automata Theory, Language and Computation, Addison-Wesley.

[KAR95] Karlaplem, K. and Li, Q. (1995): Partitioning Schemes for Object-oriented Databases. In: Proc. of 5th Int'l Workshop on Research Issues in Data Engineering Distributed Object Management, pp.42--49.

[KIM91] Kim, W. et al. (1991): A Distributed Object-oriented Database System Supporting Shared and Private Databases. In: ACM TOIS, 9(1), pp.31--51.

[LAM91] Lamb, Ch. et. al. (1991): The ObjectStore Database system. In: CACM, 34 (10), pp.50--63.

[OBJ90] Objectivity Inc. (1990): Objectivity Database Reference Manual, Menlo Park, CA., USA.

[OZS94] Ozsu, M. T. et.al. (1994): Distributed Object Management, Morgan-Kauffman Publishers.

[TEE88] Teeuw, W.B. & Blanken H. K. (1988): Joining Distributed Complex Objects: Definition and Performance. In: Data & Knowledge Engineering, 9, pp.63--96.

[WUL90] Wu, Y. and Lewis,T.G. (1990): Parallelism Encapsulation in C++. In: Proc. of ICPP'90, Vol. 2, pp.35--42.

[ZAN85] Zaniolo, (1985): The Representation and Deductive Retrieval of Complex Objects. In: Proc. of VLDB, Stockholm, Sweden.

[ZOD94] Zodnik, S. (1994): What Makes object-oriented Database Management Systems Different? In: Advances in Object-oriented Database Systems, Springer-Verlag.

Extending Path Expression to Tree Expression in OODM

John W.T. Lee and Stephen C.F. Chan
Department of Computing
Hong Kong Polytechnic University
Hung Hom, Kowloon
Hong Kong

Abstract. One of the benefit of Object-Oriented Data Models (OODM) over Relational Data Model is its ability to represent relationship between objects directly, without resorting to concepts of keys and value-based joints. The navigational referencing from an object through a series of object-valued attributes is used commonly in OODMs in the form of path expressions (PE). It plays a role in defining queries, views and constraints. PE can be viewed as a special case of conceptual graph (CG). With this perspective, the capability of PE as a graph-based referencing mechanism has not been fully exploited in current OODMs. In this paper, we examine the semantics of PE as CG, and introduce an extended form of PE called tree expression (TE) which can provide more effective referencing within the framework of a general OODM. It will be demonstrated that TEs can by itself be used as a language for query and constraint specification.

1. Introduction

One of the benefit of Object-Oriented Data Models (OODM) over Relational Data Model is their ability to model relation between objects using object-valued attributes. This makes possible direct referencing of objects which are values of another object's attribute without resorting to explicit value-based joints on keys. Such object-valued attribute referencing can be repeatedly applied forming a series of attribute, commonly referred to as path expression (PE). It provides a succinct and natural way of referencing derived properties of an object related through an attribute chain and is used in many OODMs [BAN89, BER92, DAY89, KIF89, KEM94]. In some models, e.g. [KIF89], it is also used as a proposition in Boolean expressions.

The semantics of a PE can be most easily defined using a graph model of an OODB. The graph interpretation of an OODB is used in many models [BEE89, KIF92, SU93, WUW92]. In general the interpretation treats objects as nodes in the graph while attributes name the path between these nodes. The objects referenced by a PE is then the set of terminating nodes reached by following the named path starting with the head object of the PE. A more complete system using graphs for data and knowledge representation is Conceptual Graph (CG) which is based on Peirce's existential graph [SOW84]. We can regard PE as a special case of CG. Given this perspective, the capability of PE can be substantially extended, making it an effective tool for specification of queries, views and constraints. In this paper, we show how such an extended PE, which we call tree-expression (TE), modelled with CG semantics can be used in various modelling situations.

In the following section, we first consider a general OODM as a basis for our discussion in the paper. We will examine some of the extensions of PEs in various OODMs. In section 3, we provide a CG interpretation for OODB and the PE. Section 4 discussed how we proposed to extend PE to TE with semantics defined using CGs. We conclude with Section 5 where we will look into the role of such TE.

2. Path expressions and a general OODM

The use of PE makes very little assumption on the underlying OODM. In this paper, we will use an OODM, which we refer to as general OODM, that only contains a basic set of features common to most OODMs. We look at path expression in this context together with some proposed extensions of PE as described in [BER92, KIF92].

Our general OODM consists of the followings :

a. Set of objects

Object can be either lexical, like 1, "abc", 1-Jan-95, or non-lexical like the person John, the Accounting Department etc. Objects are identified by object identifiers. Lexical objects are identified by their values. Non-lexical objects and their properties are the basic object of interest in the universe of discourse in a database.

b. Type lattice

An object may belong to one or more types. Types form a lattice with the supertype/subtype relation. Objects belonging to a type also belongs to all its supertypes (i.e. inclusion semantics). We use a type to reference its extension (the set of objects belonging to the type) as well, and therefore do not distinguish type from class. We assume there is a most general type, $\mathfrak{S}$, which is supertype of all types, and an absurd type, Ω, which is the subtype of all types and with null extension.

c. Attributes

Non-lexical objects have attributes. We assume the most general form of attribute relation, a mapping from one object type to another. Thus an attribute

A: $T_1 \rightarrow T_2$ defined on type T_1 with a range in T_2 is a mapping $A \subseteq T_1 x T_2$. With this interpretation, there is no need for distinction between single-valued and multi-valued attributes. Attributes defined on a type is also defined on all its subtypes (i.e. attribute inheritance). We also assume attribute names to be unique so that if an attribute is defined on two objects, they belong to some common type on which the attribute is defined.

An OODB instance, D, can be interpreted as a graph, where objects formed the nodes of the graph, and with named edges corresponding to the attribute mappings between the objects.

A path expression $o.A_1.A_2...A_n$ consists of a starting object (or object variable) o and a series of attribute names A_1, A_2, ... A_n. The interpretation of such expression is the set of objects o_n such that there exist a path (o, o_1, o_2,... , o_{n-1}, o_n) (called the ground instance of the PE) in the OODB instance where $(o_{i-1}, o_i) \in A_i$. When the PE is used as a proposition, it is true when such a ground instance can be found in the database instance.

In [BER92, KIF92], a number of extension is made to increase the expressiveness of path expression. These include :

- Attribute variable
  Where the path expression can include a variable in a position of an attribute. This can be used to retrieve schema information. For example Joe.X will be satisfied when X is substituted by an attribute name which the object Joe has.

- Closure of an attribute
  Where an attribute can be assumed to occur an unspecified number of times in the path expression. For example, John.supervisor* = John. supervisor or John.supervisor.supervisor, etc.

- Selectors
  Where a specific object can be named as a node in the path expression so that the ground instance must include the object in the particular position. For example, ComputerDept.Staff[Mary].Child can be used to reference the children of a specific staff Mary in the ComputerDept.

- Quantification
  Where the quantifiers $\forall$ and $\exists$ can be added before an attribute name in the path. This states a condition an intermediary node of the path must satisfy. For example the expression :

  $$x.\forall Staff.\exists Child.Age > 18$$

would be satisfied by any department x in which all staff has some children aged over 18.

- Methods
  Where methods occur in place of attributes. In many OODMs, attributes are just consider as a special case of method (i.e. parameterless method with no side effect). Thus inclusion of methods in a path expression is a natural extension to the construct.

In this paper, we will be only concentrating our discussion on the structure of the PE, selectors and qualitifications in the context of our general model.

3. CG as interpretation of OODM & PEs

3.1 CG and OODB

Conceptual Graph, as introduced by John Sowa [SOW84], provides a graph based formalism for modelling the conceptual world, describing relations between concepts in a way which is "... logically precise, humanly readable, and computationally tractable..." [SOW92]. As an instrument for conceptual modelling, it shares the fundamental concepts mentioned in our general OODM. Indeed the use of CG as a basis for deductive OODB was proposed in [WUW92]. The following illustrates some of the basic CG features :

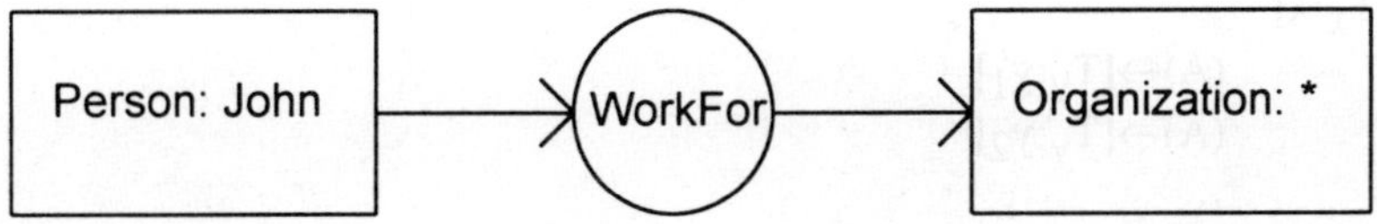

In linear form :

u: [Person: John]→(WorkFor)→[Organization: *]

- There are two types of nodes in CG, viz. concept ([Person: John] and [Organization: *] in above), and relation ((WorkFor) in above). They correspond approximately to entity and relationship in the Entity-Relationship model. The two types of nodes are linked to one another by directed arcs.

- A concept consists of a type (*Person* and *Organization*) and a referent (*John* and *). The referent may be an individual marker like "John", denoting some specific individual, or a generic marker "*" representing some unspecified referent. Generic markers are often omitted in a graph.

- Types in CG have similar meaning to those used in OODMs. They represent classification of objects with similar properties. The type lattice is as described in our general OODM.

- A CG, as a logical proposition, can be translated to predicate calculus by a formula operator ϕ. Thus for the CG above

$$\phi u = \exists x\ (\text{person(John)} \wedge \text{organization}(x) \wedge \text{workfor(John}, x)).$$

The reader is referred to [SOW92, SOW93, SOW84] for more detail description of CG. An OODB instance D can be regarded as a CG. We will denote the CG for D by $\gamma(D)$. We will call this the OODB instance graph. The graph is generated as follows.

- For each non-lexical object o in D, we create a graph consisting of a single individual concept, c = $\gamma(o)$, with type(c) equal to the most specific type of the object, and referent(c) the object-id of o.

- For each single-valued attribute A: $T_x \rightarrow T_y$ of an object x of type T_x in the OODB with value y, we create a graph

  $$[T_x{:}x] \rightarrow (A) \rightarrow [T_y{:}y].$$

  If the attribute is multi-valued with values y_1, y_2, $\ldots y_n$, then the CG corresponds to

  $$\begin{array}{ll} [T_x{:}x]- & \\ & (A) \rightarrow [T_y{:}y_1] \\ & (A) \rightarrow [T_y{:}y_2] \\ & \ldots \\ & (A) \rightarrow [T_y{:}y_n]. \end{array}$$

- The OODB instance graph $\gamma(D)$ is the CG (possibly disconnected) formed by joining the set of CGs generated above, on all equal individual concepts with the types restricted to the most specific type of the individual markers.

In this interpretation, object, object id and attribute correspond in the CG to concept, individual marker and relation respectively. The underlying type lattice in CG will be the same as those in the OODB. Where there is no ambiguity, we will use these terms inter-changeably.

3.2 Path expression and conceptual graph

A path expression o.p consists of an object o at the head of the expression, followed by an attribute path p, of attributes joined by the operator '.'. In order to interprete the path expression in CG, we will first construct for p the CG correspondence $\gamma(p)$ in terms of its attribute components.

We will define a join operator '.' in CG. For two CGs u and v, the concept join on concepts c_u of u and c_v of v is defined as follows.

Definition. Concept Join.

Let c_u be a concept in u
c_v be a concept in v

and c_u and c_v are compatible concepts [SOW84], i.e.

- $type(c_u) \cap type(c_v) > \perp$, i.e. their maximal common subtype is not the absurd type.
- The referents of both c_u and c_v conform to $type(c_u) \cap type(c_v)$.
- If one of the referent is individual marker i, the other is either i or *.

Then the concept join, $u(c_u).v(c_v)$, of u and v on c_u and c_v is given by

- restricting c_u and c_v to the common concept c' where type(c') is $type(c_u) \cap type(c_v)$, and referent(c') is the individual marker i, if one of the referent of c_u and c_v is i, else it is the generic marker *. We denote the resulting graphs u' and v' respectively
- joining u' and v' on c'.

This is the maximal join of u and v on compatible projection on the common generalization [$type(c_u) \cup type(c_v)$: *]. We will further define a serial join for linear CGs.

We define the head and tail of a linear CG as follows. For a linear CG of the form

$$u : [T_0] \rightarrow (A_1) \rightarrow [T_1] \rightarrow (A_2) \ldots . \rightarrow (A_n) \rightarrow [T_n]$$

$[T_0]$ = Head or root concept, denoted by head(u)
$[T_n]$ = Tail or end concept, denoted by tail(u)

Definition. Serial Join.

For two linear CGs u_1, u_2, the serial join $u_1.u_2$ is the concept join of the two CGs on tail(u_1) with head(u_2).

To construct the CG for the attribute path p, for each attribute A: $T_x \rightarrow T_y$, we create its corresponding CG $\gamma(A) = [T_x] \rightarrow (A) \rightarrow [T_y]$. The CG representation of an attribute expression $A_1.A_2...A_n$ can now be defined by

$$\gamma(A_1.A_2...A_n) = \gamma(A_1).\gamma(A_2) \ldots \gamma(A_n)$$

That is, the CG formed by applying the concept join to the tail concept of A_1 to the head concept of A_2 (Note: the two concepts may not be the same, but necessarily compatible in order to be satisfiable), etc. in sequence, giving a graph of the form

$$[T_0] \rightarrow (A_1) \rightarrow [T_1] \rightarrow (A_2) \ldots . \rightarrow (A_n) \rightarrow [T_n]$$

A path expression can now be defined in terms of the corresponding λ-expression in CG :

$$\gamma(o.A_1.A_2...A_n) = \lambda x\ \gamma(o).\gamma(A_1.A_2...A_n).[♋:x]$$

or simply

$$= \gamma(o).\gamma(A_1.A_2...A_n).[\lambda].$$

For example :

γ(CS.Staff.Study.Name)
= [Department: CS].[Unit]→(Staff)→[Employee].[Student]→(Study)→[Course].
[Course]→(Name)→[String].[λ]
= [Department: CS]→(Staff)→[StudentWorker]→(Study)→[Course]-
(Name)→[String: λ]

where

Staff: Unit→Employee
Study: Student→Course
Name: Course→String
[Department]≤ [Unit]
[Employee]∩[Student] = [StudentWorker]

A path expression evaluates to the set of objects which when substituted into the λ position produce a CG which is a CG generalization of (i.e. provable from) the OODB instance graph γ(D).

4. Extending the power of PE

4.1 The CG perspective of PE

As can be seen in the above, a path expression can be considered a special case of λ -expression in CG which is linear, with the λ-variable in the tail concept. This perspective suggests the expressiveness of path expression can be improved by extending its structure to incorporate other capabilities of CGs. In the following, we define a more general form of path expression which we will call tree expression. We discuss how it extends the path expression with reference semantics derived from its CG interpretation.

4.2 The Tree expression

As its name implies, we extend the linear path form of the path expression to a tree structure by providing branching representation. We represent such attribute tree expression, for example, in the form

Staff(Supervisor (Name, Post), Child(Study, Age))

which corresponds to the conceptual graph :

```
[Department]→(Staff)→[Employee]-
                          (Supervisor)→[Employee]-
                                           (Name)→[String]
                                           (Post)→[String],
                          (Child)→[Person]-
                                           (Study)→[School]
                                           (Age)→[Numeric].
```

The leading concept [Department] is called the root or head concept as in the case of attribute expression. The basic syntax of the tree expression is formally defined in the Appendix using BNF.

The tree expression allows the inclusion of selectors in various positions as in [KIF92]. However our selector takes the form of a concept in CG:

[Type: Referent {θ ObjectValue}]

where

Type = object type, may be omitted if ♋
Referent = an object variable, object value or the generic marker *
θ = comparison operator >, <, ...

ObjectValue = lexical objects like numeric, string,... or object id of non-lexical object

We will omit various parts of the term as long as there is no ambiguity. Thus [<12] is the contracted form for [♋: *<12].

The selector term can be inserted into the attribute tree at the root or in any position after an attribute. This insertion is interpreted as the concept join of the tail concept of the corresponding attribute graph with the selector concept. For example, if the attribute Age is Age: Person→Numeric, then

Age[<18]

is interpreted as the CG

[Person]→(Age)→[Numeric:*<18]

The tree expression is then an attribute tree with a λ-variable in one of the selector term. As an illustration, the following tree expression references "The name of academic staff in the Computer Department with a child age under 18"

ComputerDept.Staff[Academic](Name[λ], Child.Age[<18]) (Ex. 1)

with its meaning given by the CG

[Department: ComputerDept]→(Staff)→[Academic]-
(Name)→[String: λ]
(Child)→[Person]→(Age)→[Numeric:*<18]

To be consistent with the commonly used path expression, we will drop the λ-variable if it is at the end of a linear (degenerate) tree expression, and drop the [] at the head of the expression if there is no ambiguity, as in the above example.

4.3 Extensions in the tree expression

In this section, we see how the constraints of path expression is relaxed to the tree expression and their meaning under CG.

a. Input and output object position

Basically, a path expression is a composite function consisting of sequential application of attribute functions. The input object always correspond to root concept of the corresponding linear CG, while the output corresponds to the tail concept, as in

ComputerDept.Staff.Child

which correspond to the CG

[Department: ComputerDept]→(Staff)→[Person]→(Child)→[Person: λ]

As a CG, a tree-expression may take an input object at any concept position and output object at any position indicated by the λ-variable. Thus in the following example, the referenced objects is not at the terminal position of the expression :

ComputerDept.Staff[λ].Child

with the CG interpretation of

[Department: ComputerDept]→(Staff)→[Employee: λ]→(Child)→[Person]

refers to the "Staff of Computer Department and who has a child".

Similar, the input object is also not restricted to the first position of the expression but any position along the path (or tree), as in

Staff[λ].Child[John]

where the input object is at the end of the expression, with interpretation

[Department]→(Staff)→[Employee: λ]→(Child)→[Person: John]

which references "The person(s) who is staff in a certain department, and whose child is the person John".

We may even provide no input object at all, so that

Staff[λ].Child

refers to "All persons who are staff of some department, and who has a child".

b. Object type & objects as selectors in path expression

In [KIF92], the PE can include an object selector with an attribute thus restricting the node the path must pass through. Such selection can be generalize to selection by object type instead of specific object. Selection by type is important in OODM because there are more opportunities for representing information by type, and not by attribute value. Thus an Academic can be considered as a sub-type of Person rather than a Person, say, with attribute Job = 'teaching'.

In the tree expression, the selection of any object in the tree can be by type or object value. For example:

ComputerDept.Staff[Academic: λ].Child.Age[<18])

with CG interpretation

[Department: ComputerDept]→(Staff)→[Academic: λ]-
(Child)→[Person]→(Age)→[Numeric:*<18]

references "The academic staff of computer department with a child aged under 18". The selector [Academic] is a type constraint restricting the search to a subtype of Person who is staff of the department. The second is a range constraint [<18] for the attribute value of Age.

c. Branching out of path expression

The path expression only permit us to select objects along a linear attribute path. If we need instead the value of another related attribute of some object in the path, we have to go back to the query language construct of a OODM. This often involves introduction of additional artificial variables. By providing branching in a path expression to tree, such referencing can be incorporated into the tree expression. As shown in the initial example (T1) :

ComputerDept.Staff[Academic](Name[λ], Child.Age[<18])

which references "The names of academic staff in the Computer Department, and who has a child aged under 18."

d. Types and derived attribute

In [SOW84], Sowa used λ-expression to define a sub-type from another type (the genus) basing a differentiating CG (the differentia). With the CG interpretation of tree-expression, we can use a tree expression to define a type. For example :

[Dependent] = [Person: λ].Age[<18]
and [Academic] = [Person: λ].Job["Teaching"]

which said "Dependent is a Person whose Age is under 18", and "Academic is a Person whose Job is teaching". Using type contraction and expansion, the example (T1) can be rewritten as

ComputerDept.Staff(Job["Teaching"], Name[λ], Child[Dependent])

Such expansion and contraction can be useful in database integration, where an expression can be interpreted differently under different DB application model environment.

The path expression is in a sense a derived attribute of the root object in the expression. The same interpretation can be made of the tree expression. We can define a derived attribute, corresponding to relation abstraction in CG, using a tree expression in the form

StaffWithDependent = Staff[λ].Child.Age[<18])

which says StaffWithDependent is a Staff with a Child Aged under 18. Using relation contraction, (Ex. 1) can be rewritten as

ComputerDept.StaffWithDependent[Academic].Name

4.4 Quantification and use of tree-expression as constraint

Conceptual graph is a system of logic and a graph can be interpreted as a proposition, a truth-valued function. The ϕ operator translates a CG to an equivalent predicate logic expression. All generic markers are considered existentially qualified. For example :

[Department: ComputerDept]→(Staff)→[Academic]→(Child)→[Person]

can be translated into predicate logic as

$$\exists x \exists y\ (\text{Department}(\text{ComputerDept}) \wedge \text{Academic}(x) \wedge \text{Person}(y) \wedge \text{Staff}(\text{ComputerDept}, x) \wedge \text{Child}(x,y))$$

The universal qualifier ∀ can be converted into existential form by the equivalence

$$\forall P \equiv \neg\exists\neg P$$

It can be used in conceptual graph as a short-hand notation to simplify expressions. We permit the use of ∀ in any object position in the tree expression, applying the same semantics as those of the CG with ∀ put in the corresponding position.

[Department: ∀].Staff[Academic].Teach

correspond to the CG

[Department: ∀]→(Staff)→[Academic]→(Teach)→[Subject]

or "In every department, some academic staff teaches some subject".

In [KIF92], quantifier is used to restrict binding of values to variables in intermediate node of a path. Such quantified path expression provides additional selection capability in the intermediate nodes of the path where set valued attribute is involved. We incorporate that semantics into our tree expression with similar meaning. The ∀ can thus be placed before any attribute in the tree expression as in quantified path expression. The formal meaning of that is (we only describe here the case where there is only one such qualifier.) :

- assume the attribute qualified is P in the tree expression, ...∀P...
- disconnect the tree by cutting it at the concept node range(P), duplicating it in both sub-graphs. Assume the part containing the root concept is u, and the other subtree with range(P) as root is v.
- Introduce x as referent(range(P)) of both u and v, i.e. x is the co-referent. The CG of the quantifier is equivalent to

$$\neg[u \neg[v]]$$

or $$u \Rightarrow v$$

For example :

[ComputerDept].Staff.∀Teach.Level[Master]

correspond to the CG

[Department: ComputerDept]→(Staff)→[Person]→(Teach)→[Subject: x]
⇒ [Subject: x]→(Level)→[Master]

or "All subjects taught by staff in ComputerDept are of master level".

As proposition, the tree expression can be used to specify constraints whose truth value is to be maintained. The following constraint says "In every department, every academic staff teaches some subject."

[Department: ∀].∀Staff[Academic].Teach

The universal qualifier can be used with the other application of tree-expression discussed above, viz. referencing, type and relation definition.

5. Conclusion

In the above, we have introduced an extension of path expression, the tree expression, and its semantics in the form of conceptual graph. The tree expression, given its CG perspective, provides an effective tool in object oriented modelling for specification of queries, views and constraints. It eliminates much of the need for introducing artificial variables in specifications, making them more natural and easy to understand. Indeed, tree expression can be used as foundation for a complete data model based on its CG semantics. Schema information can be defined simply by tree expressions as in :

[Person](Name[String], Age[Integer>0], Child[Person])

Query can be specified by tree expressions using selection variables, linked by co-reference variables and logical connectives. Constraints and views can be similarly defined. CG provides a clear logic basis for the such system. We are currently developing a system in support of such model.

References

[BAN89] F. Bancilhon, S. Cluet, C. Delobel, "A Query Language for the O_2 Object-Oriented Database System", Proceedings of the Second International Workshop on Database Programming Languages, June 1989, R. Hull, R. Morrison, D. Stemple, pp 122-138.

[BEE89] C. Beeri, "Formal Models for Object Oriented Databases", Deductive and Object-Oriented Databases - Proceedings of the First International Conference on Deductive and Object-Oriented Databases (DOOD'89), W. Kim, J Nicolas, S. Nishio, eds., pp 405-430.

[BER92] E. Bertino, et. al, "Object-Oriented Query Languages: The Notion and the Issues", IEEE Transactions on Knowledge and Data Engineering, June 1992, IEEE Computer Society, pp. 223-237.

[CAR94] B. Carbonneill, O. Haemmerle, "Standardizing and Interfacing Relational Databases Using Conceptual Graphs", Proceedings of 2nd International Conference on Conceptual Structures, ICCS'94, W.M. Tepfenhart, J.P. Dick, J.F. Sowa, eds., Springer-Verlag, 1994, pp. 311-330.

[DAY89] U. Dayal, "Queries and Views in an Object-Oriented Data Model", Proceedings of the Second International Workshop on Database Programming Languages, June 1989, R. Hull, R. Morrison, D. Stemple, eds., pp 80-102.

[KEM94] A. Kemper, G. Moerkotte, Object-Oriented Database Management :

Applications in Engineering and Computer Science, Prentice-Hall 1994.

[KIF92] M. Kifer, W. Kim, Y. Sagiv, "Querying Object Oriented Databases", Proceedings of the 1992 ACM SIGMOD International Conference on Management of Data, ACM Press, pp. 393-402.

[SOW84] J.F. Sowa, Conceptual Structures - Information Processing in Mind and Machine, Addison-Wesley 1984.

[SOW92] J.F. Sowa, "Conceptual Graphs Summary", Conceptual Structures: Current Research & Practice, T.E. Nagle, et. al., eds., Ellis Horwood 1992.

[SOW93] J.F. Sowa, "Relating Diagrams to Logic", Conceptual Graphs for Knowledge Representation, Processdings of the First International Conference on Conceptual Structures, ICCS'93, G.W. Mineau, B. Moulin, J.F. Sowa, eds., Springer-Verlag 1993, pp. 1-35.

[SU93] S.Y.W. Su, M. Guo, H. Lam, "Association Algebra: A Mathematical Foundation for Object-Oriented Databases", IEEE Transactions on Knowledge and Data Engineering, Oct 1993, pp. 775-798.

[WUW92] V.Wuwongse, B.C. Ghosh, "Towards Deductive Object-Oriented Databases Based on Conceptual Graphs", Conceptual Structures: Theory and Implementation - 7th Annual Workshop Proceedings, July 1992, H.D. Pfeiffer, T.E. Nagel, eds., pp 188-205.

Appendix

Basic syntax of a tree-expression in BNF

The basic syntax does not include various contracted forms, defaults, quantifier and sophisticate selectors involving set comparison in our full syntax.

tree-expression ::= [<object-selector> '.'] [<attribute-path>] ['(' <tree-expression>
{',' <tree-expression>} ')']
attribute-path ::= <attribute-term> {'.' <attribute-term>}
attribute-term ::= <attribute-name> [<object-selector>]
object-selector ::= '[' <type-name> [':' <referent-term>] [<op> <referent>] ']'
referent-term ::= '*' | 'λ' | <referent>
referent ::= <object-id> | <object-variable> | <lexical-value>
op ::= '=' | '<>' | '<' | '>' | '>=' | '<='

Translating basic tree-expression to CG

For any linear CG of the form

$$u : [T_0]\rightarrow(A_1)\rightarrow[T_1]\rightarrow(A_2)\ldots.\rightarrow(A_n)\rightarrow[T_n]$$

we call
$[T_0]$ = Head or root concept, denoted by head(u)
$[T_n]$ = Tail or end concept, denoted by tail(u)

For any CG of tree from

v : $[T_0]$-
    $(A_1)\rightarrow$subtree$_1$
    $(A_2)\rightarrow$subtree$_2$
    ...

$[T_0]$ = Head or root concept, denoted by head(v)

For any tree (including linear) CGs $u_1, u_2, u_3, \ldots u_n$
the parallel join $\uparrow(u_1, u_2, u_3, \ldots u_n)$ is the join on all head(u_i) of u_i.

If u_1 is linear and u_2 is a tree (not necessarily linear), the serial join $u_1.u_2$ is the concept join on tail(u_1) with head(u_2).

The following rules provide for translation of a basic tree expression to CG :

1. For an attribute A: $T_x\rightarrow T_y$
   $\gamma(A) = [T_x]\rightarrow(A)\rightarrow[T_y]$
2. For an object-selector S, γ(S) is the concept of the same form.
3. γ(attribute-term) = γ(A).γ(S)
4. γ(attribute-term$_1$.attribute-term$_2$.attribute-term$_3$...)
   =γ(attribute-term$_1$).γ(attribute-term$_2$).γ(attribute-term$_3$), ...
5. γ((tree-exp$_1$, tree-exp$_2$, tree-exp$_3$, ...))
   = ↑(γ(tree-exp$_1$), γ(tree-exp$_2$), γ(tree-exp$_3$), ...)

An S-signature Scheme on Path Dictionary for Efficient Query Processing in Object-Oriented Database Systems

Hakgene Shin
Dept. of Computer Engineering,
Chonbuk National University,
Chonju, Chonbuk 560-756,
Korea
Phone: +82-652-70-2414
(FAX: 70-8689)
E-mail :
shin@dblab.chonbuk.ac.kr

Jaewoo Chang
Dept. of Computer Engineering,
Chonbuk National University,
Chonju, Chonbuk 560-756,
Korea
Phone: +82-652-70-2414
(FAX: 70-8689)
E-
mail:jwchang@moak.chonbuk.ac.kr

Abstract. Some implementation issues such as query processing and indexing become a critical factor in the success of object-oriented database systems. To tackle the issues, we propose an s-signature scheme, which is an efficient access method for query processing, especially, when the path dictionary is used. We also compare the s-signature scheme with other indexing techniques such as path idex, path signature, and path dictionary. Finally, we demonstrate that the proposed method shows significant improvements in the retrieval operation, while at the same time producing lower storage overhead than the path index.

Keywords. OODBS, complex object, query processing, path dictionary, signature

1. Introduction

During the past two decades, relational database systems have been successful in a variety of business applications. In spite of this success, newly emerging application areas such as CAD/CAM/CASE systems, knowledge-based systems, multimedia information systems, and advanced human-interface systems compel people to accept the object-oriented database system(OODBS). As a result of the wide acceptance of OODBS, some implementation issues such as query processing and indexing become a critical factor to the success of OODBSs.

OODBSs which deal with complex objects require expensive traversal costs to process queries. Therefore, there are many studies on the indexing technique to support efficient query processing against nested objects in OODBSs. Access Support Relations(ASR) proposed in [KEM90] used a relation containing object identifiers(OIDs) on paths and key fields with the B-tree. Path index, nested index, and multiple index using an inverted file have been proposed in [BER89, KIM89, BER93]. The path index, which is recommended for an aggregation hierarchy with a long path and virtually equivalent to the ASR, unfortunately requires high storage overhead and costly index maintenance if it wants to support various key fields. We found tree signatures and path signatures at [LEE92]. However, the filtering capability of the tree signature scheme is weaken if the subtree is large. The path signature has expensive update cost and storage overhead because it has a lot of redundant signatures and OIDs. The path dictionary scheme introduced at [LEE94] has shown its lower storage overhead and its universality. In spite of the advantages, the path dictionary also lacks an efficient access method not only for the databases but also for the path dictionary itself. Therefore, it is necessary to design a new access method which utilizes the advantages of the path dictionary as well as processes diverse queries in an efficient and universal manner.

In this paper, we propose a new signature scheme, called the *s-signature* on the path dictionary to efficiently support query processing of different types of queries. For this, we generate a signature from each object in an s-expression, which is an expression scheme of the path dictionary, and superimpose those signatures to form an s-signature for the s-expression. Each s-expression may contain several paths terminating at the same object. The s-signature provides an efficient filtering mechanism, so as not to access the database at the initial stage of query processing, which is required at the original path dictionary scheme. The s-signature also provides an efficient access method for the path dictionary instead of the sequential scanning. Finally we compare our s-signature scheme with path index, path signature, and path dictionary methods, so as to show that the our scheme achieves significant improvements in the retrieval operation.

The organization of this paper is as follows. In section 2, we will review some concepts and definitions involved in the query processing of OODBS and describe some conventional indexing techniques. In section 3, we propose a new signature scheme for path dictionary. Section 4 describes a retrieval and an update algorithm using our s-signature scheme. In section 5, after discussing a cost model for evaluating some database operations and the storage overhead, we compare the s-signature scheme with the conventional indexing techniques. In section 6, we draw our conclusion.

2. Related Work

2.1 Definitions and Concepts

Let us review some definitions and concepts, which follows the leads of [BER89, KIM89, LEE94]. Fig. 1. shows a graphical representation of an *aggregation hierarchy*, and also is used to illustrate some key concepts. The class Person has three *primitive attributes*, SSN, age, and residence and two *complex attributes*, owns and name. The domain of the attribute owns is Vehicle. The class Vehicle has two primitive attributes, model and color, and two complex attributes, manufacturer and drivetrain. The manufacturer's domain is Company that consists of two primitive attributes, etc. Every object in the database is identified by a unique *object identifier*(OID). By storing the OID of an object(O_{i+1}) as an attribute value of another object(O_i), an aggregation hierarchy is established between two objects. We call O_i the *parent* object of O_{i+1}. A predicate on a nonnested attribute will be called a *simple predicate*, while a predicate defined on a nested attribute will be called a *complex predicate* or a *nested predicate*.

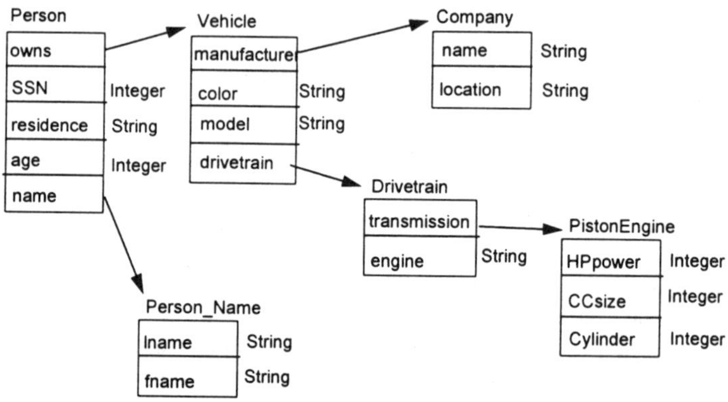

Fig. 1. Aggregation hierarchy

In a given query, for example, "retrieve all vehicles manufactured by Ford and owned by a 50 years old person" can be expressed as the following. Here, the class from which objects are retrieved will be called the *target class*, while the class involved in the predicate will be called the *predicate class*.

```
retrieve Person.Vehicle
where Person.Vehicle.Company.name="Ford"
and Person.age=50
```

There are two fundamental ways for evaluating a query involving nested attributes: *top-down* and *bottom-up* evaluations. The top-down approach, that is, *forward traversal*, traverses the objects starting from an ancestor class to a nested class, which searches in depth-first order. On the other hand, the bottom approach, that is, *backward traversal*, traverses the objects in the leaf class of the aggregation hierarchy and then toward the root class. In this paper, we assume there is no backward reference, which means a child object does not carry the OID of its parent.

To answer the above example query in the top-down approach, the system has to retrieve all of the objects in the class Person and screen out those with age 50. Then the system retrieves the Vehicle referenced by the 50 year old persons. The system then retrieves the Company objects referenced by the vehicles and checks if the company names are Ford. Finally those vehicles satisfying both predicates are returned. In the bottom-up approach, the system retrieves the objects in the class Company and checks if their names are Ford. Without the backward reference, the screened OIDs are stored in a set. Then the vehicle objects in the class Vehicle are examined to identify those vehicles made by the companies in *S*. The qualified vehicle objects are collected in a set *S'*. Finally the Person objects are retrieved to see if they are 50 years old and own a vehicle in *S'*.

As we can see from the above query processing, the traversal between a predicate class and a target class requires a high processing cost. To overcome this cost, several indexing schemes have been proposed, i.e., path index, tree and path signatures, and path dictionary.

2.2 Indexing Techniques

Path Index

Given a path, a path index on the path *P* is defined as a set of pairs *(O,S)* where

S={p < j-1 > p_i such that:
$p_i = O_1, O_2, \ldots O_j$ is a nonredundent instantiation(either partial or not) of the path;
$O_j = O$ (that is the ending object of p_i)}

The first element of the pair *(O,S)* is the index key. For instance, let us consider the objects in Fig. 1. The path index will contain the following pairs:

(Ford,{Person[3].Vehicle[5], Person[7].Vehicle[5],Person[4].Vehicle[12] })
(GMC, {Vehicle[6],Vehicle[9]} ...) ...

Tree and Path Signature

The signature file techniques have widely been advocated as an efficient access method to deal with new applications demanding a large amount of textual databases [FAL88, FAL92] and multimedia databases [BAR90]. A signature is an abstraction of the information stored in the attributes of an object, which is a superimposed bit string generated from the attribute values. Formal representation of the query processing can be described as below.

$$Si \text{ Ç } Sq = Sq$$

where *Si* is a set of object signatures and *Sq* is a query signature.

Based on the above signature scheme, tree signature and path signature have been proposed in [LEE92]. For every class *C* in the aggregation hierarchy, the tree signature scheme has an entry <*sig, oid*> in a signature file. The *sig* is the signature of every object *O* in *C* and the *oid* is the *OID* of *O*. The filtering capacity of the tree signature scheme is degraded when the subtree is large because a signature for an object *O* is created from all of the primitive values in the subtree of objects rooted at *O*. The path signature scheme creates signature files for a single path. The signature files created for the classes on a path will support the evaluation of queries involving any classes on the path and their attributes. The path signature of complex attributes located on the path are generated by superimposing the signatures of its nested attributes. The signature file S for every object O in C has an entry <*sig, oid_list*>, where *sig* is the signature of O and *oid_list* are the object identifiers of O and its nested objects located in the path. Details of the tree and path signature are found in [LEE92].

Path Dictionary

OODBSs use OIDs embedded in complex attributes as the main mechanism in accessing nested objects. So the path dictionary extracts the complex attributes from the database to represent the connections between objects. Formally, a path dictionary is created for a path, $C_1, C_2, \ldots, C_n$ in the aggregation hierarchy. A path dictionary is a secondary file containing nesting information about the objects in the classes along the path [LEE94].

To represent the connection information along the aggregation hierarchy in the path dictionary, an s-expression scheme is also described in [LEE94]. The s-expression scheme encodes into a recursive expression all paths terminating at the same object in a leaf class. The definition of s-expression is as follows:

$S_1 = O_1$, where O_1 is the OID of an object in class C_1 or null.
$S_i = O_i(S_{i-1}[,S_{i-1}])\ 1 < i <= n$, where O_i is an s-expression for the path $C_1, C_2, \ldots, C_{i-1}$.

```
Company[1](Vehicle[5](Person[3],Person[7]),Vehicle[12](Person[4]))
Company[2](Vehicle[6],Vehicle[9](),Vehicle[11]())
Company[3](Vehicle[3]())
Company[4](Vehicle[4](),Vehicle[7](Person[1],Person[6]))
Company[5](Vehicle[1](Person[2]),Vehicle[2](Person[8]),Vehicle[8](Person[5]),Vehicle[10]())
((Person[9]))
...
```

Fig. 2. S-expression scheme for a path dictionary

For instance, Fig. 2. shows an example of the s-expression. In Fig. 2, the s-expression maintains all the linkage information for the objects located on the path Person.Vehicle.Company. Since we assume each primitive attribute has only one value, the advantage of the s-expression scheme is that every object on the path appears only once in the path dictionary and that it provides an efficient traversal means along the aggregation hierarchy.

However the path dictionary scheme does not have an efficient access method for the database and the path dictionary file itself. So when a query has C_t as the target class and C_p as the predicate class, this scheme does sequentially search the database for OIDs satisfying the C_p. Once the qualified OIDs are available, the scheme again does sequentially search the path dictionary to locate the s-expressions that contain the qualified OIDs.

3. S-signature on s-expression

In this section, we propose a new signature scheme and how to apply the new scheme to the path dictionary. First, we will describe the s-signature scheme and later describe the way to combine the s-signature with the path dictionary. Finally, we will introduce an example query processing using the s-signature scheme.

3.1 S-signature

As we have seen in the previous section, there is a main bottleneck in the path dictionary scheme, that is, sequential scanning of the database and the path dictionary. To resolve the problem, we need an efficient access method for the path dictionary and the database. The access method must:

- support fast scanning of the database and the path dictionary.
- support different types of queries.
- have low storage overhead.

The path index, which is the first candidate, is not appropriate because the path index expects a primary or a secondary key field to be used. This feature of the path index does not satisfy the second requirement. In other words, in the OODBSs with complex attributes, we can not always predict which key attribute will be used to access the database. On the other hand, since the path dictionary only contains the linkage information for the objects, that is, OIDs, in the paths, we can not directly compare the predicate given in a query with the path dictionary. Therefore, while we use the linkage information of the aggregation hierarchy in the path dictionary, which provides fast traversal means and processes different types of queries, we need to develop a new signature scheme on the path dictionary, so as to use the advantages of the path dictionary as well as to provide a means of fast access.

Before describing the new signature, let us again look at the s-expression in the path dictionary. The s-expression encodes into a recursive expression all paths terminating at the same object in a leaf class. In other words, within an aggregation hierarchy, there may be many paths terminating at the same object. This is called reference sharing and has a major impact on the cost of query processing [BER93].

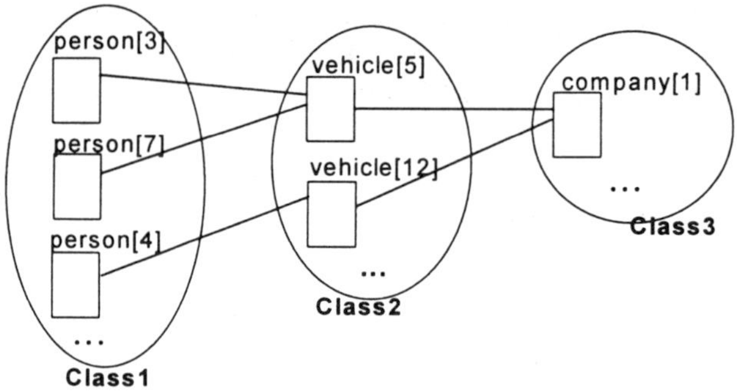

Fig. 3. Paths with reference sharing

Fig. 3. shows possible paths terminating at the same object, Company[1], which we can find at the first s-expression in Fig. 2. For every path terminating at the same object of the aggregation hierarchy, we create a signature for the paths represented by an s-expression. Basically the signature is extracted from attribute values of the objects in the s-expression. We call this the s-signature in compliance with the s-expression. Since the s-signature extracted from the object values, we can compare any given query predicate with the s-signature. The construction algorithm of the s-signature for an s-expression can be clarified as follows:

Algorithm : const_s_sig
Input : s-expression
Output : s-signature

1. retrieve every objects contained in the s-expression.
2. create the signature of each object by ORing the signatures made from primitive attribute values.
3. superimpose all the object signatures to form an s-signature.

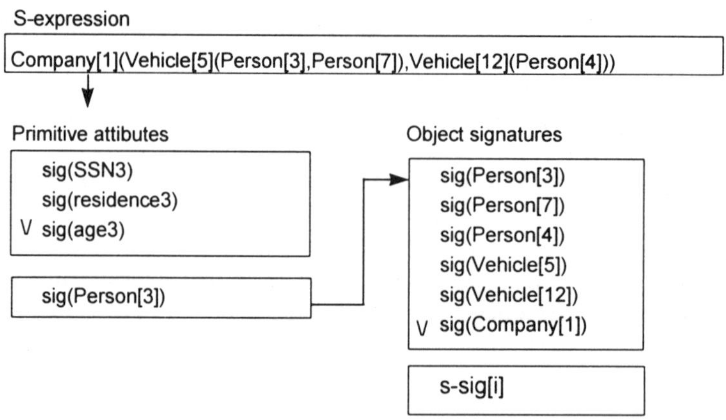

Fig. 4. Generation of s-signature

The algorithm, const_s_sig and Fig. 4. show how to generate the s-signature from the previous example s-expression in Fig. 3. As Fig. 4. shows, we extracted the signature from every primitive attribute values in an object, so that an object signature may represent the object in the database. Whenever a query predicate contains any attribute from the object, the query can be processed without scanning of the database. Besides, since we superimpose the all the object signatures from an s-expression to form an s-signature, the s-signature represents all the objects in one s-expression. Therefore, the s-signature provides the filtering mechanism of s-expressions in the path dictionary. In other words, once we find whether an s-signature matches the signature generated from the query predicate or not, we don't have to scan the path dictionary. We just use the pointer from the s-signature in the s-signature file to the s-expression.

The s-signature generated based on the s-expressions can be stored in an s-signature file. Fig. 5. depicts that every signature in an s-signature file has an entry *<s-sig(i), pointer_s_expression>* in the file. The *s-sig(i)* is the signature of objects found in an s-expression and the *pointer_s_expression* is the pointer to the corresponding s-expression.

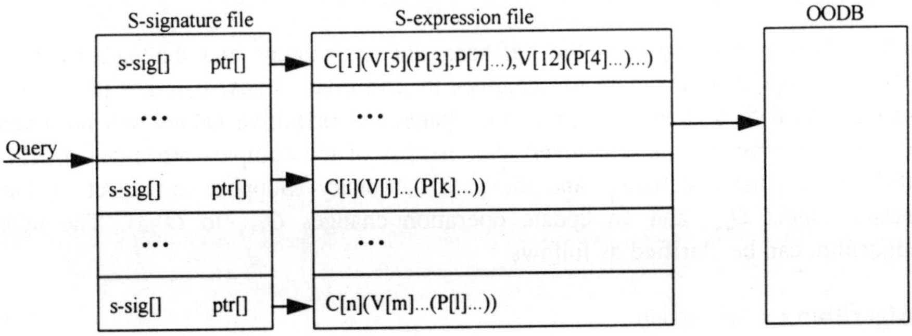

Fig. 5. S-signature scheme on s-expression

The s-signature scheme on an s-expression file can filter out candidate s-expressions without sequential search for a database and also find an OID specified in a query out of the path dictionary. Those processes are considered as the most time consuming tasks in the conventional path dictionary approach. Besides, for the fast search for the s-signature file, a bit-sliced signature file scheme [FAL88] instead of a bit-string one can be adopted for an implementation of the s-signature file.

3.2 Query Processing with S-signature

Now, we discuss how to use the s-signature scheme for retrievals and updates. We assume that the s-signature for each s-expression is available.

Retrieval

Let's say there is a query Q that has C_t as the target class and C_p as the predicate class, where $1<t,p<n$. The retrieval algorithm can be clarified as follows:

Algorithm : s_sig_retrieval
Input : query Q with C_t and C_p
Output : set of objects retrieved by a query

1. Compute the query signature for the query 1.
2. Match the query signature against the s-signatures to select candidate s-signatures and their pointers to s-expressions.
3. Read the s-expressions pointed by the selected pointers.
4. Based on the qualified OIDs in the s-expressions, obtain OIDs of C_t.
5. Retrieve the objects.

The s-signature scheme avoids searching the database sequentially. In addition, the s-expression avoids accessing any objects between C_t and C_p in the database.

Update

When there are changes in the database, the s-signature and the path dictionary should be updated. If there are changes in primitive values, it is not necessary to change the path dictionary because the changes of primitive values will not change the links among objects. However, the changes of the complex attributes should be reflected on the s-signature and the path dictionary. Suppose an object O_i has a nested object O_{i+1} and an update operation changes O_{i+1} to O'_{i+1}. The update algorithm can be clarified as follows:

Algorithm : s_sig_update
Input : object O_i of which attribute values have been changed
Output : s-signature file and path dictionary after updating object O_i

- If only primitive attribute values have been changed:
  1. retrieve objects in an s-expression where O_i is found
  2. generate s-signature with the objects
  3. rewrite the signature into the s-signature file

- If the complex attribute value of O_i has been changed from O_{i+1} to O'_{i+1}:
  1. find all s-expressions containing the OIDs of O_{i+1} and O'_{i+1} using the s-signature file
  2. every occurrence of O_i and its ancestor list are removed from the ancestor list of O_{i+1}.

3. insert them into the ancestor list of O'_{i+1}
4. retrieve the objects in the s-expressions containing O_{i+1} and O'_{i+1} respectively
5. generate s-signatures of the objects in each s-expression respectively
6. rewrite the s-signatures into the s-signature file

At the stage 1 in each case, the s-signatures of the object, O_i, O_{i+1} and O'_{i+1} can be used to avoid full scanning of the database.

3.3 Example

Let's examine an example retrieval operation with the s-signature scheme. The sig_retrieval algorithm describe the general procedures of the retrieval operation and Fig. 6. depicts the relations between related components. We use the example query given in section 2, which is "retrieve all vehicles manufactured by Ford and owned by a 50 years old person". In the query, there are two predicates, Person.age=50 and Person.Vehicle.Company.name="Ford". First, we generate query signatures from the predicates and compare the query signatures with s-signatures. Then, the matched signatures will be selected from the s-signature file.

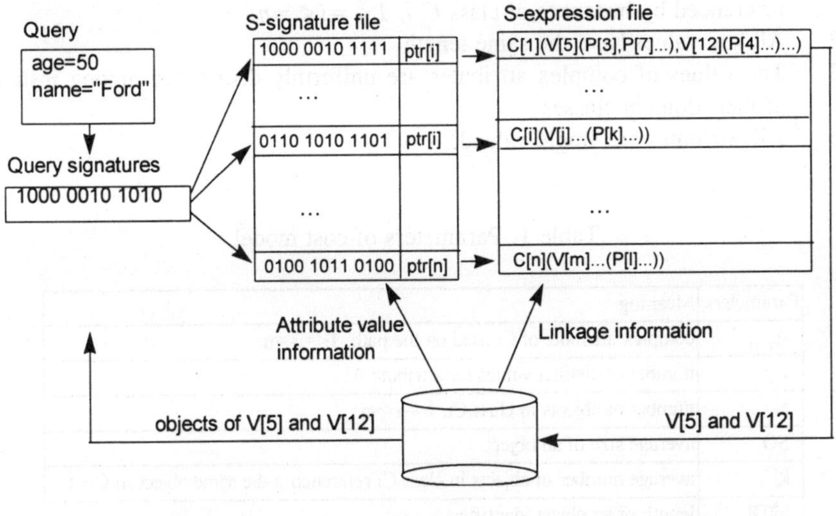

Fig. 6. Query processing with s-signature scheme on s-expression

Here, we suppose an arbitrary length of the query signatures and the s-signatures for simplifying the explanation. Secondly, in Fig. 6., the query signature, 1000 0000 1010, matches with the s-signature, 1000 0010 1111, so the s-expression, Company[1](Vehicle[5](Person[5],Person[7]),Vehicle[12] (Person[4])), pointed by the pointer of the s-signature will be retrieved. By using the pointer to the s-expression, we don't have to scan the path dictionary. In the s-expression, Company[1] is the OID of the object which satisfies the query predicate, Person.Vehicle.Company.name="Ford", and at least, one of Person[5], Person[7], and Person[4] is the OID of the object which satisfies the query predicate, Person.age=50. Finally, the query result will be the objects of V[5] and V[12]. As we have seen, first the query processing uses the signature of attribute values in the s-signature file and then uses the linkage information in the path dictionary.

4 Cost Models

This section describes a cost model for retrieval and update to estimate performance of the proposed scheme and presents storage overhead. To formulate the cost model, we adopt some common parameters from [BER89, LEE94] and introduce some new parameters as Table 1. Since a page is the basic unit for data transfer between the main memory and the external storage device, the cost model is based on the number of I/O access, so as to estimate the retrieval, update, and storage overhead. All lengths and sizes are in bytes. For fair comparison with the other schemes such as the path index, the path signature, and the path dictionary, we also assume the following:

1. There is no partial instantiation, that is, each instance of a class Ci is referenced by instances of class C_{i-1}, $1<=i<=n$.
2. All key values have the same length
3. The values of complex attributes are uniformly distributed among instances of their domain classes
4. All attributes are single-valued.

Table 1. Parameters of cost model

Parameters	Meaning
A_i	complex attribute of Ci used on the path, 1<=i<=n
D_i	number of distinct values for attribute Ai
N_i	number of objects in class Ci, 1<=i<=n
SO	average size of an object
k_i	average number of objects in class Ci referencing the same object in Ci+1
UIDL	length of an object identifier
P	page size
pp	length of a page pointer
OFFL	length of an offset field in the path dictionary
SL	length of the start field in the path dictionary
FSL	length of the free space field in the free space directory
EL	length of EOS
Fs	size of an s-signature

Table 2. Parameter values of the cost model (bytes)

Parameters	Values
P	4096
UIDL	8
pp	4
OFFL	2
SL	2
FSL	2
EL	4

We adopt the parameter values in [BER89, LEE94] shown as Table 2. To compute the size of the path signature and s-signature, we use the formulae found in [FAL92] as follows:

$$Fd = 2^{-m}$$
$$F*ln2 = mD$$

where m is the number of bit set by '1' in a signature and Fd is also drop probability. F means the size of signature and D indicates the number of distinct noncommon words per document. In this case, the distinct words represent attributes in objects on the paths.

4.1 Retrieval Cost

To answer a query Q with C_t, C_p, $1<=t,p<=n$, the s-signature scheme has to retrieve the s-signature file, then the s-expressions pointed by the s-signatures will be retrieved. Finally the s-expression with the verified OIDs will be scanned to find the C_t. The number of pages needed for retrieving the s-signature file, NPS, is:

$$NPS = \begin{cases} \left\lceil N_n / \lfloor P/Fs \rfloor \right\rceil & \text{if } Fs <= P \\ N_n \lceil Fs/P \rceil & \text{if } Fs > P \end{cases}$$

The average number of objects in an s-expression, $NOBJ$, is:

$$NOBJ = 1 + k_{n-1} + k_{n-1}*k_{n-2} + \ldots + k_{n-1}*k_{n-2}*\ldots * k_1$$

Thus, the average size of an s-expression, SS, is:

$$SS = (SL*n) + (UIDL + OFFL)*NOBJ + EL$$

Therefore the number of pages accessed for object retrieval, *SSR*, is:

$$SSR = NPS + \lceil SS/P \rceil$$

4.2 Update Cost

In this section, to make the analysis simple, we do not include the costs due to page overflow caused by update operation. Update operations have two cases. First, only primitive values have been changed, which does not require the change of the path dictionary. Second, the complex attribute value has been changed. Since the second case is a superset of the first case, we describe the cost model of the second case.

To update the domain of O_i from O_{i+1} to O'_{i+1} that are in different pages, the s-signature file scan is necessary at first. Then, the s-expressions for O_{i+1} and O'_{i+1} have to be retrieved. After switching the ancestor list of O_{i+1} to O'_{i+1} and rewriting new s-expressions, it is necessary to retrieve objects in the new s-expressions and generate s-signatures. Finally the old s-signatures are updated. So, the number of the retrieval pages of the s-signature and corresponding s-expressions for O_{i+1} and O'_{i+1} is:

$$NPS + 2\lceil SS/P \rceil$$

If the bit-sliced signature scheme is applied to scan the s-signature file, the cost will be reduced. In addition, $\lceil SS/P \rceil$ page accesses are necessary for rewriting the s-expression, $\lceil SO/P \rceil$ for reading objects in the s-expression, and $\lceil FS/P \rceil$ pages for rewriting the s-signature. Therefore the number of page accesses for update for O_{i+1} and O'_{i+1}, *SSU*, is:

$$SSU = NPS + 2(\lceil SS/P \rceil + \lceil SS/P \rceil + \lceil SO/P \rceil + \lceil FS/P \rceil$$

4.3 Storage Overhead

For estimating the storage overhead, we use the same parameter values. The storage size of the s-signature is decided upon the false drop probability, *Fd*, and the number of the logical blocks, *D*, that is, the number of objects in the path. For each s-expression in the path dictionary, there is an s-signature. Therefore, the number of terminating node, N_n, decides the number of s-signatures. Thus, the number of pages needed for all of the s-expressions in the path dictionary, *SSP*, is:

$$SSP = \begin{cases} \lceil N_n / \lfloor P / SS \rfloor \rceil & \text{if } SS <= P \\ N_n \lceil SS / P \rceil & \text{if } SS > P \end{cases}$$

The number of pages needed for the free space directory, *FSD*, which records the pages with free space and exists at the beginning of the path dictionary[LEE94], is:

$$FSD = \lceil SSP * (pp + FSL)/P \rceil$$

The number of pages needed for all of the s-signatures of objects in each s-expression is NPS as described in section 5.1. Therefore, the number of pages needed for the s-signature, *SSS*, is:

$$SSS = SSP + FSD + NPS$$

5 Performance Comparison

Based on the cost model developed in the previous section, we compare the s-signature scheme with the path index, the path dictionary, and the path signature in terms of retrieval costs. Suppose a path of 4 classes with the cardinality of N_1 equals 200000 and the average size of an object is 80 bytes. The size of the s-signature, *Fs*, depends upon the number of objects, *D*, in the path and upon the false drop probability, *Fd*. *Fd* is $1/N_n$ in the test, so that there is no false drop in theory. If $k_1=k_2=k_3=k_4=1$, the number of objects in the aggregation hierarchy is the same as the number of classes, that is, 4 in the test case. So the values of k_i representing the degree of reference sharing decide the number of objects in the path. The size of the path index also depends on the value of k_i, $1<=i<=4$ and let's assume $k_4=1$ for convenience. So we can vary k_1, k_2, k_3 to observe the change of the retrieval cost for the path index(*PIR*), the path dictionary(*PDR*), path signature(*PSR*), and the s-signature(*SSR*) methods. We assume that the query used in the first comparison of retrieval cost has C_1 as the target class, C_4 as the predicate class, and the indexed attribute as the predicate attribute. Also, we suppose the parameter k_2 only changes from 1 to 1000, while other *k* values are set to 1.

Fig. 7. shows that the s-signature scheme improves the performance of the path dictionary significantly. If the queries are applied to a predicate specified on an indexed attribute, the path index outperforms other approaches. The path signature scheme shows an almost independent degree of reference sharing, that is, the

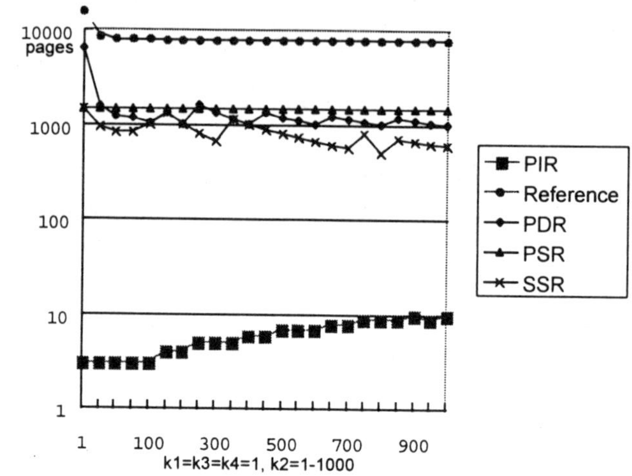

Fig. 7. Retrieval cost

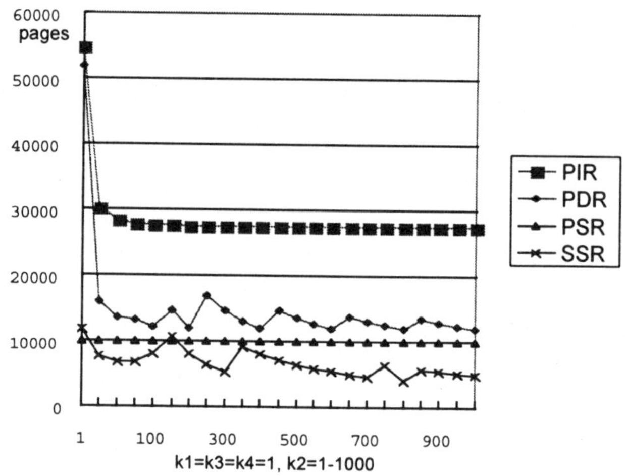

Fig. 8. General retrieval cost

changes of *k* values. However, like the path dictionary, the s-signature scheme is a more general approach than the path index because the s-signature may be used to process queries with predicate classes located anywhere on the path. When the queries are applied to predicates without index, s-signature is superior to other approaches. To show this reason, we adopt different kinds of queries used in [LEE94] as follows:

1. Three queries in which the indexed attribute of C_4 is the only predicate attribute, and each with C_1, C_2 or C_3 as the target class.

2. Three queries in which a non-indexed attribute of C_4 is the predicate attribute, and each with C_1, C_2 or C_3 as the target class.
3. Two queries in which C_1 is the target class, and each with C_2 or C_3 as the predicate class.

When the 8 different kinds of queries are given as above, Fig. 8. shows that the s-signature approach has a better overall performance than the path dictionary, the path signature, and the path index. This result has important implications, since queries in an OODBS could be very flexible, so that we can not predict which key attribute is going to be used in a query. In contrast, inverted indexes which anticipate a primary or secondary indexed key will be used in a query. Also it is impractical to use as many inverted files attributes to support various query patterns because the inverted files bring too much storage overhead. Therefore we believe the s-signature method is appropriate to the query processing involved in complex objects in OODBSs.

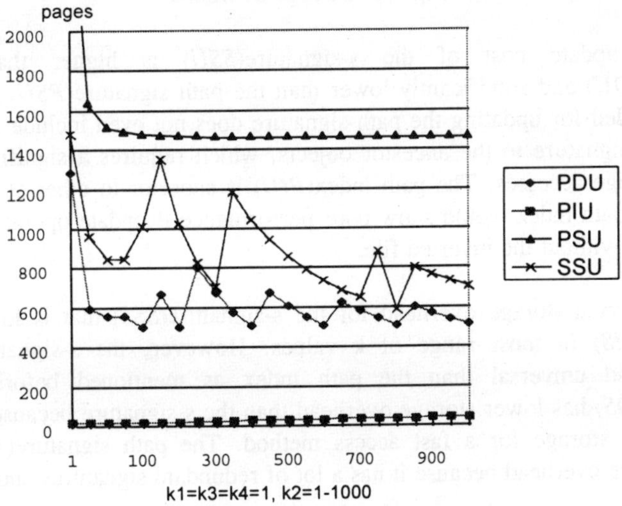

Fig. 9. Update cost

In the comparison of the four indexing schemes in terms of update costs, we use the same test assumptions used in the previous comparisons. In addition, for simplicity of the comparison, we also assume all update operations are applied to complex attributes, which is the worst case. If the portion of update operations upon primitive attributes is increased, the update cost(*SSU*) shown in Fig. 9. will be reduced.

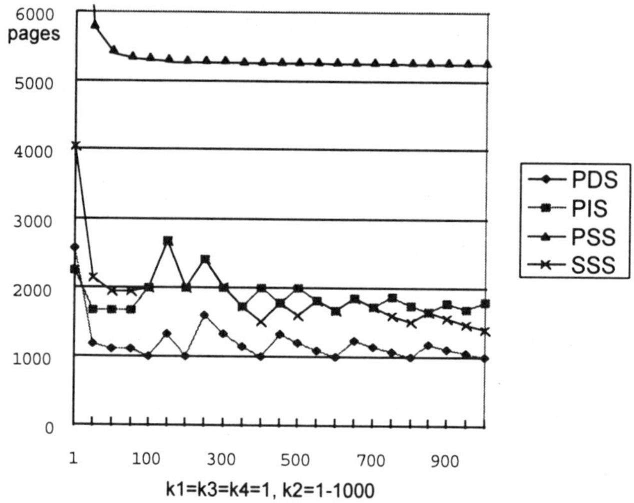

Fig. 10. Storage overhead

shows the update cost of the s-signature(*SSU*) is higher than the path dictionary(*PDU*) and significantly lower than the path signature(*PSU*). The number of pages needed for updating the path signature does not even include spreading the update of a signature to the ancestor objects, which requires a significantly higher number of page accesses. The path index(*PIU*) is superior to other schemes in this test. But the path index would show poor performance if update operation applies to the attributes without the inverted file.

Fig. 10. shows a storage overhead for the s-signature(*SSS*) that is lower than the path index(*PIS*) in most range of k values. However, the s-signature is more applicable and universal than the path index as mentioned before. The path dictionary(*PDS*) has lower storage overhead than the s-signature because it does not have the any storage for a fast access method. The path signature(*PSS*) has the highest storage overhead because it has a lot of redundant signatures and OIDs.

6 Conclusion

The acceptance of OODBSs required an efficient query processing scheme such as good indexing of the predicate class. Since queries in an OODBS could be very flexible, we could not predict which key attribute would be used in a query. However, the inverted file methods anticipate that a key field will be used in a query. The path dictionary encoded the connection information of class aggregation hierarchy and showed an effective way to process different kinds of queries. But it suffered from the lack of an efficient access method. In this paper, we proposed the s-signature scheme on the path dictionary and developed cost models for retrieval, update operations and storage overhead. Using the cost model, we compared the s-signature with other schemes under different degrees of reference sharing and demonstrated its efficiency and universality for different kinds of queries. Based on the results, we showed the s-signature method is appropriate to the efficient query processing in OODBSs. At present, we are studying the implementation issue of the s-signature using the bit-sliced signature file.

References

[BER89] Bertino, E. and Kim, W. (1989): Indexing technique for queries on nested objects, IEEE Trans. Knowledge and Data Engineering, 1(2), pp.196--214

[BER93] Bertino, E. and Guglielmina, C. (1993): Path index: An approach to the efficient execution of object-oriented queries, Data and Knowledge Engineering, North Holland, 10, pp.1--27

[FAL88] Faloutsos, C. and Chan, R. (1988): Fast Text Access Methods for Optical and Large Magnetic Disks: Designs and Performance Comparison, In:Proc. 14th International Conf. on VLDB, Long Beach, Calif., pp. 280--293

[FAL92] Faloutsos, C. (1992): Signature Files, in Information Retrieval: data structure and algorithms, W.B. Frakes, R. Baeza-Yates, eds., PTR Prentice-Hall, Englewood Cliffs, NJ, pp. 44--65.

[KEM90] Kemper, A. and Moerkotte, G. (1990): Advanced query processing in object bases using access support relations. In:Proc. of the 16th VLDB Conference, Brisbane, Australia, pp.290--301

[KIM89] Kim, W., Kim, K.C., Dale, A. (1989): Indexing techniques for object-oriented databases, in Object-Oriented, Concepts, Databases, and Applications, W. Kim and F.H. Lochovsky, eds., Addison-Wesley, Reading, MA, pp. 371--394.

[LEE92] Lee, W.C. and Lee, D.L. (1992): Signature File Methods for Indexing Object-Oriented Database Systems, In:Proc. of the 2nd International Computer Science Conference, Hong Kong, Dec. pp. 616--622

[LEE94] Lee, D.L. and Lee, W.C. (1994): Using Path Information for Query Processing in Object-Oriented Database Systems, In:Third International Conference on Information and Knowledge Management, Gaitherburg, MD, pp. 64--71

[RAB90] Rabitti, F. and Zezula, P. (1990): A Dynamic Signature Technique for Multimedia Databases, In:Proc. of ACM SIGIR Conf. on Research and Development in Information Retrieval, pp.193--210

Query Translation: The Query Interoperability Approach

Carlos Wong & W.S. Luk
School of Computing Science
Simon Fraser University
Burnaby, B.C. V5A 1S6
Canada
(Email: carlos@cs.sfu.ca, woshun@cs.sfu.ca)

Abstract: Interoperable system is an information-sharing system which does not have any integrated schemas. Query Interoperability is an approach to assist the user in interacting with multiple, dissimilar DBMSs in an interoperable system with respect to schema browsing and querying. In [ZHA95], an object-oriented common data model and schema (or DDL - data definition language) translation methods have been presented with the emphasis on dealing with many existing relational and object-oriented DBMSs. This paper deals with the querying (or DML - data manipulation language) aspects of the query interoperability approach. In particular, a canonical form for representing nested queries is devised. Algorithms are presented to show how O_2 and ObjectStore queries may be mapped into the canonical form and vice versa. The issue when the query language of the DBMS lacks the query nesting feature is also dealt with.

1 Introduction

According to [BRI92], information-sharing systems are classified into six categories, on the basis of the degree of coupling of the component systems. They range from systems with a single global schema at one extreme to ones without any notion of integrated schema at the other extreme. The latter ones are called *interoperable systems*. There is very little discussion on these systems in [BRI92], except that they lack some fundamental features of databases, due to the absence of global schemas. This paper is about interoperable systems. for convenience all component systems of an interoperable system are considered to be database management systems (DBMSs) themselves, although our work can be extended to include non-DBMS systems, such as file system or even spread-sheet.

The trade-off between integration and autonomy is a crucial issue in information-sharing systems. By autonomy, we mean the amount of work each site has to perform in order to maintain the prescribed level of information sharing. While most articles in the literature are in favor of some form of integration, there are situations that integration of any form may not be possible or desirable, especially when the number of component database system is large and the frequency of schema modifications is high. According to [KAR94], there are over 100 molecular biology databases which need to share information under the Human Genome Project. These databases have complex data structures, which are constantly changing because new experimental techniques are constantly being developed [DAV94]. Maintenance of integrated schema in any form would be difficult. This paper takes the position that autonomy is preferred over integration, and seeks a level of integration which is necessary to effect information sharing with minimal reduction in the autonomy of the individual component DBMS.

The main disadvantage of interoperable databases is of course the lack of capability to query remote DBMS since the necessary schema is not already transformed to a common format. This is particularly true when the user needs to work with schemas from multiple sites, i.e. a multi-site query. Since the end user is generally considered to be incapable of handling this task of integration, an integrated view of data from different sites are deemed necessary. However, we will argue that the lack of integrated schema is not as critical as it normally appears. In general, schemas from different sites may not be easily integrated into one due to the fact that the meaning of an attribute in one schema may differ from that of the attribute of the same name in other schemas. This is generally known as *semantic heterogeneity*. Much research has been done to discover ways to integrate schema algorithmically, but thus far, no completely satisfactory solution has been found. As stated in [SHE92], human intervention seems necessary, at least for the time being, to integrate schemas from different component databases. Thus, it appears interoperable databases take the 'lazy' approach to schema integration. Instead of reconciling the differences by system administrators in advance, i.e., the 'eager' approach, the interoperable system allows the users to do the job of resolving conflicts due to semantic heterogeneity. While this may be a too intimidating task for the end user to undertake in general, a case can be made that users with in-depth domain knowledge, e.g. molecular biologists, are in a better position to seek relevant information sources, and discern subtle differences between similar attributes, provided adequate support is provided on the computing side of the task. Indeed, our goal here is to ensure knowledge workers be provided with adequate support to carry their tasks independently. The current GUI (graphical user interface) technology has gone a long way to allow them to interact comfortably with the (local) database system. The emphasis thus should be on improvements in browsing and remote-site querying capabilities. We propose that the user is given the same local view of each (unintegrated) component DBMS, i.e. the query interoperability approach. This is how our work is different from most articles on interoperability, although we do share similar techniques, especially in the area of schema/query transformations.

Our earlier paper [ZHA95] has initiated the concept of query interoperability. In addition, we have presented our scheme for schema transformation, which basically adopts the ODMG-93 object data model as described in [CAT94], as the common data model, into which all different data models may be mapped. However, the object query language of the ODMG93 standard is not specific enough for our purpose of achieving query interoperability. The objective of this paper is then to present a query model, which will accommodate most existing DBMS.

The rest of this paper is organized as follows. In Section 2, the concept of query interoperability is explained in more detail. Query Exchange Centre (QEC), the software tool that enables query interoperability is also described. In Section 3, we briefly summarize OOCDM (Object-Oriented Common Data Model), which is central to schema transformation. In Section 4, OOCQM (Object-Oriented Common Query Model) is introduced. Examples of how the model works for query languages of three different DBMSs are presented. In Section 5, we compare our work with other similar work. Section 6 is the concluding section.

2 Query Interoperability & QEC

The lazy approach to schema integration is preferred when the schemas involved are subjected to frequent changes and the user is expected to be a knowledgeable worker. On the other hand, the burden is on the user to perform schema integration when a query is posed on remote databases. The motivation here is to reduce the amount of work the user has to go through to pose such a query. Normally, the user without any pre-built integrated schema, has to

I. import the schema(s) from remote site(s)
II. pose query against the remote database to retrieve the required data
III. create an integrated schema on the local DBMS
IV. import the retrieved data into the local database
V. pose the query on the integrated schema

Query interoperability is a method to simplify these steps, or to make it easier for the user to work with. Consider the case of querying a remote DBMS, when the remote DBMS may be different from the local one. The remote schema will likely be quite different, and the user, even a knowledgeable one, may find it difficult to understand. It will be much easier for the user if the remote schema may be transformed so that it appears in the same format as the local schema. The user will then be able to pose a local query against this transformed schema. The query is then translated into an equivalent query for the remote DBMS. The answer is then transformed into local data format. The whole scheme involves a software module which is capable of schema/query/data transformation as required by the above steps. We shall call it the *Query Exchange Centre* (QEC), where the term "query" is being interpreted broadly to include data definition and data manipulation languages (DDL & DML). The whole process of querying a remote DBMS is shown in the following diagram (Figure 1):

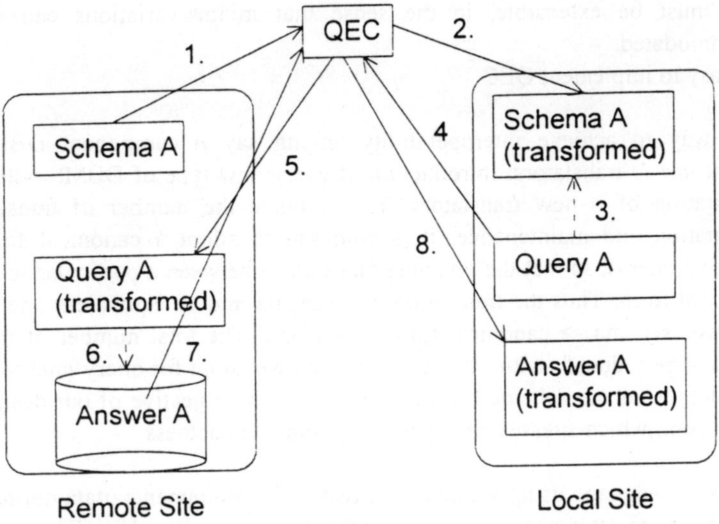

Figure 1

1. & 2.	Schema translation
3.	Query formation
4. & 5.	Query translation
6.	Running query against the (remote) database
7. & 8.	Data (Answer) translation

Multi-site querying is a fairly straightforward extension of the above plan. Once the remote schema(s) are imported into the local database, the remote schema and the local schema are effectively integrated, once the semantic meanings of the remote schemas have been ascertained. The user is now in a position to pose the query on these schemas, as if they are all local. This query will then be processed as a multi-site query. This step should not be difficult, since it is similar to many query processing algorithms proposed for information sharing systems with global schemas.

The presentation of Query Exchange Centre (QEC) in this paper is more conceptual than physical. In this paper, it is considered as a gigantic switch, which performs all required functions concerning transformation of schema and queries. Each component DBMS corresponds with only the QEC. In practice, this may not be desirable or feasible. It is likely that there will be an intelligent agent which is attached to each component DBMS to handle its interoperability needs. In this paper, however, we are concerned with only its functionalities, and how they are realized. For the rest of this section, we will discuss the common data model, the metadata language, and the transform schemes. Our aim is to demonstrate that our design of QEC achieves the following goals:

1. QEC must be capable of working with most existing database systems.

2. QEC must be extensible, in the sense that minor variations can be easily accommodated.
3. It is easy to implement QEC.

A naive way to achieve interoperability among say *n* component DBMS is to implement *n(n-1)* translators. Introduction of every new type of DBMS will result in implementation of *n* new translators. To minimize the number of translators for implementation and maintenance, it is common to adopt a canonical form for a schema (or a query), so that the mapping takes place between a particular schema and the canonical form. Thus the translation of a schema into an equivalent one is a two-step process: schema -> canonical form -> schema. The total number of translators required will be reduced to $2n$. It is the approach we adopt for query interoperability. What distinguishes our scheme from others' lies in the objective of our design of the canonical form, which stresses on extensibility and compactness.

Since a query language usually consists of two main components: data definition and data manipulation language, so does the canonical form we adopt. They are called Object-Oriented Common Data Model (OOCDM) and Object-Oriented Common Query Model (OOCQM) respectively. The OOCDM has been described in detail in another paper of ours ([ZHA95]). We will nonetheless present a brief summary in Section 3, with emphasis on the parts that are related to OOCQM.

3 OOCDM

We define a data model as a set of modeling primitives with which to determine the semantic aspect of the data definition language (DDL). A common data model is a data model which contains most if not all modeling primitives that may be used in the collection of all database systems covered in this study. It is also object-oriented, in two ways. First, the common data model described here contains all common modeling primitives found in most object-oriented databases. In fact, our model draws heavily from the object model of ODMG-93 ([CAT94]), both in concepts and terminology. ODMG-93 is an object database standard submitted by a consortium of five OODBMS vendors, for the purpose of interoperability among OODBMS. Nonetheless, our model is not a subset of the ODMG-93 object model. Ours differs because ODMG-93 is meant to be the standard DDL specification for all OODBMSs, whereas the OOCDM must consider all widely-used DBMSs, including RDBMS. We modify the ODMG-93 object model to incorporate features commonly found in extended relational databases, such as SQL3, the upcoming SQL standard [MEL92].

The OOCDM is called object-oriented also because we choose to describe the data model in an object-oriented fashion. The OOCDM can be described at two levels: the basic-object and meta-object levels, i.e. basic-object model and meta-object model. At the basic-object model, the primitives are about modeling real-world objects. At the meta-object level, each modeling primitive is an (meta)-object itself and has a set of properties and a set of operations. Each property in turn is a meta-object. For example,

User-Defined Type is a modeling primitive (MP). As a meta-object, it has a number of properties, such as Attribute and Relationship. An example of the operation is a Create procedure which specifies the syntax associated with User-Defined Type. As a property of User-Defined Type and therefore a meta-object, Attribute has a number properties, such as Domain and Integrity-constraint, and so on. Consequently a hierarchy of meta-objects are formed. Fig. 2 shows the top level of this hierarchy.

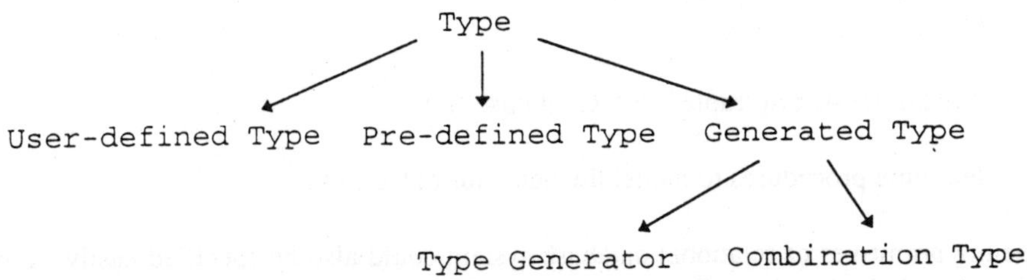

Figure 2

A meta-object language (MOL) is designed as a specification language for OOCDM, as OOCQM. For convenience, it may be considered as a subset of C++, in particular with the similar syntax. Every meta-object is defined as abstract data type (or class, in C++), with a default specification. It is in this sense that the OOCDM can be considered a class library. To map the data model of any specific DBMS into the OOCDM, one can use the MOL to express its specifications in terms of the OOCDM class library. In do so, the default class specification of any class member can be used as it is. It is also possible to override the specification of any class member, or to add new specifications to the library, or to combine any of the above techniques. In particular, given a modeling primitive of the DBMS, say MP, the database administrator, who is presumed to be the one to write the specification, will do the following:

1. If there exists a modeling primitive (meta-object) in OOCDM that matches MP in both semantic and syntax (as specified in the create function), we are done with MP and proceed to the next primitive.
2. If there exists a modeling primitive in OOCDM that matches MP's semantic but not its syntax, override the default syntax by a create statement.
3. If no primitive in OOCDM matches MP's semantic, the specification of MP has to be described using the meta-object language and added to the OOCDM.

For example, consider the specification of O_2. the modeling primitive 'class' in O_2 has the same semantic as User-Defined Type. The create statement also dictates the syntax of 'class' correctly, therefore nothing have to be done for this primitive. Now consider the O_2 primitive 'INT', which denotes integer of 4 bytes. Semantically, it matches the meta-object Int3. Suppose their syntax does not match, then the default syntax have to be overridden by

Int3::Create("INT").

Now consider the primitive 'tuple', which does not match any meta-object in OOCDM. However, we can add the subtype Tuple to Type Generator. To do so, we described tuple as, using the meta language,

```
Tuple : Type_Generator {
      list(Attribute)     Contents;
}

Tuple::Create("tuple", "(", Contents, ")")
```

and added some procedures to model the behavior of Tuple.

Modeling primitives of relational database system could also be specified easily. For example, 'relation' and 'attribute' match, respectively, User-Defined Type and Attribute in semantic. One simply has to override the default syntax:

```
User-Defined-Type::Create("create table", Type.Name,
                                    "(", list(Attribute), ")", ";")
Attribute::Create(Name, Domain)
```

3.1 DDL Canonical Form

The DDL Canonical Form is the internal representation of a schema that conforms to the OOCDM. Assuming that the DDL specifications of all relevant DBMS have been defined, we now discuss the process of translating a schema from one DBMS to another one. The first step of the process is to send the schema in question to the QEC, which translates it into one in the DDL Canonical Form. The Create function is in essence the parsing algorithm which transforms the schema into a number of instances of modeling primitives. For example, execution of the User-Defined-Type::Create function for table against a table definition will result in a name of the table and a list of attributes and the information associated with each attribute. Since all modeling primitives of the DDL in question are defined according to OOCDM, the outcome after executing all necessary Create functions is in canonical form.

To convert the schema in DDL-CF to the schema of a given DBMS requires more work, because modeling primitives that are not applicable to the DBMS must be translated into some things that are acceptable to the DBMS. For example, there are some data types in our OOCDM that are not supported by relational databases. An example is the 'tuple' used by O_2. A more problematic incompatibility between object-oriented model and the relation model is the embedding of objects within an object in many object-oriented models. Although extended relational models do allow nested structures within records, the usual relational model still lacks this feature. In this case, an augmentation procedure is required to convert from OOCDM to a form that a RDBMS will understand. [MEN93] addresses the problem of translating object schema to that of relational. We adopt a similar approach in converting schema from canonical form to that of RDBMS. During the process of such a conversion, necessary information would be stored so that appropriate modification could be made to upcoming queries posed by the RDBMS user.

4 OOCQM

Notice that the DDL described in Section 3 already contains a provision for data manipulation. Operation, according to OOCDM (and ODMG-93) serves the same function as the stored procedure in many RDBMS. A remote user can execute the operation by specifying the said operation name associated with the object class to the QEC. Since the operands of the operation are all typed according to OOCDM, the translation of operands will proceed in a similar way as the schema translation.

The DML of the query language is in effect a specialized operation that may be attached to class definition. The purpose of this operation is to provide a declarative way of data retrieval. Consequently, our OOCQM, following the familiar SELECT...FROM...WHERE, consists of three parts: the specification for what to be retrieved (SELECT), the specification of the collection which could be a horizontal and/or vertical subsets of the SELECT portion, and the specification of the criterion according to which the FROM is selected. This primitive is modeled by `Query_block`, a meta-object and may be specified using the meta-object language (MOL):

```
Query_block {
        list(Query_Exp)     Targets        // SELECT
        list(Source_Exp)    Sources        // FROM
        Predicate_Exp       Predicates     // WHERE
}
Source_Exp {
        IDENTIFIER          Newname
        Query_Exp           Source
}
```

Notice that the domain of both `Targets` and `Sources` is essentially (a list of) `Query_Exp`, `Source_Exp` being a domain with provision for renaming. This allows the OOCQM to encompass a greater variety of models. Indeed, the definition of a query expression, i.e. `Query_Exp` is very similar to what was stated in ODMG-93. Our current definition comes from [ZHA94] where the ODMG-93 definition has been suitably modified to work in our environment. One of the ramifications of this definition is that `Sources`, the operand after FROM, can be a list of query expressions, i.e. a list of query blocks. This nesting feature has significant impact on the internal representation of the OOCQM, i.e. the DML Canonical Form. This will be the focus of Section 4.1. `Predicate_Exp` can be a fairly complicated meta-object too. We assume that `Predicates` is in disjunctive normal form $q_1 \vee q_2 \vee ... \vee q_n$ where each q_i has the form $p_{i1} \wedge p_{i2} \wedge ... \wedge p_{im}$. It is possible for any p_{ij} to contain query block. However, since nesting of query blocks inside `Predicates` may be handled in a similar manner as nesting of query blocks in `Sources`, which will be discussed in greater details later, we will not elaborate further on the issue of nesting in `Predicates`.

For a DBMS with a more restrictive query language facility, the domain can be overridden for tighter type checking. For example, for most RDBMS do not allow nested queries, the domain of `Sources` may be restricted to a list of `Identifier`, i.e. name.

For the rest of this section, we will focus on constructing a DML Canonical Form (Section 4.1). We will show that this canonical form is appropriate by providing schemes for translating O_2 (Section 4.2) and ObjectStore (Section 4.3) queries respectively to and from the canonical form. The translation of the operands in a query, i.e. `Targets`, `Sources` and `Predicates` is assumed to be done through the DDL translation scheme which is discussed in [ZHA95].

4.1 DML Canonical Form

The DML Canonical Form, i.e. the internal representation of a (retrieval) query within the QEC, is quite different from that of DDL Canonical Form, which is derived directly from the OOCDM. This is possible because the properties of a meta-object in DDL are independent of each other. For example, the translation of the `Attribute` in DDL, a property of the meta-object `User-Defined Type`, is independent of what is in `Operation`, another property of the meta-object. However, the same is not for the properties of the meta-object `Query_Block`. In fact, all the properties inside appear more like operands of a function for `Query_Block`. For this reason, the detail of a DML query will be stored in a graph format, due to the query nesting feature of the OOCQM. The translation cannot be done by considering properties individually. As a result, procedures are required to convert a query *to* and *from* the canonical form.

To simplify the presentation of the DML canonical form, we consider only class as the only one instance of `User-Defined Type`, which roughly corresponds to table in relational databases or to class in C++. We use the term 'attribute' or 'member' to denote the characteristics of a class. (By 'member', we mean the member characteristics of a class, not the member functions, which is sometimes called 'method'.) Attributes/Member may be simple or complex. Simple attributes/members are those of having primitive types — int, real, char, etc, while complex attributes/members are those of user-defined types — i.e. another class.

We call the DML canonical form, the *canonical graph*, due to our graph-theoretic presentation, even though it would eventually be represented by some appropriate data structure. The canonical graph represents an instance of `Query_Block`, which we simply call *query*. It consists of a set of vertices (CV), a set of directed edges (CE), and a set of operators (CO) that operate on edges. Each *vertex* represents a class, a simple attribute (or 'member', in C++) of a class or a query. We divide CV into three mutually exclusive sets, CVC, CVM, and CVQ accordingly to differentiate classes, simple attributes of classes, and queries — CVC containing vertices representing classes, CVM containing vertices representing simple attributes, and CVQ containing vertices representing queries. (CVQ vertices would be discussed in greater details later.) Each vertex is named with the name of the class or the attribute it represents. A CVC vertex may also be annotated to reflect the constraint set upon it by the query. Finally, a vertex can be highlighted. A highlighted vertex $v \in$ CVM indicates that the value of its associated attribute is to be returned by the query; these vertices correspond to the SELECT clause of a query. On the other hand, a highlighted vertex $v \in$ CVC, or CVQ indicates that its associated class is a source from which the query draws information; these vertices correspond to instances of `Source_Exp`.

Vertices may be connected by *edges*. A connection between two vertices v_1 and v_2 may be classified into one of the following three cases.

Case 1: $v_1 \in$ CVC and $v_2 \in$ CVM with v_2 being a simple member of the class v_1.

This is represented by an arrow drawn from v_1 to v_2.

Case 2: Both $v_1, v_2 \in$ CVC.

Subcase (a): v_2 is a complex member of v_1.

This is represented by an arrow drawn from v_1 to v_2. The arrow is labeled by the name of the member

Subcase(b): v_1 has a member of Set(v_2), or, in general, Collection(v_2).

This is represented by a thick arrow drawn from v_1 to v_2. The arrow is labeled by the name of the member

Case 3: Both $v_1, v_2 \in$ CVM.

This kind of connection arises when v_1 is compared to v_2: v_1 *comp* v_2, where *comp* is one of $\{=, \neq, \leq, <, >, \geq\}$. In this case, an arrow is drawn from v_1 to v_2, and labeled with *comp*. (If v_2 is compared to v_1, reversed to direction of the arrow.)

Additional constructs are devised to support the semantic of universal quantification and existential quantification. Universal quantification such as 'for all *member* in *collection*' is represented by putting an '$\forall$' inside the vertex representing the collection in question (see Figure 3). Similarly, existential quantification such as 'for some *member* in *collection*' could be represented by putting an '$\exists$' inside the collection. Other commonly used constructs that can be used to build a query in canonical form, are described in Figure 3.

Canonical	Description
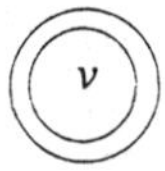	vertex representing a class v
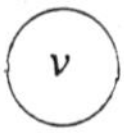	vertex representing a simple attribute v (i.e. member of primitive type such as int, char, real, etc.)
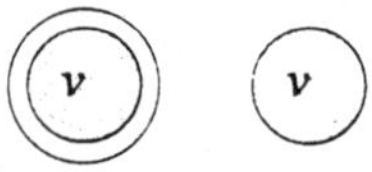	highlighted vertices marking the attributes to be returned by the query and the classes upon which the query operates
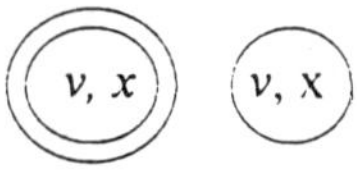	vertices renamed with 'x'
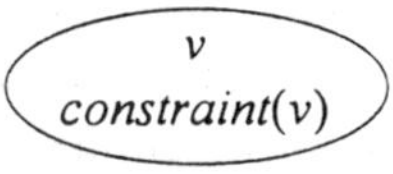	vertex with constraint; *constraint(v)* is any constraint that depends on the value of v only (e.g. $v < 100$)
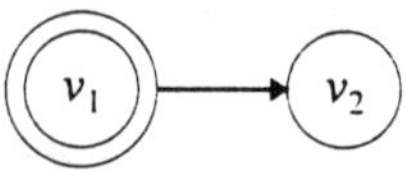	class v_1 with simple attribute (member) v_2
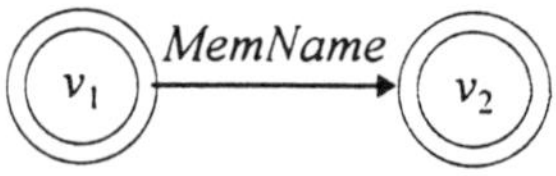	class v_1 with complex attribute (member) *MemName* of class v_2
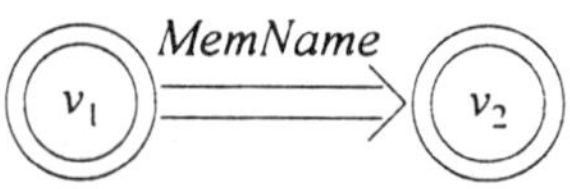	class v_1 with complex attribute (member) *MemName* of type Set(v_2)
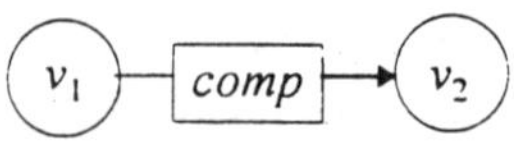	comparison between values of two simple attributes v_1 and v_2: v_1 *comp* v_2, where *comp*$\in \{=, \neq, \leq, <, >, \geq\}$
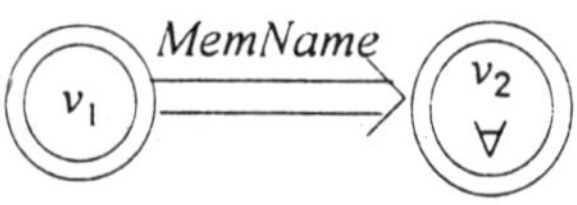	graphical representation of 'for all v_2 in v_1.*MemName*
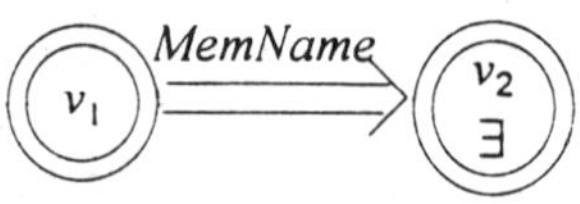	graphical representation of 'for some v_2 in v_1.*MemName*
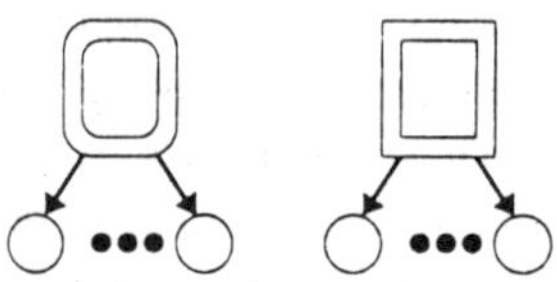	graphical representation of queries

Figure 3. Some common canonical components for building queries.

Recall that we have assumed that `Predicates` are in disjunctive normal form: $q_1 \vee q_2 \vee ... \vee q_n$ where each q_i has the form $p_{i1} \wedge p_{i2} \wedge ... \wedge p_{im}$. In its current form discussed in this paper, the canonical form can handle only the case where n=1. However, the more general cases can be easily handled by labelling each constraint with the corresponding subscript of the query to which it belongs. For example, p_{ij}'s canonical representation can be labelled with the number *i*.

Since a query can be treated as a class object with its returned attributes treated as class members, we represent a query in canonical form in a manner similar to that of a class. Namely, a query is represented by a CVQ vertex, a double-lined rectangle. Attributes returned by the query are represented by CVC (single-lined) vertices that are connected to the CVQ vertex with directed edges. Inside the CVQ vertex are the canonical representation of the `sources` upon which the query operates and the constraints imposed by the query. Figure 4(a) shows the canonical form of a simple query. This query, and the nested ones, in this example are presented in a form that is similar to most SQL, except that we have used the syntax '*z* rename_of *w*' to indicate explicitly that *z* is a rename of the object *w*, where *w* may be a class name or a query. Since the only class in the FROM clause is the object *w*, it is the only object drawn inside the CVQ vertex. The selected attributes *a*, *b*, and *c* are duplicated outside the CVQ vertex to reflect the fact that they are now members of the CVQ vertex. The advantage of treating a query as a class object is that nested queries can be represented easily without additional constructs. Figure 4(b) shows the canonical representation of a query with the query nested inside its FROM clause. Note, from the diagram, that, as far as the outer level of the query is concerned, the nested query is simply a class object (renamed to *y*) with attributes *a*, *b*, and *c*; activities inside the nested query are transparent to the outer query. Figure 4(c) shows a multi-level query with constraints imposed upon attributes at different levels. The point to emphasize here is that treating a query as a class object allows a consistent way of representing constraint, regardless whether the attributes involved are simple members of a class or selected attributes returned by a query. Finally, it should be mentioned that, in order to focus on the query, it is not necessary to show members (attributes) not involved in the query. Thus, in examples in Figure 4, it is not necessary to show the attribute *w.d*.

Queries can now be translated from and to the canonical form by matching query components with canonical components. QEC assumes such translations are provided by the users through the implementation of two functions: to_canonical translates queries to canonical form while the function from_canonical translates canonical form to queries in the corresponding DML format. Since our canonical form closely resembles the object predicate graph given by [MEN93] and [YU95], which address, in details, the transformation of such a graph from and to the relational queries, we will not be addressing such a translation here. It suffices to point out that there exists a one-to-one mapping between the canonical form and the predicate graph, and hence a translation of the canonical graph to and from a relational query is possible. The following discusses briefly how the to_canonical and from_canonical functions can be implemented for O_2 and ObjectStore.

4.2 Translating To and From Canonical Form: O_2

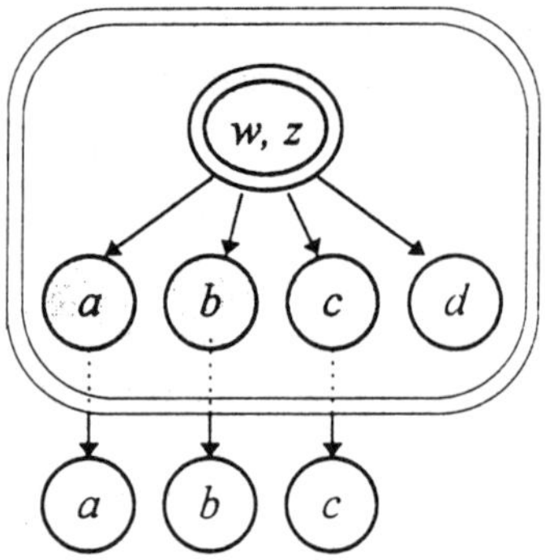

(a) Canonical form representing:
SELECT z.a, z.b, z.c
FROM z rename_of w

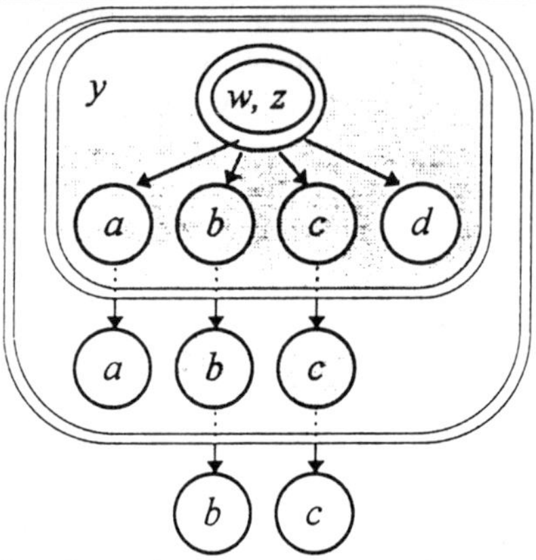

(b) Canonical form representing:
SELECT y.b, y.c
FROM y rename_of
(SELECT z.a, z.b, z.c
FROM z rename_of w)

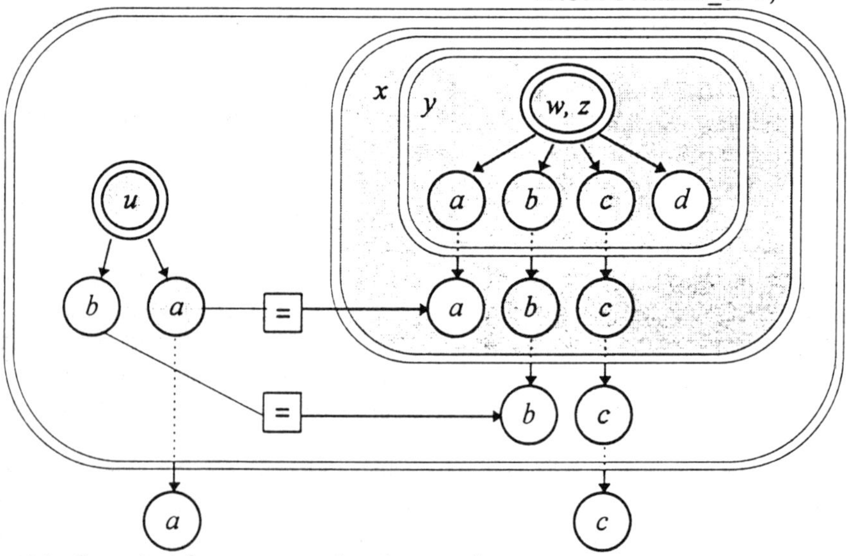

(c) Canonical form representing the nested query:
SELECT u.a, x.c FROM u, x rename_of
(SELECT y.b, y.c
FROM y rename_of (SELECT z.a, z.b, z.c FROM z rename_of w)
WHERE y.a = u.a)
WHERE u.b = x.b

Figure 4. Examples showing how (nested) queries can be represented in canonical form.

The implementation of these conversion functions is easier for O_2 users, due to the similarity between the canonical form and O_2 DML. We begin with the following to_canonical function.

Query_Block::to_canonical(Targets, Sources, Predicates)

{

Starting from the innermost level of the query, repeat the following steps until the outermost level of the query is converted.

1. Use a CVQ vertex to represent the current query, encompassing the graphical representations of all queries that are nested within the current query. Unless specified otherwise, all canonical form to be generated in steps 2 to 5 go inside this CVQ.
2. Using CVC vertices, form a graphical representation of each of the classes specified in the Sources, labeling them with their renames, if present. Nothing has to be done for a nested query encountered in the Sources since its canonical form should already exist.
3. Using the appropriate vertices and edges (CVM vertices and single-lined arrows for simple members, and CVC vertices and double-lined arrows for complex members), show the descendants of the classes just drawn in step 2. Vertices for members that are not involved in the query need not be drawn.
4. For each expression/constraint in Predicates, put the corresponding constructs on the graph as follow:

   (i) For a simple constraint on simple attribute, annotate the corresponding vertex with the constraint.

   (ii) For a comparison between two simple attributes, link the corresponding vertices with an arrow, labeling it with the appropriate comparison operation (See Figure 3).

   (iii) For an universal quantification ('for all x in y'), put an $\forall$ operator on the appropriate CVM or CVQ vertex.

   (iv) For an existential quantification ('for some x in y'), put an $\exists$ operator on the appropriate CVM or CVQ vertex.

   If the constraint involves objects that are defined in outer levels of the query, this step has to be deferred, since the vertices represented those objects are not drawn yet.
5. Highlight the vertices representing the simple attributes in the Targets clause. Duplicate these vertices (with the duplicates put outside the current CVQ vertex) and link them to the current CVQ vertex with single-lined arrow to reflect the fact that these are now the members under the query vertex.

}

We have actually used this function to arrive at the canonical form seen in Figure 4(c) from the following O_2 query.

SELECT u.a, x.c

```
FROM u, x in ( SELECT y.b, y.c
               FROM y in ( SELECT z.a, z.b, z.c
                           FROM z in w)
               WHERE y.a = u.a))
WHERE u.b = x.b
```

Figure 4(a) represents the resulting canonical form after applying steps 1 to 5 to the innermost level of the query (Select z.a, z.b, z.c From z in w). Figure 4(b) shows the result after the next level is also translated. Since the translation of the constraint 'y.a = u.a' requires a yet-to-exist vertex for the object u, this translation has to be deferred. Figure 4(c) gives the final result.

For transforming from canonical forms to O_2 queries, we start off from the outer levels of the canonical form and work inward. The following function gives the details for such transformations. We will use the term 'referable' to describe any path name that started with (i) the rename (or the name, in case where a rename does not exist) of a class represented by vertex at the current or any outer level of the query, or (ii) the rename of the u's (see step 3) at the current or any outer level of the query. Furthermore, we call such starting names (classname or rename) the 'header'.

Query_Block::from_canonical()
{
Start with the outermost level of the query, repeat the following steps until the innermost level of the query is converted.

1. /* form the FROM clause */
   Let v_1, ..., v_k be the set of highlighted CVC or CVQ vertices at the current level. For each $v_i \in$ CVC, let s_i be the string "*classname*$_i$", where *classname*$_i$ is the name of the class represented by v_i; let s_i be "*rename*$_i$ in *classname*$_i$" in cases where a rename exists. For each $v_i \in$ CVQ, let s_i be "*rename*$_i$ in (*query*$_i$)" where *query*$_i$ is the resulting query after applying steps 1 to 7 to v_i. Form the clause "From s_1, s_2, ..., s_k".
2. /* form the SELECT clause */
   Let w_i, ..., w_m be the set of highlighted CVM vertices at the current level. For each w_i, let n_i be the name of the path that leads from any v_j to w_i. (i.e.
   n_i = *classname*$_j$.*attribute*$_1$.*attribute*$_2$...*attribute_represented_by_w*$_i$ or . n_i = *rename*$_j$.*attribute*$_1$.*attribute*$_2$...*attribute_represented_by_w*$_i$.) Form the clause "Select n_1, ..., n_m".
3. /* form the universal and existential quantifiers */
   Let o_1, ..., o_n be the set of $\forall$ or $\exists$ operations at the current level; let u_1, ..., u_n be the corresponding CVC or CVQ vertices upon which o_1, ..., o_n operate. For each $o_i = \forall$, form a universal quantification expression uq_i = "for all *rename*$_i$ in *set*$_i$", where *rename*$_i$ is a rename for the class/query represented by u_i. If $u_i \in$ CVC, *set*$_i$ is the referable name for u_i; otherwise, *set*$_i$ = (*query*$_i$), where *query*$_i$ is the resulting query after

applying steps 1 to 7 to u_i. In the same manner, for an existential quantification expression eq_i = "exist $rename_i$ in set_i" for each $o_i = \exists$.

4. /* form the predicates */
   For each constraint imposed on a CVM vertex of the current level, form a predicate p_i = "*name comp constant*", where *name* is a referable name for the vertex, *comp* is the appropriate comparison operator, and *constant* is any constant. For each constraint imposed between a CVM vertex of the current level and a CVM vertex of an outer level, form a corresponding predicate p_i = "$name_1$ *comp* $name_2$", where $name_1$ and $name_2$ are the referable names of the two vertices in concern.

/* At this point, all expressions that go under the WHERE clause have already been formed. Steps 5 to 7 arrange these expressions so that all references can be instantiated when the query is executed. */

5. Partition the predicates into maximum number of groups (G_i) such that no predicates from different groups contain referable names that have the same header, other than those that appear in the FROM clause or at outer levels. (e.g. 'x.son.age > 5' and 'y.gender = "M"' should belong to different groups while 'x.son.age > 5' and 'x.gender = "M"' should be in the same group unless 'x' already appears in an outer level or in the FROM clause.)
6. Distribute each *uq* and *eq* into some groups defined in step 5 according to the following criteria: *uq* (or *eq*) belongs to G_i if the *rename* in *uq* (*eq*) is the header of a referable name involved in some predicates, *uq*, or *eq* already in G_i. (e.g. for the example in step 5, 'for all x in z.u' belongs to the group containing 'x.song.age > 5', but not to the group containing 'y.gender = "M"'.)
7. Let $q_{i1}, q_{i2}, ..., q_{ig}$ be the *uq* or *eq* in group G_i and $p_{i1}, p_{i2}, ..., p_{ih}$ be the predicates in G_i. Arrange the quantification expressions so that the header of any referable name involved in q_{ij} does not equal to the rename in q_{ik} for any k>j. (This guarantees that, for example, 'for all x in z.a' goes before 'for all y in x.b'. This ordering is necessary for 'x.b' to make sense.) Form W_i = "q_{i1} (q_{i2} ... (q_{ig} (p_{i1} and p_{i2} and ...and p_{ih})) ...)". Finally, form the WHERE clause of the query: "Where W_1 and W_2 and ...".

}

For an example, consider the schema on the Book Database in Appendix I. Suppose an RDBMS user wants to 'find the titles of all books about mathematics satisfying the following criteria: all its authors have written, before this book is published, some physics books that are published by a publisher having a branch in Vancouver'. To accomplish this task, he poses a relational query to the QEC. Using the DML specification for the relational site (which should include the to_canonical and from_canonical functions), QEC then transforms the query into canonical form. Figure 5 shows a probable canonical form for such a query. Following the from_canonical function specified above for O_2, the QEC can obtain the corresponding query as follows. First, seeing that 'book, b1' and 'book, b2' are the only highlighted CVC vertices, the first step yields the following FROM clause:

FROM b1 in book, b2 in book

For step 2, the only highlighted CVM vertex is 'title'. The prefix 'b1.' is necessary to make the name referable. We thus obtain the SELECT clause:

SELECT b1.title

There are three ∀/∃ operators. Correspondingly we form the three quantification expressions:

uq_1: for all a1 in b1.authors_list
eq_1: exist a2 in b2.authors_list
eq_1: exist c2 in b2.published_by.locations

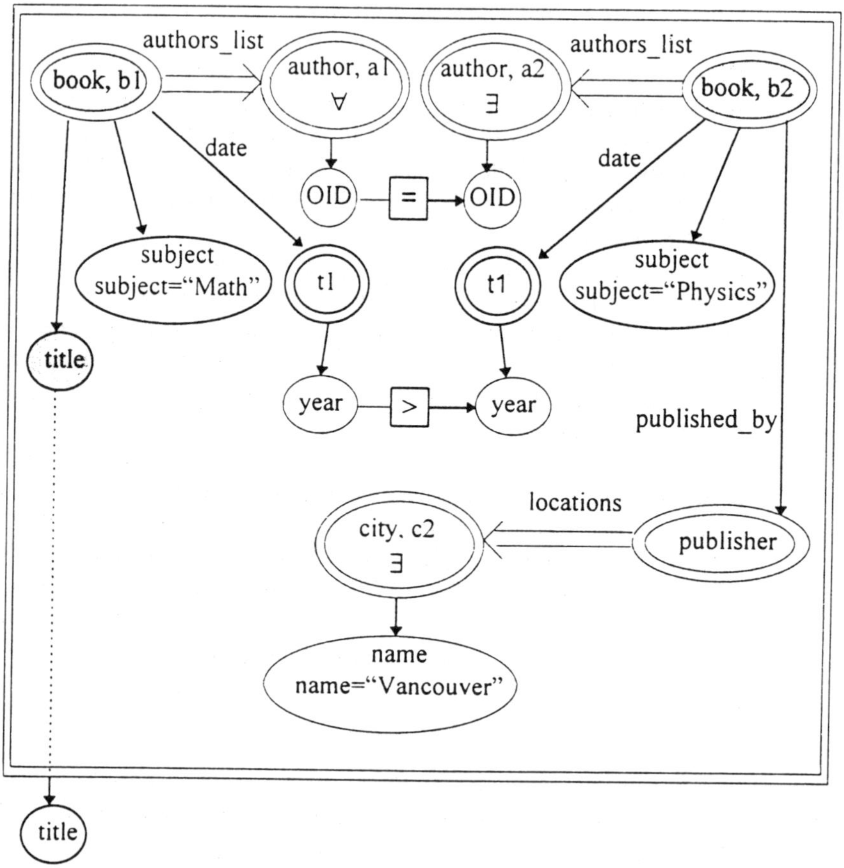

Figure 5. Canonical representation of the query 'Find the titles of all books about mathematics satisfying the following criteria: all its authors have written, before this book is published, some physics books that are published by a publisher having a branch in Vancouver'.

Again, notice that appropriate prefixes are required in order to make the references to 'authors_list' and 'locations' referable. Following step 4 and 5 we translate and group the five constraints into the following predicates:

G_1: b1.subject = 'Math'
G_2: b2.subject = 'Physics'
G_3: b1.date.year > b2.date.year
G_4: c2.name = 'Vancouver'
G_5: a1.OID = a2.OID

Notice that all 'c2.name', 'a1.OID', and 'a2.OID' are referable since c2, a1, and a2 are aliases that appear in the above quantification expressions. Since the headers 'b1' and 'b2' already appear in the SELECT clause, step 5 allows the first and the third predicates be put into different groups even though they contain referable names ('b1.subject' and 'b1.date.year') that have the same header ('b1'). According to step 6, both uq_1 and eq_1 are grouped into G_5 since their renames ('a1' and 'a2') are the same as the headers of some referable names ('a1.OID' and 'a2.OID) in the predicate in G_5. For the same reason, eq_2 is grouped into G_4. Applying step 7 results in the desired query:

```
SELECT b1.title
FROM   b1 in book, b2 in book
WHERE  b1.subject='Math' and
       b2.subject = 'Physics' and
       b1.date.year > b2.date.year and
       exist c2 in b2.published_by.locations            (eq2)
             (c2.name = 'Vancouver') and
       for all a1 in b1.authors_list                    (uq1)
             (exist a2 in b2.authors_list               (eq1)
                   (a1.OID = a2.OID))
```

The order of uq_1 and eq_1 is not important, since the header of the referable name in uq_1 ('b1') does not equal to the rename in eq_1 ('a1'), and vice versa.

4.3 Translating To and From Canonical Form: ObjectStore

The relatively simple conversion of O_2 queries from and to the canonical form is due to the similarity of the two's semantic. However, not all query languages share the same similarity with the canonical form. Since we have attempted to capture most of the semantics of most query languages when choosing the canonical form, it is not surprising that more than a few query languages may not support some of the semantics in the canonical form. In such cases, it is necessary to augment the languages in question so that query interoperability is possible. In this section, we look at such a language, ObjectStore's query language [LAM91], and briefly discuss how it might be augmented in order to perform the to_canonical and to_canonical function.

The typical format of a ObjectStore query is:

```
(Sources)[: Predicates :]
```

where `Sources` is a collection of objects, which could be another query, and `Predicates` has the form

$$\text{Predicate}_1 \ \&\& \ \text{Predicate}_2 \ \&\& \ \ldots \ \&\& \ \text{Predicate}_n$$

with each predicate being either a constraint on simple members of objects at outer levels or another query. In the latter case, the predicate is evaluated to TRUE if the result of the query is not an empty set; in other words, it is equivalent to an existential quantifier. Consider an example of an ObjectStore query (on the Book Database in Appendix I) that 'finds all books written by Tom on the subject cooking and published by a publisher having a branch in a city with population greater than 500000'.

book::extent[: authors_list[: name == "Tom" :] && subject == "Cooking" &&
publisher->locations[: population > 500000 :] :] *(OSQ1)*

where book:extent is ObjectStore's way of saying 'the set of all books'.

The above query is nested in ObjectStore's terminology since one of the predicate is a query. Another kind of nesting occurs when `Sources` is a query. The following shows such a query, which accomplishes the same task as the *OSQ1*.

((book::extent[: authors_list[: name == "Tom" :] :])[: subject == "Cooking" :])
[: publisher->locations[: population > 500000 :] :] *(OSQ2)*

However, all queries like that of *OSQ2* can be written in the form as *OSQ1*, where no `Sources` clauses are nested. Therefore, for the rest of the section, we assume that `Sources` is not nested.

It is not difficult to see that the ObjectStore query language is, semantically, a subset of the canonical form. Therefore, all ObjectStore queries could be represented in canonical forms. The following to_canonical function shows how the conversion could be done. Figure 6 shows the canonical form resulted from applying the function to *OSQ1*.

`Query_Block`::to_canonical(`Targets`, `Sources`, `Predicates`)

{

Starting from the outermost level of the query, repeat the following steps until the innermost level of the query is converted.

1. Use a CVQ vertex to represent the query. Unless specified otherwise, all canonical forms to be generated go inside this CVQ vertex.
2. Use a CVC vertex to form a graphical representation of the class specified in Sources. Highlight the vertex.
3. Using the appropriate vertices and edges (CVM vertices and single-lined arrows for simple members, and CVC vertices and double-lined arrows for complex members), show the descendants of the class just drawn in step 2; vertices for members that are not involved in the query need not be drawn.
4. Highlight and duplicate the CVM vertex representing the OID attribute of the class drawn in step 2. Put the duplicate outside the CVQ vertex and link it to the CVQ vertex to reflect the fact that the query is returning a set of pointers.

5. For each expression/constraint in `Predicates`, put the corresponding constructs on the graph as follow:
   (i) For a simple constraint on simple attribute, annotate the corresponding vertex with the constraint.
   (ii) For a comparison between two simple attributes, link the corresponding vertices with an arrow, labeling it with the appropriate comparison operation (See Figure 3).
   (iii) For a predicate that takes the form of a query (i.e. `Sources[: Predicates :]`), locate the CVC vertex representing the `Sources`. If such CVC vertex does not exist, create a new vertex by repeating step 2 and 3 above. In any case, generate a rename for the CVC vertex and also mark it with a universal quantifier.

}

The conversion from the canonical form to ObjectStore query, on the other hand, is more difficult, due to the limitation of ObjectStore query. There are two major operations in the canonical form that are missing from ObjectStore. First, since ObjectStore queries always return the references of only one class of objects (or more

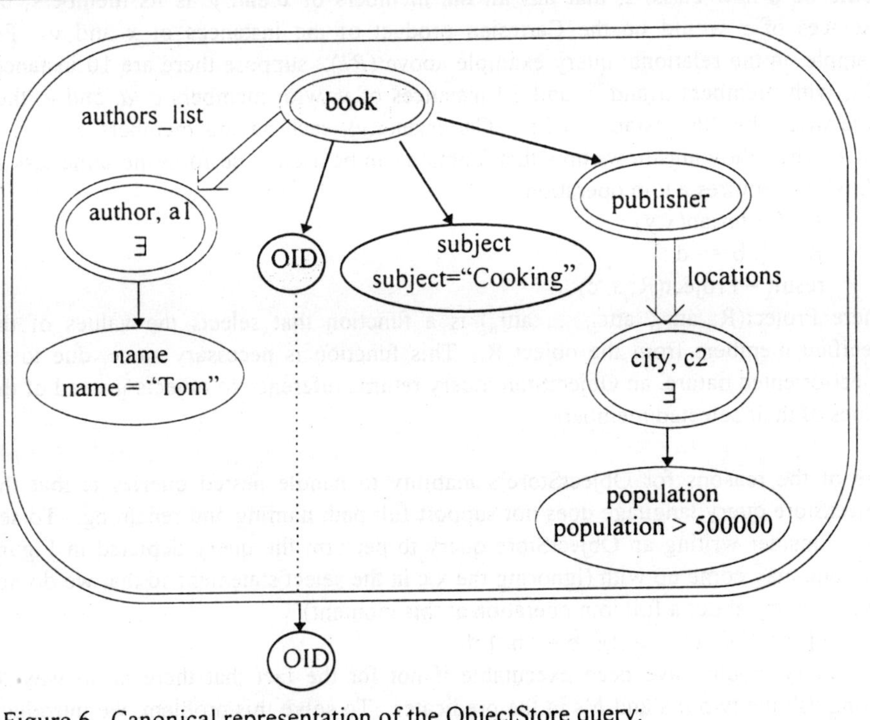

Figure 6. Canonical representation of the ObjectStore query:
book::extent[: authors_list[: name == "Tom" :]
&& subject == "Cooking" &&
publisher->locations[: population > 500000 :] :]

accurately, their pointers), they can only perform semi-join operations, but not full join operations. For example, it is not possible to write a ObjectStore query that would perform the same task as the following relational query:

```
SELECT x.a y.c
FROM x y
WHERE x.b = y.d                                   (R1)
```

Second, ObjectStore queries cannot handle the kind of query nesting as depicted by the canonical form and other query languages. As we can see from Figure 6, a nested ObjectStore query does not correspond to a nested canonical form. In general, a nested canonical form cannot be converted to a single ObjectStore query.

It is thus clear that augmentation (in the form of programming codes) is required for ObjectStore to execute general queries expressed in canonical forms. Due to space limitation, we shall not present the full, general-purposed algorithm for augmentation here, but to give some ideas and examples as how the missing semantics could be simulated using ObjectStore's programming language (C++).

The join operation can be simulated in ObjectStore by writing a function Cartesian(x,y) that takes the Cartesian product of two classes x and y. The result would be a new class, z, that has all the members of x and y as its members; the instances of z would be the Cartesian product of the instances of x and y. For example, in the relational query example above ($R1$), suppose there are 10 instances of x, with members a and b, and 20 instances of y, with members c, d, and e, then there would be 200 instances of z = Cartesian(x,y), each having members a, b, c, d, and e. The following shows how this function can be used to perform the same task as $R1$, which requires a join operation.

```
z = Cartesian(x,y)
R = z[: b == d :]
result = Project(R; a, c)
```

where Project(R; $attr_1$, $attr_2$, ..., $attr_n$) is a function that selects the values of the specified members from the object R. This function is necessary since, due to its object-oriented nature, an ObjectStore query returns reference to objects instead of the values of their selected members.

One of the reasons for ObjectStore's inability to handle nested queries is that the ObjectStore query language does not support full path naming and renaming. To see why, consider writing an ObjectStore query to perform the query depicted in Figure 4(c), one may come up with (ignoring the x.c in the select statement so that we do not have to worry about a full join operation at this moment):

```
u[: ((w[])[: a == a :])[: b == b :] :]
```

This query would have been executable if not for the fact that there is no way to distinguish the two a's and b's in the predicates. To solve this problem, we introduce the Rename(obj) function, which renames all members of obj by prefixing the members' names with 'obj_'. For example, if an object u has members a and b, then u would have members u_a and u_b after the execution of Rename(u). Suppose also that there is a function Dename(obj) function that removes the prefix of the renamed members of *obj*. The following shows how these functions allow the query in Figure 4(c) be carried out in ObjectStore:

```
z = w
Rename(z)// z now has members z_a, z_b, z_c, z_d
y = Project(z; z_a, z_b, z_c) // y has members z_a, z_b, z_c
Rename(Dename(y))                    // y now has members y_a, y_b, y_c
Rename(u)
y_u = Cartesian(y, u)
tmp = y_u[: y_a == u_a :]
x = Project(tmp; y_b, y_c)   // x has members y_b, y_c
Rename(Dename(x))                    // x now has members x_b, x_c
u_x = Cartesian(u, x)
tmp = u_x[: u_b == x_b :]
result = Project(tmp; u_a, x_c)
```

5 Literature Survey

There are other articles about interoperable systems. A few of them has subscribed to the same view on integration vs. autonomy as expressed here. [GOH94] is devoted to reasons why integration approach to information-sharing system (e.g., integrated schema approach) may not be always the most suitable approach. It proposes a context interchange solution whereby the representation and interpretation of data will be conducted under a set of pre-existing assumptions. For example, all currencies in the answer of the query must be in US currency. [WID92] introduced the concept of mediators in an information-sharing system, which relies on intelligent agents acting on behalf of the individual component DBMS (in our terminology) to resolve syntactic and semantic differences among each other. More details in this approach can be found in [QIA94] which describes methods to reason about a given query.

There are many articles on query translation and canonical forms. Most of them consider the problem in abstract, without references to existing DBMS, especially OODBMS and RDBMS. We will consider a few of them that are more relevant to this paper. In [QIA95], a canonical deductive database is proposed as a uniform representation of object-oriented databases (or common data model in our terminology). A given object-oriented query is mapped into this format, which is then translated into a relational query. The emphasis is on query optimization prior to the translation step and efficiency of the translation algorithm. In [MEN93] a scheme of translating an object-oriented query into relational query is presented, and in [YU95], a reverse process is described. [MEN95] proposes a theory to translate from relational queries to hierarchical queries. Their model for hierarchical queries is different from OOCQM. In addition, issue of converting hierarchical queries into a query language of a specific DBMS is not discussed in detail.

6 Conclusion

In this paper, we construct a canonical form for data manipulating queries which may contain nested queries. This canonical form is capable of handling queries from existing DBMS, which have very different query languages. Together with the common data model presented in our previous [ZHA95], we have presented a concrete design on how a query exchange centre may be implemented as a tool for knowledgeable workers to achieve query interoperability over an autonomous heterogeneous database system.

Acknowledgment: This research was partially supported by a research grant from Natural Science & Engineering Research Council of Canada and Centre for Systems Science, Simon Fraser University

References

[BRI92] Bright, M.W., Hurson, A.R., and Pakzad S.H., "A Taxonomy and Current Issues in Multidatabase Systems", IEEE Computer, Vol. 25, No. 3, 1992

[CAT94] Cattell, R.G.G., "The Object Database Standard: ODMG-93", Release 1.1 Morgan Kaufmann, Publishers, 1994.

[DEU91] Deux, O., et al, "The O2 System", Comm. of the ACM, Vol.34, No.10, October 1991.

[DAV94] Davidson, S.B., Kosky, A.S., and Eckman, B., "Facilitating Transformations in a Human Genome Project Database", Proc. Of 3rd Inter. Conf. On Information and Knowledge Management", Gaithersburg, MD, November 1994

[GOH94] Goh, C.H., Madnick, S.E., and Siegel, M.D., "Context Interchange: Overcoming the Challenges of Large-Scale Interoperable Database Systems in a Dynamic Environment", Proc. Of 3rd Inter. Conf. On Information and Knowledge Management", Gaithersburg, MD, November 1994

[KAR94] Karp, P.D., "Report of the Meeting on Interconnection of Molecular Biology Databases", Artificial Intelligence Center, SRI International, CA, 1994

[LAM91] Lamb, C., Landis, G., Orensten, J., and Weinreb, D., "The ObjectStore System", Comm. of the ACM, Vol.34, No.10, October 1991.

[LIT90] Litwin, W., Mark, L., Roussopoulos N., "Interoperability of Multiple Autonomous Databases", ACM Computing Surveys, Vol. 22, No. 3, 1990

[MEL92] Melton, J., Editor. "(ISO/ANSI) Working Draft Database Language SQL(SQL3)" ISO, ANSI, July, 1992.

[MEN93] Meng, W., Yu, C., Kim, W., et al, "Construction of a Relational Front-end for Object-Oriented Database Systems." Proc. of IEEE Data Engineering Conference, 1993.

[MEM95] Meng, W., Yu, C., and Kim, W., "A Theory of Translation From Relational Queries to Hierarchical Queries", IEEE Transactions on Knowledge and Data Engineering, Vol. 7, No. 2, April 1995.

[QIA94] Qian, X., and Lunt, T., "Semantic Interoperation: A Query Mediation Approach", Technical Report SRI-CSL-94-02, Computer Science Laboratory, SRI International, April 1994

[QIA95] Qian, X., and Raschid, L., "Query Interoperation Among Object-Oriented and Relational Databases", Proc. of IEEE Data Engineering Conference, Taipei, Taiwan, March 1995

[SHE89] Sheth, A., "Attribute Relationships: An Impediment to Automating Schema Integration." In Workshop on Heterogeneous Database Systems, Chicago, 1989

[WID92] Widerhold, G., "Mediators in the Architecture of Future Information Systems", IEEE Computer, Vol. 25, No. 3, 1992

[YU95] Yu, C., et al., "Translation of Object-Oriented Queries to Relational Queries", Proc. of IEEE Data Engineering Conference, Taipei, Taiwan, March 1995

[ZHA94] Zhan, J., "Automatic Generation of Query Language Front Ends", M.Sc. thesis, School of Computing Science, Simon Fraser University, May 1994

[ZHA95] Zhan, J., Luk, W.S., and Wong, C., "An Object-Oriented Approach to Query Interoperability", Proceedings of 6th International Database Workshop, Hong Kong, March 1995

Appendix I: Book Database Schemas

O_2 Schema of the Book Database

```
class book {
    type tuple(  title: string
                 authors_list: set(author)
                 subject: string
                 published_by: publisher
                 pub_date: tuple(month:
                   integer; year: integer))
    }
class author {
    type tuple(  name: string)
    }
class publisher {
    type tuple(  name: string
                 locations: set(city))
    }
class city {
    type tuple(  name: string
                 population: int)
    }
```

ObjectStore Schema of the Book Database

```
class book {
    public:
    *char             title;
    <Set> *author     authors_list;
    *char             subject;
    publisher         published_by;
    t1                date;
}
class author {
    public:
    *char             name;
}
class publisher {
    public:
    *char             name;
    <Set> *city       locations;
}
class city {
    public:
    *char             name;
    int               population;
}
class t1 {
    public:
    int               month;
    int               year;
}
```

Towards a Method for Schema Translation from Relational to Object-Oriented Databases

Brian Siu
Division of Technology
City University of Hong Kong
Tat Chee Avenue, Hong Kong
E-mail: tcbksiu@cityu.edu.hk

To-yat Cheung
Department of Computer Science
City University of Hong Kong
Tat Chee Avenue, Hong Kong
E-mail: cscheung@cityu.edu.hk

Abstract. This paper proposes a method that maps relational schema to OODB schema. The method consists of five phase - initialization, decomposition, classification, generalization, and identification. Each phases refines the schema to include semantic enhancements, engaging the user where necessary to resolve semantic ambiguity.

Keywords.. Interoperation, methodology, object-oriented database, relational database, schema translation.

1. Introduction

With more and more viable OODB products emerging in the commercial world, and more RDBMS vendors incorporating various OODB features into their next-generation products, it will be the trend for more organizations to have a mix of OODB and RDB applications. There are two approaches to adapting to OODB technology. The first is to convert all existing RDB to OODB by using a re-engineering approach [FON94]. The second is to use a multi-database whereby multi-database operations are allowed to access both the RDB and OODB. In both approaches, schema translation from RDB to OODB is needed.

Schema translation from one database model to another, e.g., from RDB schema to OODB schema, enables database interoperability in a multi-database environment. The ideal situation is to provide a multi-database model that allows users to access different databases without concerning the underlying models. Basarlou and Gangopadhyay [BAR92] discussed the technical problems relating to the use of different data models, e.g., relational data model, object-oriented data model; and different transaction processing methods. They proposed a unifying framework for multi-model multi-database systems, namely, M(DM), by using a combination of first-order logic, object-orientation, and a set of metatypes that capture and express data-model constructs in second-order logic. Hsiao [HSI89] provided an early insight into the need for a heterogeneous DBMS environment and operations. The benefit of using heterogeneous database systems is that the user can write transactions in the data language and utilise data in the data model with which the user is familiar. For example, the user can access data from a hierarchical database as if it is a relational database. This idea is important. Database users should be able to write query transactions to access both the relational database and object-oriented database without regard to the data structure of the underlying DBMS being used. Fig. 1. shows a schema translation process.

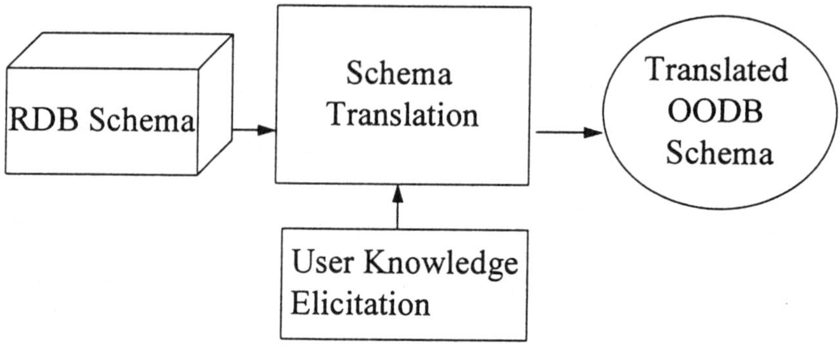

Fig. 1. Schema translation from RDB to OODB.

The translated OODB schema can be used for (1) database conversion, and (2) database interoperation. Papers on schema translation include, for example, Meng et.al. [MEN93] constructed a relational front-end for object-oriented database systems. Narasimhan et al. [NAR93] mappings from ER or relational schemas to OO schemas. Kwan, Fong and Li [KWA95] and Premerlani and Blaha [PRE94] also describe methods for translating from relational into ER schemas. A comprehensive method is needed for schema translation from relational to object-oriented databases.

2. Methodfor Schema Translation from Relational to Object-Oriented Databases

We propose a method that maps relational schemas to OODB schemas [CHI93]. The method consists of 5 phases. The final phase consists of ten steps to cater for different types of relations in a relational schema.

Phase I: Initialization

- Resolve attribute conflicts on homonyms(*) and synonyms (*)

(*) Example homonym (two attributes with same name but different meaning):
A customer can be either a company customer or a company employee
for example, a customer may purchase goods from the University's computer centre,
he can also be an employee in teaching support staff of the University.

Example synonym (two attributes with different names but the same meaning):
examples are, a loan borrower is a bank customer
he can also be an account holder in the bank.

Algorithm:

```
begin
    for each pair of relations A and B, do
        for each X ∈ (attr(A) ∩ attr(B)), do
            if A.X and B.X have different data types or size
                then begin
                X in A and B are homonyms
                Clarify X in A and B
                end
    for each pair of input relations A and B do
        for each pair(x,y), X ∈ attr(A) and Y ∈ attr(B), do
            if x≠y and X.A and B.Y have the same data type and size
                then begin
                X and Y are synonyms
                Clarify X, Y
                end
end
```

Phase II: Decomposition

- Decompose input relations into relations in third normal form

Algorithm:

```
begin
    for input relations A, B ...... N, do
        for each input relation A, do
            if there is partial dependency and/or transitive dependency
            then decompose relation A into relations A1 and A2 by eliminating
            these dependencies
end
```

Phase III: Classification

- Classify relations and attributes into different relation types and attribute types

Algorithm:

```
begin
    for input relations A, B ...... N, do
        for each input relation A, do
            if Primary-Key(A) does not contain a key of another relation
            then relation A is a "Primary Relation Type 1";
                i.e., Primary-Key(A)⇒Primary key of relation A = Strong
            relation
            if Primary-Key(A) is partially formed by containing a key of another
            relation
            then relation A is a "Primary Relation Type 2"
```

i.e., Weak relation

if Primary-Key(A) is fully formed by concatenation of primary keys of other relations

then relation A is a "Secondary relation Type 1"

i.e., Relationship relation without its own key

if Primary-Key(A) is partially formed by concatenation of primary keys of other relations

then relation A is a "Secondary relation Type 2"

i.e., Relationship relation with its own key

if Primary-Key(A) is an attribute in the key of a Primary relation and also an attribute in the key of a Secondary relation

then Primary-Key(A) is a Primary Key attribute

else Primary-Key(A) is a General Key attribute (+)

if attr(A) is a foreign key

then attr(A) is a Foreign Key Attribute

else attr(A) is a Non-Foreign Key Attribute

end

(+) Example

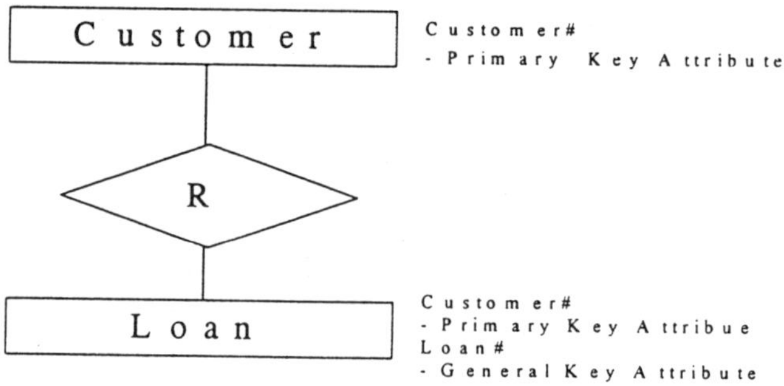

Fig. 2. Classification of relations Loan and Customer.

Phase IV: Generalization

- Generate Inclusion Dependencies

Algorithm:

begin

for each pair of Primary Relations of Type I, A and B **do**

for each $X \in (Key(A) \cap Key(B))$ **do**

if user specifies ID: $A.X \subseteq B.X$

then relation A is a Subclass Relation, B is a Superclass Relation

else A is a Superclass Relation, B is a Subclass Relation

end

Phase V: Identification

- Identify classes and methods
- There are 10 steps in this phase

Step 1: Primary Relation of Type 1 → Class

Relation:		*Class:*
Person (name, address)	→	**Class** Person
		properties
		name: String;
		address: String;
		end Person.

Explanation: Given a relation "person" in RDB, a corresponding class "person" is created in the OODB. The attributes of the relation are transformed into properties of the class.

Step 2: Primary Relation Type 1 plus Foreign Key Attribute → Class + Association

Relation:		*Classes:*
Employee (emp-name, address, supervisor-name*)	→	**Class** Employee
		properties
		emp-name: String;
		address: String;
		supervise: Employee;
		end Employee

Explanation: In the relation "employee", the employee may be a Supervisor which is also an employee. This association is turned into the property "Employee.supervise".

Step 3: Binary Relationship → Class + Association

Case 1: 1:1 relationship (see Fig. 3.)
Two Primary Relations Type 1 plus Foreign Key → Attribute Class + Association

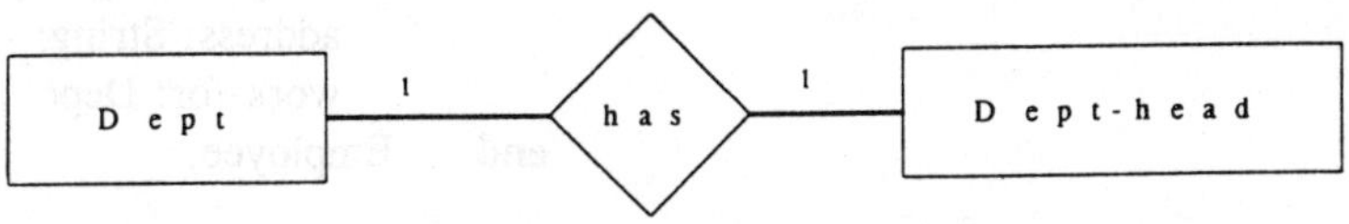

Fig. 3: EER model (attributes not shown).

Relation: *Classes:*

Dept (dept-name, head) → **Class** Dept
properties
dept-name: String;
head-by: Dept-head;
end Dept.

Dept-head (head-name,address) → **Class** Dept-head
properties
head: Dept;
head-name: String;
end Dept-head.

Explanation: The 1:1 relationship has been reduced to "head-by: Dept-head" in class "Dept", and "head" in class "Dept-head".

Case 2: 1: n relationship (see Fig. 4.)

Two Primary Relations of Type 1 plus Foreign Key → Attribute Class + Association

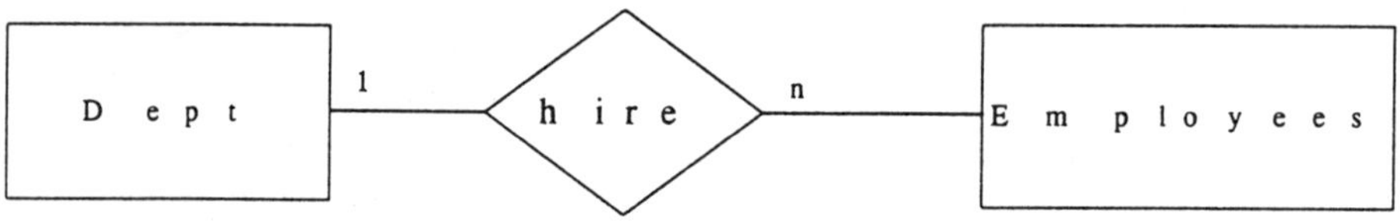

Fig. 4. EER model (attributes not shown).

Relation: Classes:

Dept (name,head) → **Class** Dept
properties
dept-name: String;
head: String;
hire: set (Employees);
end Dept.

Employee (emp#,address,dept-name) → **Class** Employee
properties
emp#: Integer;
address: String;
work-for: Dept
end Employee.

Explanation: This is a one-to-many relationship. Dept can hire many employees. This is indicated by the association "Dept .. hire: set of Employees ..." in class "Dept", and association "Employee .. work-for ..." in class "Employee".

Case 3: Two m : n relationship (see Fig. 5.)

Two Primary Relations Type 1 plus One Secondary Relation Type 1 →
Attribute Class + Association

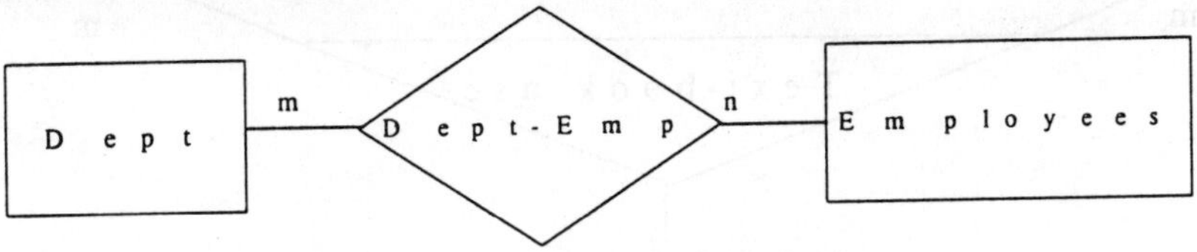

Fig. 5. EER model (attributes not shown).

Relation:		Classes:
Dept (dept-name, head)	→	**Class** Dept **properties** dept-name: String; head: String; hire: set (Dept-Emp); **end** Dept.
Employee (emp#, address)	→	**Class** Employee **properties** emp#: Integer; address: String; work-for: set (Dept-Emp) **end** Employee.
Dept-Emp (dept-name, emp#, hours)	→	**Class** Dept-Emp **properties** hire: Employee; hired-by: Dept; hours: Integer; **end** Dept-Emp.

Explanation: The relation "Dept-Emp" shows a many-to-many relationship. Dept can hire many employees. One employee may belong to more than one department. This is indicated by the association "Dept .. hire: set (Dept-Emp) ..." in class "Dept", and by the association "Employee ... work-for: set (Dept-Emp) ..." in class "Employee", and in class "Dept-Emp". The 3 relations have been converted to 3 classes.

Step 4: Ternary Relationship Relation → Class + Association (see Fig. 6.)

Three Primary Relations Type 1 plus one Secondary Relation Type 1 →
Attribute Class + Association

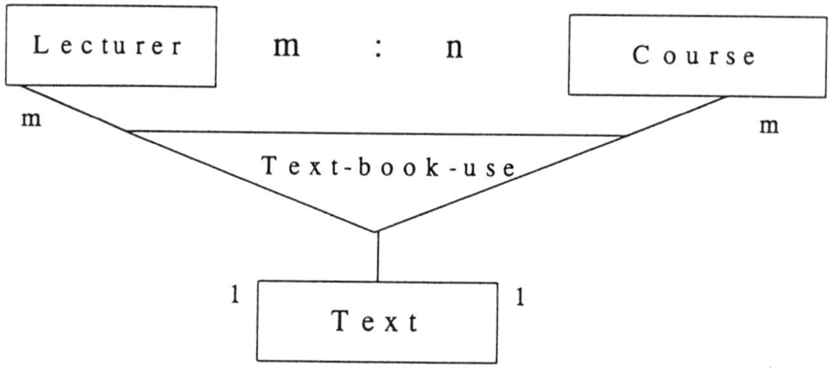

Fig. 6. EER model (attributes not shown)

Relation:		*Classes:*
Lecturer (l-name, address)	→	**Class** Lecturer **properties** l-name: String; address: String; uses: set (Text-book-use); **end** Lecturer.
Course (class#, subject)	→	**Class** Course **properties** class#: Integer; subject: String; course-texts: set (Text-book-use); **end** Course.
Text (text-book-name, publisher)	→	**Class** Text **properties** text-book-name: String; publisher: String; used-for: set (Text-book-use); **end** Text.
Text-book-use(l-name,class#, text-book-name)	→	**Class** Text-book-use **properties** assigned by: Lecturer; assigned to: Course; text-book: Text; **end** Text-book-use.

Explanation: The 4 relations have been converted to 4 classes. The ternary relationship is indicated in the class "text-book-use" by the associations: "assigned by: Lecturer", "assigned to: Course", and "published by: Text".

Step 5: Subclass and Superclass Relations → Class + Inheritance (is-a relationship) (see Fig. 7.)

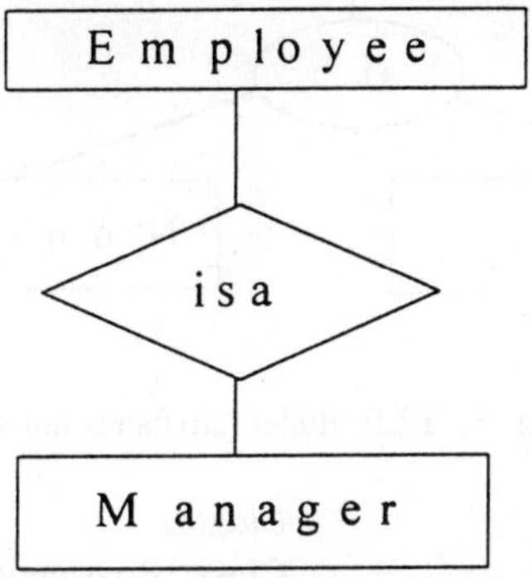

Fig. 7. EER model (attributes not shown)

Relation:		*Classes:*
Employee (e-name, address)	→	**Class** Employee **properties** e-name: String; address: String; **end** Employee.
Manager (m-name, age, salary)	→	**Class** Manager **inherits:** Employee; **properties** age: Integer; salary: Integer; **end** Manager.

Explanation: Manager is a subclass of class "Employee". The is-a relationship is indicated in the class "Manager" by the inheritance link "inherits: Employee".

Step 6: Generalization Relation → Class + Inheritance + Method

Case 1: Disjoint generalization (see Fig. 8.)

Two Subclass Relations plus One Superclass Relations →
Class + Inheritance (is-a relationship)

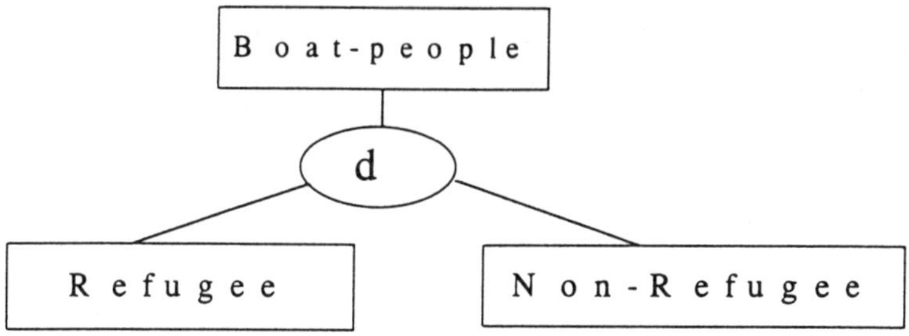

Fig. 8. EER model (attributes not shown).

Relation:		*Classes:*
Boat-people (<u>name</u>, age)	→	**Class** Boat-people **properties** name: String; age: Integer; **end** Boat-people.
Refugee (<u>name</u>, qualification)	→	**Class** Refugee **inherit** Boat-people **properties** qualification: String; **operations** add: if not exist in Non-Refugee then create Refugee **end** Refugee.
Non-refugee (<u>name</u>, source-country)	→	**Class** Non-Refugee **inherit** Boat-people **properties** source-country: String; **operations** add: if not exist in Refugee then create Non-Refugee **end** Non-Refugee.

Explanation: In a disjoint situation, the converted relations are shown in the classes by inheritance and by methods (operations). In the class "Refugee", the method creates an object of class Refugee only after testing that the person is NOT a non-refugee. In the class "Non-Refugee", the method creates an object of class Non-Refugee only after testing that the person is NOT already a refugee.

Case 2: Overlap Generalization (see Fig. 9.)
Two Subclass Relations plus One Superclass Relation → Class + Inheritance (is-a relationship)

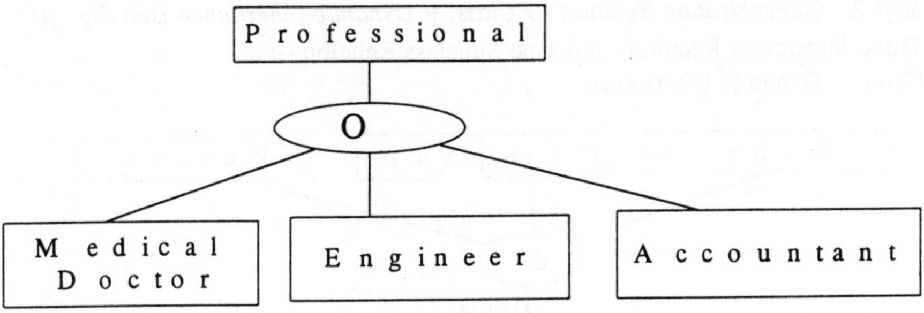

Fig. 9. EER model (attributes not shown).

Relation: — *Classes:*

Professional (name, ..) → **Class** Professional
 properties
  name: String;
  ...
  ...
 operations
  If update
  Then
   update ALL (medical doctor, engineer, accountant) with same primary key
  .
end Professional.

Doctor (name, ..) → **Class** Doctor
 inherit: Professional;
 properties
  ...
end Doctor.

Engineer (name, ..) → **Class** Engineer
 inherit: Professional;
 properties
  ...
end Engineer.

Accountant (name, ..) → **Class** Accountant
 inherit: Professional;
 properties
  ...
end Accountant.

Explanation: In an overlap situation, a professional may be both an engineer and an accountant. In the case of update to the class "professional", the update is propagated to instances of all other classes that have the same primary key.

Step 7: Categorization Relation → Class + Dynamic Inheritance (see Fig. 10.)
Three Superclass Relations plus One Subclass Relation →
Class + Dynamic Inheritance

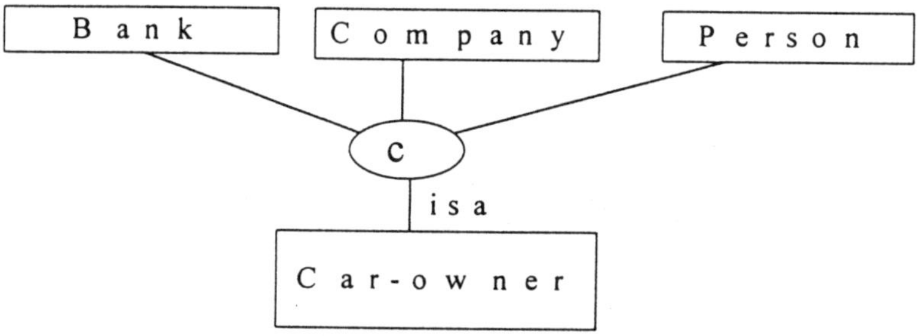

Fig. 10. EER model (attributes not shown).

Relation:		*Classes:*
Bank (<u>ownership#</u>, ...)	→	**Class** Bank **properties** ownership#: Integer; ... **end** Bank.
Company (<u>ownership#</u>, ...)	→	**Class** Company **properties** ownership#: Integer; ... **end** Company
Person (<u>ownership#</u>, ...)	→	**Class** Person **properties** ownership#: Integer; ... **end** Person.
Car-owner (<u>ownership#</u>, <u>license#</u>)	→	**Class** Car-owner **inherit** (Bank, Company, Person) **operation** case Car-owner is Bank: address ← Bank.address Company:address ←Company.address Person: address ← Person.address age ← Person.age **end** Car-owner.

Explanation: In this situation, either of "Bank", "Company", or "Person" can be car-owner. The relationship is indicated in the class "Car-owner" by dynamic inheritance using the method (operation). If car-owner is bank, update bank address; if car-owner is company, update company address; if car-owner is person, update person address as well as person's age

Step 8: Aggregation Relation → Classes + Associations *(see Fig. 11.)*
Two Primary Relations Type 1 plus Two Secondary Relations Type 1 →
Class + Association

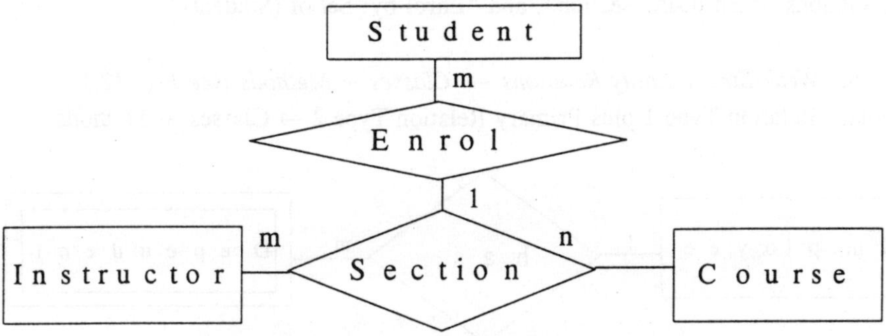

Fig. 11. EER model (attributes not shown).

Relation: → *Classes:*

Instructor (<u>instructor-name</u>,.....) →

Class Instructor
  properties
    instructor-name: String;
    ...
end Instructor.

Course (<u>course#</u>,.....) →

Class Course
  properties
    course#: Integer;
    ...
end Course.

Section (<u>instructor-name</u> , <u>course#</u>, section#) →

Class Section
  properties
    taught-by: Instructor;
    belong-to: Course;
    section#: Integer;
end Section.

Student (<u>student#</u>, ...) →

Class Student
  properties
    student#: Integer;
    ...
end Student.

Enrol (instructor-name , course#, student#, grade) → **Class** Enrol
properties
Enrol-in: Section;
Enrol-by: Set (Student);
grade: String
end Enrol.

Explanation: In this situation, the aggregation relation "Section" is indicated in the class "Section" by the associations: "taught-by: Instructor", and "belong-to: Course". The aggregation relation "Enrol" is indicated in the class "Enrol" by the associations: "Enrol-in: Section", and "Enrol-by: Set of (Student)".

Step 9: Weak/Strong Entity Relations → Classes + Methods (see Fig. 12.)
Primary Relation Type 1 plus Primary Relation Type 2 → Classes + Methods

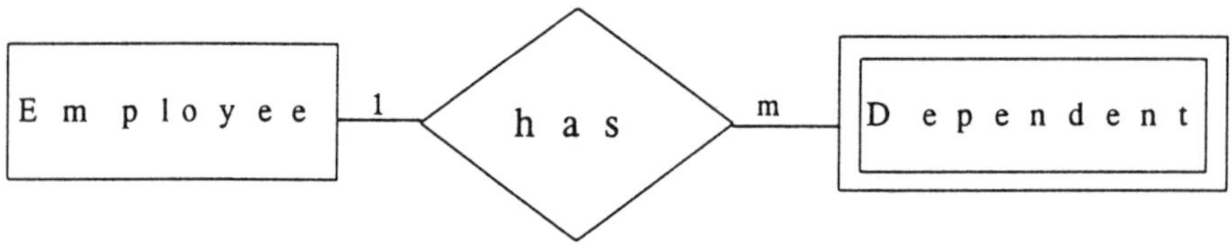

Fig. 13. EER model (the double box shows that it is a weak entity).

Relation:		*Classes:*
Employee (emp#,...)	→	**Class** Employee **properties** emp#:Integer; has: Set (Dependent); **operations** delete: if delete (Employee) then delete (Dependent) **end** Employee.
Dependent (name,emp#,) where emp# ≠ null	→	**Class** Dependent **properties** name: String depends-on: Employee **operations** add: if exists (Employee) then create (Dependent) **end** Dependent. (note: Keep RDB constraint in OODB)

Explanation: In this situation, the RDB constraints are kept in the OODB: in the class "Employee" by the method (operations) "delete: if delete (Employee) then delete (Dependent)", and in the class "Dependent" by the method (operations) "add: if exists (Employee) then create (Dependent)".

Step 10: Identifier inclusion relationship → Composite Object (see Fig. 13.)
Pirmary Relation Type 1 plus Primary Relation type 2 → Composite Object

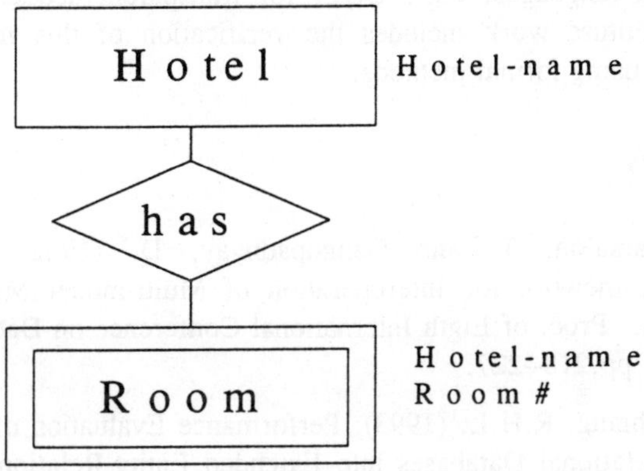

Fig. 13. EER model (the double box shows that it is identifier dependent)

Relation:		*Classes:*
Hotel (<u>Hotel-name</u>,...)	→	**Class** Hotel

```
Class Hotel
        properties
          own: Set of room;
          hotel-name: String;
        operations
            delete: delete all rooms
end   Hotel
```

Room (<u>Hotel-name</u>, <u>Room#</u>,...) →

```
Class Room
        inherits: Hotel
        properties
          room#: Integer;
          ...
        operations
          add: if exists (Hotel)
                    create (Room) +
                    add room to Hotel.own
end   Room
```

Explanation: In this situation, if the class "Hotel" is deleted, then delete the set of rooms owned by this Hotel. Also if a room is added then the hotel must exist.

3. Conclusion

This paper has proposed a method for schema translation from relational databases to object-oriented databases. Schema translation is one of the important processes in a multidatabase environment. It is used both in database conversion and database interoperation. In the case of database interoperation, the translated object-oriented database schema can be used as input to a database gateway that processes data manipulation languages, e.g., OQL, for transparent access to existing relational databases. Future work includes the verification of this method by prototyping approach or using formal methods.

References

[BAR92] Barsalou, T. and Gangopadhyay, D. (1992): M(DM): An Open Framework for Interoperation of Multi-model Multi-database Systems. In: Proc. of Eigth International Conference on Data Engineering, ICDE-8, pp.218--227.

[CHI93] Chiang, R.H.L. (1993): Performance Evaluation of Reverse Engineering Relational Databases into Extended Entity-Relationship Models (MDM): An Open Framework for Interoperation of Multi-model Multi-database Systems. In: Proc. of Eigth International Conference on Data Engineering, ICDE-8, pp.218--227.

[FON94] Fong, J. and Kwan, I. (1994): An Re-engineering Approach for Object-Oriented Database Design. In: Proc. of First IFIP/SQL International Conference on Software Quality and Productivity, Hong Kong, Chapman and Hall, pp.139--147.

[HSI93] Hsiao, D.K., Neuhold, E.J., and Sacks-Davis, R., (eds.) (1993): Interoperable Database Systems (DS-5), IFIP, North Holland, Elsevier Science Publishers.

[KWA95] Kwan, I., Fong, J. and Li, Q. (1995): A Methodfor Reengineering Relational to Object-Oriented Database Systems Via an Extended E-R Model. In: 6th International Conference of Database and Expert Systems Application Conference, DEXA 95, London. September.

[MEN93] Meng, W., Yu, C., Kim, W., Wang, G., Pham, T., and Dao, S. (1993): Construction of a Relational Front-end for Object-Oriented Database Systems. In: Proceedings of Nineth International Conference on Data Engineering, ICDE-9, pp.476-- 483.

[NAR93] Narasimhan, B., Navathe, S.B., and Jayaraman, S. (1993): On Mapping ER and Relational Models into OO Schemas. In: Proc. of Entity-Relationship Modeling Conference. Springer Verlag

[PRE94] Premerlani, W.J., and Blaha, M.R. (1994): An Approach for Reverse Engineering of Relational Databases. Communications of the ACM, May, Vol. 37, No. 5, pp.42--49.

A Distributed Object Database's Basic Design Issues

Xiuzhen Zhang
Department of Computer Science
Beijing Polytechnic University
Beijing 100022, P. R. C

Joseph Fong
Department of Computer Science
City University of Hong Kong
Tat Chee Avenue, Kowloon
Hong Kong

Abstract Distributed Object Database(DODB) is a relatively new topic deserving further research. There are not mature technologies in the design of a DODB system up to now. This paper gives a discussion on the basic issues, single logical view, distributed object management, and global query optimization, of the design of a DODB.

Key Words Distributed database design, Object database

1 Introduction

Object Databases(ODBs) have been commercially available for at least four years and have found usage in a wide variety of application domains. Many organizations have mixtures of ODBs in different branches. These ODBs may be heterogeneous in the sense that they are provided by different vendors or same ODBs with different versions. Distributed Object Database Management Systems(DODBMSs) have evolved to provide a mechanism for users to transparently access objects everywhere in the network.

The traditional "top-down approach" can only be used when a Distributed Database(DDB) system is designed from scratch[CER84]. We start by designing the global schema, and proceed by designing the fragmentation of the database and allocating the fragments to the sites of the network, creating the physical images. The design is completed by performing, at each site, the "physical design" of the data which are allocated to it.

As mentioned earlier, with network and database technologies in use for years, today's DDB systems can not be DDB systems from scratch. On the contrary, they are collections of widely distributed database systems that span geographical areas, hardware platforms and database architectures. They are characterized by the loosely coupled applications, diverse data models and more local autonomy. Even if all the component databases base on the same data model, e.g., object model, they are ODBs provided by different vendors or same ODBs with different versions.

So, a working definition of today's DODB can be "a collection of sites connected by a communications network, in which each site is a component ODB in its own right but the component ODBs have agreed to cooperate so a user at any site can access objects in the network as if the objects were stored in the user's own site". As the component databases are existing heterogeneous ODBs, some new topics, e.g., single logical view and distributed object management, arise. Also, some of the traditional design issues of a DDB system, e.g., global query optimization , require reexamination and close evaluation now within the object paradigm. This paper will discuss the basic issues, single logical view, distributed object management, and global query optimization, of the design of a DODB.

2 Single Logical View

The most ambitious requirement of such a DODB system is the capability of providing a view of the system which is transparent not only to data distribution, but also to heterogeneity of component ODBs. To achieve this, a means is needed to resolve the differences in data representation and function between local ODBs. Different representations of semantically similar data may include different naming conventions, formats, data structures, levels of abstraction, and/or completeness/consistency of the data. Various approaches [GAR95], [JAM95], [KAM95], [KOH93], [MIS95], [MUH95], [NAV95], [RED94], [SUZ95], [TOW95] exists, which can be classified into three broad categories -- total integration, partial integration and interoperability[RED94].

2.1 Global Schema Approach

With the total integration(global schema) approach, a global schema is created . Under this paradigm, we takes the independently developed local schemata, resolves semantic and syntactic(structural) differences between them, and creates an integrated summary of all the information from the union of the local schemata by integrating schemata of the component databases. The global schema is just another layer, above the local external schemata, that provides additional data independence. Global users essentially see a single, large, integrated database. A major difference, however, is the lack of global control over local decisions. The global schema is usually replicated at each system node. Global schema design is also referred to as view integration. Efforts in this approach can be found in [GAR95], [KAM95], [KOH93], [RED94], [SUZ95], [TOW95]. The most excellent work is done by Reddy et al.[RED94]. Compared to existing procedures, this four-layered schema architecture for virtual integration of component databases lays greater stress on resolving semantic incompatibilities among the component database schemata and data inconsistencies among data in the local databases. Reddy's procedure of schema integration is based on the object-oriented approach, but it doesn't require that all the component databases base on the Object Model.

2.2 Language Approach

The interoperability(language) approach places much emphasis on query rather than on integration of schemata[MIS95], [BRI94]. It puts most of the integration responsibility on the user, but alleviates the problem by giving the user many functions to ease the task and providing a great deal of control over the information. In general, the language approach shifts the burden of integration from global DBAs(the global schema approach) to users and local DBAs. The language approach trades a level of data independence (the global schema hides replication, heterogeneity, and location information) for a more dynamic system and greater control over system information. The Summary Schemas Model(SSM) is proposed in Bright's paper[BRI94] as an extension to DDB system to aid in semantic identification. The SSM uses a global data structure to abstract the information available in a DDB system. This abstracted form allows users to use their own terms(imprecise queries) when accessing data rather than being forced to use system-specified terms. The system uses the global data structure to match the user's terms to the semantically closest available system terms. The SSM draws heavily from previous work in large-system user interfaces and in linguistic theory, it does not concern much with the underlying data model of the component databases.

2.3 Comments

The global schema and language approaches are the two extremes of achieving a single logical view of a DODB system. The partial integration approach is between these two extremes[NAV95], [MUH95], [JAM95]. The global schema approach fits tightly into the definition of single logical view of DODB. However, there are some prominent defects of the global schema approach. First, despite the methodologies, algorithms, and heuristics which have been defined to help automate parts of the schema integration process, this process is still very human labour intensive. Second, a global schema can be a very large data object. The sheer size can make it a problem to replicate at nodes with limited storage facilities. The popularity of personal computers and small DBMSs which may want to join the system makes this an important problem. Third, global DBAs must also maintain the global schema in the face of arbitrary(since the local DBMSs are autonomous) changes to local schemas. The literature is largely silent on how this is done. The language approach[BRI94] is an attempt to resolve these problems associated with the global schema approach, but it strays away from our traditional DDB definition. We believe much research work, especially on the semantic resolution of the component ODBs, still needs to be done before the most excellent approach can be found.

3 Distributed Object Management

For a truly distributed network, persistent objects residing in component ODBs require a permanent means of identification that is unique across the networks.

3.1 Object Identity in Network

Objects must be identified uniquely across the entire network. This is crucial for maintaining database integrity and ensuring that proper transaction management can take place. A unique identity across the network ensures that the object can be accessed no matter where it is currently in use. Unique identification of objects is also very important for maintaining different versions of objects. The network-unique identity should include the name of the component ODB, class identifier, object ID(local), creation date and time, and so on. Object identity is assigned on creation and remain unchanged.

3.2 Identical but different objects

Objects may be identical but have different identities, this is quite different from that in a DRDB. When copying an object, the new object may have a unique identifier. This implies that the objects may be identical with respect to all their attributes, but are still different because of a unique identifier. Prefixing an ODB name to the identity achieves this uniqueness for multiple copies of the same object.

3.3 Versioning

Objects may have one or more versions. A version number is stored with each object that is incremented every time an object attribute is updated. When an application requests a local ODBMS to access an object, a message is sent to the object's owner to verify that the local copy is the current version of the object. If the local copy is an older version, the current version is retrieved from the owner. This model of version control ensures that the application programs always operate with the latest version of the object and, to the extent possible, realize a performance benefit from the local copy.

4 Global Query Optimization

An access operation issued by an application can be expressed as a query which references global objects in the global schema(called global query). The DODBMS has to transform this query into simpler queries which refer only to component database objects(called local queries). There should be different ways to transform a global query into local queries which are equivalent in the sense that they produce the same result. Among a set of correct query expressions, selecting one which corresponds to the best value of a specific goal function(e.g. communication cost, data storage cost) is the subject of the optimization of access strategies. However, most of the literature is largely on the DRDB(Distributed Relational Database) side, e.g., [MAR95], few attempts are reported on how these things can be done in a DODB.

4.1 Translation of Global Query to Local Queries

Since there are still no commonly accepted object algebra and object calculus to serve as the formal or mathematical foundation for the design of object query languages and query processing and optimization, the translation of global query to local queries becomes a rather difficult work. There are no equivalence transformation rules as in RDB queries. The most straightforward outline, following the global schema approach, is to provide an additional control component, known as the global controller. The global controller maintains the definition of the global schema and acts as a coordinator and translator: it receives a global query, possibly in a user specific language; translates it into an equivalent query on a common-model query into subqueries to the corresponding local database sites for processing; collects the results; identifies and resolves data content conflicts; reformats the result; and sends it back to the originating site.

4.2 Query Optimization

Query optimization, in both nondistributed as well as distributed environments, has been a subject for significant research and development. AI and expert system techniques have been utilized for query optimization. Primary tasks in query optimization are access path selection for joins and developing an optimal plan for joining data objects. While most research has been performed on optimizing RDBs, query optimization has not been a subject of major importance for ODBs, not mention DODBs.

A query execution plan describes the internal sequence of operations for executing a query. For RDBs, depending on the implementation, it is either in the form of a tree(the leaf nodes are tables and nonleaf nodes are operations), or in a canonical form(e.g., in Ingres). The tree form or the canonical form is created by parsing and compiling the query into the internal representation. This step reduces the query into an abstract view of the high-level operations(such as join, projection, sort and so on). Then, possible low-level processing methods are chosen and all possible plans can be generated. Finally, all possible plans are evaluated and the optimal plan can be formed.

Object databases do not lend themselves easily to traditional approaches to query optimization due to their inherent lack of tightly defined structure. In conventional RDBMSs, AI techniques are often used for query optimization. Even so, it may not be able to relocate data very easily due to the inherently rigid structure of a RDB. This, however, is not so in an ODB. Due to encapsulation, objects have a greater freedom to move. It is just from this point that we believe AI techniques can be of greater value in query optimization of ODBs and DODBs.

5 Conclusion

DODB is a new research topic, the design of a DODB system is not a trivial matter. What we have discussed is only the basic things of the various design issues of a DODB system. Many other aspects, such as transaction management, database administration affairs etc., have to be taken into consideration for the design of a successful DODB system.

References

[AND92] Andleigh, P. K., Gretzinger, M. R.(1992). Distributed Object-oriented Data Systems Design. Englewood Cliffs, N. J., *PTR Prentice Hall.*

[APE88] Apers, P. M. G.(1988). Data allocation in distributed database Systems. ACM Transactions on Database Systems, Vol. 13, No. 3, pp. 263-304.

[BER89] Bertino, E., Negri, M., Pelagatti, G.. Sbatella(1989). An object-oriented approach to the interconnection of heterogeneous databases. NSF Workshop on Heterogeneous Databases, Evanston, IL, 1989.

[BRI94] Bright, M. W., Hurson, A. R., Pakzad, S.(1994). Automated Resolution of Semantic Heterogeneity in Multidatabases. ACM Transactions on Database Systems, Vol. 19, No. 2, June 1994, pp. 212-253.

[CER84] Ceri, S., Pelagatti, G.(1984). Distributed Databases: Principles and Systems. *McGraw-Hill Book Company.*

[DAT87] Date, C. J.(1987). Twelve Rules for a distributed Data Base. Computerworld, June 8, 1987.

[GAR95] Garcia-Solaco, M., Saltor F. and Castellanos, M.(1995). Extensional Issues in Schema Integration. Proceedings of the 6th international Hong Kong Computer Society Database workshop, Database Reengineering and Interoperability, Kowloon, Hong Kong, March 1995.

[JAM95] James, E. A.(1995). A Database Integration System and an Example of its Application. Proceedings of the 6th International Hong Kong Computer Society Database Workshop, Kownloon, Hong Kong, March 1995.

[KAM95] Kamel, M.(1995). Identifying, Classifying, and Resolving Semantic Conflicts in Distributed Heterogeneous Databases: A Case Study. Journal of Database Management, Vol. 6, No. 1, Winter 1995.

[KOH93] Koh, J.-L., Chen, A.L.P.(1993). Integration of Heterogeneous Object Schemas. Proceedings of the 12th International Conference on Entity-Relationship Approach, December 1993.

[MAR95] March, S. T., Rho, S.(1995). Allocating Data and Operations to Nodes in Distributed Database Design. IEEE Transactions on Knowledge and Data Engineering, Vol. 7, No. 2, April 1995.

[MIS95] Missier, P., Rusinkiewicz, M., Silberschatz, A.(1995). Providing Multidatabase Access -- an Association Approach. Proceedings of the 6th international Hong Kong Computer Society Database workshop, Database Reengineering and Interoperability, March 1995.

[MUH95] Muhlberger, R. M., Orlowska, M. E.(1995). A Business Process Driven Multidatabase Integration Methodology. Proceedings of the 6th international Hong Kong Computer Society Database workshop, Database Reengineering and Interoperability, March 1995.

[NAV95] Navathe, S. B., Donahoo M. J.(1995). Towards Intelligent Integration of Heterogeneous Information Sources. Proceedings of the 6th international Hong Kong Computer Society Database workshop, Database Reengineering and Interoperability, March 1995.

[RED94] Reddy, M. P., Prasad, B. E., Reddy, P. G., Gupta, A.(1994). A Methodology for Integration of Heterogeneous Databases. IEEE Transactions on Knowledge and Data Engineering, Vol. 6, No. 6, December 1994.

[SUZ95] Suzuki, G., Yamamuro, M.(1995). Schema Integration Methodology Including Structural Conflict Resolution and Checking Conceptual Similarity - Conceptual Graphs Approach Proceedings of the 6th international Hong Kong Computer Society Database workshop, Database Reengineering and Interoperability, March 1995.

[TOW95] Towell, E., Haseman, W. D.(1995). Semantic Resolution in Multi-Database Environments, Journal of Database Management, Vol. 6, No.3, Summer 1995.

A Case Study on the Capability on Object-oriented Database under UNISQL

Pong Chee Hoi
IBM China/Hong Kong
Corporation
E-Mail: apong@vnet.ibm.com

Abstract

The project report summerizes a studying on the possibility, pros and cons of migrating the Business systems of EPSON HONG LIMITED from a relational database to an Object-oriented database (UNISQL). Base on these hands-on experience, I comment UNISQL's features with reference to Object-oriented standards. listing both its strengths and weakness; I also point out some suggestions for the later version of UNISQL and draw the following conclusions: although UNISQL is not mature, it has many potential advantages, and therefore conversion of EPSON database from relational model to Object-oriented model should be carried out as soon as possible.

1. Introduction

Epson Hong Kong Limited (EHK) is primarily in the business of trading EPSON computer, printer products and electronics. EHK has experienced rapid growth over the past few years and have recognize a need for improvement on their existing information systems in order to support the continued growth in the coming years.

As object-oriented data model allows the representation of not only data, and relationships and constraints on that data, as the relational data model does[ELM89]; but also the encapsulation of data and programs that operate on the data, and provides a uniform framework for the treatment of arbitrary user defined data types. Using the data modeling tools available within Objected-oriented database (OODB), users can define, store, and manipulate multi-media data, including audio, Video, and images[COY91] [THU92]. Since, there are some who say that OODB will eventually replace relational database for most application, I was commissioned by EDP manager to take Sale and Distribution system as the pilot-runner to evaluate them in terms of advantages and disadvantages of an Object-oriented approach.

By examining the fundamentals and motivations behind this pilot project, this report outlines some of the major design and implementation issues involved under UNISQL environment. Once design issues are discussed , object-oriented models are implemented. This project also describes how to interact with the UniSQL/X databases. This interaction including how to create database objects, how to modify the database schema, and how to manage data. In addition, this report will contained the evaluation on the degree of confirmation for UNISQL to the standard of Object-oriented database. As a conclusion, solution and suggestion for Epson's project on UNISQL will be discussed. The major tasks of this project includes,

a) Study the theory of Object-oriented (OO) database approach;
b) Design the database schema in OO approach;
c) Implement the database on the UNISQL platform;
d) Evaluate the pros and cons of OO approach based on the on-hands experience;
e) Built user interface for order maintenance to demonstrate that OO-database is extremely suitable for processing of multi-media data, including audio and video information.

2. Features of Object Oriented Database

The basic building blocks of an object-oriented Database are objects. A Database is divided into sets of interacting objects. Objects are abstractions of elements in a problem domain and are designed to reflect their behavior. OODB contains the following features:

2.1 Object Identity

Object Identity is used to distinguish objects regardless of their characteristics or physical location and to facilitate sharing of object. Most of the conventional DBMS, including DBMS, requires that each record instance be uniquely identified by content.

2.2 Object Typing

Object Typing is the ability to define new object types and to create associate objects with one or more object types (whole-part) support for object instances and classes;

2.3 Inheritance

Inheritance supports for Generalization and Specialization Hierarchy : the ability to define subtypes and supertypes so that subtypes inherit the attributes and operations of their supertypes (specialization of operations with data).

2.4 Encapsulation

Recognizing the need for a specific set of operators to be defined for each complex object type, a number of database systems allow the definition of a new object type not only to give the structure of that class of object, but also to define the set of operators with which the user can access and manipulate such objects. We can say that the operators are encapsulated with the structural definition of the object. By ensuring that the defined methods for an object providing the only way to access that object, we build an interface to the object which is user defined, specific to each class of object, and hides the implementation of the object from users of the object.

2.5 Whole-part relationship

Composite objects can be reflect by whole part relationship.

2.6 Object sharing

Object sharing is the capability of different object to share parts of their contents. Reduce storage overhead and maintain data integrity

2.7 Handling bulky data

OODB support for multimedia data, i.e. ability to capturing, storing, and manipulating multimedia data.

2.8 Abstraction

When modeling abstract object, many system systems ignore the internal structure of the objects completely and hide the internal structure of the object within an attributes of that object. Specific advantages which arise from direct support for abstraction (the ability to devise a model a model of a problem in terms of the data items and operators which are most suited to our needs) include: Data hiding, Data independence, Modularity and reusability.

3. Overall Relationship amongst Epson Order Processing Objects

After Object-oriented Analysis [COA91a] [COA91B], a set of objects are identified to be important for EPSON's order and Distribution System. Figure 1 defines the overall relationship between these objects in this mini-project [BRA93] [BRO91]. The relationship between <Vendors>, <Customers> and <Companys> is generalization and specification (GS). Class <Vendors> inherits all the arrtibutes and methods of class <Companys> in addition to its features such as *AmtReceivable*. Class <Customers> encounter the similar situation as <Vendors>.

<BusinessPartners> are the companys who perform both purchasing and selling business activities with EPSON. Therefore, its has 2 parents and inherit all the properties for <Vendors> and <Customers>. This phenomenon is named as **Multiple-Inheritance** and the relation between <BusinessPartners> and its parents is also a **generalization-specification** relation.

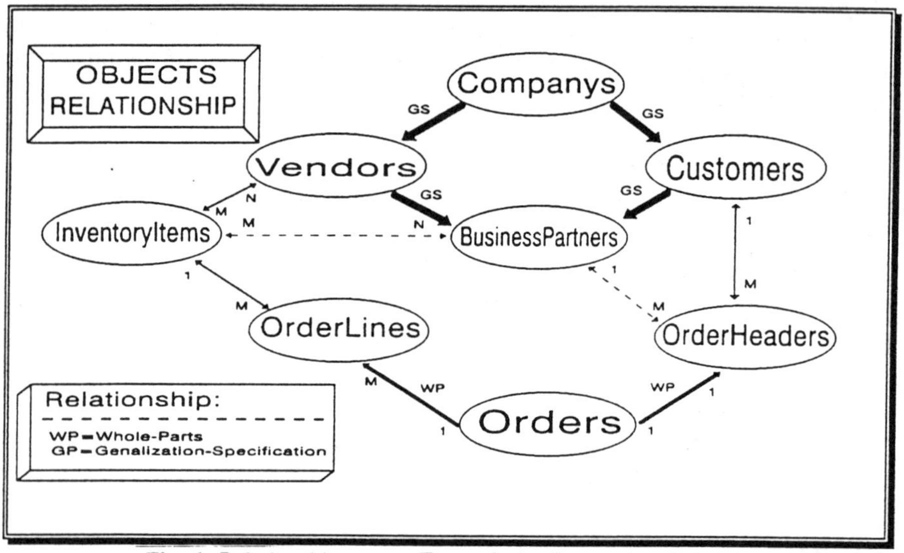

Fig. 1: Relationship among Epson Order Processing Objects

Each vendor supplies a list of stock items. On the other hand, each stock item can has a number of suppliers, thus there is a many-to-many relationship between <Vendors> and <InventoryItems>. Since <BusinessPartners> is a specification of <Vendors>, Many-to-Many is hold indirectly between them.

Each order can simply be divided into 2 parts: **Order Header** and **Order Details.** Order Header contains the general information about an order, such as order date, customer code, term and currency, etc. Order Details contains *a set* of order lines. Each order line contains one item information of to be ordered, including the item number, quantity, unit price and status. Hence, there is a **Whole-Part** relationship between <Orders> and its sons: <OrderHeaders> and <orderLines>.

Since each <OrderLines> can only contain one inventoryItem, and the same <InventoryItems> instances can be included in many <OrderLines> instances, the relationship between <InvemtoryItems> and <OrderLines> is 1-to-many.

Also, each order only contain 1 customer normally, but each customer can issue multiple orders, the relationship between <OrderHeaders> and <Customers> is 1-to-many. <BusinessPartners> and <OrderHeaders> also has the same 1-to-many relationship since <BusinessPartners> is a specification of class <Customers>.

4. Hands-on experience through case study of UNISQL

OODB has a list of features, including Generalization-Specification relationship, Whole-Part relationship, multiple inheritance, method implementation, Trigger definition, multi-media information handling capability, etc. My hands-on experiences on these features on UNISQL [HUG91] [UNI93A] [UNI93B] will be discussed below:

4.1 Support for generalization/Specification Hierarchy

The generalization/Specification hierarchy is used to define the type, subtype, and the type relationships between various entities. Within **Gen-Spec Structures**, inheritance applies, with an explicit representation of more general Attributes and Services followed by pertinent specialization's. Refer to Epson's model, class <Companys> is a generalization of class <Customers> and <Vendors>, while <Customers> and <Vendors> is the specification of class <Companys>. As a result, <Customers> and <Vendors> inherit all the attributes and methods owned by <Companys>. Moreover, they have their own specialized features in addition to their parent, <Companys>.

4.2 Support for Composite Objects

Any class which has a composite instance variable is a composite class. The instances belonging to such a class are composite object together with its components forms a hierarchy called the **IS-PART-OF (composite)** hierarchy. The link from a composite object to its components is called a **composite link**. All these included objects are grouped together to form a the composite object. This relationship is named as Whole-part relationship. In Epson's case, Class <Orders> is a composite object. It contains attribute OrderNo, sub-class object <OrderHeaders> as well as a set of <orderLines>.

4.3 Multiple Inheritance:

To demonstrate the capability of implementation of multiple inheritance under UNISQL, I create a new class <BusinessPartners> which **inherits** all the properties of Class <Customers> and <Vendors>. The new class has one additional attributes <Balance>, where <Balance> = <AmtReceivable> - <AmtPayable>. Since <BusinessPartners> has 2 superclasses, it has inherited the some attributes from its parents more than once. Since the common attributes are of the same domain, a resolution must be specified with the INHERIT clause.

4.4 Flexibility on Alternating the definition of object classes

Theoretically, it is easy and flexible for us to make dynamic changes to the schema in OODB. Changes to the schema will often involve modifying the definition and/or inheritance hierarchy of existing classes. UNISQL provides ALTER statement for us to add, drop, or change the attributes, methods and triggers in a class, or to establish or remove a superclass link.

4.5 Object Instantiation

UNISQL does not provides means for instance sharing. Object with Whole-part relationship is instantiated by means of nested INSERT. The instantiation for UNISQL sometimes result in data duplication. Since data redundancy always lead to waste of disk space, difficulty of updating and weakness of data referential integrity.

4.6 Method

Under UNISQL, methods are software routines that you can write to extend or customize the functionality of the Object-Oriented database system. This software routines are actually programs that are written in C and are invoked by the UniSQL/X CALL or EVALUATE statements. In addition, we can also invoke a method indirectly by executing a SQL query statement. When a method is invoked, the program is loaded and **dynamically linked** with the running application by the dynamic loader. The method is then executed and any values that are generated by the method are returned to the caller.

The SQL/X language supports two types of methods: **class methods** and **instance methods**. Inheritance rules for methods are similar to the inheritance rules for attributes. A subclass inherits class and instance methods from its superclasses. A Subclass may shadow the definition of a class or instance method from its superclasses. Conflict resolution rules for method names are the same as the conflict resolution rules for names of attributes.

4.7 Trigger

A **Trigger** is a system object that provides a mechanism for the insertion of user-defined operations during the processing of a database request. The following list highlights some of the ways in which triggers are commonly used:

- notify that an event has taken place
- prevent unauthorized access to a class.
- perform cascading deletes
- gather and maintain statistics
- assign circular references
- perform parallel updates
- enforce integrity constraints and session constraints

A trigger can alter a user request or it can simply record information. When a constraint is being violated, a trigger can change the behavior of the offending request. If a trigger is used to gather session statistics, it simply records information with altering the user request.

4.8 Disjoint/Overlapping Specification

Disjointness Specification specifies that the subclasses of the specialization must be disjoint. This means that an entity can be a member of at most one of the subclasses of the specialization. If the subclasses are not disjoint, their sets of entities may overlap; that is, the same entity may be a member of more than one subclass of the specialization. To demonstrate the properties of **Disjoint and Overlapping Specification,** I modified the relationship among Epson's classes to include objects: <ServiceProviders>, <ServiceLines> and <ItemLines>:

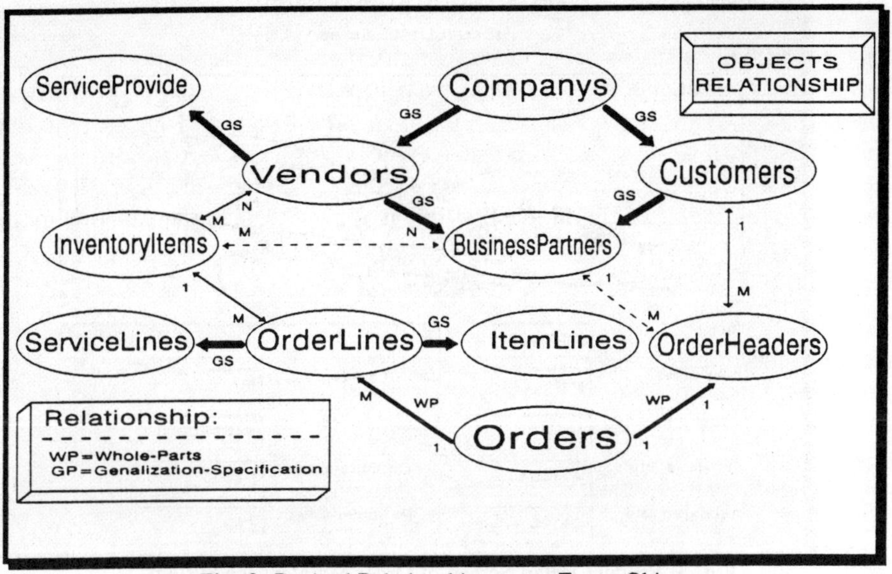

Fig. 2: Revised Relationship among Epson Objects

4.8.1 Overlapped Specification:

In EPSON case, relationship between <BusinessPartners> and <ServiceProviders> is a **overlapped specialization** of superclass <Vendors>. Actually, both of them are specialization of <Vendors> and own all the properties of their parent class. <BusinessPartners> is specialized in that its instance also contains all the properties of <Customers>. Therefore, they can acts as both Vendors and Customers. On the other hand, <ServiceProviders> are <Vendors> who can only provide services. Since a instance of <BusinessPartners> can also be an instance of <ServiceProviders>, this is a **Overlapping Specification.**

4.8.2 Disjoint Specification:

On the hand, every order line can be a **service line** with description and amount, or a **item line** with item no and quantity. To demonstrate this property, I restructure the <OrderLines> schema to include 2 subclasses : <ServiceLines> and <ItemLines>. So, an instance of <OrderLines> can either an instance of <ServiceLines> or an instance of <ItemLines>, **but not** both. This is a typical example of **Disjointness specification.**

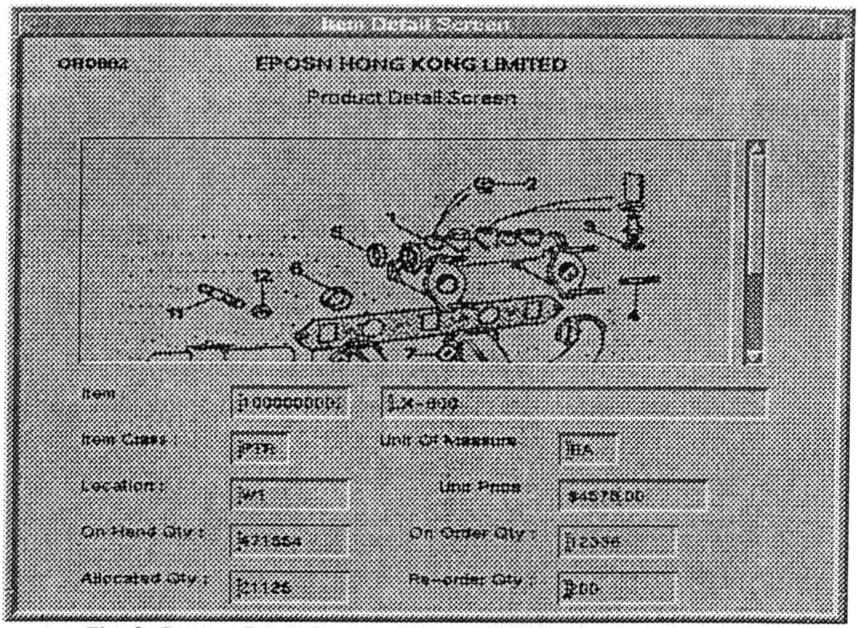

Fig. 3: Product Detail Screen of Order Maintenance System

4.9 Support for Multimedia Data

A major requirement for object-oriented database is the representation of **multimedia** data. This will include extensibility, where new multimedia device as well as new functions on multimedia information can be incorporated with ease. The fundamental building block of multimedia support is the **Generalized Large Object** (**GLO**) class. GLOs allow many different types of unstructured data to be saved in the database. In addition, An **Agent** class exists to enhance the functionality of GLOs and support interaction with data-producing programs. Creating objects with multimedia data has been discussed on section <Object Instantiation>. Now, to demonstrate the capability of UNISQL in handling multimedia information, I have built an application using **Object Master** which facilitate user to carry out order maintenance. User can use this application to browse orders including multimedia data, such as Order Delivery Instruction and Photos of items. Object Master is a tool provided by UniSQL that allow user to rapidly develop database applications with a minimum of traditional coding. It accomplishes this by accelerating the tasks of:

- application organization and assembly;
- user interface development
- multi-media manipulation

As an example, this window shows the **product name, item number, price, and description** for the product that is highlighted in the table in the main window. An image of the product is also displayed. Changes made to this information automatically update the same information in the main window.

5. Conclusion

The objective of this mini-project is studying the pros and cons on migration Epson's information system from relational database into Object-oriented database. After the project, I found that Object-oriented approach is more superior than relational approach for multimedia information management (data structure, method). The object-oriented database is efficient on storage and manipulation of large objects and multimedia data such as text, image, voice, graphics and video. In addition, users can also periodically update the multimedia database so that information contained in it accurately reflects the real world.

The cornerstone of the object-oriented database is that it provides a more natural way to model many real world situations. The important point here is that the model obtained by using an object-oriented approach will be a more direct representation of the situation, providing a better framework for understanding and manipulating of complex relationships which may exist. Object-oriented development methodologies can facilitate the production of high quality systems of increasing complexity.

UniSQL owns most of the Object-oriented database features. For example, I have experienced the creation of classes and instantiation of objects. UniSQL provides flexibility for us to create class and object in different environments, such as under command mode and interactive mode. The corresponding query statement can be saved and reused later.

In addition, UniSQL supports Whole-Part (IS-PART-OF) relationship. In addition, UniSQL supports Generalization-Specification relationship by means of inheritances. UniSQL also allows multiple inheritance that a class has more than one superclasses. Moreover, UniSQL also facilitate user to define Overlapping specification and Disjoint specification.

Besides, UniSQL provides Trigger function for insertion of user-defined operations during the processing of a database request. Method is a must for OODB. UniSQL provides method by C routines

To demonstrate UniSQL has the capability in handling multi-media information, I have created an Order Maintenance System using Object Master for user to browse and update order information. This application has the ability to handle multimedia data such as product image and delivery handling message. UniSQL can also supports many conventional database features. For example, I has found out UniSQL allowing one-to-one, one-to-many and many-to-many relationship between different objects. Under UniSQL, we also can alternate the definition of created classes easily. We add\change\delete new attributes, methods, superclasses, subclass, triggers as well as constraints any time we liked. In addition, Object instance of the updated classes will be automatically carry out data conversion.

Although Object-oriented database is better than relational database, the cited advantages are balanced by corresponding limitations and drawbacks. The limitations outlined before included:

No formal semantics. A great attraction of the relational data model is that it has a sound mathematical basis;

Loss of relational simplicity. One of the attractions of relational database systems is that the model of data which is supported is sufficiently simple to allow end users to defines their own database schema, or to write simple queries;

No general query language. An important requirement of many design applications is support for general as hoc queries

In this mini-project, I have got some hands-on experiences on UniSQL. UniSQL is claimed to be an Object-oriented database. However, I am not hundred percent agree with this declaration. I feel that UniSQL is not a truly Object-oriented database. Indeed, it is a unified version of relational and object oriented data model built on the platform of a relational database. In other word, UNISQL is the extension of relational database, with query language enhance to manipulate the data item.

It is also cumbersome to update/insert the multi-media data, such as audio, video information. Although the most common data manipulation language in UNISQL is SQL, however, it is very inconvenient that we cannot use SQL to display multimedia data. One possible solution is to attempt to modify SQL by providing extensions to the language in order to accommodate multimedia information. This approach has two possible problems. First, can SQL syntax be modified to accommodate multimedia information and not violate relational theory? Second, assuming it can be adequately modified, how long will it take to develop agreement on the new syntax standards, and what does one do in the meantime?

Anyway, after the hands-on experience on this mini-project, I found that Extending a conventional relational DBMS to include objected-oriented concepts is possible. Base on my hands-on experience and research study, even though UniSQL is not a truly Object-oriented database, I think UNISQL has confirmed the Object-oriented standards to a large extend. Although UNISQL is not mature, it is have many potential advantages and the conversion of EPSON database from relational model to Object-oriented model is highly recommended and should be carried out as soon as possible.

Bibliographic References

[ELM89] R. A., Elmasri, and S.B., Navathe, *Fundamentals of Database Systems*. The Benjamin/Cummings Publishing Company, Inc [1989]

[COY91] J. P. Coyne, *Relational databases and Multimedia Repositories*, MultiMedia Review,[Fall, 1991]

[THU92] B. Thuraisingham, *On Developing Multmedia Database Management System Using the Object-Oriented Approach,* MultiMedia Review, Vol3:No 2, [Summer 1992]

[UNI93a] UniSql/X Database Management System User Manual, UniSQL Inc., [1993]

[UNI93b] UniSql/X Database Management System Object Master Manual, UniSQL Inc., [1993]

[HUG91] J. G. Hughes, *Object-Oriented Databases*, Prentice Hall, [1991]

[COA91a] P. Coad and E. Yourdon, *Object-Oriented Analysis*, Prentice Hall, [1991 2nd Ed]

[COA91b] P. Coad and E. Yourdon, *Object-Oriented Design*, Prentice Hall, [1991 2nd Ed]

[BRA93] K. S. Brathwaite, *Object-Oriented Database Design - Concepts and Application*, Academic Press, [1993]

[BRO91] A. W. Brown, *Object-Oriented Databases - Applications in Software Engineering*, McGRAW Hill International [1991]

Building The Virtual Enterprise With OO Technology

Stuart Seow
Computer Associates International Limited
Hong Kong

Abstract

Object oriented technology is becoming increasingly important in the new generations of applications that are emerging. Companies are assessing the Internet as a way to bypass traditional infrastructures that add cost to products and prevent them from forging bonding relationships with clients. Object oriented web-enabled tools, multi-media authoring and browser-centric tools and ODBMSs are technologies that are in demand to enable these companies to process and display information in highly original ways. This paper discusses current trends in object oriented technologies and presents a real world implementation which integrates these technologies for the development and deployment of networked multimedia business applications.

Introduction

The use of database information technology has rapidly evolved from supporting back office administration to providing the foundation for mission-critical enterprise systems. The very landscape of computing is changing with a new class of applications emerging. Applications in the networked client/server environment are placing unprecedented demands on the database management systems that support them. New technologies are needed to support the changing application landscape. Databases need to have unprecedented flexibility, power, speed and robustness.

While the current database market is centered around relational technology, most agree that the future for object database technology is tremendous because it allows us to better represent the real world. Traditional database technology is very good at handling classical data — small amounts of text, numbers, date and time values — organized in tabular structures. The relational systems were designed to satisfy the requirements of traditional business management systems. The way they describe data, in the form of tables, corresponds well to the type of data manipulated by these applications. Other technologies such as free-text retrieval systems and document image processing systems have emerged to handle information that is less rigidly structured. However, in many specialised applications, none of these technologies have proved suitable so application designers have traditionally crafted their own data management solutions.

The pace of object orientation adoption has increased dramatically in the past year. Surveys have shown significant increases in the number of organisations with production object oriented systems, as well as a similar increase in organisations having immediate plans to adopt object orientation. The object-oriented paradigm for program construction builds on the simple premise that software organized along modular, self-contained "objects" is more maintainable, extensible and reusable than the conventional "action-oriented" approach where software is divided around procedural lines. Instead of concentrating on what functions need to be performed, the focus is shifted to the entities on which functions have to be performed. The object-oriented design methodology leads to an architecture that is based on objects every system or subsystem manipulates. With the simultaneous decrease in the cost of hardware and increase in the power of machines, new applications which handle real world data have appeared. The emergence of graphics workstations with multimedia capability interconnected by local networks has resulted in distributed processing and user interfaces that are more friendly. In the new world, data needs behavior in the form of methods, to allow binary information to represent business processes. We need to manage new data types, arranged in new structures. The object oriented paradigm for software construction can be applied just as effectively to a database management system. The only difference is that in the database management system, the objects in question are persistent and outlast the invocation of any individual program.

Why are object databases needed?

There are two main categories of database applications: those that involve storing large amounts of static data, such as parts information in an inventory system, and those that are process-intensive and involve complex dynamic data, such as engineering data, where the structure of the data is intertwined closely with the structure of the program. Traditional (relational and hierarchical) databases are well equipped to manage static data for relatively simple applications where the structure of the data remains mostly static after the data analysis. In such applications, once the database has been set up, the schema does not evolve much over time. Relational databases are designed so that there is a strict separation between data and programs that use the data and they provide data persistence, mechanisms for data sharing, and data security. For applications where the schema of the data is likely to change, and where the data are complex or n-dimensional, conventional databases are usually not flexible enough or efficient enough. Such is the case in research environments where the goal is to design new systems. In these environments the design process is iterative, causing both the structure of the data (schema) and the structure of the program to evolve over time. Design systems typically build objects from other objects. Tthey need multiple levels of abstraction consisting of multiple components and need to be able to look into these components. The design task is shared among several designers. Designer will be modifying a certain part of the design and referring to the surrounding parts; there is a need to share component designs, and also to note that this sharing follows a certain pattern.

Object-oriented databases (OODB) are systems that can be used to store and retrieve objects and to provide facilities to manipulate stored objects. OODBs make it possible to store in a database a complete object as it exists in memory, without having to change the structure and representation of the object. It is possible to store and retrieve complex objects. One of the benefits of an OODB is the ability to build into the database knowledge about the data it contains, about data interrelationships, and about operations on the data. Objects can be related to other objects through inheritance, link, and embedded relationships. OODBs have the ability to maintain relationships between objects once these relationships have been established. Client applications accessing an ODBMS do not have to specify the relationships because they already exist in the database. The strengths of ODBMS can be summarised as follows:

- Suitability when data and relationships are irregular and complex
- Tightly coupled, relatively transparent object oriented programming language interfaces
- Designed to take advantage of PC/workstation architectures, in terms of local memory and disk
- Integration of non-DBMS data sources and applications

Clients of OODBs tend to have complex, evolutionary sets of data. Examples are knowledge-based systems, CAD/CAM design systems, program support environments and CASE tools. Typically these applications generate a lot of graphical information which creates problems with relational databases. It is not of course true that all multimedia applications need an object database. For example, to store photographs of people in a simple personnel file, a relational database with so-called *binary large objects* (blobs) might be quite satisfactory. Equally, a straightforward library of sound or video recordings might be held quite adequately in operating system filestore. An object database comes into its own when the same multimedia object is accessed, referenced or published in many different ways, and when a variety of different media are encountered in the same system.

Jasmine

In January 1996, Computer Associates announced Jasmine, a breakthrough technology for easy development and deployment of networked multimedia business applications, which combines world-class object database technology with a revolutionary multi-media application development environment. Jasmine is the first and only industrial strength object-oriented database that features a multi-media, Internet/Intranet-enabled application development system. Jasmine represents the next generation in database technology. By enabling companies to process and display information in highly original ways, Jasmine spurs customer demand, lowers development costs, and provides managers with the flexibility to respond to the most daunting business challenges.

Jasmine is a complete turnkey operation designed to meet rigorous time-to-market schedules. Whether you represent business data with a multimedia interface, build business logic, or store complex data in the database system, Jasmine is consistently object-oriented. This is important because objects can be engineered once and reused again and again, enabling the rapid creation and distribution of increasingly complex applications. Adapting these systems to meet changing business requirements is also easy because only the affected building blocks need to be altered. This eliminates the need to rewrite large amounts of the application, and permits the creation of highly flexible business systems.

Object-Oriented Database Engine

Jasmine's object-oriented database engine provides the robust foundation needed for multimedia applications on the Internet, and for electronic commerce specifically. It provides the integrity, security, transaction management and performance of an industrial-strength database. Object-oriented database technology is particularly well suited to handling the complex data structures and large data volumes required for today's multimedia applications. Unlike the unstructured blobs indiscriminately added to relational databases, the object system understands the inherent structure in large objects like video, sound and images, and provides facilities for analysing and processing the data.

Jasmine provides all the capabilities expected in a modern object-oriented database:

- Multiple inheritance
- Instance properties and class properties
- Instance methods and class methods
- Native support for sets with set-level methods

Methods are defined in a rich object-oriented language with native syntax for processing database objects, searching the database and navigating sets. This removes any barrier between programming and the database: methods operate in the database under the full control of the transaction and security management systems. Jasmine supports methods written in C or C++, leveraging existing expertise and allowing for recycling of existing logic. Jasmine will also provide support for writing methods in Java, the language emerging as one of the premier forces for Internet application development.

Jasmine includes an extensive class library with support for multimedia data and other complex data types, including images, frame animation sequences, audio of different types, video of different types, rich text and page layouts. Useful by themselves, the built-in classes also provide a foundation for extensibility, as the parent for derived classes designed for specific application needs. In addition to the foundation classes provided by Computer Associates, third-party developers will also provide several class libraries to provide a broad foundation for application development.

Most organisations today have large investments in applications using relational databases, and many also have hierarchical or Codasyl databases or indexed-sequential files. Some have extensive text or image databases. The idea of integrating all this data into a single central database has long been abandoned: the different systems have to coexist and have to interchange information with each other.

Jasmine provides integral support for legacy databases, including relational systems such as CA-OpenIngres, Oracle, Sybase, Informix and SQLServer, as well as mainframe databases including CA-IDMS, CA-Datacom and DB2. By presenting legacy data as objects, this integration allows methods of Jasmine objects to seamlessly refer to data used in existing business applications, ensuring that new applications can be deployed without requiring the reengineering of the entire business. Jasmine integrates especially closely with CA-OpenIngres, providing seamless transaction management, security management and replication management across CA-OpenIngres and Jasmine data.

Multimedia is fine for end-user applications, but utility functions -- maintaining inventory, setting prices, publishing catalogues, dispatching shipments -- often need to access the database from standard programming languages, using standard client server connectivity architectures. The Jasmine database provides APIs for access from C, C++ and Smalltalk. OLE controls (OCXs) also open the database to Visual Basic and other development systems that support OLE.

Jasmine provides an automatic HTML renderer that provides text and form access to Jasmine objects, their links and methods from a standard Web browser. While less powerful than the multimedia Jasmine plug-in, the HTML renderer does permit customisation of the appearance with templates designed with HTML authoring tools.

Application Development Environment

Jasmine provides an integrated application development environment for visual, object-oriented, multimedia authoring with an extensive collection of multimedia classes, including image processing, advanced video, sound, algorithmically generated background music, and voice recognition. The system provides tools for browsing and editing the classes and objects in the database, and for creating and editing multimedia applications.

The Class Browser is used for defining and editing classes and their methods. It visually presents all the classes in the database, and their inheritance relationships, properties and methods. The database stores objects of all classes, both those that can visualise themselves in multimedia applications and those that are used as hidden "back room" objects. The method editor is used to define the methods -- programs that belong to a class and execute on the server. The methods are defined with a rich object-oriented programming language that provides all the facilities expected in a modern development system, including built-in support for navigating object collections.

The Object Browser provides for inspecting, defining and editing objects in the database. It presents all properties of an object in a visual interface, including references to other objects; multimedia properties are displayed graphically. Multimedia objects contain many types of multimedia properties: photographs of products, testimonials from clients, explanations of how to install or use a component, engineering drawings, and sales pitches. The Object Browser includes a "resource wrangler" with a simple drag-and-drop interface for storing multimedia resources - images, animation sequences, video, and audio.

When developing an application, you create scenes by arranging objects. The user can interact with the objects; objects can play sounds, videos and animations; and the application can transition from scene to scene. The objects, both passive objects like backgrounds and furniture, and active objects like the boots, saddle and cowboy in the scene above, have their own properties and behaviour, and can take action both within the client-side multimedia application and on the server by executing methods.

All the classes, objects and queries are shown in an Add Object window. You place them by simply dragging them onto the scene. Placing a specific object in a scene is useful for furniture, backgrounds, interactive controls such as buttons, and special services such as a shopping cart or checkout counter. Placing a class or query in the scene is used for dynamic situations when the application needs to show many objects, for example when browsing a product catalogue.

The behaviour of an object -- how it responds to user interaction, database messages and other events - is defined in terms of a simple event-action metaphor, requiring no scripting. Events include everything from mouse clicks to "lingering" mouse pointers, timers going off, animation and video starting or ending, and messages sent from other objects. Objects can take many kinds of actions, including showing graphics, playing animation, audio or video, changing the scene, and sending messages to other objects. For objects of a class with methods defined in the database, executing a server-side method and responding to its result is as easy as playing a video or starting an animation. Actions can refer directly to methods and properties of the object itself as well as other objects in the database.

The system also provides expression evaluation, conditional logic and looping whenever more complex user interaction requires it. But really complex business logic does not belong in the multimedia front-end; it is done in server-side methods with all the power and robustness of the object-oriented server and its object-oriented language. The Jasmine execution environment provides the framework for running the client side of the applications: it controls animation and multimedia, co-ordinates user interaction with internal activities, handles the timely retrieval of multimedia resources from the database and communicates with the server for method execution.

The execution environment can operate in two modes. In standalone mode the multimedia application executes on the computer like any other client/server application. This mode is most often used to create a unique environment for the user, presenting a self-contained environment for a special purpose. Common applications include electronic catalogues on CD-ROM and kiosk systems. In this configuration, the execution environment communicates with the server through any communications protocol available. In integrated mode as a plug-in in a Web browser, the Jasmine execution environment allows the multimedia application to be used as an "applet" within an HTML page. Web-based multimedia applets may be used for anything from simple "eye candy," animation used for excitement or entertainment, to sophisticated electronic commerce. In this configuration, the execution environment communicates through HTTP, the standard protocol underlying the Web. Unlike some of the early Web plug-ins, Jasmine does not require downloading of large monolithic animation files: its communication with the server is optimised for incremental download to minimise bandwidth demands and exploit the caching mechanisms of Web browsers, proxies and servers. In either case - when operating standalone or as a browser plug-in -- the Jasmine execution environment may be controlled from the outside. Web browsers with JavaScript or VBScript will be able to interact with the Jasmine multimedia applet, and other applications written in Visual Basic or other OLE-enabled languages can also access and control the Jasmine execution system.

Summary

Until now, there has been hesitation to move to object database systems because of the unclear pathway for evolution. Many commercial ODBMS suffer from scalability issues, lack of support for industry standards and lack of performance to support design and development of large-scale systems. Revolutionizing information technology, Jasmine delivers the first and only industrial-strength object-oriented database that features a multimedia, Internet/Intranet-enabled application development system. Jasmine is unique because of the synergy afforded by its many features. It exploits the countless opportunities to integrate the Internet (or the company Intranet) with a broad array of business strategies, functions and technologies. Jasmine is complete and because all functions are seamlessly integrated in a cohesive, visual fashion, Jasmine significantly boosts a programmer's productivity. Developers can easily build applications that mirror the complexities of day-to-day business activities. Jasmine, which combines business processes and data into a cohesive object model, allows developers to solve high-level problems simply by assembling pluggable components into solutions. Built on a foundation of proven technologies from Computer Associates and Fujitsu, Jasmine applications inherently exhibit the high standards of integrity, reliability and performance that mission-critical business functions demand.

DRDA Implementation

Aaron K.D. Sze
Information Technology Services Dept.,
Hong Kong Government,
15/F, Wanchai Tower,
Harbour Road,
Hong Kong.

1. Introduction

The acronym DRDA stands for Distributed Relational Database Architecture. It is a set of open protocols from IBM that software developers can follow to develop solutions for accessing the distributed relational data on like or unlike platforms operating on machines of the same or different make. DRDA supports the standard Structured Query Language (SQL) to provide easy access to the connected systems. And among these connected systems, DRDA coordinates the communications.

A large project was in need of a system which could integrate their existing databases and provide many other new functions. During the planning stage of the new project, it was determined that a client/server based application rather than the traditional host based CICS/DB2 application is most suitable.

So, why client/server and DRDA? First of all, the users' data involve a large amount of information presented in Chinese characters which could be well handled by a PC with a Chinese operating environment like Chinese Windows. Secondly, a Windows based application could integrate with the users' Office Automation (OA) environment. The availability of development tools which allow for fast development also favour the choice of client/server.

For DRDA, its efficiency was the major reason why it was adopted. For many middleware products, the data are translated into an intermediate format, which is independent of platforms, before transmission. On the receiving end, the data are translated from their intermediate format to the target format after having been received. Substantial overheads could be induced by doing so. However, for DRDA, the sender does not perform any translation. It is the responsibility of the receiver to carry out the translation to an acceptable form when necessary.

The DRDA application to be discussed is an online system consists of

i) PC clients running Chinese Windows;
ii) DRDA gateway running on UNIX platform; and
iii) DB2 running on MVS host.

(See Figure 1.)

All of the presentations and application logic reside on the PC while all of the data reside on the host, except for some static data such as code tables.

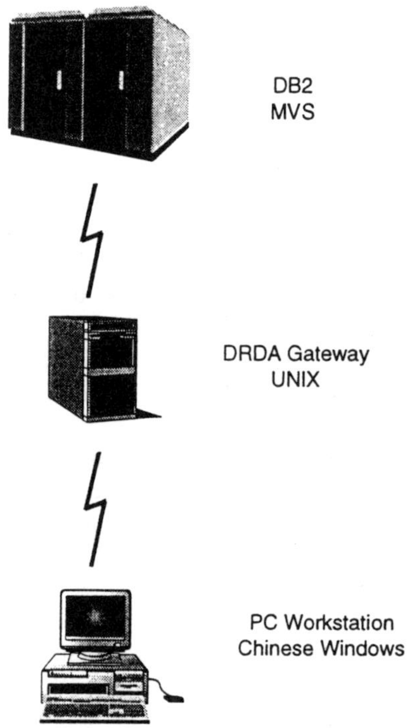

Fig. 1. DRDA Project Environment

So, according to the Gartner Group, our application should be classified as Remote Data Management even though DRDA actually supports Distributed Database applications. (See Figure 2.)

2. User Authentication

In the DOS environment of the PC clients, there is no product to manage users and groups locally. So, the authentication is done at 'Connect' time. The user needs to issue a 'Connect' statement to the DRDA software with the user id and password to establish his/her identity. But where the user id and password validation is performed depends on how the database is defined at the DRDA gateway and client workstations.

For our application, the user id/password are captured by application programs running on the PC. The application then issues a 'Connect' to the database on behalf of the user.

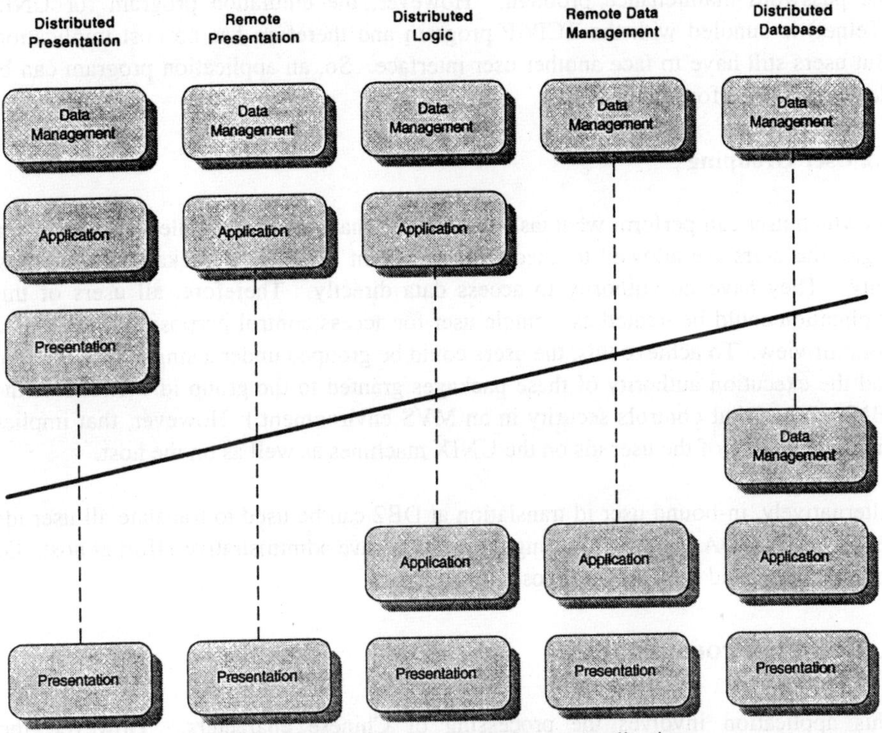

Fig. 2. Classification of Client/Server Application

On the system side, we have the options to check the user id/password at the DRDA gateway or at the MVS host. If they are checked at the gateway, we have the option to allow the host to accept the user id without further checking.

2.1 User Authentication Options

First, consider user id and password checking at the MVS host. This is the natural extension of the host-centric computing paradigm. Since practically all data reside in the DB2 database at the MVS host, this would seems an obvious choice. Furthermore, this provides a central security control and eliminates the need for user id/password synchronization across multiple machines in the case of UNIX (as there are more than one UNIX machines).

However, there is one problem in this approach. When the password expires, the user can no longer connect to the database; and there is no facility in DRDA for password maintenance. The only way is to provide terminal access to users for this purpose.

The drawbacks are the additional cost for emulation software or terminal and another user interface for users.

So, let's consider user id and password checking at the DRDA gateway. This also has the password maintenance problem. However, the emulation program for UNIX (Telnet) is bundled with the TCP/IP program and therefore has no cost implication. But users still have to face another user interface. So, an application program can be developed to perform the task.

2.2 User Grouping

As which user can perform what task and access what data is controlled by application logic, the users are allowed to execute the relevant application packages on the host only. They have no authority to access data directly. Therefore, all users of this application could be treated as a single user for access control purpose from the DB2 point of view. To achieve this, the users could be grouped under a single RACF group and the execution authority of these packages granted to the group id. (RACF is the IBM product that controls security in an MVS environment.) However, that implies the maintenance of the user ids on the UNIX machines as well as on the host.

Alternatively, in-bound user id translation at DB2 can be used to translate all user ids sent from a DRDA gateway to a single user id to save administrative effort at host. Of course, the second method was chosen.

3. Chinese Processing

This application involves the processing of Chinese characters. However, the representation of Chinese characters are different on the two platforms where the data are input and stored. On the host side where the data are stored, Chinese characters are represented in DBCS while on the PC where the data are input and displayed, they are in Big-5.

In principle, the DRDA architecture allows for the transparent access of data and therefore has provided for data translation. However, DB2/MVS does not support the translation from Big-5 to DBCS codes. So, the Big-5 codes are treated as binary data and no translation is done, i.e. the Big-5 codes are stored in their original Hex values in DB2.

This solves the problem for the online system. However, batch processing is run on the host and requires the printing of Chinese characters. In order to print the Chinese characters, they need to be in DBCS.

To overcome this, we have three options. First, let's consider storing the DBCS codes along sides the Big-5 codes. The obvious drawback is the additional storage required to store the additional set of Chinese codes. Also, there are problems synchronizing the two sets of codes.

Another option is to store only DBCS codes. As discussed earlier, DB2/MVS won't translate Big-5 codes to DBCS codes. So, we have to find a way around this. One method is to include codes in the PC program to do the translations. However, this would make the program too large.

So, we decided that the translation should be done by the printing programs. This would prolong the batch runtime but after some testing, it was found to be acceptable.

4. Conclusion

Although we have encountered a few problems, DRDA seems to have delivered what we had expected. The application is now being implemented in phases and the phases so far implemented have been running smoothly. We also found that the overheads of DRDA is very small.

Oracle 7 Release 7.3 Universal Database

Doug Farber
Oracle Systems Hong Kong Ltd.
Rm. 1401, 14/F,
Evergo House,
Wanchai,
Hong Kong.

Abstract: The world is entering the New Information Age. Throughout history, each quantum leap in the availability of and access to information has enlightened people and expanded business opportunities. Time and time again, information has proven itself to be an unequaled source of power for both individuals and business. Acting as a large multimedia library of information, the Oracle Universal Database (UDBMS) has the ability to manage and deliver real-time data such as video and audio, unstructured text, and traditional relational data. By delivering relational and multimedia support together with powerful and versatile indexing and processing capabilities, the UDBMS opens up opportunities for a new generation of applications that combine many different types of data, including video, audio, text, and spatial, as well as analytical data and objects. The UDBMS can integrate and deliver this data to one, tens, or thousands of users over any network, including the Web.

Any Data, Any Application, Any Scale

The key to the UDBMS is flexibility. Businesses now can start developing with the most popular, secure, and manageable relational database engine to build integrated systems by adding the pieces needed to create an ideal application development foundation.

The UDBMS improves access and manipulation of information. Support for any number of local or remote users is built in. Access and analysis tools provide all levels of users with immediate access to the information they need. When combined with other solution components, the UDBMS provides the flexibility to deploy a wide array of applications. Executive decision support, order-entry, on-line sales, or integrated Web systems can be built from the same technology base, reducing installation, support, and training costs, and making it easier to deploy new applications faster.

Heralding the Dawn of Network Computing

The Information Age will require a computing model that fully exploits the potential of powerful servers and high-speed networks. Low-cost end-user devices that support a rich graphical environment and will be able to download most or all of their software from servers over a network. The UDBMS is optimized for the arrival of Network Computing, with the power to store and deliver any kind of data to any kind of Network Computer.

Enabling the Information Age

The UDBMS breaks new ground in storing and delivering rich data. It lays the foundation for a dramatically different class of applications that integrate relational, text, video, and spatial, and Web-based information. A vast array of implementation services will focus on helping customers streamline business transactions, optimize day-to-day productivity, and maintain the highest possible levels of service. The UDBMS will change the way enterprises operate and companies do business in a new Information Age of vivid color, rich sound, and perpetual motion. Businesses will comfortably cruise the burgeoning Information Superhighway and maintain critical competitive advantage in their respective industries.

The UDBMS is geared to developing any application:

- Data Warehousing
- OLTP
- Distributed
- Internet Commerce

The UDBMS enables advanced relational and "unstructured" data types across all of the customer's key application requirements.

- Structured: Relational
- Unstructured: Video, Audio, Text, Analytical/OLAP, Spatial, Web

To be applied to any scale of application and provide the optimum architecture that ensures a successful deployment at any scale of database size, type of platform, or number of databases.

- Small to Very Large Database (VLDB)
- Small number to very many databases
- Individual PC to massively parallel systems

Business Value Proposition

Lowest Risk

The UDBMS reduces the customer's risk in developing and deploying any type of database application based on proven database technology and vast a application base. Migration or adoption of the UDBMS is the lowest risk decision. The UDBMS technology is proven across virtually ever type of application the customer would like to develop and deploy. To provide for a wealth of data types and heterogeneous connectivity freedom of choice of third party tools, applications and utilities to ensure the most comprehensive solutions enhance the UDBMS.

Maximum Leverage

For an effective applications development environment, having a UDBMS maximizes the customer's leverage of resources across applications development, applications maintenance, and systems management. Enabling complex data types and multimedia greatly enhances current and under development application solutions in an integrated architecture, allowing skills to be completely leveraged.

Greatest Value
Scaleable performance across the customers, platforms and data types eliminates the need for specialized databases, proving the ultimate value in an enterprise-wide database. A UDBMS provides our customers with the maximum value in a database by allowing the customer to develop all of their applications with a single architecture, eliminating the need for special purpose database engines.

Internet Integration
It is essential that a UDBMS be Web/Internet enabled, allowing customers today to leverage the Internet across a wide of applications, providing an integrated, web-enabled database that can be leveraged across all applications.

Data Warehousing

The most widely applicable database application is Data Warehousing. Taking operational and demographic data, load it into a peripheral database and use the information to make better Informed, highly tactic intelligent decisions.

Any Source
Expand the performance of warehousing applications beyond parallel features by adding support for many new query types. A UDBMS can optimize performance against this multimedia of DW queries and sources

Bit-mapped indexing - Provides order of magnitude performance improvement for to a new range of queries, where bit mapped indexing optimizes performance.

Enhanced star queries - improves performance for specialized star or snowflake queries where many small tables are unifies with large "fact" tables. Eliminates the need for specialized star query processors.

Any Data

- Multiple data types need to be available to the Data Warehouse by adding capabilities to add unstructured data types to applications.
- Spatial Data Capability - extends the Warehouse to add spatial queries, particularly useful for Geographical Information Systems (GIS).
- Free Form Text Searching - Adds advanced text management capabilities using sophisticated linguistic rules and theme based searching.
- On Line Analytical Processing - Adds management of analytical data for OLAP (on-line applications processing) applications.
- Video Server Integration - Enables a Data Warehouse application to be extended to add retrieval of video elements.

Any Scale

- Major optimization capabilities are needed to enhance server performance for all parallel queries.
- Improved parallel performance should be extended to loosely coupled systems such as massively parallel computers.
- Adaptable queries - for loosely coupled systems, improves load balancing by better sharing of querying workload between CPUs.
- Parallel aware optimizer with histograms - Improved performance of all queries by better optimizing use of system resource for multi-processing systems and by better understanding the distribution of data according to the value of the data.

Any Access

- platform capability, both on the front and back end, to ensure maximum accessibility. A Data Warehouse requires Internet access to provide wider access to applications. Systems need cross

Business Value Proposition of UDBMS

Investment protection & leverage

- Software investment
- Applications development knowledge
- Systems and DB administration

A UDBMS enabled Data Warehouse maximizes the leverage of the customer's technology investment by supporting the widest range of DW applications. A wide range of performance features are needed to accommodate ad hoc application requirements. The UDBMS has the widest range of features for data warehousing, ensuring maximum performance by integrating an advanced cost optimizer with parallel, bit mapped and star query features.

Minimize long term cost of ownership

- Systems management and database administration
- Applications maintenance
- Minimizing the administration and complexity associated with Data warehousing applications, allows the lowest cost of implementation and fastest time to market
- DW technology features need to be integrated within the UDBMS, ensuring ease of implementation and management. Separate servers to provide features such as bit-mapped indexing technology.
- Overcomplicating implementation and systems management complicates administration and increase the level of complexity of the application.

Minimize risk, maximize user satisfaction

Fastest time to market

Adapt to per-planned and ad-hoc requests
Easily scale to increase performance
Utilizing a UDBMS minimizes risk in implementing data warehousing applications. By dynamically automating partitioning and other parallel performance tuning, maximizing performance automatically.
Use of advanced parallel query technology ultizes dynamic partitioning to minimize costs of administration, to maximize efficiency of system hardware by performing automatic load balancing of both pre-planned and ad hoc queries. Oracle also uniquely adds new "adaptive" query features to further improve load balancing on loosely coupled systems such as MPPs.

OLTP Solutions

Performance

- Reduced use of system resources - improves the throughput/performance of OLTP applications where high availability or scalability to MPP or cluster system environments is required.
- Optimized "code path" improves the overall OLTP throughout and scalability by improving the efficiency of the UDBMS server in performance transactions.

Reliability & Availability

- Refined locking for Parallel Server - improves the throughput/performance of OLTP applications where high availability or scalability to MPP or cluster system environments is required.

Scalability

- Support of the XA(distributed OLTP) should be standard to our parallel server technology. XA support for Parallel Server - add an industry standard interface for connecting OLTP monitors such as Tuxedo, increasing the number of users and connections that a UDBMS can support.
- A UDBMS expands the data types available to OLTP applications for "rich content" applications. Text, Video, and Spatial Data Options - The addition of "rich content" transactional applications using audio, video, or other new media types emerges.

Business Values Proposition

Investment protection & leverage

- Software investment
- Applications development knowledge
- Systems and DB administration
- A UDBMS maximizes the leverage of the customer's technology investment by supporting the widest scale of OLTP applications.

- Establish the foundation for the support of rich context OLTP applications in the future which may include multi-media and other unstructured data.
- A UDBMS provides the maximum performance, reliability, availability and scalability in an open database by supporting all range of transaction processing applications.
- The database must support large OLTP sites deployed across multiple industries, with large use populations and transaction performance.

Minimize long term cost of ownership

- Leading systems and database administration to minimize cost of operations.
- Scaleable architecture with leading features to ensure investment protection for applications as needs increase.
- Minimize the administration and complexity associated with OLTP applications, allowing the lowest cost of implementation and maintenance.
- The UDBMS's OLTP technology is integrated with the core architecture of the database, ensuring complete compatibility of all features.
- The UDBMS is designed to support the availability and administration requirements of small and large production database applications.
- UDBMS provides on-line, parallel administration features such as backup, restore and recovery of data to support mission critical environments.

Minimize risk, maximize user satisfaction

- Provide leading customer services for OLTP to ensure quality implementation and maintenance.
- Scaleable architecture to ensure user performance and headroom as user populations increase.
- Combines a scaleable software technology and a services organization focused on the deployment of business critical applications to minimizes the risk in implementing open systems OLTP.
- UDBMS brings three key differentiaters for customer's interested in minimizing the risk of production systems in an open platform environment:
  => Experience: Having a product that has evolved over time to address core business needs and has built a strong foundation for data type enhancement.
  => Services: Extensive consulting, support and training organizations are required for assisting in the deployment of business critical applications.
  => Proven scaleable technology: Having extensive experience in deploying across a wide array of parallel configurations.

Distributed Solutions:

Flexible

- UDBMS eases deployment of the largest variety of distributed applications with the most extensive toolkit of RDBMS technologies for supporting:

=> Branch Automation
=> Intent Integration
=> Enterprise Information Access
=> Mobile Workforce

- Synchronous Replication(part of Symmetric Replication Option) expands a customer's choice of replication configurations.
- Heterogeneous Replication enables replication between non-Oracle and Oracle databases, easing interoperability for applications such as data marts.
- Mobile Technology expands the applications network using client-agent-server architecture to improve performance on mobile or bandwidth constrained LAN's.

Manageable

- An integrated architecture ensures ease of deployment, management and compatibility of features.
- Consistent database services across distributed sites, such as backup/recovery, security and native language.
- Oracle adds integrated support of new media types to distributed applications, including video/audio and text management.
- Groupware and Workgroup products provide an easy to use, easy to manage, and easy to install integrated departmental solution, enabling simplified branch automation of distributed workgroups.
- Enterprise Networking Option adds network security, authentication, DCE support and native naming services, ensuring secure distributed applications that are easy to install and administer.
- Text, Video/Audio and Spatial Options - adds support for integrating new media into all distributed applications.

Minimize long term cost of ownership

- Comprehensive and open systems management and database administration solutions.
- Low maintenance cost through automated software distribution.
- Minimize cost of management through a comprehensive database and systems management environment that allows centralized or remote management of distributed sites.
- Software distribution and license management ensures the lowest cost of deployment of future applications and upgrades across distributed sites.
- Accommodate a maximum number of third party systems management solutions.
- Provides a single, comprehensive management architecture that supports all of the key management requirements of enterprise wide distributed applications.
- Fully compliant with SNMP, the industries leading management standard, ensuring integration with other third party console environments.

Minimize risk, maximize user satisfaction

- Fastest time to market
- Integrated software technology for compatibility and ease of use.
- Integrated database technology across client-server, server-server, web and mobile applications minimizes the risk of deployment.
- Compatibility of features, integrated workgroup suites and consolidated administration ensures the fastest time to market for distributed applications maximizing user satisfaction.
- Comprehensive tools for deploying distributed applications, including web/Internet, mobile and other client-server configurations.

Electronic/Internet Commerce

Security & Reliability

- Leverage database security capability to add additional layers of security. Utilise database-centric encryption, authorization, and authentication facilities.
- Utilise architectural constructs such as failover, replication, and integrity constructs to ensure maximum uptime of WEB based applications.

Performance

- Ensure tight integration with existing systems and WEB enabled applications.
- Minimize the network traffic by utilizing performance enhancements such as client-side validation, load balancing, intelligent network packet exchange.
- Build WEB based systems on powerful back-end engines to ensure dynamic content and speedy response times.

Availability

- Build on backup and recovery mechanisms already deployed in database applications and apply them to the WEB.
- Maintain WEB links and intelligent data on usage and behavior to understand tendencies of WEB visitors. Customize functions for target audience.

Scalability

- File-based WEB systems are inherently limited. Leverage parallel constructs and scalability aspects of a UDBMS to allow applications maintain and improve performance as the size of the deployment rises.

New Application Opportunities

Using a UDBMS makes using the Web a reality for dynamic production database applications, enabling the next generation of content rich applications.

Video

Video Server Option - enables the integration for real time multi-media "stream" data into UDBMS and WEB based applications, including video and audio elements. Video Server Option enhances Oracle solutions and brings new types of applications capability, where relational tables can be combined with multi-media elements.

- Web-video applications
- Interactive Customer Kiosks
- Medical Imaging Systems
- Training on Demand
- Electronic Catalogs
- Video help or instruction management

Text

Text Server Option - provides leading text management capabilities for web and existing client-server application types. Provides all of the elements of text management to UDBMS applications, including context sensitive search, text summarization and classification.

- Web-based text management
- Document Archiving Application
- Search and Retrieval
- Text reduction/summarization

Spatial

Allows the integration of spatial, coordinate oriented applications to be built using UDBMS technology. Using a patented HH index compression encoding technology, Spatial Option provides a new performance metric for advanced application types such as GIS.

- Geographical Information Systems(GIS) utilizing front end mapping technology
- Demographic analysis
- Scientific data
- Temporal analysis

Analytical

Adds the ability to analyse data in a multi-dimensional form, ideal for end-user analysis applications such as On-line Application Processing (OLAP). Adds major capabilities in multi-dimensional views, what-if analysis and historical analysis.

- On-line Application Processing
- What-if analysis

  Multi-dimensional data views and analysis

UniSQL and World Wide Web

Andrew Lam
ITIS Technology
Rm. 401, 4/F, Centre
9 Hung To Road, Kwun Tong,
Hong Kong.

Abstract: UniSQL offers a high speed management for HTML, WWW, GIS, CAD/CAM by combing the On-Line Complex Processing Technology. UniSQL is designed for allowing complex application store and complex data; compound data; multimedia data retrieval. Combining the relational and object database architecture, UniSQL is leading the advance technology. Advance features of UniSQL:

- Multi Vendor Database Integration
- Multimedia Integration
- Natural support for object-oriented programming languages C++ and smalltalk
- Support double-byte character set. Examples: Chinese and Japanese

Object-Oriented Middleware

Ray Ruff
Sybase Hong Kong Ltd.
33rd Floor, NatWest Tower,
Times Square
Causeway Bay,
Hong Kong

Abstract: Computing technology is becoming more object-oriented to increase development productivity, reduce maintenance costs, handle often-changing requirements, and manage complex data and applications. Database customers want these benefits without reinventing or redeploying their existing systems. Interoperability between relational and object-oriented tools is a market requirement. Using technology that will map object-oriented models to existing relational data, object-oriented middleware combines robust, reliable, production quality systems with object-oriented software design.

Through the Sybase Open Client, Open Server architecture, the integration of object-oriented development techniques with existing relational databases can be achieved now to enable the more advanced client development environments to be immediately used with existing relational and legacy datastores to provide a smooth transition to an object environment. This object-to-relational mapping technology supports data transparency in a multi-tiered application architecture.

Object Relational Databases : Towards a Universal Server

Tony Banham
Informix Greater China Regional Office,
2801, Central Plaza,
Harbour Rd.
Wanchai,
Hong Kong.

Introduction

It is generally recognised that the traditional Relational Database Management System (RDBMS), while excellent for simple alphanumeric data storage and transactions, is not structured to deal with more complex data objects and operations. This fact has effectively defined a whole class of applications for which the RDBMS cannot be used. However, the relational concept - and its non-procedural APIs - are so well suited to standard commercial data processing that the RDBMS is still growing in popularity.

At the same time, a new class of database capable of handling complex objects and operations, the Object Oriented Database Management System (ODBMS or OODBMS), has evolved. These databases have shown themselves very capable in handling those applications which are beyond the scope of the traditional RDBMS. The ODBMS approach however, has some clear drawbacks :

- Relatively poor performance for commercial OLTP / DSS
- Poor Scalability
- Conceptually far more difficult to use
- Business-wise, a riskier proposition

This paper shows that there is a middle approach, the so-called Object-Relational Database Management System (ORDBMS), which is capable of evolving to the point where it combines the best of the RDBMS and ODBMS worlds.

What is an Object Relational Database ?

We will start by looking at the types of data, and types of operations on that data, in common use today. Michael Stonebreaker ("Object-Relational DBMS - The Next Wave") has pointed out that there are four quadrants forming a query complexity/data complexity matrix. Retrieving simple data (such as a named spreadsheet file) can be handled by a computer's operating system. Querying simple data - for example, listing the names of a company's employees - can be handled by a traditional relational database.

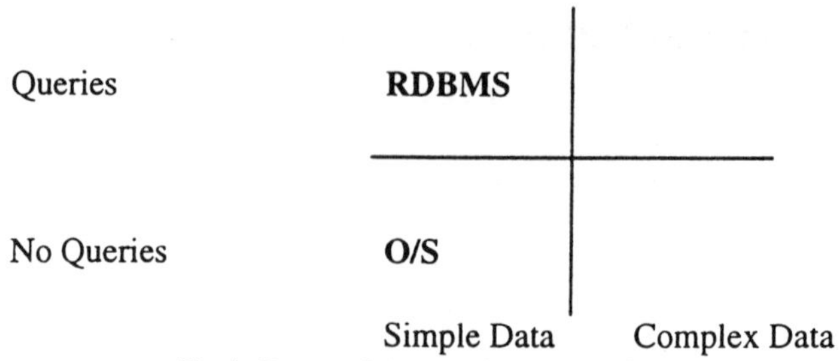

Fig 1: Data and Access Quadrant - O/S, RDBMS

The RDBMS has the great advantage of being based on a conceptually simple model. Mentally picturing data as sets of two-dimensional tables seems to come very naturally. And while SQL may not be perfect, the concept of a non-procedural physical-location-transparent querying language is also relatively easy to grasp.
While the datatypes handled by an RDBMS (numbers, characters, times, dates, etc.) are rather limited, they are appropriate for the book-keeping, and clerical applications which computing has today penetrated most successfully.
The weakness of the RDBMS, of course, has been in the handling of any data type outside this narrow range. Most RDBMS kernels today can handle some sort of 'large object' or BLOB type, which might more accurately be labeled 'other'. The problem with this data type is that it is too general purpose. The engine understands nothing about the data being stored in it, and the programmer and DBA often use it as a file structure for which their applications need to provide all the processing logic. While undesirable, this can be done to a degree - but the engine is still not capable of querying on the contents of these BLOBs, or optimising query paths based on content, as the content is itself transparent to the engine.
If a traditional relational system has extensions for types and functions, they are added as an afterthought. This type of architecture will never provide high-performance or good integration with other database facilities, neither does it provide a standard method for the addition of new datatypes.
The development of new data objects within the traditional RDBMS structure has also been obstructed by the RDBMS vendors' (and their customers', and their hardware partners') preoccupation with raw performance. Instead of adding new capabilities, many vendors have recently focused on shortening code paths and increasing efficiencies for handling large volumes of users, large volumes of data, and large volumes of transactions.
In summary, today's RDBMSs have evolved to do what they do best, better ! The BLOB has become a catch-all for all other datatypes and the onus has been put on the programmer/DBA to try and make the best use of it if they want to store other datatypes in the database.

To fill the glaring gap in capabilities, the ODBMS was created. The design imperative was simple - to be able to efficiently store the data types beyond the capabilities of the RDBMS. This type of database has been of great interest to users who habitually deal with complex data types (CAD/CAM, GIS, Multi-Media, etc.).

Queries	**RDBMS**	
No Queries	**O/S**	**ODBMS**
	Simple Data	Complex Data

Fig 2: Data and Access Quadrant - ODBMS

However, while achieving their basic aim, the ODBMS vendors have not been able to match the RDBMS in terms of normal commercial usage. Large databases (>50GB, say), and large user and transaction counts are currently beyond their capabilities. The lack of a standard non-procedural API, such as SQL, has also slowed down the adoption of this technology, and popularity has been limited by the fact that complex data type descriptions are by definition conceptually less simple than the relational model.

Furthermore, for performance reasons, the designers of these systems have generally placed persistent storage in the same address space as the client, and this leads to security issues.

The trade-offs inherent in ODBMSs are clear. While the storage and retrieval of complex objects is fast and efficient, they demonstrate relatively poor scalability and usability for typical commercial applications.

What is required is a combination of the best aspects of both Object and Relational technologies. This is where the Object-Relational Database Management Systems (ORDBMS) fits in. This architecture must allow for complex queries on complex data types.

Queries	**RDBMS**	**ORDBMS**
No Queries	**O/S**	**ODBMS**
	Simple Data	Complex Data

Fig 3: Data and Access Quadrant - ORDBMS

Unlike the BLOB approach to complex data storage offered by the RDBMS, the ORDBMS should not require the applications to contain all the object logic. This can be encapsulated in the ORDBMS itself in the same way that date/time logic is encapsulated in today's RDBMSs.

From a business standpoint, perhaps the most significant factor in the uptake of this technology will be its API's similarity to today's RDBMSs. An Object/Relational non-procedural language (such as SQL3) is merely an evolution of existing SQL, rather than a dramatically different interface as provided by ODBMSs. Not only do decision makers feel happier dealing with existing technologies, but also the users require less extra knowledge and training.

The trade-offs of today's ORDBMSs are that although they handle complex queries on complex data extremely well, the performance and scalability achieved for conventional OLTP and DSS - although far superior to existing ODBMSs - is weak compared to the best of current RDBMS architectures.

The Universal Server

This situation has led Informix to propose a 'Universal Server', an extension of the existing Informix high-performance RDBMS (the OnLine Dynamic Server) with the ORDBMS technology of Illustra Information Technologies Inc., a company - having developed the most evolved of the existing ORDBMSs - which was purchased by Informix Software at the end of December 1995. In this section we will briefly describe the heritage of Illustra's architecture.

The two dominating aspects of Illustra's architecture are the facts that :
- It has an SQL-based client/server structure
- Objects of unlimited complexity can be defined by DataBlades which are 'plugged into' the database engine.

In combining the SQL API with the capability of user defined functions and abstract datatypes, Illustra has managed to include the best of both worlds. A successful marriage has been achieved between RDBMS features for OLTP, DSS, security, & recovery, and the ODBMS requirement for high performance operations on complex data. This fact also makes it relatively simple to merge the product with an existing RDBMS framework.
Illustra provides all the features expected in a relational database, but is also just as object-oriented as existing ODBMSs - it provides all the features that make Object-Orientation (OO) appealing.
Datatypes of any kind can be created, including brand new datatypes not built on any pre-existing datatypes. Illustra includes arrays and sets as well as the rows familiar to relational users. This provides a very high degree of flexibility in creating data types that accurately model real objects.
To manipulate these types the developer can build functions, either in C or in SQL, and embed them in the database, where they are available to all users of the server. OO programmers often call these User Defined Functions (UDFs) "methods".
Inheritance, encapsulation and polymorphism are the three major features of OO programming that are responsible for much of its benefit: faster development, higher quality, lower maintenance, more reusability.
Illustra assigns to each object an Object ID which is permanent over the life of the object. Developers can use this OID to provide the kind of navigation available in Object DBMSs.

In building OO applications, it is important to simplify as much as possible. Function overloading lets the developer create a function that performs a certain action (say display an image), and then create another function of the same name that performs the same action on another datatype (say display a video clip). The developer need only remember that "display" displays things, and leave the system to work out which version of display to use for the current type of data. Operator overloading lets the developer assign functions to operators so that they naturally fit into SQL syntax.

Using these features, Illustra supports a number of pre-packaged data domains. These are called Data Blades. DataBlades define new object types, new functions, new display methods, new access methods, and give optimizer guidance

DataBlades allow unlimited functional extensibility. Similar in concept to class libraries in development tools, they allow the ORDBMS vendor, other independent software vendors, and end-user IT departments to each add functionality as required. These modular extensions can then be used in any combination to add to the capabilities of the database engine.

DataBlades are the key to providing high-performance operations on complex data. They allow the functions of the database to match the structure of the data types. For example, although B-Tree indexes are excellent for range or equality searches on alphanumeric data, they are all but useless for multi-dimensional spatial data, a problem which is solved by allowing the definition of new index methods within a DataBlade ('R-Tree', in the case of spatial data).

In summary, Illustra combines extensibility with performance in a paradigm little removed from the classic SQL world. Three key ways in which performance is gained are :

Server-side functions

Filtering data on the server side avoids moving unqualified data to the client. In the OO world, where complex objects may be measured in megabytes of data, this can save a great deal of network traffic.

If it is possible to select just three out of 10,000 20MB images on the server side - before passing them to the client - then a saving of 199.940GB of data transmission will have been achieved !

Functional indexing

Functional indexing speeds access to data based on function results. This indexing can vary internally depending on the structure of a particular data type. For example, a B-Tree index could be created on the function density(volume,weight) for iron ore analysis in the commodities market.

Extensible access methods

B-trees are not good for every thing. Although B-Tree indexing is excellent for equality or range searches, it is all but useless for multi-dimensional spatial data. New access methods added in DataBlades can enable queries which would be totally impractical in a normal RDBMS.

Through these technologies Illustra maintains a relatively consistent performance independent of object complexity. Although the best-of-breed RDBMSs still outperform Illustra for simple data types, their performance degrades fast as the complexity increases. The Universal Server will add best-of-breed alphanumeric performance to best-of-breed extensibility.

Options Facing RDBMS Vendors

In conclusion, let us summarize the various options open to database vendors today. We have shown in this paper that there is no 'one size fits all' in the database world today. Each type of database, for example ODBMS, shows advantages in some areas of operations, and disadvantages in others. The way forward lies in somehow combining the best of the ODBMS and RDBMS ideas.

While some database vendors are attempting to do this by having a different type of server for each data domain (i.e. one for alphanumeric, one for large text objects, one for video, one for multi-dimensional, etc.), this cannot be taken seriously as a long-term solution. Questions of performance, integrity, and distributed joins discredit the theoretical capability of handling all data types.

The long-term solution must be to have a single database capable of handling all data types, present and future, with acceptable performance for everything from OLTP to CAD/CAM.

Today, the ORDBMS comes closest to providing the answer, but as we have seen, too many bread-and-butter RDBMS capabilities are currently missing from today's ORDBMSs. The only practical solution appears to be to extend today's RDBMS offerings, not by some bolt-on object wrapper, but by embedding the capabilities of the ORDBMS.

This opinion, endorsed by many partners and analysts, led Informix to its December 1995 acquisition of Illustra with the long-term aim of producing a Universal Server capable of proving functionality and performance across the spectrum of database needs.

In the interim, Informix is working to marry the capabilities of the Informix-OnLine Dynamic Server RDBMS and the Illustra ORDBMS by creating an Informix 'gateway' to be plugged in to Illustra. This will give the closest integration between the two systems allowing applications access to both simple and complex data through transparent distributed joins between the two database engines.

This 'virtual' Universal Server will ensure transparent interoperability between Illustra and all Informix OnLine 7.x (and above) engines, while at the same time protecting the investment of users of both products (developers can migrate DataBlades and applications to the Universal Server). Informix customers will be able to exploit advanced Web, Multimedia, Spatial and other customised Illustra extensions, while Illustra customers can start to exploit DSA scalability

However, the final aim is to fully integrate the two engines into one single product. Fortunately Informix had been working on an 'Extensible Framework' - similar in concept to Illustra's DataBlades - for over a year before the acquisition was announced. This will greatly facilitate the merger of the two systems into a true 'Universal Server'.

The Universal Server will be a highly-scalable Object Relational server combining Illustra's extensibility with the Dynamic Scalable Architecture's scalability. The Universal Server will address whole new set of applications while redefining both the rules for complex DSS and the evaluation criteria for RDBMS OLTP applications development.

Conclusion

Architecturally the solution of merging the Informix-OnLine Dynamic Server RDBMS with the Illustra ORDBMS is extremely elegant, and it creates the first opportunity for a single database kernel to offer all the data management needs of an organisation within a practical implementation. The Universal Server will have both the high-performance of a modern RDBMS, and the extensibility of an ORDBMS.

Using Multistage Retrieval and Hybrid Adaptation to Build a Case-Based Reasoning System for Pilot Production

Tzu-Fu Chiu**, Jackie Archibald* & Colin Hardy*
* School of Computing and Information Systems, University of Sunderland, U.K.
** School of Computing and Information Systems, University of Sunderland, U.K. & Tamsui Oxford University College, Taiwan, R.O.C.

1. Introduction

In general manufacturing industry, product design and pilot production are usually complicated and time-consuming procedures, especially in made-to-order factories. This is because, their products are non-standard, and differ in line with the orders made. According to the product specification, the pilot-production procedure applies available material, existing machinery, and effective methods to examine if the specification can be transformed economically to be a real product. Within the pilot production procedure, there are several crucial factors which affect the success of a final product, such as: reviews of the drawings, confirmation of the material specification, preparation of the auxiliary tools, and the prediction and prevention of the possible defects/failures. Therefore, in order to increase the efficiency and productivity of pilot production work, a computer system based on the case-based reasoning (CBR) paradigm, will be built to assist the engineers to perform their jobs more smoothly [KUM95].

2. Method --- Case-Based Reasoning

Case-based reasoning is a new approach to problem solving and knowledge engineering, that has received a lot of attention over the last few years.
A case-based reasoner solves new problems by adapting solutions that were used to solve old problems [RIE89]. That is, case-based reasoning solves a new problem by remembering a previous similar situation, and by reusing information and knowledge of that situation [AAM94].

3. Multistage Retrieval and Hybrid Adaptation

Most industrial products are composed of components. These components may in turn be made up of other parts, and so on, down to the elementary component. We propose a multistage retrieval technique technique [KOL93; BRA95] to allow the reasoner to draw out the most similar case, level by level, from any initial level down to a lower level. Theoretically, this procedure may be extended from any n-level to (n+1)-level, should this become necessary.

In order to fit the characteristics of the specific domain, our hybrid adaptation method is employed to transform the previous defect-description, cause-of-defect, and the corrective-action for the new situation. This is to be done by combining the causal model-based [KEH92; DOH94] and adjusted criteria rule-based methods [DUT93] together. Within them, a causal model deals with the relationship of possible defects between part and process, as well as the relationship of possible defects between process and machine. Meanwhile, adjustment criteria rules handle the relevant data about the interrelationship amongst the specification and precision of parts, as well as the variety and condition of the machine.

4. System Architecture for the Application

A new conceptual ES architecture [CHI95], based on the proposed methods (multistage retrieval and hybrid adaptation), has been developed for manipulating the process and FMEA data in the pilot production. The system architecture is depicted in Figure 1.

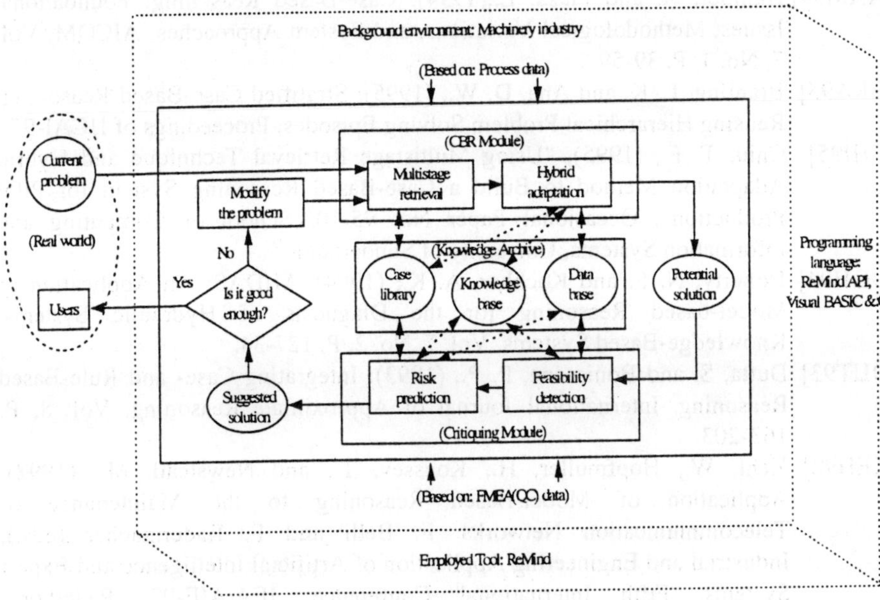

Figure 1 : Conceptual System architecture

The main functions of the system are:

(1) to retrieve the most similar case for the input problem;
(2) Transform the retrieved case to be a potential solution for the current problem;
(3) Detect the feasibility of the potential solution;
(4) Predict the risk of the potential solution;
(5) and generate a final suggested solution for the user;

(6) if the suggested solution is not good enough, the user is allowed to modify parts of the input problem, and then rerun the system till an acceptable solution obtained.

5. Application in Industry

Expert systems are domain-dependent methodologies. Having established the system architecture, a collaborating factory (an automobile component manufacturer) has been found to implement the system architecture in a real industrial environment. Meanwhile, through this proposed framework, we will utilise the existing pilot-production experience to assist manufacturing engineers for FMEA prediction and trouble-shooting in their daily work. The prototype system is now under development, and the implementation and evaluation of the system, will be carried out in the industrial environment (i.e. in the collaborating factory).

References

[AAM94] Aamodt, A. and Plaza, E.,(1994): Case-Based Reasoning: Foundational Issues, Methodological Variations, and System Approaches. AICOM, Vol. 7, No. 1, P. 39-59.

[BRA95] Branting, L. K. and Aha, D. W., (1995): Stratified Case-Based Reasoning: Reusing Hierarchical Problem Solving Episodes. Proceedings of IJCAI-95.

[CHI95] Chiu, T. F., (1995), "Using Multistage Retrieval Technique and Hybrid Adaptation Method to Build a Case-Based Reasoning System for Pilot Production", Occasional Paper No. 95-10, School of Computing and Information Systems, University of Sunderland.

[DOH94] Doherty, N. F. and Kochhar, A. K., (1994): MIDAS: An Application of Model-based Reasoning for the Diagnosis of Hydraulic Systems. Knowledge-Based Systems, Vol. 7, No. 2, P. 127-34.

[DUT93] Dutta, S. and Bonissone, P. P., (1993): Integrating Case- and Rule-Based Reasoning. International Journal of Approximate Reasoning, Vol. 8, P. 163-203.

[KEH92] Kehl, W., Hopfmuller, H., Koussev, T., and Newstead, M., (1992): Application of Model-Based Reasoning to the Maintenance of Telecommunication Networks. F. Belli and F. Radermacher (eds.), Industrial and Engineering Application of Artificial Intelligence and Expert Systems, Fifth International Conference, IEA/AIE-92, Paderborn, Germany, P. 79-88.

[KOL93] Kolodner, J., (1993): Case-Based Reasoning. Morgan Kaufmann Publishers, Inc.

[KUM95] Kumar, H. S. and Krishnamoorthy, C. S., (1995): A Framework for Case-Based Reasoning in Engineering Design. Artificial Intelligence for Engineering Design, Analysis and Manufacturing, Vol. 9, P. 161-182.

[RIE89] Riesbeck, C. K. and Schank, R. C., (1989): Inside Case-Based Reasoning. Lawrence Erlbaum Associates, Inc.

A Temporal Probabilistic Object-Oriented Data Model

Bingning Dai John G. Hughes David A. Bell
Faculty of Informatics
University of Ulster at Jordanstown
Newtownabbey
Co. Antrim, BT37 0QB
Northern Ireland, UK.
E-mail: B.Dai, JG.Hughes, DA.Bell@ulst.ac.uk

Abstract. In order to capture both uncertainty and temporality in the world models (databases) of intelligent systems interacting with the real world, this paper presents an extended Object-Oriented (OO) data model. Making full use of the built-in types in the ODMG Object Model, no addition to the Object Query Language (OQL) is necessary.

1 Introduction

The knowledge about the world of intelligent systems interacting with the real world is not only uncertain due to sensor errors, etc., but also temporal because the world is dynamic. Although there have been some work in temporal databases (DBs) ([TAN93]) and OO models dealing with uncertainty, this work is an initial effort to bring together the research and considers AI as well. Having chosen the object model of ODMG-93 ([CAT94]) as the underlying object model, [KOR94]'s idea of modelling attribute uncertainty is implanted into our model. Then the model is further extended to incorporate both *valid time* and *transaction time* ([JEN94]).

2 Overview of the ODMG Object Model and the OQL

2.1 The ODMG Object Model

The ODMG Object Model supports most of the characteristics of an object data model described in [PIS93]. The type hierarchy of the object model is rooted at the type *Denotable_Object*. *Set* and *Structure* are built-in collection type generators.

2.2 The Object Query Language (OQL)

The ODMG OQL is a declarative language. It deals with complex objects without privileging the set construct and the *select-from-where* clause. Its two important characteristics are: 1) An OQL query is a function which, when applied to the input, delivers an object whose type may be inferred from the operator contributing to the query expression; 2) An object identity uniquely distinguishes the object from all other objects within the domain in which the object was created.

3 The Extended Object Model

3.1 Uncertainty Modelling

Besides attribute uncertainty, in an OO data model, there is uncertainty related to class hierarchies, i.e. uncertain *downward* and *upward* classification ([KOR94]). Only attribute uncertainty is considered in this paper. The probability theory is applied here for its well understood semantics and suitability in intelligent systems.

Definition 1: Assume: $\mathcal{T}$ is the set of all the type names defined in an application environment and T_P is a real number type taking values from the interval [0,1]. *A probabilistic attribute value* is a set$\{<d_1, p_1>, \ldots, <d_n, p_n>\}$, where d_i and p_i are instances of $D(\in\mathcal{T})$ and T_P respectively ($i=1, \ldots, n$), and all p_i's sum up to 1. "$\perp$" is added to every domain to represent any unknown instance of an object type.

3.2 Incorporating Temporal Information

The two types of special temporal information in temporal DBs are: *valid time* and *transaction time* ([Jensen94]). The two approaches to model temporal data in OO DBs are *attribute versioning* and *object versioning*. Attribute versioning is applied.

Definition 2: Assume: 1) $\mathcal{T}$ is a set of all the type names defined in an application environment; 2) $\mathcal{Time}$ is a set of the names of all the temporal data types. *A temporal probabilistic attribute value* is a set $\{<u_1, vt_1, tt_1>, \ldots, <u_n, vt_n, tt_n>\}$, where each u_i is a probabilistic attribute as defined before, d_i, tv_i and tt_i are instances of $D\in\mathcal{T}$, $Vtime\in\mathcal{Time}$ and $Ttime\in\mathcal{Time}$ respectively ($i=1, \ldots, n$).

3.3 The Extension to ODMG Data Model

A new type named *TPAttribute*, i.e. *Temporal Probabilistic Attribute* is added to the built-in type hierarchy of the ODMG Object Model to carry out the modelling. It is a subtype of type *Attribute*. It refines the following inherited operations:

```
set_value(new_value: Immutable_Set(Immutable_Structure(e1: T, e2: Float)),
        valid_time: Timestamp)
get_value() →existing_value: Immutable_Set(Immutable_Structure(Immutable_Set
    (Immutable_Structure(e1:T, e2:Float)), valid_time:Timestamp, trans_time:Timestamp))
get_value(predicate: String) →latest_value: Immutable_Structure(e1: T, e2: Float)
```

It defines new operations as follows:

```
get_value_series(predicate: String) → existing_value: Immutable_Set(Immutable_Structure
    (Immutable_Set( Immutable_Structure (e1: T, e2: Float)), time: Timestamp))
get_valid_time(value: T, predicate: String) →Immutable_Set(valid_time: Timestamp)
get_trans_time(value: T, predicate: String) →Immutable_Set(trans_time: Timestamp)
```

Set_value adds a probabilistic value, its valid time, and the system generated transaction time. *Get_value* returns probabilistic values according to *predicate*. The predicates for *get_value* and *get_value_series* are temporal constraints, while those for *get_valid_time* and *get_trans_time* are probability thresholds.

3.4 Summary of the Examples

All of the query examples have exploited *TPAttribute* without addition to the OQL. This has made full use of OO paradigms. It is critical to support intelligent systems.

4 Related Work

Our work is distinctive for it integrates time and uncertainty into one object model. The handling of temporal information is similar to *time series* in [SEG93]. As to the work in AI, e.g. [HAN94], an intelligent agent's state of information over time is lost. Here both rollback information (transaction time) and historical information (valid time) are stored in its world model (DB) and can be used at any time.

5 Future Work

In our model, temporal uncertain semantics is straightforward at present. Issues like uncertainty in class hierarchy and update mechanism still need to be explored.

References

[CAT94] Cattell, R.G.G., (ed.) (1994): The Object Database Standard: ODMG-93, Release 1.1, San Francisco, California, Morgan Kaufmann.

[HAN94] Hanks, S. and McDermott, D. (1994): Modelling a Dynamic and Uncertain World I: Symbolic and Probabilistic Reasoning about Change. In: Artificial Intelligence, 66(1), pp. 1--55.

[JEN94] Jensen, C.S., Clifford, J., Elmasri, R., and et al. (1994): A Consensus Glossary of Temporal Database Concepts. In: SIGMOD RECORD, March, 23(1), pp. 52--64.

[KOR94] Kornatzky, Y. and Shimony, S.E. (1994): A Probabilistic Object-Oriented Data Model. In: Data and Knowledge Engineering, 12, pp. 143--166.

[PIS93] Pissinou, N., Makki, K., and Yesha, Y. (1993): On Temporal Modelling in the Context of Object Databases. In: SIGMOD Record, September, 22(3), pp. 8--15.

[SEG93] Segev, A. and Chandra, R. (1993): A Data Model for Time-Series Analysis. In: Theories and Methods of Spatio-Temporal Reasoning in Geographic Space, LNCS No. 639, Springer-Verlag, pp. 191--212.

[TAN93] Tansel, A.U. and et al., (eds.) (1993): Temporal Databases: Theory, Design & Implementation, Benjamin/Cumming Publishing Company, Inc.

Design and Implementation of an Object Management Module for a PDA

Chang-ju Lee, Sang-ui Yoon, Sang-goo Lee
Department of Computer Science, Seoul National University
Kwanak-gu Shillimdong
Seoul, Korea

Abstract

We present in this paper algorithms for an object management module (OMM) of a PDA (Personal Digital Assistant). The OMM is responsible for efficiently storing and retrieving objects (or records) used by application programs of a PDA. Since most operating systems of PDA supply only low level memory management functions to allocate and deallocate memory blocks, each application program must have its own memory management capability to arrange its data objects into memory blocks. This results in enlarged sizes and increased implementation costs of application programs. We have designed and implemented an OMM that manages data objects from every application.

Key words : PDA (Personal Digital Assistant), Memory management

1. Introduction

Small computers such as laptop computers, electronic notebooks and PDAs (Personal Digital Assistants) are becoming ever more affordable. PDA generally has a small capacity of memory due to its small size and limit of power supply. For example, the PDA which we target in our research has a main memory of 256KB and has no auxiliary storage devices such as hard disks. Accordingly, it is essential that the limited amount of memory of a PDA be managed efficiently.

The OS (operating system) of our target PDA is VRTXmc [MIC90], developed by Microtec Research, Santa Clara, California, USA. Since VRTXmc supplies only low level memory management functions to allocate and deallocate memory blocks, each application program must have its own memory management capability to arrange its data objects into blocks. This results in enlarged sizes and increased implementation costs of application programs. In addition, it would be very difficult to coherently manage main memory. In order to solve this problem, we have designed and implemented an OMM that sits between the OS and the application programs and manages data objects from every application. Application programs call the OMM functions to insert, delete and retrieve data, and the OMM implements these functions through low level functions of VRTXmc. Although various studies have been presented concerning memory management, none have addressed the exact problem that we face [GIO87, KNU73, MAT77].

An object (or record) is the unit of data which is read or stored in main memory. *An object set* is a set of objects of the same sort that belong to an application program. In VRTXmc, memory is divided into a number of partitions and each partition into a number of equal size blocks. The block is the basic unit of allocation and deallocation. The configuration of each partition which is composed of the partition size, block size, number of blocks in the partition cannot change at run time. VRTXmx supplies functions to allocate and deallocate blocks for a given partition. The OMM is responsible for mapping the variable size objects onto blocks and for keeping track of object sets.

2. Algorithms for the Object Management Module

We have developed four different algorithms for object management. The 'brute-force' algorithm simple appends objects and runs compaction when deletion occurs. The 'object-link' method tries to minimize internal fragmentation by linking blocks of different sizes to fit the given object. The 'partition allocation' algorithm assigns one partition to each object set and manages them separately. The 'hybrid' method has shown the best performance in space and time combined, and is explained below.

In the 'hybrid' method, objects of an application program are stored in data partitions and the information of an object set is stored in a special partition which we call the catalog partition. Each data partition is used exclusively by an object set but the number of data partitions of an object set is dynamic. The number of partitions should not be less than the maximum number of object sets so that every object set can be assigned at least one partition. Every data partition is of the same size and has one block.

OMM stores the address of the End of Set marker in the catalog partition to speed up insertion. To insert an object, OMM first gets the address of the End of Set from the catalog partition. If this data partition has enough space, the object is inserted at that position. If there is not enough space, OMM carries out memory compaction. If the compaction cannot produce enough room, OMM looks for an unused data partition, and if any, it links the data partition to the current partition. An overflow occurs when there is no unused data partition left.

In searching an object, OMM just walks through the chain of partitions assigned to the object set. In order to delete an object, the search routine is used to find the object to be deleted and the object is replaced by delete marks.

3. Performance

Since the object sizes have great effect on the performance of the OMM, we classified all application programs into three kinds of programs on the basis of object size and constructed simulation models by varying the relative composition of the different classes. Figure 1 shows results from one of the models. In both (a) and (b) of Figure 1, the horizontal axis reflects a percentage of total sum of objects in memory. In (a) the vertical axis is the percentage of objects in memory used to store objects. Therefore, the nearer the value is to 1, the better the memory usage. In (b), the vertical axis shows time (in microseconds) needed to insert an object.

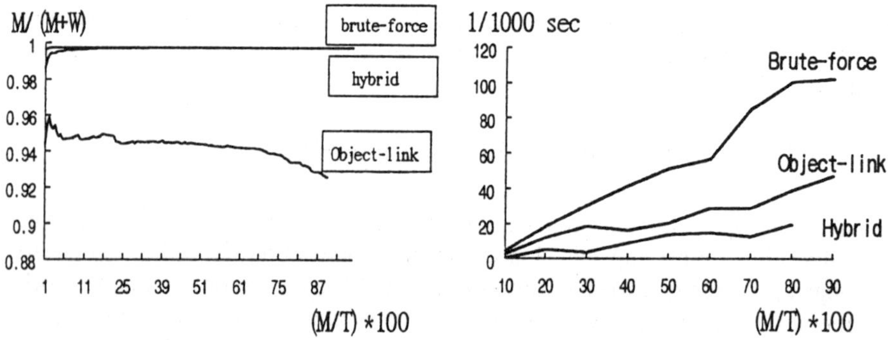

(a) Memory Utilization

(b) Execution Time (Insertion)

Figure 1. Performance Results

4. Future work

There are three main areas of future work. First, we need deeper understanding of the actual data sets of the application programs of a PDA. Second, the OMM should be tightly integrated into the OS. There are certain amount of redundancy between the OMM and VRTXmc's memory management module (such as book-keeping). If OMM functions were supported directly by the OS (with access to low level internals), efficiency is expected to improve both in space and time. Third, the OMM should be extended to include other types of memory. Flash memory is becoming the prime candidate for high speed secondary memory for PDAs. Data objects will be stored in these devices and the OMM should be able to cope with such diversity.

References

[GIO87] Gio Widerhold, *File Organization for Database Design*, McGraw-Hill, Inc., 1987.

[KNU73] Knuth, D.E., *The Art of Computer Programming: Fundamental Algorithms*, Vol. 1, 2nd Ed., Addison-Wesley, 1973.

[MAT77] Matick, R.E., *Computer Storage Systems and Technology*, John Wiley & Sons, 1977.

Variable Knowledge Based System

Li-Guo Wang[1]

South Bank University, London SW8 2JZ

Abstract: To integrate data, knowledge and reasoning within a general computing framework we present a method of variable knowledge based system. It deals with the relation of abstract syntax and dynamic semantics for knowledge representation and reasoning. An abstract knowledge model is presented as a uniform framework to hold various data and knowledge and a dynamic semantics is presented to interpret the abstract model to different data, knowledge and their reasoning.

1. Introduction.

In the recent years and in the area of computer science application and artificial intelligence *integration* has attracted increasing attention. However, a radical limitation is that most work are restricted to the particular host system by its technical details such that the interesting academic aspect of the integration is concealed. To find the essential content of the problem and to set up a foundation for integration of different systems we take an abstract view point -- concentrating on the abstractions of systems and their relation. For this we present the concept and method of variable knowledge based system.

2. Abstract Knowledge Model and its Dynamic Semantics

Following Winston's (1984) definition: knowledge representation is:

> *a set of syntactic and semantic conventions that make it possible to describe things*

we present a general syntax and semantics combination to represent various data, knowledge and reasoning.

Abstract Knowledge Model: <akm> ::= <id> [<akm_list>]
<akm_list> ::= nil | <asm>, <akm-list>

By the definition abstract knowledge model is an abstract syntax. Its structure is recursive. The base case is "id" (identity) and the step case is "id" followed by a list of "akm" (abstract acknowledge model). By the syntax all the relationship among the knowledge structure and sub-structure are expressed through the relationship between "id" and sub-id.

Abstract Semantics Framework:

$$\Phi (\langle id \rangle) = \langle id \rangle$$

$$\Phi (\langle id \rangle [\langle akm\text{-}list \rangle]) = \vartheta (\Phi ((\langle id \rangle) [\Phi (\langle akm\text{-}list \rangle)])$$

$$\Phi (nil) = nil$$

[1] The research is supported by EPSRC GR/J42175. Email: lgw@dcs.ed.ac.uk

$$\Phi (\langle akm\rangle, \langle akm\text{-}list\rangle) = \varsigma (\Phi (\langle akm\rangle), \Phi (\langle akm\text{-}list\rangle))$$

This is a framework. It merely describes a general structure to be ready to fit by various concrete semantics. For this it leaves "id" unchained but has opened ϑ and ς for the relation between knowledge and sub-knowledge. Different interpretations to ϑ and ς will lead to different knowledge and reasoning. These interpretations are activated by data.

Dynamic Semantics: It is data driven. The same data can be interpreted to different meanings. Therefore, knowledge and reasoning are only determined in the system running process.

A further advantage is that we can use the framework to describe not only knowledge and reasoning but also meta-knowledge and meta-reasoning; not only system but also the relation of systems and so on. This sets up a foundation to automatically integrate various data, knowledge and reasoning in a general computing framework. Let us give three different semantics to illustrate.

(1). Logical Knowledge Scheme:

Syntax: logic-knowledge ::= clause-base [clause-set]
clause-set ::= nil | | clause, clause-set
clause ::= rule [predicate-list]
predicate-list ::= nil | predicate, predicate-list
predicate ::= name [term-list]
term-list ::= name [term-list]
term = constant | variable | function [term-list]

Semantics: The main part is as below:

α (predicate-list) = $\forall x,y,\ldots,z.$ β (predicate-list)
β (predicate, predicate-list)= γ (predicate) $\Leftarrow$ γ (predicate-list)
γ (predicate) = predicate
γ (predicate, predicate-list) = predicate $\wedge$ γ (predicate-list)
Here, x, y, ..., z are all the variables in predicate-list.

Above, the abstract knowledge model is interpreted into Prolog.

(2). Network Knowledge Scheme:

Syntax: network-knowledge ::= connection-base [connection-set]
connection-set ::= nil | connection, connection-set
connection ::= relation | [term, term]
term ::= constant | variable | function [term-list]

Semantics: The key is α (.relation [term1, term2])= relation (term1, term2)
i.e. two "term1" and "term2" have a "relation".

Above, the abstract knowledge model is interpreted into Semantics Network.

(3). Structured Knowledge Scheme:

Syntax: structured-knowledge ::= frame-base [frame-set]
frame-set ::= nil | frame, frame-set
frame ::= titl [attribute-list]
attribute-list ::= nil | attribute, attribute-list
attribute ::= slot [value]
value ::= constant | frame-structure

Semantics: It is quite directed.

Above, the abstract knowledge model is interpreted into Frame.

3. Connection of Variable Knowledge System

To connect two system ,say **S1** to **S2**, we introduce the third system **C**:

connection-system [connection-variable [$x, y, \ldots$ z],
connection-channel1 [sys1-interface1, x],
connection-channe2 [sys1-interface2, y],
...,
connection-channen [sys1-interfacen, z]]

The important point is that the **C** is also an instance of the abstract knowledge model.

4. Operation of Variable Knowledge System

We can integrate several systems **S1, S2,...,Sn** to gain a integrated system **S**:

S = integration [**S1, S2, ..., Sn**]

Again, the **S** is also an instance of the abstract knowledge model.

However, we can have two different semantics to interpret the **S:**

(1). Declarative Semantics: $S_1 \wedge S_2 \wedge \ldots \wedge S_n$

(2). Procedural Semantics: $S_1 \rightarrow S_2 \rightarrow \ldots \rightarrow S_n$

Here, $R \wedge S$ means the conjunction of two statements (system),.*i.e.* both are held simultaneously; $R \rightarrow S$ means the concatenation of two systems, *i.e.* first do **R** then do **S**.

5. Conclusion and Further Work

We have completed a test system which includes three knowledge representation and reasoning: Prolog, semantics-network and frame. The test system is based on the C++ and ObjectStore. Further work will focus the structure and operation of meta-knowledge and meta-reasoning.

6. References

[DS86] David A. Schmiodt, Denotational Semantics, Allyn and Bacon, Inc. 1986

Author Index